Assessing Learning in Universities

Table of Contents

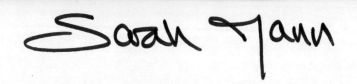

THE UNIVERSITY OF
NEW SOUTH WALES

Assessing Learning
in Universities

Peggy Nightingale

Ina Te Wiata

Sue Toohey

Greg Ryan

Chris Hughes

Doug Magin

Professional Development Centre
University of New South Wales

with the support of the
Committee for the Advancement of University Teaching,
Department of Employment, Education and Technology

PROFESSIONAL
DEVELOPMENT
CENTRE•UNSW

Published by
University of New South Wales Press
Sydney 2052
Telephone (02) 9398 8900
Fax (02) 9398 3408

National Library of Australia
Cataloguing-in-Publication entry:

   Assessing learning in universities.

   Bibliography.
   Includes index.

   ISBN 0 86840 408 x
   1. Education, Higher—Aims and objectives.
   2. College students—Rating of.
   I. Nightingale, Peggy. 1942-.

378.16

Printed by Southwood Press, NSW.

The project

A project team comprised of staff of the Professional Development Centre at the University of New South Wales accepted a commission from the Australian government-funded Committee for the Advancement of University Teaching (CAUT) to produce the materials in this package.

The team was concerned first of all, to attract university teachers to the package, and secondly, to persuade them to adopt assessment strategies which both encourage the student learning outcomes they desire and allow teachers to evaluate the success of their teaching in terms of those outcomes. Using case studies, the materials now before you demonstrate and explain how such strategies can be used.

Intended outcomes of the project

The overall aim of the project (as specified by the CAUT Project Brief) was to "produce a series of user-friendly materials designed to be of practical assistance in assessing and examining for university teachers in a wide range of discipline and multi-disciplinary subject areas". Specific objectives of the project team were:

1. to synthesise the literature on assessment in higher education so as to make it accessible and relevant to the teachers of a wide variety of disciplines;

2. to develop materials which not only provide models of assessment processes but also relate assessment to curriculum design and pedagogy and to the enhancement of student learning;

3. to develop materials which address principles of good practice at the level of school or department as well as at the level of individual subject, thus encouraging the exercise of academic leadership;

4. to develop materials which encourage consideration of alternatives to traditional methods of assessment in the various disciplines;

5. to develop materials which will suit the needs of individual academics who wish to consider modest changes to their practice as well as the needs of individuals or groups who wish to expend considerable energy in a major reappraisal of their practice;

6. to develop materials which will assist colleagues working in academic staff development or educational development to offer workshops, seminars and programs of study on assessment issues.

The ultimate test of whether these objectives have been achieved begins as the materials are made available to academic staff throughout Australia. They have, however, been trialled and evaluated and refined throughout the 18 months of the project's life.

Recruiting assistance

From the beginning CAUT pressed the project team to involve as many others as possible in the project and to publicise the work in progress.

Our first step was to write to the Deans of all Faculties in Australian universities inviting them to nominate Faculty members involved in interesting or innovative assessment practice. This initial broad sweep was followed by:

- publicity for the project through the national press, inviting academics to contribute examples of their own practice or to join our feedback group and comment on the project as it progressed;
- workshops in many Australian universities and at the annual conferences of the Higher Education Research and Development Society of Australasia (HERDSA Inc) as well as overseas (New Zealand, South Africa and USA) explaining the project and seeking contributions;
- approaches to individuals known to us (including past and present students in our postgraduate program in university teaching) who we knew were doing innovative and worthwhile things in assessment.

Eventually we had a self-selected mailing list of over 500 academics throughout Australia. Some became contributors of case studies and/or other materials, and their names are listed in the Appendix; the rest formed our "Feedback Group".

Finding an organising principle

Clearly, our brief from the Committee for the Advancement of University Teaching was broad. The project team began by considering the range of issues which confront teachers when thinking about assessment. We developed a multi-dimensional framework representing the range of starting points from which one might enter the discussion about assessment. Dimensions included:

- the range of assessment tasks, techniques for assessing students' work;
- the choice of assessor (including the role of students in assessment);
- the functions of assessment in the educational system including the diagnostic, formative and summative roles of assessment;
- The technical, philosophical and resource issues - including such aspects as the choice between grading systems which are standards based (criterion-referenced) and those which are designed to rank students by comparing their performances (norm referenced);
- the kinds of learning (or learning outcomes) which should be consciously assessed - knowledge, technical and professional skills, intellectual skills and abilities such as critical thinking and problem solving, personal attributes and values.

We knew we did not want to organise our materials around disciplines or specific assessment techniques, but it was hard to picture a different structure. Initial focus group meetings explored all of the dimensions of assessment listed above but kept returning to the last one - the importance of determining the characteristics and abilities that are expected of graduates of our courses. In the process of designing an assessment system, this decision proves to be the key. Once it has been determined what abilities and characteristics (knowledge, skills and attitudes) we believe our graduates ought to have, then many of the other decisions fall naturally into place. In terms of what to assess we will be looking for evidence of the full range of abilities that we expect of graduates. The kind of evidence we want helps to determine the how and who of assessment.

In keeping with this emphasis on student learning outcomes, the project team began a long process of collaborative research and consultation to determine the kinds of abilities which might be considered desirable across programs of study within higher education. We began by looking at what had been recently written about the goals of higher education, and we asked many university teachers in workshops to list and discuss the abilities which they believed their graduates ought to have. Our first attempt at a list of core abilities was sent to our feedback group. Their advice helped to refine and modify the initial work until we arrived at the eight clusters of abilities which now provide the structure for this package.

These clusters of abilities we identify as:

- thinking critically and making judgements
- solving problems and developing plans
- performing procedures and demonstrating techniques
- managing and developing oneself
- accessing and managing information
- demonstrating knowledge and understanding
- designing, creating, performing
- communicating.

We believe that these eight ability groups represent the areas in which most academics would like to see their students make significant progress throughout their university education and which ought, therefore, to form the basis of assessment. The case materials have been organised into eight modules which show how these broad abilities might be assessed in a number of ways in a range of disciplines.

Applying the organising principle

Case study materials were collected throughout 1994 and helped to validate and refine our ability groups. One of the difficulties which we encountered with some of the case studies was the decision regarding which ability group they belonged to. Many of the cases here are, in fact, descriptions of 'integrated' or 'authentic' assessment. These terms, which have recently appeared in the assessment literature, refer to assessment tasks which are closely modelled on real life situations (hence 'authentic'). They may take the form of complex simulations, case studies, role plays or multi-faceted projects and are used to assess a range of knowledge, skills and attitudes in the one assessment task (hence 'integrated'). Our problem was where to place such complex assessments. Where, for example, to put the portfolio assessment which was being used to assess knowledge and understanding, communication skills and the ability to evaluate one's own learning? Where to put the objective structured clinical examination which was used to assess nursing skills, the ability to communicate with patients, the ability to solve clinical problems and prepare patient management plans? We resolved these dilemmas by selecting what seemed to be the most significant (or heavily weighted) of the abilities being assessed and assigned the case study to that group. Many of the cases could have been placed in more than one module.

Between case studies we have written discussions of issues which are prompted by consideration of the practices described. Sometimes we offer advice based on the literature on student learning and assessment to help readers develop their own practice. Because a technique like self-assessment might have been discussed in several different modules, we have done a lot of cross-referencing.

We also include:

- a glossary of commonly used terms,
- an index which includes disciplines covered by case studies and the common techniques, and
- an annotated bibliography.

Sometimes it seemed to us that we had chosen one of the most difficult ways imaginable to organise these materials. However, we were looking for a way to encourage people to break free of the traditional methods of assessment in their disciplines. If we had structured the package around techniques or around disciplines, we feared people would turn only to the section that seems most relevant to their own discipline, or to a technique already commonly used. The abilities we are trying to foster in our students are common to all disciplines, and we hope focussing on them will lead people to consider, be challenged and stimulated by practice in other areas very different from their own. Responses from people who have tried out parts of the package have encouraged us to persist. While we hope you will read this whole package of materials, we think it will be possible for you to enter and re-enter the package at almost any point and weave your way through it.

In addition to the Table of Contents and Index, each module is preceded by an overview to help readers find their way around the materials. Case study titles and the discipline they come from are listed in those overviews as well as the assessment issues and the techniques covered by the discussion sections.

Acknowledgements

We wish to pay tribute to the academic staff from all over Australia, and New Zealand, who contributed case studies and responded to our requests for more information and comments on our work in progress. They are listed in an Appendix to these materials. Without them we would not have produced materials which are alive with real practice.

Not all of the materials collected could be used. In some cases a number of individuals had independently chosen very similar strategies and it was a matter of choosing one good example from the variety offered. We sought examples from the widest possible range of disciplines and so we sometimes rejected good materials from a discipline which was well represented in favour of a similar case from a discipline which had not been represented.

We are very aware that we have not captured all that is out there. Even as we prepare these materials for press, we keep hearing of new ideas and different practices that we would have liked to include. We also hear from contributors that they have already modified or developed the practice we report, or found something even better.

In addition to all of those contributors, we had a Steering Committee comprised of Professor Don Anderson and Professor Michael Jackson from CAUT, and Professor Neil Baumgart and Associate Professor Penny Little who reviewed these materials as they were developed and offered wise counsel on their contents.

Dr Lee Andresen, formerly on the staff of the Professional Development Centre, assisted with development of the bid and the original articulation of the abilities to be included in modules.

Dr Jim Tognolini, Director of the Educational Testing Centre at the University of New South Wales, offered advice throughout the project and his expertise on educational measurement.

Mr Lindsay Hewson, Senior Lecturer in the Professional Development Centre, has advised on the design of the materials and helped supervise their production. We value his good taste and good humour as well as his skills as a designer of instructional materials.

Ms Jan McLean, Lecturer in the Professional Development Centre, helped with literature searches and contributed to discussions of approaches to this work.

Ms Lynne Bruce, Ms Debbie Owen, Ms Anne-Maree Austen, and Ms Shirley Yeoh made up the administrative staff of the Professional Development Centre. They have contributed directly and indirectly to this project; without them, the project team would never have been able to fulfill their many other obligations while completing this work.

Finally, we must thank the Committee for the Advancement of University Teaching for the $87,000 grant which extended our resources sufficiently to make the project possible, and for entrusting us with this commission. It has been an exciting project for all of us who have worked on it.

The project team

This was a team effort. None of us could have managed without the others (and all those listed above). Each of us has areas of expertise which we were able to contribute to the project, but the whole is definitely greater than the sum of the parts in work like this. We talked and developed our ideas together. We drafted sections of the materials and read each other's work and rewrote for each other, so although sections have authors, there are unseen co-authors as well. However, some people took on special responsibilities and we wish to acknowledge their roles.

Ina TeWiata was the Project Officer for the duration of this work. She maintained the database of contributors and our feedback group and all the files of contributions and resources. She kept minutes of meetings. She searched the literature and the halls of academe for contributions from unrepresented disciplines. She produced newsletters and mountains of correspondence, and she travelled far and wide telling people about the project and testing the draft materials with workshop groups. She wrote the module on "Thinking critically and making judgments". She compiled the Bibliography from the various references module authors had accumulated. She encouraged and she cajoled, and occasionally, she bullied the rest of the team, and always she smiled and supported.

Peggy Nightingale was Project Manager and looked after the budget and liaison with CAUT and the administration of the project. She compiled the final text, editing the materials and supervising the indexing and final production. She wrote the modules on "Communicating", on "Accessing and managing information", and on "Designing, creating and performing" (with help from Doug Magin on the "Designing" section).

Sue Toohey and Greg Ryan facilitated team meetings and gave structure to our discussions. Sue wrote the modules on "Managing and developing oneself" and on "Performing procedures and demonstrating techniques" (the latter with Doug Magin). Greg wrote the module on "Solving problems and developing plans".

Chris Hughes created the database for the project and guided novices through our bibliographic software. (Lindsay Hewson also helped those of us who constantly get into trouble with technology). Chris compiled the Glossary, writing most of it himself. He co-wrote, with Doug Magin, the module on "Demonstrating knowledge and understanding".

Introduction

(Assessment) which requires the student only to regurgitate material obtained through lectures and required reading virtually forces the student to use a surface approach to learning that material. On the other hand, (assessment) which requires the student to apply knowledge gained on the course to the solution of novel problems, not previously seen by the student, ... cannot be tackled without a deeper understanding.

Sharp quoted by Entwistle (1992 , p. 39)

In this package we present a varied selection of assessment strategies and discussion of the issues associated with employing them. Throughout the materials we are concerned to put the emphasis on what it is that teachers in particular subjects at particular stages of a program of study really want their students to know and to be able to do. That is, we are stressing the desired outcomes of learning. This emphasis was chosen because good assessment practice allows teachers to demonstrate the quality of their students' learning to others (meeting demands for accountability) and, more importantly, because we are convinced - from our own experience as teachers, as advisors of teachers, as scholars of student learning and as researchers in higher education - that there is nothing more likely to undermine teachers' objectives than ill-conceived assessment tasks.

Student learning research has repeatedly demonstrated the impact of assessment on students' approaches to learning (see Gibbs, 1992a ; Gibbs, 1992b ; Biggs, 1989 ; ...Ramsden, 1992). Ask them to understand the physics and chemistry of muscle contraction, but test them on the names of the muscles, and they will "learn" the names but not be able to explain how contraction happens. Ask students to understand narrative perspective in the novel but test them on the author's background and they will know a lot about the author and little about narrative perspective.

(Nightingale & O'Neil, 1994, pp149-50)

The changing nature of university assessment

Assessment in universities is changing - in its intent and in its methods. Traditional forms of assessment have usually focussed on ranking students according to the knowledge that they gained in a subject or course. Assessment methods were designed to let students demonstrate their knowledge in easily measurable ways so that comparisons between them were facilitated. Students' achievements were viewed in quantitative terms - "How much do they know?" - and judgments made by assessors were often assumed to be a definitive statement of the student's ability.

While much assessment still displays these characteristics, pressure for change has come in at least three areas. The first is a growing desire to broaden university education, to develop - and consequently to assess - a much broader range of student abilities. The second is the desire to harness the full power of assessment and feedback in support of learning. The third arises from the belief that education should lead to a capacity for independent judgment and an ability to evaluate one's own performance - and that these abilities can only be developed through involvement in the assessment process.

The need to assess a broader range of learning outcomes

One of the most powerful factors influencing university assessment in recent times has been a growing change in conceptions of the goals of a university education. Calls for a broadening of these goals have come from groups as disparate as national governments, employer and professional associations and educational theorists. Such ideas have received a considerable degree of acceptance within academia - for example, in 1992 the Higher Education Council, describing the desirable characteristics of graduates, refers not only to acquisition of a body of knowledge but also to mastery of the technical skills of a discipline, development of abilities such as problem solving, critical thinking and effective communication as well as development of attitudes and dispositions such as a commitment to working in groups and to ethical practice within one's discipline.

At the same time as the desirable outcomes of higher education have broadened, research into student learning has shown the powerful effect of assessment in determining the real "curriculum in action" as opposed to the espoused curriculum. For students it is their knowledge and expectations of what will be assessed that largely determines what they will learn. Activities in tutorials, labs and field work may be interesting and enjoyable, but if those activities are not assessed, they do not form part of the "real course". It follows that if undergraduate education is intended to develop a broad range of abilities, it must also assess and document students' achievements over the full range. The development and use of a much broader range of assessment methods has come about in response to this challenge.

The need for assessment to guide and enrich learning

Research on student learning during the last fifteen years has brought to the fore the central role of assessment in shaping learning - in both positive and negative directions. At worst - and far too frequently- the kinds of assessment methods chosen force students into surface learning - rote learning and regurgitation of isolated facts and formulae - quickly acquired to meet exam pressures and just as quickly forgotten. At best - provided with opportunities to apply their newly acquired knowledge to real and challenging problems - assessment provides students with the chance to learn in depth and test the limits of their understanding. University teachers who encounter research on student learning are not slow to understand the implications. They see the need to design different kinds of assesment tasks which will be significant learning experiences in themselves and which will provide the kind of feedback that leads to success for the individual and reinforces positive attitudes toward learning.

The need for assessment to support autonomy and self evaluation

While challenging assignments and informative feedback can greatly strengthen learning, they do not necessarily help students develop their own capacity for self evaluation. Many teachers have been struck by the incongruity of a system which claims to develop professionals capable of monitoring their own performance and that of their peers but which gives students the message that they do not have the capacity and cannot be trusted to evaluate their own learning. As a consequence many teachers are involving students in the assessment process and consciously attempting to develop self assessment skills.

The purposes of assessment and the challenges they present

Once in a while, most teachers wonder what would happen if there were no assessment, or at least no grading. In most circumstances the needs of the various parties force us to conclude that realistically, we will have to continue assessing and grading students' work.

Students' needs

- To know how they are doing in general (am I on track?)
- To know whether they are reaching a required standard (will I pass/graduate?)
- To have something to show to others (please employ me/ give me a scholarship)

Teachers' needs

- To know whether students are achieving the intended learning outcomes - particularly at the subject level (am I getting through? are they doing the work?)
- To prove to others that they are effective teachers (please give me tenure/ promote me)
- To certify that students can proceed to subjects for which theirs is a prerequisite (a student who passes my subject should be able to cope with yours)

Institutions' needs

- To know whether students are achieving the intended learning outcomes - particularly at the program level (are our courses effective? are our staff effective?)
- To prove to others that graduates have achieved what the institution claims they have (please continue to fund/ support us)
- To certify that students can proceed to employment, professional practice, further study (our graduates meet your requirements)
- To know whether to accept applicants into programs of study (do you have the required prerequisite knowledge? what is your level of achievement compared to other applicants?)

Community needs

- To know whether the institutions and the teachers are effective (we will continue to fund/ support you)
- To know whether individual graduates are employable, capable to practice, etc (you may work here, teach, doctor, etc)

Obvious conflicts of interest are inherent in these needs, and these conflicts lead us to consideration of some of the major issues in assessment. These are the issues which are recurring themes through our materials.

Summative vs formative assessment

Summative assessment is that which is graded - at least with a pass or fail - and counts toward the award of credit for study. Formative assessment is that which is offered as advice or feedback to students and which does not contribute marks toward their final result. Much of the time we try to combine formative with summative assessment, and usually it is desirable to do so. We want students to learn from doing assignments or tests as well as proving that they have already learned something. In addition, we often believe - probably correctly - that students will not make a real effort on work which "does not count".

Cases in the modules of this package will illustrate some ways to make summative assessment more formative and to get students to take formative tasks seriously. These include "scaffolding" or "tiering" which means breaking an assignment down into stages and requiring students to get feedback on each stage (formative assessment) before submitting the final assignment (for summative assessment). There are suggestions about ways to get students to process the feedback on graded assignments. There are also suggestions about ways to encourage students to learn through assessing their own or their peers' work.

Criterion-referenced vs norm-referenced assessment

Criterion-referenced assessment establishes standards (criteria) for specific grades or for passing or failing; a student who meets the criteria gets the specified result. Competency standards may be used as the basis of criteria-referenced assessment. Mastery learning is another example: students must demonstrate a certain level of achievement or they cannot continue to the next stage of a subject or program of study. The goal is for everyone to meet an established standard.

Norm-referenced assessment uses the achievement of a group of students to set the standards for specific grades or simply for passing or failing. The best X% of students get the best result, and the worst X% fail. "Grading on the curve" is an example of norm-referencing. Institutions often set expectations for markers that specified percentages of any class will get grades such as Pass, Credit, Distinction, and High Distinction; these institutions are requiring norm-referencing.

In practice, few assessment strategies are entirely norm-referenced or criteria-referenced. There is usually a minimum standard (albeit not always very explicitly articulated), regardless of expectations of grade distributions. In the materials which follow there are discussions of the "swings and roundabouts" of these ways of approaching establishing the standards for students' work.

Authentic or integrated assessment

In an attempt to make judgments about whether students are really able to demonstrate higher order abilities, many teachers are trying to design assessment tasks which require students to do things they would have to do in the "real world". These "integrated" or "authentic" assessment tasks often require students to demonstrate a number of skills and to apply considerable content knowledge. The assessment criteria may include attitudinal factors as well, for instance, related to demonstrating ethical behaviour or empathy.

The controversy about this sort of assessment is centred primarily on its reliability. For an assessment to be reliable, it should yield the same results if it is repeated, or different markers should make the same judgments about students' achievements. Because integrated assessment involves a complex task with many variables, the judgment of the overall quality of the performance is more likely to be open to interpretation than an assessment of a simpler task.

Although authentic or integrated assessment is likely to have high validity, there may also be a problem in this area. A somewhat simplistic definition of validity is that for an assessment to be valid, it must actually assess whatever it intends to assess; for instance, a multiple-choice test of content knowledge is not a valid test of critical thinking. It is important to recognise that especially when attempting to assess attitudes or ethical behaviour, the judgment may be valid under test circumstances but does not necessarily predict behaviour in real practice.

Recognising that authentic or integrated assessment tasks encourage students to integrate and apply their learning of subject content, some of our contributors offer innovative examples which attempt to balance requirements for reliability and validity.

Choosing assessment methods

We have spoken about the pressures for change in higher education assessment and the consequent development of a range of different approaches and methods. But how does one make a rational choice about which method to use?

While assessment serves many needs, including those of the educational institution, the community and the students, the first principle to be kept in mind is that the choice of assessment method should allow reasonable judgments to be made about the extent to which the student has achieved the aims, objectives or intended outcomes of the educational program. If, for example, the educational program claims to produce graduates who are innovative problem solvers then there should be many occasions throughout the program where students are asked to solve problems and develop innovative solutions and are assessed accordingly. Problem solving ability cannot be inferred from assessments which test only knowledge and technical skills.

Our second principle is that the assessment method chosen should support learning and not undermine it. Some of the most discouraging research on student learning has shown that students can successfully progress through all the assessments for their degree while still holding fundamental misconceptions about the principles on which the discipline is based. Resource shortages and the needs of employers and educational institutions for quick methods of ranking students and graduates may push us towards certain assessment methods which foster this. But the whole exercise of assessment is pointless if it cannot make useful judgments about student learning and if, in fact, it encourages students into ineffective learning.

Not only should assessment practice be student-centred, and based on outcomes, but the teaching program should be directed at achieving the desired outcomes in terms of student learning. Readings and lectures, practical classes and learning activities in tutorials should all be planned to help students achieve the desired goals. In short, there should be internal consistency among:

- the identified aims and and expected outcomes of the program of study;
- the teaching methods which will be used to help students achieve these aims and outcomes; and
- the way/s in which these outcomes will be assessed.

One way of establishing this consistency is to ask a number of key questions, such as:

1. What characteristics do we want to see in our graduates? What knowledge, skills, and attitudes and values will they be expected to develop?
2. What teaching methods are the most appropriate to help students to develop the knowledge, skills, and attitudes/values? What kinds of learning experiences should they undertake?
3. What kinds of tasks will allow students to demonstrate their knowledge and understanding, skills and attitudes? Can we find assessment tasks which look like the real tasks of the discipline or profession and thus have relevance and credibility for students?
4. Finally - What standard of performance should be required? What are the characteristics of successful performance?

Current practice in university assessment

The materials presented here - case studies on assessment from Australian and New Zealand institutions - form a portfolio of current practice. The teachers who devised and implemented these assessment tasks are coming to grips with the new dimensions of assessment - the need to assess a broad range of goals, to design assessments which support learning and promote personal responsibility. None of the teachers whose work is documented here would claim to have perfected the methods they use - they speak frankly about the strengths and limitations of their currrent practice. Each case study is a snapshot of a moment in our colleagues' professional life; many of them have further developed their practices. What stands out in the materials they prepared for us and the interviews we conducted with them is their passion for experimentation in search of excellence and their drive to make the whole assessment process as valuable as possible for all the players. Our contributors used student assessment as a major source of feedback on both their teaching and their assessment practice. The assessment practices they described were constantly modified from year to year in response to that feedback. We hope our readers will be inspired by their examples.

References

Biggs, J. (1989). Does learning about learning help teachers with teaching? Psychology and the tertiary teacher. Inaugural lecture, 8 December 1988. *Supplement to the Gazette*, University of Hong Kong, 20 March 1989.

Entwistle, N. (1992). *The Impact of Teaching on Learning Outcomes in Higher Education: A Literature Review*. Sheffield: Committee of Vice-Chancellors and Principals of the Universities of the United Kingdom, Universities' Staff Development Unit.

Gibbs, G. (1992a). *Improving the Quality of Student Learning*. Bristol: Technical and Education Services.

Gibbs, G. (1992b). Improving the quality of student learning through course design. In R. Barnett (Ed.), *Learning to Effect*. Buckingham: Society for Research into Higher Education and Open University Press.

Nightingale, P., & O'Neil, M. (1994). *Achieving Quality Learning in Higher Education*. London: Kogan Page.

Ramsden, P. (1992). *Learning to Teach in Higher Education*. London: Routledge.

MODULE 1

THINKING CRITICALLY AND MAKING JUDGEMENTS

INA TE WIATA

Module 1
Thinking critically and making judgments

The primary focus of this module is to illustrate assessment tasks that concentrate on the assessment of intellectual activity that is somewhat abstract in nature where reflection plays a major role, and where conclusions and action are neither obvious or immediate.

This module covers broad abilities such as:
- developing arguments
- reflecting
- evaluating
- assessing
- judging

Themes

- Defining critical thinking
- Linking aims, learning outcomes, teaching methods and assessment techniques
- Assessment for learning
- Importance of clear criteria
- Communicating the criteria
- Weighting of criteria
- Aggregation of marks
- Problematic areas
  generalisability
  teaching critical thinking
  varying background beliefs
- Indicators of quality of assessment programs/techniques
  validity
  reliability

Techniques

- Interview
- Written evidence
  essay
  report
  assignment

Case studies

1. Critical incident analysis, Business Studies
2. Critical incident analysis, Education
3. Evaluation of a change and/or innovation, Education
4. Critical evaluation of research literature, Education
5. Critique of a current concern, Applied Physical Geography
6. Reflective journal writing, Health Science Education

Module 1
Thinking critically and making judgments
Ina Te Wiata

A major area of focus in university education is the development of students' abilities to think critically and to arrive at sound judgments.

Educators in every discipline value the ability to think critically and make judgments. For example, chemists value the ability to draw sound inferences from observations, critically analyse and evaluate previous research, and generate new questions or experiments, while educators teaching English value the ability to elaborate an argument and develop its implications, understand, analyse, and evaluate arguments, support general assertions with details, and recognise the central thesis in a work (Kurfiss, 1988).

But how do we know if and when students are thinking critically?
How can we tell if our efforts to teach critical thinking are actually having an impact?

Before we can answer these questions it is necessary to have a closer look at what critical thinking might actually be, and what abilities it might encompass.

The central idea that we have adopted for this module is that

> *critical thinking is reasonable and reflective thinking that is focused on deciding what to believe or do.* (Norris & Ennis, 1990)

The purpose is to explore a situation, phenomenon, question or issue, and arrive at a hypothesis or conclusion about it that integrates all available information and that can therefore be convincingly justified (Kurfiss, 1988).

The outcomes of a critical inquiry comprise a conclusion or hypothesis and the justification offered in support of it. Although critical thinking can result in a decision, a judgment, or a proposal, other consequences include a new way of approaching significant issues in one's life or a deeper understanding of the basis for one's actions, (Brookfield, cited by Kurfiss, 1988). Or it might result in political activity, (Guyton, cited by Kurfiss, 1988)

Abilities that are included in this module include the following:
*   developing arguments
*   reflecting
*   evaluating
*   assessing
*   judging

It is worthwhile at this point to remind readers that there is overlap between this module and others in the package, particularly in the areas of solving problems and developing plans, and managing and developing oneself. Some of the many similarities between problem solving and critical thinking include, for example, identifying constraints, gathering information, and generating hypotheses. What distinguishes critical thinking from problem solving most clearly is the process of developing support for a position. Whereas problem solving is about moving from an unsatisfactory state to a more desired goal state, the goal in critical thinking is to sort, weigh and evaluate information using your own values explicitly as an underlying basis for the judgment. Other people may construct different but equally valid answers depending on their own value bases. Collins (cited by Kurfiss, 1988) reminds us that no con-of the supposedly value-neutral scientific method) is free of value assumptions. It is the place of values and ethical deliberations in the curriculum that is problematic.

Examples of assessment practices included in this module concentrate on the assessment of intellectual activity that is somewhat abstract in nature, where reflection plays a major role, and where conclusions and action are neither obvious nor immediate. In contrast, we discuss problem-solving as an activity with more concrete outcomes.

Although the module "Managing and developing oneself" may discuss a number of similar terms to those in this module, eg. reflection, evaluation, the focus is explicitly on students assuming greater authority over their own learning. This means the emphasis of the assessment tasks is on students evaluating themselves (rather than the work of others), not only in terms of their subject/course context but also with respect to the factors that might help them to become better learners.

Assessment tasks focusing on critical thinking are designed to determine the extent to which students recognise the assumptions underlying their beliefs and behaviours, and give justification to their ideas and actions. It is this justification which we as educators try to evaluate.

There are a number of theoretical underpinnings that are the bases for the approaches taken to the teaching, learning and assessment of critical thinking. For those readers who are interesting in pursuing this further, *Critical Thinking* (Kurfiss, 1988) is a useful starting point.

Taking this information into account then, how might educators clarify what critical thinking is, and how ought it to be assessed?

To help answer this let us return for a moment to the central idea mentioned earlier, that critical thinking is about reasonable and reflective thinking that is focused on deciding what to believe or do (Norris & Ennis, 1990).

In order to assess students' capability in this area competently, it is necessary for us to be more specific about what exactly we as educators are assessing.

Once again the work of Norris and Ennis (1990) is useful here. In their discussion there are four elements of critical thinking - reasonable, reflective, focused, and decision oriented. They define **reasonable thinking** as good thinking that relies appropriately upon good evidence. They emphasise that good thinking is not arbitrary but leads in general to the best conclusions or judgments. **Reflective thinking** is that which examines the reasonableness of both one's own and others' thoughts. It is believed to be stimulated by a "perplexed" situation (Dewey, cited by Kurfiss, 1988). Critical thinkers are also those who **consciously** seek and use good reasons. The third part of the central idea of critical thinking that we have adopted for this module is about focus. **Focused thinking** suggests that critical thinking is consciously directed. It is purposeful as it does not occur accidentally or without reason. And finally, the focus of critical thinking is about making a judgment, ie. judgment could also be thought of as reflective thinking turned to controversy (Dewey, cited by Kurfiss, 1988). That is, it involves selecting, weighing, and deciding.

To carry out the process of thinking critically and making judgments effectively, Norris and Ennis (1990) argue that one needs both abilities and dispositions.* Stating these abilities and dispositions as explicitly as we are able helps serve as a basis by which to assess our students. For example, abilities include those required to analyse an argument, judge the credibility of a source, identify assumptions, judge the soundness of information, and so on. However, a person may have the abilities for critical thinking and making judgments, but for some reason not use them. So the term disposition refers to those attitudes, commitments and

---

* These writers use the latter terms somewhat differently from how we have chosen to use them for the assessment modules.

tendencies to act: for example, a commitment to open mindedness, and trying to be well informed. Dispositions include aspects such as ensuring that all assumptions are open to questions, divergent views are actively sought, and the investigation is not biased in favour of any particular outcome. The abilities and dispositions described by Norris and Ennis (1990) are broad criteria by which we as educators can make decisions. Once again we can use these dispositions to provide us with guidance in assessing our students' ability to think critically and make judgments.

It needs to be remembered that while critical thinking is a process, it is a process used to deal with some content. The content might be part of a university subject, or a situation or problem in everyday life.

It is important to note here that one significant unresolved aspect is whether critical thinking is subject/discipline specific or a generalisable skill. That is, to what degree does learning the skills of argument enable students to reason effectively in various disciplines? The notion of generalisability, as well as other problematic aspects of the teaching and assessing of critical thinking, are discussed in a later section in this module, 'Issues for consideration', and in Module 2, "Solving problems and developing plans".

Let us now consider the case studies that typify assessment of the abilities encompassed within this module. (You may remember those abilities include: developing arguments, reflecting, evaluating, assessing, judging).

Case study 1
Critical Incident Analysis

Case study from Business Studies
Ina Te Wiata and Phil Ker, Auckland Institute of Technology

In the course of discussing the assessment of critical incident analysis these educators highlight the importance of clarifying assessment criteria and ensuring congruence between course aims, learning outcomes, teaching methods and assessment tasks. The following case study is based on written material, including course documentation (Auckland Institute of Technology, 1992) plus follow-up discussions with the contributors.

Context

This example is located in the context of a Bachelor of Business degree. The four year degree program is capability-based with 'critical and reflective thinking' being two of the core capabilities (abilities). The first three semesters are based on an integrated business studies curriculum, with students specialising in specific subjects, eg. accounting, management, or marketing in later semesters. The assessment task described here forms one of the assessment tasks for the compulsory co-operative education component (work placement, which is done through a negotiated learning contract), which occurs in either semester 6 or 7 of the program.

Each of the assessment events is linked to one or more of the co-operative education program's five learning outcomes. These outcomes are broad- based statements that indicate what the learners will be able to do by the end of their co-operative education module, ie. students will be able to:

1. Demonstrate a critical understanding of the nature, structure, and dynamics of the workplace in which they have undertaken their co-operative programme;

2. Critically analyse and reflect upon the co-operative experience;

3. Demonstrate critical thinking skills in the context of a specific situation encountered during the co-operative education programme;

4. Demonstrate oral presentation skills appropriate to the business context in which they have been operating;

5. Contract for, and complete, specific duties in a chosen area of professional activity.

Each of the outcomes has a number of assessment criteria which provide further detail as to what is expected of learners. The assessment task described in this case study is linked to that outcome which states that students should be able to, "demonstrate critical thinking skills in the context of a specific situation encountered during the co-operative education programme".

The assessment program is standards-based (criterion referenced), and no norm referencing takes place. Students' grades are decided by judging how well their performance meets a number of stated criteria.

Abilities being assessed

The abilities (referred to as capabilities in this case study) being assessed are"critical thinking" and "reflective thinking". The critical incident interview offers a way of assessing these capabilities directly, as they are applied in the context of the work placement.

Assessment procedure

Students are required to demonstrate their critical thinking skills in an interview with their Academic Supervisor and a peer Academic Supervisor.

(The latter is another academic member of staff who is currently supervising or has previously supervised, a co-operative education student). The students need to be able to discuss critically a significant incident that has occurred during their co-operative experience. The critical incident may be a problem, an event, a particularly interesting interaction, or a particular organisational success or failure that the student has been part of or has observed.

Critical incidents would usually have been recorded in a journal (Holly, 1984) throughout the semester; and students generally practice sharing these journal entries with their academic supervisor as the placement progresses. This is one way of ensuring that students clearly understand what constitutes a "critical incident". (Most students will have kept a journal throughout the semester but this is not a formal requirement.) The emphasis is on demonstrating the required ability (ie. thinking critically and making judgments) during the interview. Students may provide written material (to support their thinking and judgments) prior to the interview, and may use a combined approach (ie. written, oral, diagrammatic) during the interview to demonstrate the extent to which they have developed the capacity to reflect, think critically and make judgments. Students are also expected to demonstrate that they have engaged in self assessment of their ability in this area.

The interview procedure

The students may bring a support person with them, although this person may not be another student currently enrolled in the co-operative education module. The role of the support person is to provide moral support for the student and is an attempt to redress the power imbalance inherent in the interview approach, given that there are two staff members involved.

➤

The Academic Supervisors and peer Academic Supervisors familiarise themselves prior to the interview with any written material on the incident that has been provided by the students. They also clarify their own roles and the process for the interview. Before the interview commences the students are introduced to the peer Academic Supervisor, and the role of each person is clarified and articulated. The peer Academic Supervisors serve mainly as a quality management check of both the content and process of the interview, rather than as primary assessors of the students' capability. The students are also referred once again to the criteria by which the interview will be marked.

The interview proper begins with the Academic Supervisors asking the students to explain and analyse the incident that has occurred during the time of their work placement. This usually takes about 10 minutes, after which time the Academic Supervisors, having made sure that the students have no more to add, will ask broad questions in an attempt to probe for further information. After the Academic Supervisors believe they have probed as much as they can (without giving students the "answer"), the peer Academic Supervisors are invited to clarify any points which might help them advise Academic Supervisors on marking the student interview. Before the interview is terminated, the students are asked for any final comments and given a short debriefing on how the interview went. They are asked to return the following day to receive their marks and feedback. The marking sheets have spaces for comments by the Academic Supervisors and peer Academic Supervisors (ie. in justification of the allocated mark), as well as the students (who may wish to disagree and possibly appeal). Marking sheets must be signed and dated by all parties.

Students are prepared for the critical thinking assessment interview in several ways:

- they have opportunities to practise exercises similar to that which they will undertake for summative purposes;
- they are coached on the process of the interview;
- they are able to attend forums which are set up for discussion on any/all aspects of their assessment tasks.

The criteria for assessment

Students are assessed against criteria which are known to them at the commencement of the semester. These criteria are based on the work of Norris and Ennis (1990). In assessing the ability to think critically and make judgments, the focus is on the extent to which students can demonstrate they

(a) have identified and challenged any underlying assumptions relevant to the action/behaviour/reactions to the incident, and can explain them;

(b) recognise and can explain different perspectives on the issues arising from the incident;

(c) can offer alternative explanations for what they have observed;

(d) can articulate what they have learned from the incident and why.

Full marks (15) are awarded where students demonstrate well developed critical and reflective skills. (This means all of the above criteria must be present, as appropriate.)

Half marks (= pass). Here some elements of critical thinking and reflective thought are demonstrated. Incidents are taken beyond mere description. The skills identified above have started to develop. (Not all the above criteria need to have been met for half marks.)

Marks between 7.5 and 15 are awarded to reflect the extent to which the student's skills have been demonstrated. This is a matter of the professional judgment of the academic supervisors, who must agree on the mark to be allocated.

Students who do not secure a pass are given one opportunity to resubmit for assessment.

Marks and grades

The assessment task is weighted at 15% of the total marks for the module. The other assessment events that comprise the remainder of the assessment program in the co-operative education module, are a written report (45%), workplace evaluation (25%), and an oral presentation (15%). (The latter assessment event is described in Module 8, section 2, 'Communicating Orally'.)

In order to be credited for the co-operative education module, students must 'pass' the critical thinking interview and oral presentation separately, and when these marks are amalgamated with the other two assessment tasks (written report and work performance) there must be a 50% mark or more to enable students to progress to the next semester.

Strengths and limitations

Students and assessors both found the assessment exercise worthwhile, and useful in enhancing their ability to think critically and to make judgments. This was summed up particularly well by one student who said,

> I can see now that the journal, critical thinking exercise, and report (written) were frameworks that helped me and perhaps even forced me to put into words what I experienced. They make me analyse situations in the workplace that normally I would have just accepted.

> ....The most valuable learning for me was through relating with people - in this case it is so much harder to measure what you have learnt, especially when there are no right or wrong answers. I realised in my critical thinking interview the short-comings of my own critical thinking and how I needed to develop those skills even more.

> *(Te Wiata, 1993)*

A number of issues arose out of this assessment event. Opportunities were provided to both staff and students to familiarise themselves in advance with the requirements of the critical thinking exercise, but not all chose to attend and, consequently, some difficulties were encountered. However this was not a widespread problem and tended to resolve itself once the various parties realised that their difficulties could have been avoided if they had prepared themselves prior to the interview. There was also some initial awkwardness with the interview procedure, and uncertainty, particularly from the academic staff. This was addressed through having appropriate support mechanisms such as having access to an assessment and curriculum specialist at all times, as well as coaching and training sessions. These support mechanisms meant that the academic supervisors queries could be answered in a prompt and timely manner. As the supervisors became more experienced with this type of assessment, these problems diminished. ■

Comment

Clarifying criteria

The assessment of students' ability to think critically and to make judgments itself requires assessors to make judgments. Using assessment criteria, as noted above, means that all parties to the learning process have a clear idea about how the assessment will be performed. Kurfiss (1988) emphasises the importance of students understanding the criteria used to evaluate their work. She regards this as a primary element for students learning to think critically. Documenting these criteria, along with other course information, is an attempt to make assessment requirements as "publicly" accessible as possible. Explaining and illustrating the criteria for students and using examples of good and not-so -good work also serve to further enhance students' ability to think critically. Open discussion with participants (students, employers, academics, administrators) means, among other things, that any biases (personal, professional and theoretical) can be addressed and issues clarified. This was, according to the contributors of this case, especially important for this particular assessment event as the attempt explicitly to develop and assess critical thinking had not been attempted before. Both the specific definition of critical thinking and the process for assessing this capability needed to be negotiated and agreed to by all participants before the co-operative education module commenced.

Congruence of aims, methods, and outcomes

An analysis of Case Study 1 shows that the assessment event is congruent with:

- the **aim** of the degree, ie. that graduates will be confident, adaptable, life long learners who have a broad understanding of business and are well-prepared for professional practice through the development of a number of capabilities;

- the **learning outcome**, "demonstrate critical thinking skills in the context of a specific situation encountered during the co-operative education program"; and

- the **teaching method**, ie. reflective records, usually journals (with which students practise communicating incidents to their Academic Supervisors.)

Achieving this congruence is essential when designing a course and assessment program. (For an initial discussion of this topic readers should refer to the the 'Introduction' to this package of materials.)

Theoretical underpinnings of the case study

Before leaving this case study, it is important to highlight the theory underpinning this program and its assessment event. What follows is a very brief account of the background of the Bachelor of Business co-operative education program.

The co-operative education program is about bridging the gap between the worlds of the educational institution and practice (work) and is based on an experiential model of learning. It treats learning as an holistic process, and attempts to provide "...conceptual bridges across life situations" (Kolb, 1984) .

The work of a number of writers was used to develop the curriculum for this program. For example, Kolb (1984) and Boud (1988) were especially useful for information on experiential learning and reflection. Because the business studies program endeavoured to prepare students for the demands of professional practice, Schön's work (1983) on the reflective practitioner was also particularly helpful. It provided an appropriate strategy and structure to take account of the "varied topography of professional practice" (Schön, 1990) .

Having chosen Schön's work as a basis for initiating students into the world of professional practice, it was necessary to determine what might be the most appropriate strategies for assessing the outcome we expected students to achieve, that of critical and reflective thinking. It was here that the work of Norris and Ennis (1990), Brookfield (1987) and Benett (1989; 1993) were invaluable. The first three writers provided information on what critical thinking might be "all about", as discussed in the first section of this module. Benett's work assisted in providing both a theoretical perspective for assessing workplace learning and in addressing the issues of validity and reliability in the assessment of that learning.

The next case study is an example of critical incident analysis in which students offer their reflections in writing.

Case study 2
Critical incident analysis

Case study from Education,
Neal Sellars, James Cook University

This case study focuses once again on assessment as a learning experience for students. The information presented below is an edited version of written material provided by the contributor.

Context

This case study is set in the context of an education program, the Bachelor of Education (Primary). The assessment task, described below, is one of the assessable activities in a core education subject in the third year of this four year degree program. The final year includes extended time in schools and is regarded as a "professional year". The component encompassing this assessment event is titled Professional Development, and is taught primarily in workshop mode with an accompanying lecture strand.

Abilities being assessed

In this educator's words, "the focus in this critical incident task is on the teacher as decision maker". The abilities being assessed are similar to those described in the first case study in this module, and include reflection, critical thinking, exploring and evaluating alternatives.

Assessment procedure

Students select a critical incident which they have observed and/or participated in either as student teachers in schools (during practice teaching or "school experience", as it is called at James Cook University) or as a student (tertiary, secondary or primary), and write a factual, objective description of the incident. They then reflect on the decision made by the teacher (who may be themselves, as student teacher), and critically evaluate this decision.

➤

The critical incident is defined as an incident which makes an impact on the student teacher in terms of their learning about teaching. The fact that they recall the incident they select as a basis for this task from a range of other incidents is evidence that it is regarded as significant for them.

It is important to have a shared understanding with students as to what might constitute a "critical incident". You may remember that in the previous case study, the meaning of "critical incident," although set in a business studies context, had a similar meaning to that just described. In both cases the meaning of the term is clearly communicated to students.

Students share their written description of the incident with a group (3 or 4) of fellow students, who collectively explore aspects of the decision and alternative actions. Students subsequently review their original decision and make an evaluation of the decision based on this review and reflection. For example, students may decide to support the original decision, or alternatively, choose another option. The rationale or justification for the decision advocated is an important component of the critical incident report.

The criteria for assessment

These are as follows:
- Description of incident - clarity and adequacy
- Relevance of incident as an opportunity to learn about teaching
- Final reflection on incident - degree of insight and quality of analysis
- Summary of learning outcomes - insight into decision making in teaching
- English expression - clarity, correctness

NB Because of changes in the assessment program in this Professional Development subject, this task will in future not be assessed, but will be classified as a non-assessable subject requirement.

Strengths and limitations

The strengths of this type of assessment event included the following:
- drawing on the student's own experience in schools;
- disciplined writing requiring students to describe objectively before evaluating;
- exploring alternatives rather than looking for a recipe for teaching, a "one-right-way" to approach teaching;
- sharing with colleagues, thus fostering collaborative skills;
- revealing the value in reflecting on teaching.

The limitations highlighted are two-fold:
- some students choose incidents in which decisions are rather clear-cut and which do not offer much opportunity to explore alternatives;
- some students' reflection tends to be at the narrowly technical level, with little consideration of the rationale behind the chosen action.

■

Comment

The exercise just described is viewed by the educator who submitted the case as primarily a teaching device, a learning experience for students rather than a testing device. That is, this educator had in mind a focus on student learning as opposed to student testing when he developed this exercise.

You may recall that the results of these assignments are also used for summative purposes (ie. the marks count towards the final grades). This case study demonstrates once more how curriculum can be designed to serve both ends/goals, ie. enhancing learning and grading.

Another method of assessing the abilities included in this module is to ask students to undertake a critical evaluation. The two case studies that follow illustrate this process. In both of these cases assessment is via written work, and contributes at a significant percentage to a final grade. Both of these case studies require students to think critically and examine particular situations, and use appropriate resources in order to evaluate (eg. the impact of a change) and/or formulate recommendations.

3

Case study 3
Evaluation of a change and/or innovation

Case study from Education,
Andrew Sturman, University of Southern Queensland

The information that follows is an edited account of materials provided by the contributor along with follow up discussions (via email). The educator who provided this case study wishes to acknowledge the work of Kerry Kennedy who was responsible for the initial development of this unit.

Context

The unit of work dealt with in this case study is taken mainly by students studying the Bachelor of Education (Studies), to upgrade an original 3 year Bachelor of Teaching. Other students who may also select this unit are those studying the Graduate Diploma of Education and the Master of Education. The unit is taken over a 16 week period and is only available in an external mode.

Assessment procedure

Students are asked to write an essay evaluating the impact of a major policy change (which they have identified) on a school, the problems it has faced and the success it has had in translating policy intentions into practice. It is expected that the evaluation of change should be in terms of the students' own secondary school or one with which they are familiar. The argument here is that the quality of the evaluation is likely to be closely related to the understanding the student has of the reform in question.

➤

Marks and grades

Equal weighting is given to the description and evaluation parts of this assessment task.

The description of the changes should:

*   be placed in broad policy terms;

*   make reference to policy intentions as expressed in reports, government papers and/or legislation.

The assessment of this part of the task then has some specific expectations, for example:

*   is there a reference to policy reports?

*   is the report mentioned up-to-date etc?

As mentioned earlier the evaluation of the change has to be in terms of the student's own secondary school, or one with which they are familiar. Students are specifically asked to address a number of aspects:

*   the impact the change has had on the school;

*   the problem(s) if any, that have occurred;

*   the degree to which the policy intentions have been successfully translated into practice.

Equal weighting is given to each of these aspects.

Strengths and limitations

The educator notes that while it is relatively unproblematic to assess whether each of the above aspects has been addressed, the quality issue remains one of professional judgment.

Other broader issues focus on the assessment program for the whole subject of which this essay is part. The rest of the unit assessment is made up of a critical review of selected articles/papers (15%), and a written final examination (55%).

Some of the strengths for this assessment program include:

*   the differential weighting of the assessment items which enable students to become familiar with the objectives of the unit of work without the risk of early failure;

*   the assessment items being designed to encourage students to display a critical understanding of key features of education rather than only tap factual recall.

The main limitation identified was the use and heavy weighting of the exam, and the fact that students are not obliged to pass all items of assessment, (ie. marks are aggregated for a final result). Where this leads to students passing the unit through doing well in the exam, but poorly with the first pieces of assessment, students are sometimes requested to do supplementary work in the areas where they were performing badly. (The issue of aggregating marks is discussed more fully in Module 7, 'Designing, creating, performing')

■

Case study 4
Critical evaluation of research literature

4

Case study from Education
John Watts, Central Queensland University

The information below has been developed from written materials provided by the contributor. These include the initial case study as well as supplementary data.

Context

This case study involves third year students in the Bachelor of Teaching (Primary). Students have completed one mathematics curriculum unit in their first year, and they will complete a further mathematics curriculum unit at the end of their third year.

Assessment task

The assessment task is a major assignment which is structured into four parts: development of a contract 10%, literature surveys 30%, written presentation 40%, and oral presentation 20%. The assignment requires students to examine critically contemporary school issues and/or topics in mathematics research. They are then required to formulate consequent implications for teaching, learning and assessment practices in school or tertiary mathematics. Five pages of literature references concerning various current issues in mathematics are distributed to students as a catalyst for their thinking.

Part 3, the written presentation, provides students with the opportunity to use their own ideas (but related to the literature), and implications (and often recommendations) are formulated from the preceding conclusions emanating from their literature surveys. The rationale for the heaviest weighting on this written part of the assignment is that it is more important for students to engage in critical judgments about implications and recommendations for teaching, learning and assessment, than it is to simply draw conclusions from the literature. The assessment tasks are sequenced so that the literature survey occurs before students spend three weeks fieldwork in schools, and fieldwork resources and experiences may be used by them to help prepare the third part of their assignment.

Overall, the assignment sequence endeavours to assist students to develop their abilities to critically analyse and reflect on a current issue, using various perspectives distilled from the literature, ideas and feedback from peers, along with their own fieldwork experiences and ideas.

Clarifying the criteria

Seven criteria are supplied as guidance for students for assessment purposes.

The criteria are:
- Focus, eg. single informing theme
- Completeness, eg. breadth and depth of reading, main ideas and 'fact' ascertained
- Presentation, eg. referencing, headings, paragraphing
- Grammar, eg. spelling, syntax, punctuation
- Structure, eg. orderliness, logic, 'outline', proper beginning and ending, conciseness, headings
- Argument, eg. clarity, critical evidence, limited use of jargon and cliches, technical terms explained, reasonableness
- Appropriateness, eg. educational setting

➤

Within each of the criteria there are four minimum standard levels ranging from "a consistently high level of competence evidenced" (Standard 4) to "some level of competence evidenced, satisfactory for a passing grade" (Standard 1).

The class works through the criteria and discusses the relative weightings for each. The four main criteria chosen by students are usually focus, completeness, structure and argument. Accordingly these criteria receive the most weighting.

Marks and grades

Results are then translated into Grading levels - see below:

GRADING LEVEL	COMBINATION OF STANDARDS
High distinction	Standard 4 in the four main criteria, and not lower than standard 3 in the remaining criteria
Distinction	Standard 4 in three main criteria, standard 3 in the remaining main criterion, and not lower than standard 2 in the other criteria
Credit	Standard 3 in three main criteria, and not lower than standard 1 in the remaining criteria
Pass	Minimum standard 1 in all criteria

Formative feedback is also provided on any drafts that are submitted prior to the final handing in of assignments.

Strengths and limitations

Strengths of the assignment noted by the educator who provided this case study include comprehensiveness, student interest, flexibility, structured design, workability, scholarly activity, validity, presenting assessment tasks so that their sequence and format assist students to demonstrate their optimum performance, and integration of assessment tasks. Limitations include restricted library skills of some students, need for further development of criteria based assessment, and lack of time to cover all interests in one cohort.

Another good way of reinforcing learning through assessment is to draw on issues or topics that are current and relevant for students at a particular time. The next case study offers an example of this.

Case study 5
Critique of a current concern

Case study from Geography
Ian Prosser, University of New South Wales

The account that follows is for the most part an edited version of the material provided by the contributor. The 'Comments on Marked Assignments' are reproduced here in the form that the project team received them.

Context

The Bachelor of Science in Applied Physical Geography provides the context for this particular case study. The subject encompassing this assessment event is "Soils and Landforms" which is conducted during one session in the second year of the degree program and is compulsory for all Applied Physical Geography students. Assessment is carried out through an essay or report, the marks of which contribute 20% of the total assessment for the subject.

Abilities being assessed

This particular assessment task is designed to assess students' ability to "construct a coherent argument, and critically evaluate a complex topic". The educators responsible for this subject believe that it is important for students to graduate with this ability in order to assess the state of knowledge of any topic. This is especially so if they are to embark on careers in research, public policy, land management, and the like, which are frequently destinations of Applied Science graduates.

The assessment task

An essay/report is set on a topic of current debate and/or community interest, in relation to the subject material: for example, whether the community concerns over erosion after the January 1994 bushfires were justified or not. Students were given a few references to start them on a literature search, and a one day field trip was conducted to a site of the fires. They were also given the assessment criteria (see below) with the topic and were encouraged to present their paper in the form they considered most appropriate.

Criteria for assessment

Assessment criteria provided by the educators are as follows:

- Ability to find and refer to published work that contributes to understanding fire, runoff and erosion.

- Ability to construct an argument on the validity of concerns over fire-induced runoff and erosion on the basis of the scientific evidence. You will find many opinions but little consensus in the literature on whether fire accelerates erosion and runoff. Therefore, you will have to analyse the validity of each study, its limitations and assumptions using your knowledge of runoff and erosion processes. For example, are there any good reasons why the results of two studies appear at first to contradict each other? Then you can come to your own conclusions.

- Presentation of your argument as a logical sequence of ideas, supported by evidence and/or case studies and illustrations. Sentence structure, grammar, spelling and quality illustrations all contribute to a professional quality presentation. You can complete the assignment as either an essay or as a report with various sub-headings.

- Referencing in accordance with the Student Guide distributed in first year. All sources of information must be properly referenced.

Marks and grades

In an attempt to provide quality feedback with maximum efficiency (for teaching staff), individual comments on the reports were kept to a minimum but more complete explanation and advice was given to students in a comments sheet (see below) outlining common strengths and weaknesses in relation to the assessment criteria. Individual comments on the reports focused on the strongest and weakest features.

➤

Ian Prosser, 1994

GEOG3051 SOILS AND LANDFORMS
FIRE AND EROSION ESSAY
COMMENTS ON MARKED ASSIGNMENTS

This handout gives you advice on common problems encountered with the assignment in addition to the individual comments. You should compare these comments with your essay to assess which comments are most relevant.

The overall standard of assignments was higher than in my previous experience. Many students demonstrated that they had spent considerable time and had used initiative in researching the topic. Many assignments were also very clearly and convincingly argued, with supporting evidence provided. Assignments that met these two criteria were given the best marks. The top mark awarded was 19/20.

I accepted arguments that believed concern over erosion was not justified and arguments that believed they were justified. Your mark reflects how well your argument was made and the evidence you provided. The essential questions that needed to be addressed were:

(i)   How natural is the current fire regime in the Sydney region (see note 1)?
(ii)   Under what conditions do fires accelerate runoff and erosion (see note 2)?
(iii) What are the consequences of increased runoff and erosion (see note 3)?

Specific comments

A: Content

1.   Some essays neglected to discuss whether the fires were natural or not. If they are natural then the resultant erosion is also natural. If people have increased the intensity or frequency of fires then the subsequent erosion is a form of human impact. The frequency of high intensity fires has probably increased in modern times.

2.   Rainfall intensity in the months immediately following the fires is a crucial control on whether there will be rapid erosion or not. This is best demonstrated by comparing the results of Blong et al. (1982) with Atkinson (1984). Many essays did not make the difference clear or did not recognise the extreme rainfall conditions described by Atkinson.

3.   Some essays seemed to assume that any runoff or erosion was a bad thing, rather than accepting that runoff and erosion are natural processes that shape landscapes. The important question is whether runoff and erosion are accelerated to the extent that they have a negative impact on ecosystems or our society.

4.   You must stick to the question. Some of the references included material on soil chemical changes, vegetation changes, and nutrient studies. Whilst these are interesting topics they should only be included where they are of relevance to erosion.

5.   Many students took the opportunity to refer to the data provided on the field trip. This is admirable but you should include the data as a diagram or table and refer to specific examples in the text. eg. do not just state that there was more runoff from the unburnt site than the burnt site. Be more specific and factual. Say something like: " In the first storm following the fire the burnt runoff plots yielded 10 times more runoff than the unburnt plots even though there was only 7 mm of rainfall (Table 1)."

6.   Erosion rates are expressed in the dimensions mass/area/time, eg. tonnes/hectare/year. Many of you omitted time, probably because Atkinson (1984) also makes this mistake. 10 t/ha is rapid erosion if it is over one month, but is nothing unusual over a whole year.

Figure 1.1

Comments sheet
Ian Prosser

B: Presentation

7. An essay is a coherent argument using the literature as supporting evidence. The articles need to be compared and contrasted and you should only include information relevant to your argument. The date of the fire reported by Atkinson is not particularly relevant, for example. A summary of each paper you read does not make a very interesting essay.

8. Do not use extensive quotes, use your own words. This relates to the point above of presenting an argument rather than a summary of each paper.

9. Paragraphs should contain the development of individual ideas, and you create a new paragraph when you start to discuss a new aspect of the topic. In general you might have 2-4 paragraphs per page.

10. Many small errors in spelling or grammar could be corrected by reading your essay before it is submitted.

C: Referencing

11. All references cited in the text must be in the reference list, but the reference list should not contain any uncited reading. References are listed in alphabetical order and include the names of all authors. The publisher and place of publication are given for books. The volume and page numbers are given for journal articles.

12. If you are referring to work cited in a later paper, and you have not read the original paper then the citation in your text should be of the form"(Smith, 1969 cited in Walker et al. 1986)".

13. In your text, do not give the page numbers except when giving a direct quote, just give the surname of the author and the year of publication. There are two citation styles:

(i) "Smith (1989) recorded accelerated erosion following fire at Liverpool " or

(ii) "Accelerated erosion was recorded following fire at Liverpool (Smith, 1989)....".

14. When there are two authors give both surnames: e.g. "Strahler and Strahler, 1987". When there are three or more authors use "Walker et al., 1986" where et al. is short for et alia, which is Latin for "and others". Latin words, including species names, should be in italics or underlined. If you think the use of Latin is a bit old fashioned just substitute it with "and others".

15. If you have any doubts about referencing just follow the style of major journals such as Earth Surface Processes and Landforms or Australian Journal of Soil Research.

Figure 1.1 *(cont)*
Comments sheet
Ian Prosser

Strengths and limitations

Considerable feedback is able to be given efficiently, and written advice is given that students can refer to next time they write a report. Making the topic relevant to community concerns stimulates student interest and motivation, and helps them appreciate potential applications of the subject material. A contentious topic almost forces students to give their own opinions and not just summarise the literature.

The provision of the marking guide, 'Comments on Marked Assignments' assumes that the students make the effort to reconcile these with their own report and grade.

Although the mark is not at this stage apportioned to the individual assessment criteria this may be done in the future.

Comment

Let us now consider what some of the literature tells us about analysis and the construction of argument in relation to critical thinking.

A good starting point for readers interested in pursuing this topic further is the chapter on informal logic in Kurfiss's book, *Critical Thinking* (1988) She identifies several key concepts that are found in the texts on logic and reasoning. These concepts are as follows:

Formal arguments   these are deductive in nature, ie. their conclusions follow necessarily from their premises. For example,
(Premise)   1. If A, then B
                     2. A; therefore B
                     3. B

Informal arguments   these are inductive and involve making generalisations rather than drawing firm conclusions. Their conclusions can only be more or less probable; they can never be established as absolutely true.

Cogent arguments   rest on the premises that they are justified or warranted; there are no fallacies or errors of inference involved.

The construction of critical thinking we have used for this module includes both formal and informal logic. Whereas formal logic is concerned with the quality of reasoning (Beardsley, cited by Kurfiss, 1988), informal logic is the study of argument as it is practised in everyday life (Johnson and Blair, cited by Kurfiss, 1988). We also believe that teaching and assessing critical thinking goes beyond helping students with the "technical skills" to achieve goals, also encompassing values that those goals imply. We agree with Kurfiss (1988), that to exclude discussion of those values is to violate a fundamental purpose of helping students to improve their skills to think critically and make judgments.

The assessment exercise described in the previous case study is an example of a task that requires an informal inductive type of argument. To develop an argument of this type students require a "bank" of relevant knowledge along with the skills and dispositions inherent in our definition of critical thinking. Students need to use all of the available information relevant to the subject. Arguments that are of the informal inductive type are also dialectical; that is, the students examine and "interrogate" their knowledge base in search of possible flaws, objections or counter arguments. It is important to note that with this type of argument even a well supported conclusion can be questioned (Perkins, Allen, and Hafner, cited by Kurfiss, 1988).

Kurfiss (1988) also points out that analysis of arguments provides practice in academically important skills like reading comprehension, comparison and contrast and evaluation of ideas. Controversy compels students to confront their biases and may stimulate them to rethink their ideas, either to find new justifications or to revise them in the light of better arguments. This idea of controversy was encompassed in the previous case study, when the educators involved noted, "A contentious topic almost forces students to give their own opinions..."

In all of the previous case studies, the students' ability to reflect has been implicit (if not made explicit) in their successfully completing an assessment exercise. There are a number of ways in which students endeavour to develop this ability and the case study that follows is an example of an assessment task that focuses on one way in which students can enhance this ability.

Case study 6
Reflective journal writing

6

Case study from Health Science Education
Fran Everingham, University of Sydney

This case study was contributed to the project by the educator in a written submission and followed up with a subsequent interview.

Context

This example is located in the context of a Health Science Education program offering post-graduate studies in tertiary teaching. Students are teachers from across the health sciences who work in academic, clinical or community education settings. The assessment event that follows occurs in a Stage 1 core subject. The journal or diary is used as a bridge between private and public worlds of learning. The focus of this assessment event is on the "act" of reflection rather than the content of the actual reflection.

Abilities

In this exercise students are required to demonstrate their understanding, application and critique of the reflective cycle (Boud, Keogh & Walker, 1985). The abilities being assessed are reflection and evaluation. The intended learning outcome for students is that they be able to use the reflective cycle in their own professional context.

Assessment procedure

Students participate in a series of microskills teaching sessions during which individuals are videoed and receive facilitator and group feedback using a standardised observation sheet. Later at home students review their own videoed microskills practice and complete a self evaluation form. The video is intended to assist the student to review the microskills teaching session and engage in the process of reflection. The self-evaluation form is provided as an aid to initiate reflective writing. The students reflect on the feedback and their own self-evaluation in a journal. Finally, they write a formal report on the whole process.

As indicated in the marking criteria cover sheet reproduced below, the report covers their own reflection on their performance in the microskills teaching session, a literature-based discussion of the reflective cycle, and their own evaluation of the experience of keeping a journal. Appendices must include the feedback sheets, the self-evaluation sheet, and evidence from the journal.

Prior to the start of the Microskills module students are briefed about the assignment. In addition to the detailed written explanation provided in the 'Program Participants Guide' for all assignments, class-based explanation and clarification of assignment requirements is standard practice in the program. Where students are likely to be unfamiliar with the mode of assessment, this is introduced in class using explanation, structured learning activities and discussion. Copies of the assignment criteria are also distributed at this time.

Criteria

Assessment in the journal assignment is focused on students being able to:
(a) use the reflective cycle as an aid to recalling and recording professional experience, reviewing this and planning appropriate action;
(b) use journaling as a vehicle for written reflection;

➤

(c) draw on available evidence to inform self-evaluation in the context of professional practice; and
(d) reflect on their own approaches to learning.

Students are judged according to how they meet the criteria below. The criteria listed under 'Reflection Report' are drawn from the steps in the reflective cycle (Boud et al., 1985). Taking this approach enables a creative solution to the troubling issue (discussed later) of allocating marks to what would otherwise be private writing.

Marking Criteria:

Assignment 2: **Report on the Microskills Journal**

Name: ....

Criteria	Mark	Rating Indicator				
1. Reflection report		F	P	C	D	HD
• describes significant moments in the class video experience in terms of personal learning or insights (returns to the experience - awareness of self in that setting)		F	P	C	D	HD
• recalls and evaluates feelings associated with the event (description of events and feelings)		F	P	C	D	HD
• identifies and distinguishes factors that affected performance (critical analysis)		F	P	C	D	HD
• analysis of performance reflects integration of knowledge about microskills (synthesis)		F	P	C	D	HD
• draws on past teaching experience or recent contexts outside our classroom (association)		F	P	C	D	HD
• manages to balance personal with objective interpretation of evidence (validation)		F	P	C	D	HD
• discusses peer feedback		F	P	C	D	HD
• identifies strengths and weaknesses (evaluation)		F	P	C	D	HD
• selects aspects for improvement and indicates possible action (appropriation or integration of learning)						
Sub-total	25					
2. Critical evaluation of the reflective cycle		F	P	C	D	HD
• discussion draws on the literature		F	P	C	D	HD
• demonstrates understanding of the literature		F	P	C	D	HD
• evaluative comments						
Sub-total	5					
3. Evaluation of the reflective cycle		F	P	C	D	HD
• evaluative commentary about journaling in the context of professional development (experience as learner; implications for self as teacher)						
Sub-total	5					

Figure 1.2

Marking criteria
Fran Everingham

➤

4. Completeness of evidence		
• Appendix 1. Feedback sheets from video practice (facilitator and peers)		yes no (compulsory)
• Appendix 2. Self-evaluation from video viewing		yes no (compulsory)
• evidence from Personal Course Journal used to support discussion		F P C D HD
Sub-total	5	
TOTAL	40%	FINAL RESULT

Figure 1.2 *(cont)*
Marking criteria
Fran Everingham

Marks

The assessment task described in this case study is now worth 40% of the total marks for the subject. The educator who provided this case study drew attention to the fact that while this percentage may seem surprising to some, it was actually recommended by the student forum on program assessment procedures.

Mindful of the assessment dilemmas identified in the literature for teacher assessment of private writing, only a small percentage of the total assessment was initially allocated to this activity. Student feedback soon showed frustration about the low percentage of the total assessment mark actually allocated to this assignment. They viewed this as inadequate given the preparation and performance requirements in the microskills module on which the reflection was based, the time required to write about this experience on a weekly basis, and finally the time required to draw all of this together in a formal report that required the synthesis of evidence, knowledge of the literature and critical discussion.

Strengths and limitations

Because private reflective writing is used selectively as evidence for the final report which is submitted, assessment is a significant issue. Various questions emerge. Should a mark be allocated to such private writing? If the journal is to be submitted, will students write what they perceive the lecturer wants to read rather than honestly record and explore their own experience? If the journal is not assessable, will students bother to record their experiences and use writing to reflect on these?

The strategy used to address these issues was to shift the emphasis of what would be assessed away from the private journal writing to the more public product of report writing.

The greatest strength of this assessment exercise according to the educator who submitted this case study is that it provides a creative bridge between the private nature of reflection on practice for the purpose of learning and the public nature of assessment products.

Limitations included the following:

Some students report struggling with the concept of this more personal style of writing in the context of graduate studies and their perception that writing should follow the academic format. Others report being inhibited by their undergraduate and professional experience which put low demand on writing output and high expectation for scientific objectivity versus valuing personal experience and acknowledging subjectivity.

Other points worth noting are, first, that students indicate that journal writing and reflection may be convenient for them to overlook if not formalised as an assessment task early in their

➤

studies; and second, that in later stages of the program students confess they treated this Stage 1 assignment as a tedious course hurdle but as a consequence of accumulative experience with reflection in their studies found themselves using reflective writing independently of course requirements. Post graduation students report their final reflective writing, undertaken in the context of their Major Project, provided a level of insight, construction of a holistic view and illumination that they had not anticipated. They also report continuing to use writing as way to "sort out" their thinking about professional issues they face in their work settings. ■

Comment

Everingham notes that this particular assessment event embodies, models and facilitates many of the current concerns of teachers and educational researchers in higher education, such as,

- student centred learning
- self-assessment
- deep approaches to learning
- learning about learning
- experiential learning
- processes that underpin lifelong learning
- reflection on learning

Remember that the learning outcome for students is about using the reflective cycle, with the aim of this specific assignment to provide a context and an inducement to experience journaling and reflection.

Students are encouraged from the outset of the Health Science Education program to keep a journal. As in the first case study in this module, this is not compulsory, but rather recommended. In both of these cases the assessment event focuses on demonstration of an ability, ie. reflection, critical thinking, rather than the journal itself. Keeping a journal can be initially for many students a "difficult" experience. Time spent at the beginning of a course clarifying what the purpose of the journal is, and familiarising students with how they might use this tool, is a very worthwhile exercise. The type of professional diary or journal described in this case study is one that facilitates students' responsibility for developing their professional competence.*

In helping other educators understand more about how this subject and its assessment task were developed we would need to consider a number of factors including the following:

- the literature that was helpful in determining the structure of this educator's subject and assessment event
- the reflective cycle itself; what it is, what it means.

The educator provided the following explanation of the theoretical underpinnings of the design and operation of her case study.

The work of writers such as Boud (1988), Boud et al. (1985), Boud & Walker (1992), Holly (1984), and McAleese (1984) were particularly useful. The first four references relate to reflection and journaling, and are worthwhile considering for any educator interested in assessing in this area, irrespective of the discipline/context. (For instance, you may remember that the educators who submitted Case study 1 also used the work of some of these writers.)

---

* Journals according to Holly, (Holly, 1984) are records of impressions plus descriptions of circumstances, others, the self, motives, thoughts, and feelings. Journal writing can include the structured, descriptive, and objective notes, and/or free flowing impressionistic meanderings.

In explaining reflection and the reflective cycle, Everingham provided the following information:

> Reflection consists of those processes in which learners engage to recapture and re-evaluate their experience, to work with their experience to turn it into learning" (Boud, Cohen & Walker, 1993)
>
> Reflection as a key to undergraduate and lifelong learning in professional education is a significant feature in the assessment of students in this program where students are learning to be teachers. Reflection is studied from various perspectives: the learner constructing meaning; the teacher facilitating learning in classroom and workplace settings; the teacher as researcher undertaking action research; the professional practitioner using experiences as a source for continued professional development.
>
> The theoretical underpinnings of reflection are introduced in the subject 'Adult Learning', experienced as a key to professional skills development in the module 'Microskills Teaching', modelled and practised as a stage of processing structured learning activities in 'Planning and Evaluating Educational Experiences', drawn on as an approach to facilitating clinical practice in 'Clinical Teaching and Supervision', incorporated as a mode of self assessment in all independent learning contracts, explored as an aspect of action research in 'Managing and Evaluating Curriculum' and undertaken as a written component of the major project completed in Stage 3.
>
> Reflection is identified as a significant enabler of learning across the literature of the various overlapping fields of this program, that is, teacher education, health sciences education, education for the professions and continued professional education.
>
> The three stage model of reflection proposed by (Boud et al., 1985) is used as the basis of this initial assignment, that is, returning to the experience, attending to the feelings and re-evaluating the experience.

Issues for consideration

All six of the case studies described in this module have touched on a number of issues relating to the assessment of critical thinking. These have included such things as the importance of linking the assessment task with course/program aims, student learning outcomes and teaching method(s); ensuring all parties have a shared understanding of assessment requirements; and specifying and communicating the assessment criteria to students.

Perhaps the most significant issue for the development/teaching of critical thinking is that of generalisability. For an initial exploration of this issue readers are directed to (Ennis, 1989; Kurfiss, 1988; McPeck, 1981). The first writer offers some clarification to the confusing topic of whether or not critical thinking is specific to subjects by distinguishing among three versions of subject specificity. McPeck's book offers clarification of the concept of critical thinking, and draws out its curriculum implications. The book by Kurfiss provides a comprehensive outline of the aspects of critical thinking and the issues arising from this problematic field of study.

Another important issue is Paul's argument (in Kurfiss, 1988), that while it may indeed be possible to teach students (the skill of) critical thinking this alone is not enough. He contends that by emphasising analysis and "correction" of fallacies, such courses miss the point that irrationality is a fundamental human characteristic, inherent in the way "world views" are constructed and protected. Those who undertake courses in thinking critically then, run the risk of using their skills to rationalise their existing biases. Kurfiss (1988) states that the most fundamental limitation of courses that teach critical thinking is that the questions we ask determine the value of our inquiry, and without knowledge of the subject enquiry, it is difficult to ask intelligent questions. For this reason, she says it is not possible to substitute introductory courses on thinking for disciplinary based instruction in reasoning. However these courses do offer one avenue for initiating students into the complexities and challenges of reasoning they are likely to encounter throughout subsequent courses. This, she contends, needs to be reinforced and extended in disciplinary subjects.

Other problematic areas that need to be addressed include the varying background beliefs (eg. ethnic, religious, gender related) of assessees, and whether or not the tasks that are being asked of them are assessing different aspects of critical thinking or inadvertently testing their ideologies. These areas are particularly troublesome when using tests for critical thinking, particularly those which are commercially available. The difficulty lies in determining whether or not the test chosen is actually suitable for the intended purpose. While these tests appear to be effective in testing some aspects of critical thinking abilities, they fail, according to Ennis (1994), to address the dispositions inherent in critical thinking.

The choice of both the assessment exercise itself, and the manner by which it is evaluated are of paramount importance to the majority of students undertaking courses/subjects in higher education. The assessment of students' ability to think critically and make judgments is problematic at the outset. It becomes even more complex when other factors such as those described are taken into account. However, if we are serious about facilitating our students' abilities in this puzzling but exciting area, we must in the first instance acknowledge these difficulties/differences. Only when this is done, can we begin to work towards a fairer assessment for all.

Indicators of quality

At the beginning of this module thinking critically and making judgments were defined as a process of ***reasonable and reflective thinking that is focused on deciding what to believe or do***. The emphasis Norris and Ennis (1990) place on the process of thinking over its products is based on the fact that many conclusions of human thought may in retrospect be shown to be in error, either partly or wholly. That is, even though people may have reasoned well, the conclusions of their reasoning may have been wrong. In addition, it is not merely having information that is useful, but knowing how to use it. So we can say that the information that we collect on students' capacity to think critically and make judgments is of high quality when it allows us to decide whether or not the students' thinking processes were justified. The information that follows is based on the work of Norris and Ennis (1990) and readers are referred to their work for a detailed account of validity and reliability in relation to critical thinking.

As mentioned earlier in the introduction to this package, the traditional indicators of quality in the field of assessment have been reliability and validity: reliability referring to consistency; validity referring to trustworthiness. It is important to address both factors, as consistency does not necessarily mean the assessment event is a trustworthy one. For example, imagine a test purported to test for critical thinking in medical laboratory science (microbiology). However, to gain the correct answers students need only memorise the answers. One item may ask the question, "What are the most common bacteria that cause meningitis in children?". Students would be required to state the names of these organisms, eg. *Haemophilus influenza, Streptococcus pneumoniae*. Such a test might be highly reliable in the technical sense, but would indicate nothing about levels of critical thinking despite its intended purpose, so it is not valid.

When considering reliability in relation to critical thinking, it is therefore essential to interpret carefully the reported reliabilities of techniques for assessing this ability.

It is important to remember, too, that many factors can affect reliability of the exercise (apart from the assessment instrument itself). For example, the personal health of students, degree of motivation and so on. It is also important to note that many of the factors affecting consistency are beyond the students' control, eg. poor lighting, noise, as well as ambiguous instructions for the assessment tasks being undertaken.

Reliability as consistency is a desirable goal in gathering information on students' critical thinking. However it is by itself not enough, so another standard of quality - that of validity is required. For the purposes of assessment in this module an assessment event is valid to the extent it measures what it is supposed to measure in that situation. The phrase "in a situation" is a necessary qualification according to Norris and Ennis (1990), because an assessment task might be a valid measure of thinking critically in one situation and not another. They provide as an example the situation where a test of algebra word problems written in English is taken by students whose first language is Spanish and who have difficulty with English. This test would be less valid for those students whose first language is not English. The writers also highlight that no test is valid for all situations in which it might possibly be used.

A procedure for assessing students' ability to think critically and make judgments is valid if it can be trusted to tell us the extent to which the students have critical thinking ability. The task of judging the validity of an information-gathering technique is a task of judging its trustworthiness as an indicator of underlying abilities and dispositions. When we collect information on students' capacity to think critically and make judgments, we are primarily concerned with the abilities and dispositions that underlie their performance. Inference is required to move from the evidence of performance to statements about abilities and dispositions.

Quality information on students' ability to think critically and make judgments can be gathered using a variety of techniques; some of them have been described in this module. Whether it be by open ended questions/statements (eg. essays/reports), individual interviewing of students, reflective journals, or some other technique, each has advantages and disadvantages.

There are no magic answers or short cut methods which can replace the knowledgeable and careful application of general principles.

> *The most important principle to follow in evaluating (assessing) students' critical thinking is that the evaluation (assessment) itself should conform to the standards of critical thought.*
>
> *(Norris & Ennis, 1990)*

Conclusion

Most educators today would agree that there is considerable value in helping students develop the abilities (ie. develop arguments, reflect, evaluate, assess, judge) that we have included in this module. Too much emphasis on the "efficient" transmission of large quantities of information is, according to Kurfiss (1988) costly in the long run because it crowds out time students need to transform information into meaningful, usable knowledge.

How we teach, and therefore how we assess critical thinking, especially in the disciplines, is a field wide open for research. Other areas requiring further exploration, according to Kurfiss, include: the relationships between knowledge and reasoning abilities; instructional and institutional conditions that nuture critical inquiry; individual differences in approaches to critical thinking, especially those related to critical thinking skills; how the disposition to think arises; and the context for critical thinking.

The practice of good teaching is also an important subject of study for understanding how critical thinking can be taught and assessed. We as educators can learn a lot from those of our peers who successfully emphasise teaching and learning skills. Through talking with them, studying their planning and assessment processes, observing their classes, talking with their students, and reviewing their students' work we can enhance our own expertise in this fascinating though problematic area of education.

We hope that through this module we have helped you (the reader) to consider and reflect upon your own practice; and that we have been able to provide you with some stimulating and worthwhile information which will in turn further enhance your own skills in assessment.

References

Auckland Institute of Technology. (1992). *Bachelor of Business Course Document*. Auckland: Auckland Institute of Technology.

Benett, Y. (1989). The assessment of supervised work experience - a theoretical perspective. *The Vocational Aspect of Education*, 109(August), 53-64.

Benett, Y. (1993). The validity and reliability of assessments and self-assessments of work-based learning. *Assessment and Evaluation in Higher Education*, 8(2).

Boud, D. (Ed.). (1988). *Developing Student Autonomy in Learning* (2nd edition). London: Kogan Page.

Boud, D., Cohen, R., & Walker, D. (Eds.). (1993). *Using Experience for Learning*. Buckingham: Society for Research in Higher Education and Open University Press.

Boud, D., Keogh, R., & Walker, D. (Eds.). (1985). *Reflection: Turning Experience into Learning*. London: Kogan Page.

Boud, D., & Walker, D. (1992). *Reflection at Work*. Melbourne: Deakin University Press.

Brookfield, S. D. (1987). *Developing Critical Thinkers: Challenging Adults to Explore Alternative Ways of Thinking and Acting*. San Francisco: Jossey-Bass.

Ennis, R. (1989). Critical thinking and subject specificity: clarification and needed research. *Educational Researcher*, 18(3), 4-10.

Ennis, R. (1994). Dispositions and abilities of ideal critical thinkers; and an annotated list of critical thinking tests. Handouts from session at "Thinking" conference in Boston, 1994,

Holly, M. L. (1984). *Keeping a Personal-Professional Journal*. Melbourne: Deakin University.

Kolb, D. (1984). *Experiential Learning: Experience as the Source of Learning and Development*. New Jersey: Prentice Hall.

Kurfiss, J. G. (1988). *Critical Thinking: Theory, Research, Practice, and Possibilities* (ASHE-ERIC Higher Education Reports No. 2). Washington, D.C.: Association for the Study of Higher Education.

McAleese, R. (1984). Video self-confrontation as microteaching in staff development and teacher training. In O. Zuber-Skerritt (Ed.), *Video in Higher Education*. London: Kogan Page.

McPeck, J. (1981). *Critical Thinking and Education*. Oxford: Martin Robertson & Company Ltd.

Norris, S. P., & Ennis, R. H. (1990). *The Practitioner's Guide To Teaching Thinking Series: Evaluating Critical Thinking*. Victoria: Hawker Brownlow Education.

Schön, D. (1983). *The Reflective Practitioner*. USA: Basic Books Inc.

Schön, D. (1990). *Educating the Reflective Practitioner*. San Francisco: Jossey-Bass Inc.

Te Wiata, I. (1993). *The Experience of Learning in Co-operative Education*. Unpublished Master of Education thesis, University of Auckland, Auckland.

MODULE 2

SOLVING PROBLEMS AND DEVELOPING PLANS

GREG RYAN

Module 2
Solving problems and developing plans

The cases considered in this module focus on assessing students' abilities to solve ill-structured (or ill-defined) problems (such as those which occur in "real-life") and to plan subsequent actions.

This module covers broad abilities such as:
- identifying problems
- posing problems
- defining problems
- analysing data
- reviewing
- designing experiments
- planning
- using information (apply)
- diagnosing
- speculating
- conjecturing

Themes

- Chronological sequence in the stages of presenting a real-life problem
- Using problem based learning
- Internal consistency among curriculum design, and teaching and assessment methods
- Hypothetico-deductive reasoning
- Determining standards for different levels of competence
- Differences between the expert and the novice problem solver
- Determining levels of performance
- Establishing criteria for different levels of performance
- Learning from the assessment experience

- Assessing 'metacognition'
- The 'trade-off' between validity and reliability in assessment
- Improving marker reliability
- Advantage/disadvantage of using simulation
- Criteria for assessing the different stages of a research project
- Integrated assessment of knowledge, skills and attitudes through tasks such as history taking, physical examination, data interpretation, diagnosis, planning of treatment or care, administration of treatment, and assessment of related knowledge.
- Using video-recording for assessment of communicaton skills

Techniques

- Modified essay question
- Simulation
- Poster
- Objective Structured Clinical Assessment (OSCA)
- Written report

Case studies

7. Modified Essay Question (MEQ), Medicine
8. Simulated client interviews, Law
9. Objective Structured Clinical Assessment (OSCA), Nursing
10. Social history report, Social Work
11. Research poster exercise, Geography

Module 2

Solving problems and developing plans

Greg Ryan

Problem solving and planning abilities are important components of learning throughout life. Helping students to develop these abilities is one of the key functions of university education.

For the purposes of this module, problem solving is defined as

> *mental activity leading from an unsatisfactory state to a more desired 'goal state'.*
>
> *(Kurfiss, 1988, p28) .*

Whenever there is a gap between where you are now and where you want to be, and you don't know how to find a way to cross that gap, you have a problem. (Hayes, 1989, pxii)

A distinction is commonly made between so-called "well-structured" and "ill-structured" problems (see, however, additional comment on page 46 regarding this dichotomy). Well-structured (or well-defined) problems are conceptualised as those which are clearly stated, with all the information needed to solve the problem being available in the problem, or known to the student. An algorithm (a step-by-step procedure) exists that guarantees, if it is correctly applied, a correct (that is, generally agreed by members of a discipline community) solution to the problem. Students' abilities to use algorithms to solve well-structured/defined problems are discussed in Module 3, "Performing procedures and demonstrating techniques.

An ill-structured (or ill-defined) problem (such as a real-life situation), on the other hand, is more complex,

> *without definite criteria for determining when the problem is solved and without all the information needed to solve the problem.*
>
> *(Jackling, Lewis, Brandt, & Sell, 1990).*

In this instance, the use of heuristic problem solving procedures (which are based on general strategies rather than precise rules) may improve the chances of finding a solution, but will not guarantee a correct solution (indeed, there may be no single, "correct" solution, with members of a discipline community disagreeing on the correctness or otherwise of a particular solution). Part of the challenge of working with heuristics is knowing how and when to use them, particularly in unfamiliar situations.

The extent to which an assessment task is representative of problem solving in a particular discipline raises the issue of its validity (that is, does it measure what it sets out to measure). To use a well-structured/defined problem to assess problem solving in, say, medicine, law, nursing or social work, might be highly desirable from a reliability point of view (it could, for example, provide a consistent measure of one aspect of problem solving; and there could be a high level of agreement across markers). But if the purpose of the assessment is to test how a person can deal with the problems which typically occur in day-to-day professional practice, the test would have very poor validity. It simply does not reflect the complex, ill-defined/structured problems which a practitioner faces. (See also Introduction, Module 1 and Glossary.)

This module focuses primarily on ways in which students' abilities to solve ill structured problems, and to plan subsequent actions, can be assessed in a variety of academic contexts.

The abilities encompassed in this module therefore include the following:

- identifying problems
- posing problems
- defining problems
- analysing data
- reviewing
- designing experiments
- planning
- using information (applying)
- diagnosing
- speculating
- conjecturing

One of the strongest messages which appears throughout these modules is the need for consistency between our curriculum aims and objectives, our teaching methods, and the ways in which we assess our students. This means that we need to have thought through carefully what it means to be a problem solver in our particular discipline; that we help students to develop this ability through our teaching methods; and that this is then reflected in the way in which we assess.

There are a number of events which research shows typically occur in a problem solving process:

- finding the problem: recognising that there is a problem
- representing the problem: understanding the nature of the gap to be crossed
- devising a plan: choosing a method for crossing the gap
- carrying out the plan
- evaluating the outcome: asking "How good is the result?" once the plan is carried out
- consolidating gains: learning from the experience. (Hayes, 1989, p3)

Ascertaining events like these which are typically involved in a problem solving process within your own discipline can form the basis for the determination of criteria against which students' problem solving abilities can be assessed (and which can also guide their learning process). The following criteria could be used with ill-structured/defined problems in, say, the health and social sciences:

- identifies cues which indicate an actual or potential problem/s in the current situation;
- identifes further information needed to better understand the problem/s; and where and how this information can be obtained;
- demonstrates an understanding of knowledge concepts, and their interrelationships, which underly the problem/s;
- uses this knowledge to:
  - generate alternative ideas about the problem/s
  - pose alternative workable solutions to the problem/s (or, if the problem/s can't be 'solved', suggests how the situation could be improved);
- justifies a choice of a plan of action (and that this justification includes a moral/ethical dimension);
- carries out the plan;
- evaluates the success or otherwise of the plan;
- evaluates the problem solving strategy used.

Criteria such as these can be made available to the students at the start of session and used as the basis for the teaching of problem solving ability throughout the session. This would provide plenty of opportunity for modelling of so-called expert problem solving behaviour by teachers, encouraging students to "think like a doctor/lawyer/nurse/social worker...."

Case study 7
Modified essay question

Case study from Medicine
Jean McPherson, University of Newcastle

The first case study in this module presents an example of how consistency can be achieved between the aims of a course of study, and the way in which it is taught and assessed. The information provided by the contributor has been used as a basis for an expanded discussion of issues which are highlighted by the use of this particular assessment method .

The Modified Essay Question (MEQ) was developed originally for use in medical education, but it has potential applications in many other disciplines which are interested in a test that is particularly suitable for the assessment of problem solving skills. MEQ papers typically vary from 40-90 minutes and constitute a series of questions related to a gradually unfolding sequence of encounters with a "patient". The questions must be answered in the sequence asked (typically the test takes the form of a clinical case presented as a chronological sequence of items in a booklet), with no review of previous answers (to simulate the finite temporal sequence of decision-making in clinical practice) (Feletti, 1980) . Nor are students permitted to preview items (and subsequent data) in the case booklet.

Context

The following example of the use of an MEQ occurs in second-year undergraduate Medicine at the University of Newcastle. This program is designed, taught and assessed using the principles of problem based learning (see Glossary). There is in this program a high degree of internal consistency among curriculum design, and teaching and assessment methods.

Abilities being assessed

- Clinical reasoning
- Understanding of clinical and basic science
- Application of basic science to clinical problems

Assessment procedure

In Year 1, students complete a formal "Formative Assessment" which includes two MEQ papers, to make them familiar with the format prior to the (end of year) "Summative Assessment" which is outlined in this case study.

The first question is usually a brief patient scenario (clinical presentation); this is either repeated with the addition of new information or (ideally) reformulated as the paper proceeds and further information is provided. For example, in McPherson's MEQ:

Mrs Robyn Fields, age 32, brings her 8 month old son, Andrew, to you because of bruising, which has been concerning her for several weeks. The infant has large bruises over the limbs and several smaller bruises on the trunk.

Question 1:   (a) State the possible causes of this problem basing your answer on the likely mechanisms
                (b) For each general cause in (a), describe the key features you seek in the history or examination.

Time: 10 minutes
CT 10 minutes

Each question has a specified (recommended) time and a record of cumulative time (CT), as students have to answer questions sequentially and cannot scan the entire paper to determine their individual time allocation.

In terms of a problem solving process, the above example provides the students with the problem (bruising at particular sites on the body), and Question 1 requires that they generate causal hypotheses [part (a)] and nominate how each of these hypotheses will be tested through history or examination [part (b)], an example of a hypothetico-deductive approach to problem solving.

(You may not, of course, always provide the student with the problem. They may have to identify this for themselves. An example of this is provided in another case study in this module - using an OSCA [Objective Structured Clinical Assessment] in a nursing course.)

A detailed guide is provided to markers in order to improve the reliability of the allocated mark. For example, in relation to Question 1 above:

Model Answer: (a) Excessive trauma eg child abuse or clumsiness
                Coagulation disorder   (inherited or acquired) eg haemophilia
                Platelet disorder   numbers (thrombocytopenia)
                                       function (inherited or acquired)
                (b) (i)   Evidence of trauma eg old or recent fractures; attitude of mother, psychomotor deficit
                    (ii) Inherited coagulation disorder: family history (maternal family for haemophilia, either parent or family for von Willebrand's disease); history of bleeding from other sites (epistaxis) or on other occasions (?circumcised); evidence of joint bleeding (swelling, stiffness) Acquired coagulation disorder:evidence of eg liver disease
                    (iii) Presence of petechiae; history of epistaxis, gum bleeding; ingestion of drugs affecting platelet function. Inherited platelet disorders rare, but may be family history.

The idea of a standard of knowledge and/or ability expected at a particular level of a course is reflected throughout this MEQ. Careful consideration has been given to the developmental level of the students in deciding the depth of understanding which is expected in the students' responses. For example, the following level was determined for the responses to Question 1 earlier:

Minimum Level of Competence:
                (a) awareness of excessive trauma or defect in normal haemostatic mechanisms (coagulation, platelets) and that latter may be inherited or acquired.
                (b) includes family history, bleeding on other occasions or from other sites.

Determining this minimum level of competence requires you to identify what constitutes reasonable performance by students who are at a particular level of development within your course along, say, a continuum from "novice" to "expert" problem solver in your discipline. (See further discussion of expert vs novice on page 46.)

Assessment in this Modified Essay Question narrows as the paper proceeds; and as the problem is progressively defined, questions become increasingly specific. For example, the next section of the paper begins by providing a clear and concise re-conceptualisation of the problem (on another occasion, you may decide that the students should state this for themselves) before asking the students specifically about the investigations they would request.

Andrew Fields, age 8 months has bruising which is of concern to his mother. You consider excessive trauma and acquired and inherited disorders of coagulation and platelet function as possible causes. Although you cannot exclude the possibility of child abuse, you do not consider this likely. You are concerned that both acute leukaemia and severe haemophilia can present as easy bruising in this age group.

Question 2:   State which investigations you would request. Justify your answer by describing the results you would anticipate for each of these disorders.

Time: 10 minutes
CT 20 minutes

Model Answer: Full blood count (thrombocytopenia, neutropenia, anaemia, blast cells on blood film for acute leukaemia; normal in haemophilia)
APTT (prolonged in haemophilia, normal in acute leukaemia) with assay of Factor VIII and IX to determine whether haemophilia A or B.

Minimum Level of Competence:
FBC and APTT with correct comments on anticipated findings

You will note that by providing this re-conceptualisation of the problem, the student is receiving feedback about the hypotheses that they have generated and tested in response to the earlier Question 1.

The examples taken from this MEQ and cited above show that the early questions have focused on finding and representing the problem, in the lead-up to devising a treatment plan - requiring of the student the generation of diagnostic hypotheses and/or basic science mechanisms underlying the clinical presentation. Subsequent questions may require the application of knowledge of basic science, interpretation of diagnostic information, management issues, disease complications, ethical issues, prognosis, etc.

After completing this MEQ paper, and to help them to learn from the experience, the students are encouraged to review the paper with the "model answers" and "minimum level of competence" (MLC) as specified by the assessor. Students may comment, in writing, on the expectations of the assessor and their comments are available at the time the paper is marked. Model answers and specification of a MLC is common to all written assessment instruments in this medical school.

Although not part of the formal (mark-carrying) component of this assessment, an important opportunity has nevertheless been provided for students to reflect (albeit ex post facto) on their problem solving process. Schön (1990) refers to both this reflection-on-action and to reflection-in-action (while actually engaged in the activity) as being important mechanisms by which to learn from experience. The conscious act of thinking about your thinking (referred to as metacognition) is also an important element of the development from novice to expert problem solver, as Royer, Cisero and Carlo observe:

➤

> *Metacognitive skills for learning* Metacognitive skills are cognitive activities that allow an individual to reflect on and to control performance in a useful and efficient manner. Skilled performers within a domain possess the capability of planning their activity, monitoring the success or failure of their own activities, and altering behaviour in accordance with the monitoring activity. Less skilled performers are far less proficient at this monitoring process and, correspondingly, less successful at applying the skills they do possess.
>
> *(1993, p204)*

(For further discussion of assessing metacognition, see index.)

Marks and grades

Marking of the MEQ is on the basis of students reaching the minimum level of competency (MLC) specified for each 5 minute segment, with 1 mark being allocated for each satisfactory 5 minute MLC.

The marks are displayed graphically as well as in list/tabular form, enabling a "natural" cut-off point to be recognised. For those students in the borderline region, performance in individual discipline assessment tasks is also examined. Borderline poor scores in combination with significant deficiencies in several disciplines may be considered as an overall not-satisfactory result; in the first two years of the course, borderline scores with a maximum of two discipline deficiencies may be adjudged satisfactory but the student will have to fulfil a "directed own-learning task" in those disciplines in the following year.

Strengths and limitations

A well written MEQ assesses the approach of students to a problem; i.e. their reasoning skills and understanding of concepts, rather than recall of factual knowledge. Because of its closer approximation to actual professional practice, it has greater validity than would isolated questions on knowledge (that is, if the purpose of the assessment is to test how a person would perform in professional practice). The requirement for assessors to define a model answer and minimum level of competency and to mark in accord with these is a quality control mechanism which ensures criterion referenced assessment and promotes assessor accountability and inter-assessor reliability. (See Index for other discussion of validity and reliability, and criterion-based assessment; also refer to Glossary.) However, when writing questions, care must be exercised to avoid ambiguity. (For advice on the design, construction and marking of a modified essay question, the reader is directed to Feletti and Engel, 1980.)

Students can experience stress, as they are informed of the correct answer in the reformulation of the problem prior to the next question, but cannot turn back to correct their answer. (They may, for example, be required to hand in each section as it is completed.) To avoid students being penalised twice (for example, where the answer to one question determines the answer to a second question), the new question can be placed on the following page, and prefaced with a statement such as

> *Let us assume that your hypothesis is.....What physiological process would support this hypothesis in relation to the available information about the patient and his problem?*
>
> *(Feletti & Engel, 1980. p79)*

■

Comments

A note about the distinction between "well-structured" and "ill-structured" problems

The distinction between well-structured and ill-structured problems has been used, in this instance, for convenience and simplicity. However, as Voss and Post (1988: 262) point out, they do not necessarily "constitute a dichotomy but instead represent points on a continuum." A problem "may have well-defined constraints at some points in the solution and open constraints at other points, and whether a problem is ill-structured or well-structured is a function of where the solver is in the solution process."

The essential idea here is that initially ill-structured problems can become well-structured during the solution process. The preceding case study of the MEQ in use in Medicine is something of an illustration of this. You may recall that the assessment narrowed as the problem became progressively more defined, and questions became increasingly more specific. There would come a point in the working of this problem where the boundary between the well- and ill-structured aspects of the problem become increasingly unclear. In addition, for an expert, a problem may be relatively well-structured, but for a novice the same problem may appear to be quite ill-structured.

A note about novice/expert problem solving

A great deal of our knowledge of problem solving has arisen out of two quite different methods of investigation: the study of the performance of experts, and attempts to give problem solving abilities to computers. In more recent years, the most fruitful area of research has been the exploration of the differences between expert and so-called novice performance. The primary difference revealed by this research is that experts possess an extensive and highly organised body of conceptual and procedural knowledge (which is a combination of specific facts and procedures for utilising those facts) that is readily accessed and used in combination with superior monitoring and self-regulation skills. What is not so well established empirically, however, is "how (this) expertise is acquired, how it can be taught, and how beginning learners can be presented with appropriate experience." (Glaser & Chi, 1988, pxxi; Royer, Cisero & Carlo, 1993, p204)

In the meantime, though, one way in which to logically conceptualise this difference is in terms of a continuum of development of performance ability from the stage of novice towards expertise - i.e. from when students are first exposed to the concepts and ideas of a discipline to the level of the expert problem solver. (What should be acknowledged, though, is that the level of 'expert' may not be reached by our students until well after they graduate from our courses.)

One of the most important factors which distinguishes so-called 'expert' from 'novice' problem solving is the extent of the knowledge base which can be drawn on. "While some general strategies for problem solving may exist, skill in solving most problems depends a great deal on the extent and organisation of the knowledge base available to the problem solver" (Kurfiss, 1988: p28)

Acknowledging its importance to effective problem solving, Royer, Cisero and Carlo provide the following observation regarding knowledge organisation and structure, and include comment on the implications for assessment:

Knowledge organisation and structure. As a learner first begins to acquire a skill, the knowledge corresponding to that skill is stored as a set of unrelated or loosely related facts. As skill develops, these knowledge units become highly interconnected and structured. As a consequence, the skilled individual activates large chunks of information when performing an activity within the skill domain. In contrast, the novice activates isolated facts, definitions, and concepts.

The implication of this is that measures of knowledge organisation and structure can provide indexes of skill development. (1993, p207)

The challenge for us as assessors is to differentiate between what is meant by the expert and the novice in our disciplines; nominate the points on this continuum where we would like our students to be at different stages of our course; identify the standard of problem solving which we could reasonably expect at each of these points; help our students, through our teaching methods, to develop this level of ability; and choose appropriate methods to assess whether they have achieved this level of development.

A note about assessing metacognition

One of the central messages arising out of research into metacognition (thinking about thinking) "is that students can enhance their learning by becoming aware of their own thinking as they read, write and solve problems..." (Paris & Winograd, 1990), and it is an important component of our role as a teacher to help them to develop this ability.

Metacognition is not an easy component of problem solving activity to assess. It is, by nature, subjective - a personal awareness of an individual of how he or she is processing information. Whilst we may more easily assess the correctness or otherwise of the observable outcomes of the problem solving process - e.g. the solution - it is the subjective elements of the process which require caution with judgment. Metacognitive processes can certainly be verbalised by students (for example, in written or spoken form) through the answers which students provide to self-questioning such as:

Getting going with problem-solving

What information do I have ?
What is the problem ? How do I know this is a problem?
What are my ideas/hypotheses about the problem ? Where did these ideas/hypotheses come from ?
How can I test them ?
Do I need more information? Where can I get it ?
What is my judgment about the problem/s? How did I arrive at this judgment ?
What is my goal ?
What is my plan to achieve this goal ?

How am I doing ?

Am I using my plan or strategy ?
Do I need a new plan or strategy ?
Has my goal changed ? What is it now ?
Am I on the right track/getting closer to my goal ?
Did It Work ?
What worked ?
What didn't work ?
What would I do differently next time ?
What have I learned from this ?

(These questions were developed by the author of this module, and form part of ongoing research into the processes involved in problem based learning.)

Responses to these questions are recorded at different stages of the problem solving process. Some can be judged for 'correctness', as they were in the earlier hypothesis generation and testing within the MEQ. (You may recognise that these are also an heuristic for problem solving.) But others are less easily marked - they are far more subjective, and it may only be possible to comment on the quality or extent of the students' insights, their ability to express them, or how autonomous they were (that is, the extent to which they relied on the teacher for 'prompting').

Processes such as these are important elements of successful self-directed/self-regulated learning. Much talk occurs about the importance of our students taking responsibility for their own learning. But how often do we as teachers help them to do this? There is also compatibility between processes such as those discussed above, and Schön's (1990) notions of "reflection-in-action" and "reflection-on-action".

Further comment on case study 7

The modified essay question reported above is an example of how 'real life' problem solving can be simulated in an examination format. Just as would be required of them in clinical practice, the student had to respond to the problem presented by the patient by generating alternative ideas (hypotheses) about what may have led to the problem; identifying sources of information which would help them to test these alternatives (e.g. particular diagnostic tests); arriving at a correct diagnosis; and devising an appropriate treatment plan. Along the way, understanding of the knowledge elements of the problem were also tested.

This assessment is highly consistent with the teaching methods used within this particular problem-based course. There is extensive use of facilitated small group exploration of problem packages, similar to the one used within this MEQ. The choice of such a teaching method is, in turn, consistent with the stated aims of the course, which include the development of clinical problem solving and self directed learning ability.

While there is much to recommend assessment tasks such as the MEQ or those described in case studies which follow, a note of caution is sounded in a recent article by Swanson, Norman and Linn (1995). Surveying several different types of assessment tasks which attempt to simulate real-life, they note that:

1) test design and domain sampling is not more straightforward just becase the task imitates real-life;
2) examinees do not necessarily behave the same way in a test situation as they will/would in real-life;
3) scoring the rich and interesting behaviour of examinees can be highly problematic;
4) performance in one context does not predict performance in another very well;
5) correlational studies of the relationship between performance-based scores and other assessment methods targeting different skills typically produce variable and uninterpretable results;
6) security and equivalency of tests are extremely difficult, especially where numbers are large;
7) there are few studies of the intended and unintended impacts on teaching and learning of this type of testing;
8) selection of methods of assessment should depend on the skills to be assessed and a mixture of methods is usually to be preferred.

The next case study, taken from the discipline of Law, also tests students' problem solving ability through to the development of a plan of action - but in this case, the students are required to gather the information for themselves (by interviewing a 'client') and from this information, identify the problem. The use of a person acting as the 'client' also allows for the assessment of an additional, related communication ability.

Case study 8
Simulated client interviews

8

Case study from Law
Andrew Gonczi, University of Technology Sydney

The information presented below is an edited version of information contained within a published journal article written by Andrew Gonczi (1994) regarding competency based assessment in the professions in Australia.

Context

This case study, reported by Gonczi (1994), describes how simulated client interviews have been used to assess a particular element of problem solving ability (gathering and assessing data) for specialist accreditation as a Family Law Practitioner by the NSW Law Society.

Abilities and criteria

In Family Practice Law, abilities to be assessed include being able to:

* develop a relationship with a client (communication)
* gather and assess facts and instructions
* plan a timetable and course of action
* implement the plan
* act as an advocate
* complete the matter

Each of these abilities (or, in the Society's terms, 'competencies') have a certain number of defining elements, which, in turn, are further defined by criteria. For example, one of the elements of the first ability above ("develop a relationship with a client") is "listens effectively to client".

One of the criteria against which a student's performance would be assessed is "the solicitor is able to perceive the client's immediate needs regarding safety, children and the financial situation."

The other element is "communicates clearly and appropriately", and the performance criteria include "asks effective questions and interacts with the clients in a supportive way... adopts a non-discriminatory attitude and uses plain language to communicate..."

➤

In relation to the second ability listed above ("gather and assess facts and instructions") one element is "taking instructions from the client". The criteria against which a student's performance would be assessed include the following:

> *When taking instructions the specialist... displays thoroughness, persistence and awareness of relevance. The solicitor structures the process to assist the client to develop a history and obtains from the client an initial statment. This would include the nature of the problem, what the client wishes to achieve, the client's account of the relevant facts, the position of children and any relevant third parties and a view of the opponent's position. The solicitor draws the client's attention to any gaps or inconsistencies and checks the instructions with the client...the solicitor canvasses the question of costs (and) deals with any ethical issues arising from the instructions and keeps a clear record of the instructions.*

Assessment method and grading

The development of a relationship with a client as reflected in the taking of initial instructions was identified as one of the distinguishing features of the family law practice. This relationship depends on the possession of a range of abilities associated with: communication, gathering evidence, ethical principles, and the ability to assess facts. While the simulations focused on the students' communication abilities, the purpose of the activity was to gather and assess facts and instructions in order to effectively address the client's legal problem/s.

Six role plays were developed. While depicting men and women and different situations and problems (and basing them on actual cases can improve validity), all had the same key elements: an immediate need, long term issues, information not disclosed unless questions asked, client's hidden agenda, presentation of a problem that required non-legal solutions and others of a religious/cultural nature that required sensitive handling, an ethical issue, query on costs ('standardising' the situations in this way is important for reliability.)

Each student interviewed a trained 'actor' (a mature law student) for up to 60 minutes. The interviews were videotaped and assessed by a group of assessors who had undertaken a training session (also important for reliability). In this training, common faults of assessment were discussed and a number of videos were viewed and agreement reached on what would constitute adequate and superior performance. There were three levels of performance: failure to meet the standards, meeting the standards, and easily meeting the standards. Rating scales were developed to try to increase inter-assessor reliability.

For example, for communication, "poor performance" was described as: "does not allow client to talk freely, listens poorly, repeats questions, poor eye contact, ignores body language, uses only closed questions, does not reflect, paraphrase or summarise." "Very good performance" was: "asks effective questions to encourage the client to talk freely. Listens attentively, maintains eye contact, uses open body language, uses plain language, manages client's emotions, reflects, paraphrases and summarises."

For the gathering of information, "poor performance" was described as "haphazard, no awareness of relevance, sequence of events not established, inadequate information elicited. "Good performance" included "questioning persistent, adopts methods to test reality of the client's statements," etc.

■

Comment

You may recall that in the previous case study (the Modified Essay Question in the Medicine program at the University of Newcastle) the students were provided with a statement of the problem (bruising on various parts of the patient's body). In reality, of course, it rarely happens that the problem is given. The practitioner is required to gather their own information, and sift through it in order to identify the problem/s for her or himself, and this provides an added challenge for assessment. (This does happen in the Newcastle medical program as well - through mechanisms such as the OSCA, an example of which is outlined in a later case study.)

Ideally, this can be better assessed while the student is out in clinical practice, when faced with the real situation. There are both advantages and disadvantages in this. On the one hand, it is certainly reality (and therefore probably very high in validity). On the other hand, though, it is difficult to control variables adequately in order to, for example, provide consistency in the way the same and different students are assessed (thus the possibility of low reliability of the marks awarded). The challenge facing us, therefore, is to achieve a reasonable trade-off between validity and reliability. One way of doing this is through the use of simulation, wherein you provide a reasonable approximation of reality, but within certain broad, but controllable, limits.

Simulation, however, is a trade-off (see Swanson, Norman and Linn, 1995; see also p48. It can only approximate reality and it is difficult to create a simulation which adequately encompasses the extremely complex context in which a practitioner may have to function. One of the dimensions of difference between an 'expert' and a 'novice' performer, which Royer, Cisero and Carlo make, is that of the extent to which the student is able to take account of these other 'contiguous' and 'unrelated' events surrounding the problem solving activity:

> ***Automaticity of performance***. *When an unskilled individual is performing within an activity domain, every aspect of performance is frequently based on conscious reasoning processes. Because the cognitive system has a very limited capacity, this means that the individual's ability to process information other than that associated with the immediate problem is nil. In contrast, a skilled performer can handle many aspects of performance in an automatic and nearly load-free manner, thereby leaving a certain amount of cognitive capacity available for performing other activities such as integrating information, planning, or even performing a completely unrelated task.*

> *The ability to perform tasks in an automatic and capacity-free manner is yet another index of skilled performance. (1993, p204)*

The virtual world of the flight simulators used for pilot training may well be the most successful current means by which the complexities of real life have been captured in simulation. However, less sophisticated (but no less innovative) simulations which capture some of this complexity continue to be used most effectively in many disciplines. The following case study from the discipline of nursing also provides an example of the use of a simulated client. In this instance, though, unlike the law example, there is a repeat encounter with the client, when the student must return and actually administer some aspect of the care which had been planned.

The OSCA (Objective Structured Clinical Assessment) or OSCE (Objective Structured Clinical Examination) is used most extensively throughout the world in medicine and nursing programs. Like the Modified Essay Question (MEQ) (discussed earlier in the first case study in this module) the OSCA/E is a form of integrated, holistic assessment, and can include assessment of elements such as knowledge, problem solving, technical skills, communication, attitudes, and ethics.

It is typically a complex structure comprising a circuit of a number of stations at which different interrelated assessment events occur: events which are typically centred around one or more encounters with a 'client' (or group of clients) who have been coached to take this role. The complete examination often takes approximately 2-3 hours for a student to complete; and may also incorporate an additional take-home element. By setting a variety of tasks such as history taking, physical examination, data interpretation, diagnosis, planning of treatment or care, administration of treatment, assessment of related knowledge etc., the method assesses a candidates skills, attitudes and knowledge.

Case study 9
Objective Structured Clinical Assessment (OSCA)

Case study from Nursing
Sharon Bourgeois and Elizabeth McFarland, University of Western Sydney - Macarthur

An example of this method of assessment is described below. The information presented was provided by the contributors, and there have been only minor editorial changes made. The "Strengths and limitations" are reproduced here in the form that the project team received them.

Context

The following example of the use of an OSCA occurs at the University of Western Sydney, Macarthur, Faculty of Health, Division of Nursing, in year one of the three-year Bachelor of Nursing (a totally integrated, problem-based course - see footnote on page 72. It involves approximately 250-300 students and the twelve staff who comprise the first-year teaching team. In addition to assessing the abilities listed below, this end-of-year OSCA was designed to assess a variety of subject areas, including Biological and Behavioural Science, Nursing Skills, Nursing Theory, Social Science and Health.

Abilities being assessed

- interview skills
- enquiry and processing (problem solving) ability
- nursing skill competence
- application of knowledge
- critical and reflective thinking
- knowledge recall
- self reflection and assessment

Assessment procedure

Each student selected an appointment time for the assessment. Students were required to wear uniform, be on time for the appointment, and supply a video cassette. A number of students were assessed at one time. Five assessment stations were set up within the nursing laboratory (which was a large, simulated twelve-bed hospital ward, fully equipped, and including attached treatment and facility rooms).

Staff were allocated to stations to assess, coordinate or supervise as was necessary, depending on the requirements set out for each station. Marking of student papers was also necessary at some stations. Simulated 'patients' attended briefing (training) sessions prior to the OSCA, and debriefing sessions at the completion of the OSCA. Each patient was dressed in nightwear and stayed in bed each day for the duration of the OSCA (in this case, three days). Break times were timetabled for both staff and patients throughout each day. An academic staff member was responsible for meeting the needs and caring for the patients during the course of the day/s.

Station 1: Enquiry and processing (initial data, handover report) - 10 mins.

An audio tape contained one patient's set of information each; and each patient had a different but similar history. The tape was recorded simulating a hospital ward nursing handover report at the change of shift. A specially designed form for recording patient information was supplied to students for notetaking. Students were to process the information on the tape - identify problems, and generate hypotheses about the problems. The students could replay the tape several times during the time period allowed. Students were then accompanied to the next station.

Station 2: Enquiry and processing - testing information - patient interview - and nursing intervention - 45 mins.

A video camera was set up at the end of the patient's bed. Prior to commencement of the assessment, the video tape was primed and tested. Student marking papers for the patient interview session and the nursing intervention skills (simple dressing) were handed to the assessor by the student. The students were told to focus on their patient while the assessor performed the role of observer and assessor. The assessor was not available for questions or clarification.

Patients had been carefully briefed and had a prepared history to tell their student during the interview, in response to the questions asked by the student. A simulated wound relevant to the patient's history was temporarily bonded to the patient's skin, and covered in a dressing. A complete set of patient records was attached to the bed.

The video camera picked up sound using a microphone attached to the patient. Visual display from the camera showed the patient in bed and the side profile of the student. The assessor stood toward the end of the bed on the opposite side of the student and was not seen in the video replay. Each student was required to interview their client with their objective to assess the patient and to document a nursing history and test the hypotheses which they had formulated at the first station.

The assessor marked the student acording to an interview criteria sheet, based on the behaviours performed by the students and the students' responses during the interview.

The student then followed the interview with the required nursing intervention (to re-dress the wound), as determined by the student from the handover report, the patient history and the patient records. The dressing procedure was assessed against established and published criteria (to a safe standard determined by the academic staff and also published), contained in a "Care Activity Framework", a curriculum framework document developed specifically for this curriculum which requires students to identify the principles underlying each of the components of a nursing skill (in this case, simple dressing). (For example, the components "washes hands appropriately" and "uses a two-forcep, non-touch technique" are governed by the principle "maintenance of wound asepsis". All principles stated on the Framework had to be met during the intervention, according to the published standards. (The actual filling-out of the framework by the student occurs at Station 3.)

➤

Following the completion of the interview and the dressing procedure, the student left the patient and completed a nursing report in the patient's notes, based on the care they had given their patient, and identifying and applying legal requirements for report writing.

Station 3: Care activity framework - 30 mins.

Students were accompanied into a supervised adjacent room to complete their Care Activity Framework. This involved writing down the behaviours they had performed which were specific to their patient, applying these to the principles, and determining the rationale for each of the component behaviours. A formatted framework was supplied for the student to use with the principles already documented.

Station 4: Short-answer examination - 1 hour

This takes the form of a traditional short-answer exam, and is designed to test the student's knowledge of key concepts which are related to their patient's condition. In this instance, the exam contained science-related questions which were associated, for example, with wound healing and asepsis.

Station 5: Self reflection assessment - 20 mins.

A video cassette recorder was supplied for students to view the video tape of their patient interview (from Station 2). A self reflection summary of strengths and weaknesses was required for assessment. This component could also be performed at home if the student desired, for submission the following day.

Take home component - overnight

The take home component asked the student to process the notes and information which they had gathered during the assessment in order to formulate a detailed plan of on-going care for their patient (based on a specified format used within the Division). This was to be submitted by a set time, the following day.

Marks and grades

- Assessment in this program is competency based, and uses pass/fail grading.
- Assessment is based on published criteria, which are linked to a set of core, curriculum competencies relevant to professional nursing practice.
- Minimum standards are determined and published for all components of assessment.
- Students are required to pass a specified number of competencies to pass the year-long subject. (There is only one totally integrated subject in each of the three years of this program - Nursing and Health Studies I, II or III.)

Strengths and limitations

Some perceived strengths include:
- closely simulates real clinical situations in the assessment process (thus ensuring an acceptable level of validity);
- students perform a perceived relevant assessment;
- assessment is consistent with an integrated curriculum;
- allows the student to reflect on their own assessment;
- includes multiple assessment modes;
- a dynamic approach to assessment.

Problems perceived for this assessment include:

- making sure enough rooms are available to be used as stations. Room booking procedures were activated early in the year;

- ensuring there were enough staff timetabled to coordinate, mark, supervise and assess;

- allowing for adequate resources, such as tape recorders, video cameras, patient's facilities, equipment and supplies; and people to role-play the patients;

- allowing time for patient training (time before the assessment procedure and debriefing sessions after the procedure);

- a large amount of time and energy expended by staff - to set up and dismantle stations; and long days to assess 250-300 students in groups of 8-10;

- students displaying extreme nervousness towards the assessment procedure (briefing sessions must be held for students);

- a high cost factor - payment for patients and extra staff, and long days for academic staff.

■

The OSCA described in this case study is an example of how students can be assessed, in an integrated way and on a number of abilities, in a manner which approximates as closely as possible the realities of day-to-day professional practice. An approximation of reality is also achieved in the next case study, from the discipline of Social Work. In this instance, care has been taken to use a real situation which a social worker has handled (though mindful of privacy and confidentiality) as the basis for the information provided to the student for problem solving.

Case study 10
Social history report

10

Case study from Social Work
Rae Lindsay, University of Western Australia

The material presented in this case study has been reproduced with only minor editing. However, as with other case studies within this module, the "Comments" section has been written entirely by the module author.

Context

The Bachelor of Social Work is a 2-year, end-on degree. Students have to complete at least 2 years of an undergraduate degree with at least one year of study in psychology and one year of study in anthropology/sociology, before being eligible for admission to the program.

The unit being partially assessed by this case study is a semester length unit in the first semester of the 2-year program and precedes the first practicum. The other half of the assessment for this unit is a process recording of a mock interview conducted by the student in a practice laboratory setting.

Abilities being assessed

- ability to assess client needs and resources with a view to intervention; and
- ability to formulate objectives and plan intervention.

➤

Assessment procedure

A prepared case study is given to the students in the middle of the semester - about 6 weeks before the assignment is to be assessed. This consists of a single page of data regarding a particular client (problem, situation, background, family network, etc).

The data is obtained from a real situation that a social worker has handled but is disguised so that the client is unrecognisable. The data presented to the student is not ordered and the student will need to discern relevant from irrelevant data, identify the most important information, identify gaps in information and identify patterns that emerge.

The student is required to use theories of psychology/sociology to explain behaviour/situation. The assessment is worth 50% of the final grade for the unit. The assignment is expected to be approximately 2500 words long and is assessed by the lecturer in this unit.

The following guideline sheet is given to the students, and contains the weighting of the various components of the social history report.

IDENTIFYING INFORMATION Name _____ Address _____ Marital Status _____ Date of birth (Age) _____ Occupation _____ Religion _____ Ethnic identity _____ **REFERRAL** Source _____ Reason for Referral _____ Date of Referral _____ **PRESENTING PROBLEM including:** Precipitating factors - episodes which led to referral Prior interventions - collateral information; other attempts to elicit help Extent and duration of the problem	Case Data 10%
FAMILY IN TIME AND SPACE (genogram & ecomap)	Social History 40%
KEY PHYSICAL, PSYCHOLOGICAL, SOCIO-CULTURAL FACTORS	
ASSESSMENT SUMMARY STATEMENT	20%
OUTCOME GOALS	10%
INTERVENTION PLAN	15%
PRESENTATION	5%

Figure 2.1
Guideline sheet
Rae Lindsay

➤

Strengths and limitations

According to Lindsay, the assignment has now been used for several years and has proved to be useful in assessing the student's ability to:
1. write a clear and succinct report
2. discern significant information
3. use theory to interpret facts
4. demonstrate familiarity with the social work process.

It is limited because the student is restricted by only having written material available. In the real life situation the social worker would be able to get further information from the client and significant others.

■

Comment

This last issue is an interesting one. A number of ways can be used to introduce more of the realism of professional practice into an activity such as this. For example, students view/listen to a video/audio recording of an interview with a client; use a computer-based, interactive multimedia package to carry out an interview with a 'client'; or interview a simulated 'client' who has been coached for this purpose.

This latter option is one way in which this problem had been addressed in the OSCA/OSCE reported in the previous case study from the University of Western Sydney, Macarthur. This is a particularly interesting example, because the people who were coached for the simulation were not actors, but friends or neighbours of the staff of the Faculty of Health.

One of the drawbacks of using actors (or, more precisely, someone who has to learn a set script) is that it is (a) difficult for this script to adequately predict and cover the full range of questions which may be asked by a student during an interview; and (b) for this huge amount of material to be accurately (and consistently) recalled during repeated interviews by subsequent students. (An important factor for reliability, if this approach was being used as part of an assessment item.)

One way around this is to take a personal history from the would-be client, and search this history for points at which to build in the key aspects of the case study which you want them to adopt. During a subsequent briefing session, you then take them back through their history, and help them to insert the altered factors where they best fit with their own experiences. This way, they only have to remember the few altered factors, and their responses to the subsequent interview questions flow (seemingly) naturally from their personal experiences. This method has been used very successfully at the University of Western Sydney, Macarthur, and has obviated the necessity of employing trained actors. A note of caution, however. Because of the potentially sensitive and disturbing nature of the characteristics you may be asking your 'client' to adopt, it is very important to undertake a 'debriefing' session with them when the simulation has ended.

The next case study shifts the focus away from the sort of problem solving which occurs in day-to-day professional practice towards the more formal use of problem solving in research design and experimentation. Although it is a poster exercise (and therefore could as easily have been placed in Module 8, Section 3 - "Communicating Information Visually"), it has been included here as an example of how to assess student ability to 'do research'. The central focus of the assessment task is on the design and implementation of a piece of research, and a major emphasis in the marking is on the quality of the research undertaken. The poster is the means by which the outcome of the research process is communicated, and carries some assessment weighting in terms of presentation. Without the research having been undertaken, there would be no poster.

Case study 11
Research poster exercise

Case study from Geography
Iain Hay, Flinders University and Richard Millar, University of Wollongong

The account that follows has been taken from a published journal article (Hay and Miller, 1992) provided to the project team by Hay.

Context

Students are in their final year of undergraduate study. The discipline is Geography. The project requires that students devise and execute a peer-reviewed research exercise within a 14-week teaching session at the University of Wollongong. Each student's work culminates in the production and presentation of a poster which is also assessed by other students. The poster and presentation contribute to formal course assessment, being components of an overall assessment strategy which also includes written and oral reviews of journal articles, essays, seminar presentations and a final written examination.

Abilities being assessed

Along with the abilities associated with 'doing research', the poster exercise incorporates abilities associated with four modes of communication: literacy, numeracy, articulacy and graphicacy.

Assessment procedure

The exercise has three components:

* A piece of supervised research in which students set their own research question; design, execute and evaluate research strategies; and communicate the synthesised results of their activities to an audience
* Introductory exploration of the bureaucratic and competitive structure of the modern research environment
* Oral, written and graphical presentation of research results.

The exercise is designed to lead the students through different stages of the overall research process: development and approval of a project; peer review of project and methodology; and dissemination and evaluation of results. This pathway is followed through an overall exercise comprising six fundamental components:

1. Development of a research strategy

2. Critical assessment of peers' research strategies

Both the lecturer and other class members (up to twelve in a class) assessed each prepared research strategy according to the following published criteria:
-   Is the title clear?
-   Is the title related to the proposed subject?
-   Are the objectives of the research clearly outlined?
-   Has a valid justification for conducting this research been provided?

➤

- Is there a hidden agenda behind this research project? If so, what is it?
- Are there other good reasons for doing this research which are not outlined in the proposal?
- Can the project be achieved given the resources (e.g. time, money, information) likely to be available?
- Has a realistic timetable for completion of the project been provided? Can any suggestions for improvement be made?
- Are the research methods appropriate to the topic?
- Do any additional sources of appropriate information exist? Can extra readings be suggested?
- Other comments?

(Feedback from both peers and the teacher at this early stage regarding the nature and scope of the project is an important component of the process; and can significantly aid learning.)

3. Submission of an abstract

This 150 - 200 word abstract was submitted to the lecturer, and needed to make clear the central argument being made.

4. Production of a poster

Minimum dimensions were set at 60cm x 90cm, and three central principles were specified: attract attention; keep it short; and keep it simple. However, it was also stipulated that each poster must make a unified, coherent statement requiring no further explanation; otherwise, students may rely on the oral presentation to make their poster comprehensible to others, thereby defeating the end of developing visual communication skills. A number of points are made by the authors regarding the layout, visibility and colour, and the use of figures in posters, and the reader is referred to Hay and Miller (1992, pp207-209).

5. Presentation of a completed poster

Each student gave a 5-10 minute oral presentation of their poster to members of the class. Guidance on appropriate presentation skills is provided earlier in the session, when students are required to participate in a variety of different exercises requiring brief oral presentations to the rest of the class.

6. Assessment of peers' posters.

Copies of the criteria for the peer assessment were distributed early in the teaching session:

Content
- Has a clear statement of the question or relationship being investigated been provided?
- How complex is the project which has been undertaken? What is the 'degree of difficulty'?
- Does the poster 'stand alone', requiring no additional explanation?
- Has a thorough explanation of the question/relationship being investigated been provided? Is the explanation clear and logical?
- Are all components in the explanation given appropriate attention?

Poster Appearance
- Has care been taken in the production of the poster?
- Is all text on the poster legible from two metres away?
- How well organised is the presentation of material?
- How clearly do text and graphics transfer information? Is there room for improvement?
- Are figures/tables easily understood? Is appropriate use made of figures and tables?

➤

> Research
> - Does the poster indicate research methods and sources appropriate to the topic?
> - Are the references cited of good quality (variety, number, dates, sources)?
> - Are references appropriate?
> - Other comments?

Peer assessment of the poster is justified by the authors on three bases. First, assessment encourages students to think critically about the product being viewed. Second, assessment consolidates any new research and graphical skills which may have been developed through the course of the exercise. Third, if peer assessments are considered by academic staff in their final grade determinations for the exercise, student sympathy with the immediate problems of poster production may temper the more 'removed' and perhaps over-critical formal assessor's judgment.

The teachers' final assessment of the exercise focused on the quality of the information and the clarity of information transfer, rather than on artistic ability. However, because a good deal of time is devoted to the development of poster production skills, consideration is given to issues such as legibility from a distance and appropriateness of graphics.

Strengths and limitations

Because of the logistics of dealing with unwieldy posters and the demands on teacher time, the authors recommend not greater than a 1:20 teacher:student ratio for this exercise. The activity has been evaluated positively by the students, and includes the following points:

- its worth as an imaginative, creative and interesting change from the routine of essay after essay which can stifle the creativity they believe may be required in some occupations;

- it is one avenue by which research skills explored through the undergraduate degree may finally be practised - and in a novel way;

- the initial task of devising a research strategy and presenting it to peers is most worthwhile in compelling an early start to the project and motivating them to organise and formalise their thoughts about their proposed research;

- oral presentations of both the research strategy and the completed poster are considered by most students to be useful practice in the art of public speaking and, accordingly, are seen to have some clear vocational and social value.

Some problems, however, were noted:

- as research topics have to be devised early in the teaching session, students sometimes work on projects which reflect the attitudes and interests they hold when they enter the course, rather than any which may develop throughout the teaching session. This problem is difficult to overcome, unless students are provided with a list of potential topics from which one may be chosen. However, provision of such a list must be weighed against the benefits associated with individual determination of a topic.

- supervisory time demand may be heavy, but judicious use of assigned tutorial classes can ease this problem.

Conclusion

This module has focused primarily on ways in which students' abilities to solve ill-structured problems, and to plan subsequent actions, have been assessed in a variety of academic contexts. Each method has both strengths and limitations, and contributors have been honest in their respective appraisals.

What is most noteworthy is that each case study is an example of what problem solving can mean in the respective discipline (an important first step - define what it is before you try to teach and assess it). While there are some recognisable similarities, there are clearly many differences, and this reflects the current state of play of research into so-called 'ill-structured/defined' problem solving. Earlier work which concentrated on establishing general problem solving abilities was found wanting, for example in its "failure to show any transfer of problem solving ability from general…to contextualised problem solving" (Jackling et al, 1990, p146).

More recently, and as part of a wider questioning of the existence of general cognitive skills (and if so, whether they are transferable), is the belief that development of skills such as problem solving should occur " - *in association with the teaching of domain knowledge and be related to it*" (Jackling et al, 1990, p46)

(You will recall that one of the demonstrable differences between the 'expert' and the 'novice' problem solver discussed in an earlier section of this module was the extent and use of a domain-specific knowledge base.)

There is little doubt that it is desirable that the graduates from our university courses be able to problem solve effectively. This particular ability shows up repeatedly when groups of academics, from across the disciplines, are asked to list the characteristics which they believe their graduates should demonstrate as they leave their course of study and enter graduate practice. This is consistent with the recommendations of the Higher Education Council (1992) which were based on consultations not only within higher education, but also within industry and the professions.

What is not so clear, though, is how best to teach problem solving, and how best to assess whether or not the students are able to do it. There are, however, many promising developments. The previous case studies are examples of different approaches to assessment; and there are interesting developments in areas of cognitive and metacognitive instruction which involve, for example, direct explanation (e.g. of 'expert' thinking), 'scaffolded' instruction, cognitive coaching, cooperative learning and problem based learning. (For an overview of these methods, the reader is referred to Paris and Winograd (1990) or Boud and Feletti (1991).

To close this module, let us return to one of the consistent themes which recurs throughout this document: namely, that if it is your aim that students be able to solve the kind of problems which they are likely to encounter in graduate practice, then you should teach and assess in ways which help them to develop this ability.

References

Boud, D., & Feletti, G. (1991). *The Challenge of Problem Based Learning*. London: Kogan Page.

Chi, M. T. H., Glaser, R., & Farr, M. J. (eds) (1988), *The Nature of Expertise*. Hillsdale, New Jersey: Erlbaum.

Feletti, G. (1980). Reliability and validity studies on modified essay questions. *Journal of Medical Education*, 55, 933-941.

Feletti, G., & Engel, C. (1980). The modified essay question for testing problem solving skills. *The Medical Journal of Australia* (January 26), 79-80.

Glaser, R., and Chi, M.T.H. (1988) Overview, in Chi, M.T.H., Glaser, R., and Farr, M.J. (eds) *The Nature of Expertise*. Hillsdale, New Jersey. Erlbaum. pp.xv-xxviii.

Gonczi, A. (1994) Competency based assessment in the professions in Australia. *Assessment in Education*, 1 (1), 27-44.

Hay, I., & Miller, R. (1992). Application of a poster exercise in an advanced undergraduate Geography course. *Journal of Geography in Higher Education,* 16(2), 199-215.

Hayes, J. R. (1989). *The Complete Problem Solver*. Hillsdale, N.J.: Erlbaum.

Higher Education Council 1992. *Higher Education: Achieving Quality*. Canberra, ACT: Australian Government Publishing Service.

Jackling, N., Lewis, J., Brandt, D., & Sell, R. (1990). Problem solving in the professions. *Higher Education Research and Development*, 9(2), 133-149.

Kurfiss, J. G. (1988). *Critical Thinking: Theory, Research, Practice and Possibilities*. Washington, DC: Association for the Study of Higher Education.

Paris, S.C. & Winograd, P. (1990) How metacognition can promote academic learning and instruction. In B.F. Jones & L. Idol (eds) *Dimensions of Thinking and Cognitive Instruction*. Hillsdale, NJ: Erlbaum.pp15-51.

Royer, J., Cisero, C., & Carlo, M. S. (1993). Techniques and procedures for assessing cognitive skills. *Review of Educational Research, 63*(2), 201-243.

Schön, D. (1990) *Educating the Reflective Practitioner*. San Francisco: Jossey-Bass.

Swanson, D.B., Norman, G.R. and Lin, R.L. (1995) Performance-based assessment: lessons from the health professions, *Educational Researcher, 24* (5), 5-11.

Voss, J. and Post, T. (1988) On the solving of ill-structured problems, in Chi, M.T.H., Glaser, R., and Farr, M.J. (eds) *The Nature of Expertise*. Hillsdale, New Jersey. Erlbaum. Chap 9.

MODULE 3

PERFORMING PROCEDURES AND DEMONSTRATING TECHNIQUES

SUSAN TOOHEY AND DOUG MAGIN

The kinds of skills, techniques or procedures described in this module are usually acquired by practising a specified series of steps. Assessment is then carried out by observation and success is dependent on all or almost all of the steps being carried out effectively. Assessments may include grading based on defined levels of competence, or may be 'pass/fail' according to whether or not all steps in a set procedure have been carried out correctly. The routines may be vary in complexity (e.g. operating a basic microscope; driving a nuclear reactor). Successful performance may depend to a greater or lesser degree on (i) knowledge (ii) psychomotor skills (such as hand-eye co-ordination, manual dexterity), and (iii) attitudinal factors (e.g. care, scrupulous attention to carrying out all procedural steps).

This module covers broad abilities such as:
- computation
- taking readings
- using equipment
- following laboratory procedures
- following protocols
- carrying out instructions

Themes

- Validity and reliability and performance assessment
- Setting performance standards
- Different conceptions of the Objective Structured Clinical Examination/ Assessment

Techniques

All the assessment methods included in the case studies in this module involve some sort of performance assessment. They include:
- Use of computer software in carrying out statistical analysis
- Self assessment and co-assessment using video
- Objective structured clinical examination (OSCE)
- Mastery performance tests

Case studies

12. Continuous assessment of skill in using software package, Statistics
13. Using video for self assessment, Nursing
14. Objective Structured Clinical Examination (OSCE), Nursing
15. Mastery assessment, Medical Microbiology
16. Self-paced assessment of laboratory skills, Physics

Module 3

Performing procedures and demonstrating techniques

Susan Toohey and Doug Magin

The working title for this module was originally "Demonstrating skills". But skill is a term that we often use rather loosely. In the literature of education, skills are sometimes classified into three types: cognitive, perceptual and psychomotor. An example of a cognitive skill might be reading and interpreting plans; a perceptual skill might involve estimating distances, while suturing a wound would be an example of a psychomotor skill. But these distinctions prove not very useful in practice - not many skills fall neatly into a single category. Many of the skills taught in higher education require an integration of all three domains - students must understand the principles underlying the process, they must be physically adept and sensitive to the cues provided by the immediate environment. The health care professions provide many examples of these complex skills.

Perhaps a more useful way of classifying skills is to distinguish those that involve following a set procedure from those which are ill-defined, difficult to specify and non-routine. Interpersonal communication skills, management skills, skills of diagnosis and problem solving fall into the latter category and they will not be dealt with in this module. Instead, we limit ourselves here to the assessment of those skills which involve carrying out a clear sequence of steps and which usually require performance to a set standard of acceptability. Many skills in the health care fields fall into this category as well as skills in the operation of equipment, and in performing laboratory procedures.

From the many case studies submitted to the project, few indicated that their assessments are directed at testing such routine skills, techniques, or procedures. This may reflect a presumption that it is not necessary to devote much time or attention to training students in what may appear to be low level skills. However, as contributors in this section note, considerable amounts of practice and feedback may be necessary for students to master a skill to the level required for professional practice. Usually mastery of such skills is fundamental to more advanced work, and for this reason teachers sometimes wish to assess them independently before allowing students to proceed.

With skills of this type, the techniques or procedures to be carried out are specified, and usually a benchmark is set by which competence is judged. Assessments may include grading based on defined levels of competence, or may be 'pass/fail' according to whether or not all steps in a set procedure have been carried out correctly. The routines may vary in complexity (e.g. operating a basic microscope; driving a nuclear reactor). Successful performance may depend to a greater or lesser degree on (i) prior knowledge (ii) psychomotor skills (such as hand-eye co-ordination, manual dexterity), and (iii) attitudinal factors (e.g. care, scrupulous attention to carrying out all procedural steps). What is common to all is that a set of procedures must be followed and performed to a specified level of proficiency.

Assessing process or assessing product?

In many teaching contexts, the assessment of routine skills, techniques or procedures is carried out by observing the student performing the task. Success in the assessment requires students to follow the process or procedure, more or less exactly. Obvious examples of this can be seen in clinical areas of nursing and medicine. Assessment of process may be essential in these situations because some of the most important outcomes or products (such as a sterile piece of equipment) are not immediately apparent to the naked eye. The only guarantee that they are there is that the process has been followed exactly. There are other contexts, however, in which the process is not observed at all, and in which success in performing the skills is assessed from the outcomes of student work. For example, in the Bachelor's Degree in Industrial Design at the University of New South Wales, students are required to design and produce a consumer article using plastics as the construction material. Among the assessment criteria are that students demonstrate skill and craftsmanship in plastics construction but no attempt is made to assess the processes that they use in carrying out the work. Their level of skill is inferred from the product that they produce.

Assessing the product

An example of the assessment of skills through the outcomes of student work can be found in the following case study.

Case study 12
Continuous assessment of skill in using a software package

Case study from Statistics
Jennifer Bradley, Murdoch University

The following account is an edited version of materials submitted to the project team.

Context

Students are enrolled in a one semester first year statistics service subject offered by the School of Mathematical and Physical Sciences. The majority of students are drawn from Biological and Environmental Sciences. The course aims to develop students' capacity to tackle problems requiring statistical analysis of the type encountered in the Life Sciences. It introduces students to the basic concept of hypothesis testing using several basic tests for normal and non-normal data. Among the broader objectives of the course is the requirement that students become competent in using the computer package MINITAB for tests involving large / complex data sets.

Assessment method

Assessment falls into three components: assignments, short tests and final examination. Bradley says that the nature of the subject means that students constantly need to build upon work done earlier in the course. Therefore the assessment is continuous over the semester. Assignments are set weekly. However, not all of the questions on the assignments are formally marked and counted toward the final assessment results. Students are told which questions will be counted and which will not and are also told that tutors will keep a note of whether non-marked questions are attempted.

In place of a mid semester test, three short tests of 20-25 minutes are spread throughout the semester. Students prefer this to a mid semester test as it helps them spread their workload. There is also a final examination.

➤

To ensure total integration of the use of the computer package MINITAB it is incorporated into each component of assessment - assignments, short tests and final examination. Each weekly assignment has at least one question that requires the use of MINITAB. One of the short tests is devoted to testing the students' ability to choose the appropriate test and their ability to follow the protocols for accessing commands and running the MINITAB package. In the final examination, MINITAB output is presented and students are expected to be able to interpret the output. Bradley says that this also enables realistic problems to be used in the exam, rather than very simplistic ones, as the students are not required to perform complex numerical calculations.

While the ability to use the package effectively is not assessed in isolation from higher order skills, successful completion of the assessment tasks is contingent on being able to operate the package successfully.

Strengths and limitations

Bradley reports that integration of MINITAB into all aspects of assessment means that students do become very proficient. Students often return in subsequent years requesting computer time so that they can analyse data from the current subjects they are studying. Most tutors prefer the relatively even marking load throughout the semester and the only limitation is the pressure on the course coordinator in preparing weekly assignments.

■

Assessing the process

Where it is important that a specified procedure be followed in carrying out a task, it is usual for a written observation schedule or check-list to be used in assessing the performance. An example of a check-list used at the University of Maastricht to assess medical students' ability to carry out a diagnostic procedure can be found in an article by Verwijnen et al (1982).

(See opposite.)

Two obvious requirements for successful completion can be inferred:
(i)   the student must have learnt the procedural steps involved for conducting the examination, and
(ii)   must have previously practised the requisite skills. In this example, the procedural steps are limited and linear and, presumably the sequence is easily learnt. The focus of assessment, then, is on demonstration of the skills needed to carry out each procedure.

Vu and Barrow (1994) draw attention to the resource implications of using performance assessment of this kind, and assert that "One of the main concerns in the use of performance examinations is their feasibility when used on a large scale". They see as most problematic "the availability of a reasonable number of observations for each student to be assessed in a valid and reliable manner". Here they are making reference to training of physicians, but they remark that the problem is "common to many fields in which performance is based on direct observations" (p23).

One way of overcoming the problem of providing a reasonable number of opportunities for students to demonstrate skills has been developed at the University of Sydney through the use of self instruction and self assessment.

APPENDIX II: Example of a Skills-test Checklist

STATION No. 5

Examination of the peripheral circulation
of the upper extremities

***

CRITERIA	PERFORMANCE				
	COR-RECT	INCOM-PLETE	INCOR-RECT	NOT PERF.	UNASSES-SABLE
1. Inspection					
1.1 The skin colours of the left and right arm/hand are compared.	0	0	0	0	0
1.2 The temperatures of the left and right arm/hand are compared.	0	0	0	0	0
2. Palpation					
2.1 The carotid arteries are palpated on both sides.	0	0	0	0	0
2.2 The brachial arteries are palpated on both sides.	0	0	0	0	0
2.3 The radial arteries are palpated on both sides.	0	0	0	0	0
2.4 The ulnair arteries are palpated on both sides.	0	0	0	0	0
3. Auscultation					
3.1 The carotid arteries are auscultated on both sides.	0	0	0	0	0
3.2 The fossae supraclaviculares are auscultated on both sides.	0	0	0	0	0
4. The blood-pressure is measured on both sides. (For performance criteria see enclosed copy.)	0	0	0	0	0
5. The student comes to the right conclusions about the status of the peripheral circulation. (See data about the patient being examined.)	0	0	0	0	0

GENERAL IMPRESSION: good / average / bad

REMARKS·

Figure 3.1

*Example of skills-test
checklist*
University of Maastricht

Case study 13
Using video for self-assessment

Case study from Nursing
Julie Thorburn, University of Sydney

Julie Thorburn described her use of video-based skills assessment in a series of telephone interviews.

Context

Students in the third year subject Medical Surgical Nursing III learn clinical nursing skills in laboratories which simulate the hospital setting. Students are introduced to the skills through inquiry-based learning packages so that skills are always contextualised and students are required to relate the associated knowledge and principles to the skills being practised or assessed. Approximately 260 students are enrolled in Medical Surgical Nursing in third year.

The assessment program for this strand of the course includes: two written examinations worth 25% each; a group learning contract worth 15%; videoed skill assessment - 10%, and two objective structured clinical examinations (OSCE), one undertaken midyear, worth 10% and the other at the end of the year worth 15% of total marks. Details of the objective structured clinical examinations are provided in the next case study (see Case study 14).

Assessment procedure

While skills have been assessed for some time through the two objective structured clinical examinations, teaching staff were concerned that students were not practising the skills regularly enough and that there were bottlenecks in labs before each OSCE as students rushed to practise skills. They wanted students to manage their learning more efficiently and practise skills regularly throughout the semester.

To overcome these problems Thorburn describes how videoed self assessment of nursing skills was introduced to complement the OSCEs. Four work areas were set up in the nursing labs, each equipped with a video camera on a stand, VHS monitor, teaching video tapes which demonstrated a particular skill and a checklist of the correct procedure to be followed in performing the skill to a safety standard.

At the beginning of a four week teaching block students are introduced to the video self assessment process and instructed in the use of the camera. Students then book three 20 minute video sessions at one of the times when a teacher facilitator will be present. They work in teams of two to four depending on the nature of the skill being assessed and whether it involves a simulated patient and more than one nurse. At each practice session the student will be videoed performing the required skill by a partner. A viewing room is available following the taping session, where the student self assesses his or her tape using the checklist provided. The teacher facilitator is also available for feedback if the student requests it. When s/he is happy with the performance, the student submits the best performance, together with a completed self assessment checklist and responses to questions which require them to reflect on their experience. Students may book additional practice sessions but they may only present tapes for assessment which have been made when a teacher-facilitator is present.

The instructional tape provided to students is one which includes two versions of the skill being performed. One shows an expert (usually one of the teaching staff) performing the skill and the other version shows a competent but novice practitioner carrying out the same skill. (These examples are usually drawn from the previous year's students who performed well.) Thorburn says that students easily distinguish between the novice and expert performances but find it encouraging to see the skill demonstrated by a peer. They also comment that they appreciate that the staff are prepared to submit themselves to the same process (being videotaped performing a skill) that they are requiring of students.

Marks and grades

The video taped skill performance is worth 10% of the final mark for the subject. As students have already self assessed their performance a number of times and only submit when they feel they have achieved adequate competence, teacher marking essentially acts as a quality control mechanism. Thorburn says that the students tend to be relatively generous markers and the teacher will sometimes adjust the mark downwards if she feels that the critical elements of the procedure were not carried out satisfactorily. When students are informed that their mark has been lowered and the reason why, a typical response is to say 'I didn't realise you were going to be so pedantic!' It provides another opportunity, according to Thorburn, to emphasise the importance of following the procedure exactly in the interests of safety.

All video tapes are viewed by the teacher, largely in response to student demand. Thorburn says that when the video assessment process was being planned, they were advised by an educational consultant that it would be sufficient for a teacher to mark only a percentage of the tapes as a check on students' marking. But an earlier attempt at random marking of written work had proved highly unpopular with students so Thorburn decided that each video should be reviewed by a teacher. Thorburn says that students initially find the videotaping highly confronting and they invest so much of themselves in their performance that they want their work to be acknowledged. According to Thorburn, the marking is not particularly time-consuming at only 10 minutes per student.

Strengths and limitations

From Thorburn's point of view, the only real limitation has been the organisation involved. Initially no teacher was present during video taping sessions and bookings did not have to be made in advance, but lab staff were driven mad by the ensuing confusion and there was some suspicion that students were prompting each other through performances. Advance bookings and the presence of a teacher-facilitator to ensure bookings run to time and to provide feedback if requested, has made the process run much more smoothly. According to Thorburn the benefits to student learning are considerable. She says that students learn far more from self assessing performance than they do from watching a demonstration and that they become much better at organising their own learning. Most importantly, they get a real understanding of how much practice it takes to master a skill to the required standard.

■

Next we will look at the complementary method used for assessing nursing skills in this strand of the nursing degree at Sydney University - the Objective Structured Clinical Examination (OSCE).

14

Case study 14
Objective Structured Clinical Examination (OSCE)

Case Study from Nursing
Sally Borbasi, University of Sydney

The account that follows is based on written materials provided to the project by Sally Borbasi and on an evaluation of the OSCE published by the Faculty of Nursing at Sydney University (Borbasi, Shea, Mulquiney, Wilkinson, & Athanasou, 1993).

Context

Students in the third year subject Medical Surgical Nursing III learn clinical nursing skills in laboratories which simulate the hospital setting. Naturally, the skills are not taught in isolation - students are always required to relate the associated knowledge and principles to the skills being practised or assessed. Approximately 260 students are enrolled in Medical Surgical Nursing III in third year.

The assessment program for this strand of the course includes: two written examinations worth 25% each; a group learning contract worth 15%; videoed skill assessment - 10% (described in Case study 13), and two objective structured clinical examinations (OSCE), one undertaken midyear, worth 10% and the other at the end of the year worth 15% of total marks.

Assessment method

OSCE is a practical examination to assess competence. Unlike assessments of competence carried out in the workplace (such as the hospital ward), the OSCE uses simulation - including actor patients - to ensure that all students are assessed on the same task in the same context. Assessments of students' clinical skills during hospital placements have been found to have poor reliability and the personal relationship between the student and the clinical supervisor may have more impact on the result than the student's actual clinical performance (Borbasi, et al., 1993). The variability among real clinical situations also makes fair comparisons difficult. In the OSCE students circulate through a number of stations or simulated nursing situations. Through the use of such structured simulations, the OSCE attempts to overcome the difficulties and limitations which the workplace imposes on assessment.

In the form that has been developed at the University of Sydney the OSCE requires students to demonstrate their ability in each of the three components of clinical performance - acquisition of clinical data (assessment of the patient) interpretation of clinical data (problem identification, nursing diagnosis) and the use of clinical data (decision making and supportive, educative or therapeutic interventions). The skills demonstrated in each context must be performed to a set standard of acceptability.

Each component became the objective of one or more of the OSCE stations. Students circulated around a series of six stations, three of which required a written response and three of which involved observation of performance of psychomotor skills by assessors who used a previously prepared checklist. The time allowed at each station was five minutes, with half a minute allowed for students to move between stations.

The specific tasks

Three of the stations in this OSCE tested students on their knowledge and understanding related to the skills which were required at the 'performance' stations. One example of the stations which required students to make a written response presented students with an ECG monitor displaying a cardiac rhythm. Students were required to identify the rhythm and then to identify any treatments to be administered to this patient. Stations requiring written responses generally tested knowledge related to the 'performance' stations. Two of the 'performance' stations required students to prepare intravenous medications and one tested students' ability to communicate with patients by requiring them to explain a procedure and get the patient's cooperation.

Preparing students and assessors for the OSCE

Skills, techniques and procedures taught in the Professional Practice Strand have been analysed into their component steps or parts and prepared in the form of checklists. The checklists which will ultimately be used in assessing the students' performance are distributed to students as part of their course. They are encouraged to use the checklists during all their laboratory sessions and at independent practice sessions. In addition two practice OSCEs were provided to help students become familiar with the process and timing.

The Faculty of Nursing also introduced assessor training to improve reliability among assessors. A video was made of a student performing one of the skills. In training workshops, assessors scored the video performance using the checklist, discussed discrepancies in their scores and developed ground rules for overcoming problem areas.

Marks and feedback

Performance stations were assessed using the checklists and were weighted far more heavily than the stations which assessed knowledge and understanding and required a written response. At each OSCE a seventh and optional station was set up where students could obtain general feedback on their performance. Results from the OSCEs were combined with the other assessment components to produce an overall grade for the course (F, P, CR, D, HD).

Strengths and limitations

As a method of assessing clinical performance in areas such as history taking, examination, treatment and communication, the OSCE provides a more reliable method of assessment than 'on the job' assessment. It has the potential for testing a wide range of nursing knowledge and skills but the skills that can be tested in one OSCE are naturally limited. However, Borbasi cites Cox (1982) in pointing out that valid assessment of psychomotor skills must include actual observation of performance. Although students may be nervous when taking the OSCE, they readily accept its validity as an assessment method for clinical skills. As the Faculty of Nursing at Sydney has demonstrated, it can also accommodate a large number of students in one examination period. Approximately 260 students took the OSCE in 1994. Morning and afternoon sessions were held with four parallel circuits in each and twenty four assessors were required at each session. Assessors were all registered nurses with educational experience.

Obviously the OSCE is labour intensive and therefore expensive to run. It requires considerable development time and involvement of the whole teaching team. Its advantages lie in its high validity, good reliability and a high level of acceptance by students.

■

Comment

Two somewhat different approaches to the design of objective structured clinical examinations or assessments (OSCE or OSCA) have become apparent in gathering the materials for this project. One approach, like the OSCE described above, puts the emphasis on assessment of skills (predominantly technical skills but also including such skills as communication). Students may have to perform at as many as 20 stations and the time spent at each station is very limited, about 5 - 10 minutes only. Skills and knowledge assessed at individual stations are not necessarily related. Interaction with the client or patient is obviously limited. Bob Ribbons from the Faculty of Nursing at the University of Sydney describes this form of OSCE as a very 'tight and specific' form of assessment*.

The second approach limits the number of stations to around five to eight and students spend much longer at each station (up to 45 minutes at specific stations). All stations build on the same scenario, and require students to engage in quite complex problem solving, planning and evaluation as more data is fed to them at each station. An example of this second kind of OSCE/OSCA is given in Module 2, "Solving problems and developing plans" (see Case study 9, p52).

Assessing laboratory skills

Many of the skills developed in laboratories are required to be mastered to such a level that they become a routine which can be called upon in subsequent work. In the following case study mastery learning and assessment are used in the development of essential laboratory skills.

Case study 15
Mastery assessment

Case study from Medical Microbiology
Ina Te Wiata, Auckland Institute of Technology

The following account is based on interviews with Ina TeWiata and material from her guide for tutors, Mastery Learning and Assessment (Te Wiata, 1988)

Context

In 1989 mastery assessment principles were incorporated into tests of practical skills for students in medical microbiology laboratory classes at Auckland Institute of Technology. These students were enrolled in the then Diploma in Medical Laboratory Technology.

One of the essential skills that a medical laboratory scientist, especially those wishing to pursue a career in medical microbiology, must master is the correct use of a microscope. This skill forms part of the basis of the microbiological work that follows in the course, and once mastered is a "taken for granted" throughout the rest of the years they spend at the institution. Instruction in the use of the microscope includes access to a video "How to use a microscope", written notes to accompany this, plus individual instruction on the correct use of microscopes. Students also have opportunities to practise this skill, both inside and out of formal class time.

---

* Quoted by Valda Wiles of the Clinical Nursing Services Department at Sydney Hospital, in an unpublished paper, 'Methods of Assessment: OSCA and OSCE.'

Assessment method

Students are provided with a mastery assessment checklist (see below) against which their performance will be judged. Assessors are provided with copies of the same checklist plus notes highlighting areas that students often have difficulty with or perform incorrectly.

The exercise required students to demonstrate the correct use of a microscope, in this instance using an oil immersion objective. When students felt they had mastered this particular skill they notified an assessor to arrange a time for them to demonstrate their achievement. The assessor simply used the checklist below to tick off the steps as demonstrated by the student.

MEDICAL LABORATORY TECHNOLOGY

MASTERY ASSESSMENT CHECKSHEET

TASK: Demonstrate the correct use of a microscope
(You are provided with a Gram stained slide)

STEPS	DETAIL	MASTERY CHECK	
1.	Switch microscope on at wall		
2.	Switch microscope on at instrument		
3.	Adjust light control slide		
4.	Ensure sub-stage condenser is in correct position		
5.	Place slide on stage and position specimen appropriately		
6.	Ensure the correct objective is in place		
7.	Adjust eyepieces to suit		
8.	Adjust illumination to suit		
9.	Bring specimen into rough focus		
10.	Sharpen focus		
11.	Place oil on slide		
12.	Using correct objective refocus specimen		
13.	Show your assessor your field of view (to ensure focus of the specimen has been achieved)		
14.	Wipe oil from objective		
15.	Turn microscope off at instrument		

Figure 3.2
Mastery Assessment Checksheet
Ina Te Wiata

Marks

Two results were possible: mastery, ie. achievement of the task; or re-sit, ie. not demonstrating the skill (failure to satisfy each of the steps as per the checksheet). Students needed to have demonstrated mastery in this area within a specified time (ie. one academic session).

Strengths and limitations

Te Wiata cites research by Block and Anderson (1975) which shows that mastery methods produce better student learning because students learn how to learn and says that this is reflected in her experience. Pass rates too are usually higher, with students who would have failed under non-mastery methods achieving success. The introduction of mastery learning and assessment also had positive affective outcomes both for teachers and students. Students were more interested in the subject and more positive about it; lecturers found it rewarding to have students clearly and enthusiastically demonstrate their competence.

Difficulties with this approach revolve mainly around staff concerns rather than those of students. Considerable development time is required to prepare instructional materials and assessment checklists. Some lecturers were concerned about the class management issues involved with those students who completed modules well ahead of their peers. Te Wiata reports that she resolved this problem by providing enrichment activities which could be undertaken independently. Completing the basic skill at mastery level was sufficient to obtain a pass in the subject; satisfactorily completing enrichment activities would lead to a higher grade (credit or distinction). Alternatively, the student who had completed the unit at mastery level could use the time to work on other subjects - the choice was theirs.

■

Mastery learning and assessment
adapted from Te Wiata (1988)

Mastery learning and assessment is an educational philosophy based on the assumption that under appropriate teaching and learning conditions most students can and will learn most of what they are taught.

The achievement of mastery is strongly associated with the amount of time spent on the learning task - time taken to master a learning task is considered a significant indicator of student aptitude. Low aptitude for a subject need not necessarily imply low achievement but rather that the student will need a longer period to attain mastery.

Most institutions are organised to give group instruction with definite periods of time allowed for particular learning tasks. Whatever the time allowed by the institution and the curriculum for particular subjects or learning tasks, it is likely to be too much for some students and not enough for others.

The quality of instruction is also important. If teaching is excellent and educational materials are good the student will take less time to achieve mastery than if the teaching and materials are poor. Obviously student motivation is also a factor but the higher success rates which mastery programs achieve can do much to increase motivation.

If both teaching and student use of the available learning time were to become more effective, it is likely that most students would need less time to master a subject. There are several ways to optimise learning time: for example, the use of self-paced individualised packages slide/tape/workbook, interactive, computer based instruction, or one to one tutorial assistance.

To optimise student learning time, it is important that teachers also make the attitudinal shift away from assuming responsibility for covering all aspects of a given syllabus themselves towards creating and structuring opportunities for students to direct their own learning.

Mastery assessment is always criterion-referenced. Criterion-referenced tests are designed to assess what an individual knows or can do compared to what s/he must know or be able to do in order to perform a task or carry out a procedure successfully. An individual's performance is thus compared (or referenced) to an external criterion or performance standard. Norm-referenced tests on the other hand involve comparing one student's performance with that of others in the group in order to rank students and assign grades. (See index and glossary for further entries on criterion-referenced and norm-referenced assessment.)

Mastery tests may be given to individual students or to the class as a whole. They require that the student be able to meet a specified learning objective to a specified standard. Students who do not meet the standard on the first occasion are given more opportunities (after remediation) to re-sit the test with no penalty for passing on the second or third attempt.

Mastery tests are both formative and summative (see Glossary). They clearly indicate to students which aspects of the task they have/have not succeeded at - they also serve to certify what the student has learned.

Another case study in the development and testing of laboratory skills follows.

Case study 16
Self-paced assessment of laboratory skills

Case study from Physics
Ian Dunn, University of New South Wales

Ian Dunn provided written materials describing his assessment practices to the project and they form the basis of this account. Direct quotes are drawn from these materials.

Context

In first year physics at UNSW students are required to undertake the "Laboratory Learning Programs". These units are designed to help students develop understanding of fundamental topics and the process of scientific inquiry and to develop basic technical laboratory skills. The exercise illustrated below is an example of the assessment of basic laboratory skills. Other assessment exercises that are undertaken during this course are exploratory exercises for the understarding of specific topics, and experimental exercises for introducing the process of scientific inquiry.

➤

Students are provided with opportunities to learn and practice basic skills such as graphical presentation of results, and data reduction; linearisation of functional relationships; the estimation, propagation and presentation of errors and so on. A manual, containing all of the exercises that make up each unit, is provided to each student at the beginning of the course. Each of these units is self paced; and no link to any lecture course is presumed, ie the units are self-contained and stand alone. (More traditionally, laboratory experiments have been tied to lecture components of the course). There is a minimum set of units which each student must complete in one academic year.

Assessment method

One of the examples provided is a skills exercise that centres around uncertainty in measurement. The specific skills assessed in this example are making measurements and calculating results. The exercise has two linked aims. First, it introduces students to the more common basic measuring instruments, and helps them to learn to make measurements using each of them. Second, it is an illustration of a systematic, tabular method for presenting the results of measurements, and for calculating quantities derived from these.

Students are provided with the learning goals for the exercise, what equipment they will require, and what they need to do in order to practise and thus successfully complete the exercise. It is intended that some of this learning be done outside of class time.

Satisfactory completion is determined by a check test which occurs during a scheduled laboratory exercise. (Students are forewarned not to waste their own or the lecturer's time in attempting a check test if they haven't worked through the appropriate practice exercises in the manual.) Students (when they feel they are ready), ask one of the demonstrators assigned to the unit to assess them. Once the particular assessment exercise is satisfactorily completed students may proceed straightaway to the next exercise.

The check tests are mastery tests. They have two outcomes: (i) satisfactorily completed, meaning that the student has demonstrated mastery of the material, or (ii) repeat, meaning that the student has made a mistake in principle somewhere in the test.

Strengths and limitations

According to Dunn, one of the issues raised by this method of developing and assessing skills concerned the role of the demonstrators. They had to interact with students to a far greater extent than they had done previously (ie. in the more traditional teaching laboratory situations), and more closely saw the results of their efforts. Indeed interactions with a student at the help stage were closely followed by the student demonstrating an ability to perform. This then gave demonstrators clear evidence of the fulfilment of their goals with students. Demonstrators found it much more intensive (and often exhausting) but far more rewarding. In Dunn's view there were also considerable learning benefits for the students. "Because the assessment was entirely performance oriented, we found that the major transfer to the student was such that they became performance oriented. Further, there was a good matching of student perception to our conception of her or his learning experiences and their consequences." ■

Selecting a sample of skills for assessment

As briefly mentioned earlier, Vu and Barrow (1994) referred to the difficulty of valid and efficient measurement of performance against set standards of competence where observations are involved. Because performance assessments may be expensive to set up and time consuming to conduct, it may prove difficult to assess all the necessary skills or to provide multiple opportunities for each student to demonstrate each skill. If it is possible to assess only a sample of the skills that the student is expected to master, it is important that the skills to be tested are selected on a rational basis. Sometimes skills for testing are selected randomly or comparatively unimportant skills are selected on the grounds that if students can perform relatively obscure procedures, then they are likely to have also mastered the fundamentals. It is fairer to students and more likely to result in lasting learning if the selection of skills to be assessed is planned on a sounder basis, a point also made by Swanson, Norman and Linn (1995). Two of the best indicators that skill should be included in the assessment schedule are:

- the extent to which it forms a foundation for future work (for example the use of the microscope in microbiology) and/or

- the extent to which it is represented in professional practice.

Sometimes the latter can only be ascertained by research with practitioners to determine which skills are most likely to be called upon regularly. Bruce Cook of the Radiography Department at the University of Newcastle is one lecturer who has undertaken such research during his post-graduate work in higher education at the University of New South Wales. In the subject he coordinates, students learn to identify a wide range of medical conditions from X-rays. Far too wide a range, in fact, for all to be assessed. In order to provide a rational basis for assessment tasks, Cook interviewed many practitioners in the Newcastle area to determine which conditions were most likely to present in local practice. The list that resulted was used to determine which conditions students would be required to identify in assessment tasks.

Assessing skills - alone or integrated in more complex tasks?

The trend towards integrated or authentic assessment may see many skills assessed as part of complex assessment tasks where students are required to identify problems, plan and carry out solutions and evaluate their results, while managing the contingencies which arise. Integrated assessment has considerable advantages in providing students with realistic problems which mimic the situations that practitioners face. Students usually find these kinds of complex assessment tasks motivating and accept their validity. However, because of the elaborate nature of these assessment tasks they can usually only be used on one or two occasions in a semester. If they are used as the sole mechanism for assessing skills, they may not be able to provide the level of feedback that students need if they are to master a skill. It may be desirable to arrange other assessment for skills as a prerequisite or a co-requisite for the major assessment task. Such skill assessment need not be particularly formal - self or peer assessment against a model or a checklist is one of the methods used by contributors here. Other useful possibilities include computer simulations with built-in assessment. What is important is ensuring that students get sufficient opportunities to practise important skills and adequate feedback to ensure mastery.

Setting performance standards

As mentioned earlier, assessment of skills is most commonly criterion-referenced, requiring performance to a set standard. How to determine what that standard should be may prove difficult for some assessors.

Checklists for assessing skills are usually based on a task analysis, which is carried out by observing an expert perform the task and specifying each step in the process. It is usually necessary to observe an actual performance, or at least to step through it oneself, because for many practiced performers the process has become so automated, that they cannot necessarily describe all the steps from memory. The checklist so developed should be validated with other experts.

Once each step has been determined other indicators of acceptable quality can be determined. These might include:

- accuracy of work
- use of correct process monitoring sequences
- how systematically the work is done
- attitude, as evidenced by cleanliness, care and persistence
- use of safe procedures
- degree of physical dexterity
- speed of doing each stage of a task (Field, 1990).

Similarly, when a product is to be assessed, specifications setting out the characteristics of an acceptable product can be developed. Limits may be put on the time and resources which can be used.

Assessment of skills is usually on a satisfactory / not yet satisfactory basis but identification of criteria for different levels of performance is possible and used in some programs so that students can be graded.

One common variable, used in developing criteria for different levels of performance, is the degree of supervision required by the student. Field (1990) offers the following levels:

4   Skilled, can perform this task without supervision

3   Skilled, but requires some supervision

2   Some skill but requires supervision

1   Unable to perform this task.

Other possible variables which might be used to determine levels of performance include speed and fluidity of performance and the ability to perform in a range of different contexts and under different conditions.

References

Block, J. H., & Anderson, L. W. (1975). *Mastery Learning in Classroom Instruction.* New York: MacMillan.

Borbasi, S., Shea, A., Mulquiney, J., Wilkinson, M., & Athanasou, J. (1993). *An Investigation of the Reliability and Validity of the Objective Structured Clinical Examination (OSCE) as an Instrument for Assessing the Clinical Competence of Undergraduate Nursing Students.* University of Sydney, Faculty of Nursing.

Cox, K. R. (1982). Measuring clinical performance. In K. R. Cox & C. E. Ewan (Eds.), *The Medical Teacher.* Edinburgh: Churchill Livingstone. pp241-45.

Field, L. (1990). *Skilling Australia.* Melbourne: Longman Cheshire.

Swanson, D.B., Norman, G.R. and Lin, R.L. (1995). Performance-based assessment: lessons from the health professions, *Educational Researcher,* 24 (5), 5-11.

Te Wiata, I. (1988). Mastery Learning and Assessment. Auckland: Auckland Technical Institute.

Verwijnen, M., Imbos, T., Snellen, H., Stalenhoef, B., Pollemans, M., Luyk, S., Sprooten, M., Leeuwen, Y., & Vleuten, C. (1982). The evaluation system at the medical school of Maastricht. *Assessment and Evaluation in Higher Education,* 7, 225-244.

Vu, N., & Barrow, H. (1994). Use of standardised patients in clinical assessments: recent developments and measurement findings, *Educational Researcher,* 23(3), 23-30.

MODULE 4

MANAGING AND DEVELOPING ONESELF

SUSAN TOOHEY

Helping students to take responsibility for their own learning and development is an important goal for many teachers in higher education. It is often expressed as 'becoming a self-directed learner'. Teachers who value this ability are looking not only for skills in planning and carrying out learning projects but also a commitment to identifying and meeting one's own learning needs.

This module covers broad abilities such as:
- working co-operatively
- working independently
- learning independently
- being self directed
- managing time
- managing tasks
- organising

Section 1: Planning and managing one's own learning

Themes
- Supporting students undertaking independent learning projects
- Criteria for assessing independent learning projects
- Criteria for assessing self evaluative writing

Techniques
- Learning contracts
- The triple jump

Case studies
17. Learning contract, Education
18. Learning contract, Health Science Education
19. Triple jump, Community Health

Section 2: Evaluating one's own learning

Themes
- Helping students to think beyond 'getting the right answer'
- Criteria for assessing and grading portfolios
- Selecting and presenting evidence of one's learning
- Reliability of self assessment

Techniques
- Learning evaluation exercises in Mathematics
- Portfolios
- Self evaluation of one's own learning and experience for a job interview

Case studies
20. Learning evaluation exercise, Mathematics
21. Portfolios, Psychology
22. Practising self evaluation, Resource and Environmental Management

Section 3: Understanding and managing one's own feelings and being sensitive to the feelings of others

Themes
- Personal experience and the development of professional beliefs and values
- Criteria for assessing personal writing
- Appropriateness of grading personal writing

Techniques
- Autobiography
- Reflective journals

Case studies
23. Autobiography, Town Planning
24. Autobiography, Higher Education
25. Autobiography, Health Education
26. Journal, Occupational Therapy

Section 4: Making ethical judgements

Themes
- Ethics in the professional context
- Justifying decisions on ethical grounds

Techniques
- Case study examination

Case studies
27. Examination case study, Business Studies

Section 5: Working collaboratively

Themes
- Peer assessment
- Assigning marks to individuals for group work
- Developing the ability to coach others
- Students setting criteria

Techniques
- Group projects in curriculum design
- Group work under exam conditions
- Peer tutoring

Case studies
28. Group work, Education
29. Group work, Education
30. Group work in triple jump, Community Health
31. Peer tutoring, Business Studies

Module 4

Managing and developing oneself

Susan Toohey

Introduction

Helping students to take responsibility for their own learning and development has become an important goal for many teachers in higher education. It is often expressed as 'helping students become self-directed learners.' University teachers who value this ability are looking not only for skills in planning and carrying out learning projects but also the commitment to identifying and meeting one's own learning needs that should be the hallmark of a professional.

As well as attempting to develop in students the ability to learn independently, many teachers are also requiring students to work in groups or teams and assessing their ability to work collaboratively. While the same skills in managing time and organising tasks are required, students must also learn to recognise the different contributions that others can make and to negotiate goals and working arrangements.

Student professionals who are learning to work with patients or clients must develop sensitivity to client concerns while at the same time managing their own anxieties; they must be able to confront the ethical dilemmas which sometimes arise in practice and make considered and defensible choices. The academics and practitioners responsible for supervising students in professional placements are increasingly looking for valid ways of distinguishing and assessing such abilities in their students.

Until recently, the ability to plan and manage one's own learning and the willingness to develop both awareness and control of one's own emotions and sensitivity to the feelings of others have not been considered legitimate concerns for university education. Although some educators may have held that these were desirable characteristics for graduates, there has been some confusion in the minds of educators as to whether such qualities are innate to individuals or whether they can be consciously developed. As a consequence, the question of whether it is legitimate to assess such abilities is somewhat problematic.

Two factors have helped to push these abilities to greater prominence in recent years. One is the recognition by both researchers and theorists that development of what Howard Gardner (1993) calls the "personal intelligences" is often crucial to the effective use in society of the knowledge and skills gained in traditional university study. As Gardner summarises,

> *The less a person understands his (sic) own feelings, the more he will fall prey to them. The less a person understands the feelings, the responses, and the behaviour of others, the more likely he will interact inappropriately with them and therefore fail to take his proper place within the larger community (p255).*

In support, researchers like (Spencer, 1984) have shown that in the case of many professional occupations, it is possession of what Spencer calls the "soft skill competencies" that distinguishes the exceptional performer from the merely competent. Two of those "soft skill competencies" which Spencer found to be most significant in distinguishing the highly successful performers in a very wide range of professional and managerial jobs were critical

---

*   I wish to acknowledge the help of Jim Walker, Professor of Education at the University of Canberra, for extending my understanding of what the ability to manage and develop oneself involves.

thinking and accurate empathy. By critical thinking Spencer means the ability to:

> *make critical distinctions or inferences, cite data to support their positions, and reconcile conflicting data pro and con their inferences ie., reason probalistically or reconcile conflicting data by weighting opposing statements (p12).*

The assessment of critical thinking is discussed in Module 1.

"Accurate empathy" refers to the ability to "accurately hear the content, meaning and feeling of what another person is saying" or in some cases, not saying - that level of meaning expressed through body language and demeanour (p14). The value of accurate empathy is not in feeling sympathy for the other person but in being able to make an appropriate response because one understands accurately what the real concerns are. Assessing the development of empathy is the subject of one of the case studies presented in this module.

The second factor in the push to broaden university curricula to encompass the development of personal skills has come from employers and government. Recognising instinctively and from first hand experience that more was required to turn students into effective professionals than knowledge and technical skill, employer groups, professional associations and government bodies have pressed for a greater educational focus on "work skills", "generic competencies" or "communication". What seems to be underlying this often confusing array of terms is a desire for employees who can take greater responsibility for both their own individual work and for team work, and who can interact effectively with co-workers and clients using the kinds of empathy skills which Spencer found vital to so many occupations.

As just one example of the push for a greater focus on personal effectiveness as a goal for tertiary education, the Higher Education Council recently listed among its "desirable characteristics of quality in graduates" - critical thinking; intellectual curiosity; problem-solving; logical and independent thought; effective communication and related skills in identifying, accessing and managing information; personal attributes such as intellectual rigour and willingness to work in a cooperative manner with others; values such as ethical practice, integrity and tolerance (Higher Education Council, 1992, pp20-22).

In the past decade all of these factors have combined to push personal skills on to the curriculum in a wide range of courses, including not only the "helping professions" but disciplines as diverse as engineering, town planning and microbiology. In many cases, university teachers who have traditionally focussed on transmitting the body of knowledge and technical skills of their discipline have felt somewhat at a loss when asked to develop not only students' intellectual abilities but their personal effectiveness as well. Writers like Mezirow (1990) and Brookfield (1987) have begun to explore how personal effectiveness might be developed in the classroom and some of the programs described here have built on their work. But the uncertainty which still exists around the development of personal effectiveness is insignificant compared to the uncertainty surrounding how such abilities might be validly assessed, and whether such assessments could or should be graded and reported in combination with more conventional assessments of knowledge and skill. Fortunately for all concerned, many of the tasks used to assess these abilities also provide a simultaneous learning experience, rather than simply being used to gather evidence of student achievement. In doing so they comply with the first of Ramsden's rules for better assessment in higher education* (Ramsden, 1992) - while at the same time providing ideas and assistance to those new to this aspect of teaching and learning.

---

* Ramsden's first rule for improving assessment in higher education - "Link assessment to learning; focus first on learning, second on encouraging effort, and third on grading; assess during the experience of learning as well as at the end of it; set tasks that mimic realistic problems whenever possible; reward integration and application." (Ramsden, 1992, p210)

Abilities encompassed in this module

The abilities encompassed in this module fall into five broad groups:

Planning and managing one's own learning

This will involve posing questions for research or identifying problems to be solved; planning and carrying out research strategies and learning tasks and, where appropriate, choosing the most suitable medium for reporting results. There is obviously some overlap here with the abilities discussed in Module 5, "Accessing and Managing Information," but here we are primarily concerned with helping students take responsibility for their own learning, rather than skills such as accessing data bases and organising information. Of course in many situations both sets of abilities may be assessed through the same assignment.

Evaluating one's own learning

While planning and managing one's own learning inevitably involves some degree of self evaluation, this ability can also be called upon when the learning is largely planned and managed by others or when the individual is not involved in a formal learning environment. It may involve identifying gaps in one's knowledge and areas which need updating - dispositions and skills which are important when students graduate and vital for those graduates who begin independent professional practice. Other aspects involve being able to evaluate what one has learned, consider how current learning relates to previous learnings and choose which learning strategies are appropriate for a particular task - the skills of metacognition. Yet another aspect of the ability to evaluate one's own learning involves selecting and presenting evidence to show that one has acquired the necessary skills and expertise to pass a course or perform a particular role.

Understanding and managing one's own feelings and being sensitive to the feelings of others

Involved here is the ability to identify when one's performance may be impaired through stress, anger or other strong emotions; to develop strategies for dealing with such situations effectively; to accept feedback openly without defensiveness; to identify blocks and diversions which prevent one from working effectively and develop strategies for dealing with them; to identify the feelings and concerns of others and respond appropriately.

Making ethical judgments

In making ethical judgments students and practitioners must be both able to identify ethical problems when they arise in practice and willing to address them; they must be prepared to explore options and to make and defend decisions based on an ethical framework. Ideally they should show evidence of having developed a personal and coherent set of values which they use in professional decision making.

Working collaboratively.

Working with others involves skills in negotiating; in planning, coordinating and monitoring the tasks to be done; in giving and receiving feedback; and in resolving disagreements.

Section 1

Assessing how well students can plan and manage their own learning

One of the methods which has proved useful in developing and assessing student autonomy is the learning contract. Two examples are provided in the case studies which follow.

Case study 17
Learning contracts

17

Case study from Education
Helen Hayes, University of Ballarat

The following case study is an edited version of the written materials which Helen Hayes provided to the project together with the additional comments she made after seeing the first draft.

Context

The subject titled, "The adolescent in the school" forms part of the Graduate Diploma in Education (a one year post graduate program) at the University of Ballarat and integrates the study of adolescence with the exploration of critical teaching problems. The subject extends over the full year and is taught concurrently with several periods of teaching experience. The total number of students ranges between 25-50.

Assessment method

The major assessment task in this subject requires students to carry out a "depth study" on a topic related to the course. All facets of the project are negotiable and are agreed between teacher and student in the form of a learning contract. Aspects which are negotiated include the topic and purpose of the study; the procedures for research; the types of data to be gathered; the form of the final presentation; the date of submission or presentation; the criteria for assessment; the percentage of marks to be assigned and who will be the assessor/s. (The options in the choice of assessors include the student alone, the lecturer, the student and lecturer together or the class group. The student/lecturer combination tends to be the most popular choice.)

In Hayes' words, the abilities being developed and assessed through this approach include being able to:
* define and articulate a problem to be researched,
* design and carry out a personal learning project,
* seek out and evaluate sources of information and differing points of view,
* collate information and present it in a way which communicates with one's peers,
* specify relevant criteria for assessment of one's own work, and
* assess one's own learning and commitment.

Marks and grades

The assessment is primarily descriptive with agreed translation into a grade (A-E). If the student elects to self assess, (either alone or in conjunction with the lecturer) this must be done formally, against the negotiated criteria, in either a written self assessment or in a meeting with the lecturer. If the student elects to be assessed by the lecturer or by the class group, he or she must still provide the assessment criteria and be able to articulate what is meant by each. ■

Another example of the use of the learning contract comes from Fran Everingham at the University of Sydney in Health Science Education. Everingham's development and use of learning contracts in this program has been strongly influenced by Candy's work on developing student autonomy (Candy, 1991). In some aspects the students' choices here are even more wide ranging than at the University of Ballarat.

18

Case study 18
Learning contracts

Case study from Health Science Education
Fran Everingham, University of Sydney.

We draw together here comments from an interview with Fran Everingham and information from her written description and guidelines provided to students in the program.

Context

Students in the post graduate program in Health Science Education at the University of Sydney are required to take three electives of which two can take the form of independent study by learning contract.

Abilities being assessed

Students taking these elective subjects must be able to demonstrate that they can
• plan and manage self-directed learning projects,
• draw on theory to tackle real life problems,
• communicate knowledge effectively, and
• use reflection to inform personal judgment
in order to successfully pass the subject.

Assessment method and grading

As with the example from Ballarat, students have the choice of topic, research methods and learning tasks and the kinds of evidence they will present of their achievements.

In contrast to Ballarat where all marks are available for students to negotiate, at Sydney 40% of the available marks for the subject are reserved for those criteria concerned with planning an independent learning project and being able to reflect and learn from experience. The break up of marks is as follows:
• contract negotiation and documentation - 10%
• evidence for completion of contract - 60%
• written reflection on the experience of an independent project - 30%.

Within the 60% of marks available for evidence of completion of the contract, students have virtually complete freedom to determine the parameters of the assessment. They can identify a marker of choice (examples include themselves, their contract supervisor, a content specialist or an expert from the field or workplace); they can determine weighting of marks across all the forms of evidence they propose to submit; they can determine the criteria for marking and the weighting to be given to each criterion. Where the student proposes to evaluate the evidence and provide a mark, the contract supervisor also provides a mark and any discrepancy is negotiated. ➤

The 10% of marks available for contract negotiation and documentation are allocated by the contract supervisor against a set of criteria which describe the level of supervisor support required by the student to achieve a workable plan for independent learning and the achievement of the plan in terms of realistic time frames and production of evidence.

The self evaluation paper on the experience of learning through an independent project is also marked by the contract supervisor. Essentially the same criteria are used throughout the program for marking this kind of self evaluative writing. The criteria are based on Boud's work on the cycle of reflection (Boud, Keogh, & Walker, 1985) and are modified slightly to fit the different contexts provided by different subjects. (See Case study 6, p31 for an example of these criteria being used in a different part of the program.)

These criteria require the student to
- identify and describe significant incidents and the feelings that accompanied them;
- distinguish factors that affected their performance;
- analyse their performance in terms of their knowledge and skills and to make connections with previous experiences or different contexts;
- balance personal interpretation with objective interpretation or feedback from others;
- identify strengths and weaknesses and select aspects for improvement.

■

Comment on case studies involving learning contracts

Although students are increasingly being asked to do more self evaluative writing - sometimes in one-off papers such as this, more frequently in journals - their teachers and supervisors are often at a loss as to how or whether such writing ought to be assessed. Comprehensive criteria for the assessment of personal writing such as these are rare but provide a very useful framework both for assessors and for students. In the Health Science Education program at Sydney the fact that these criteria are used in other subjects within the course helps students to become familiar with them and to recognise their own development in the area of self evaluation.

Strengths, limitations and concerns about learning contracts

Both Everingham and Hayes attest to the high levels of motivation which learning contracts engender: the deep learning, high quality work and sense of ownership which ensues and the value which students place on being treated as 'co-learners' rather than 'students'. Hayes cites the in-depth understanding of the process of assessment, resulting from having to take responsibility for all aspects of the process, as being particularly valuable for those who are going to be teachers.

The wide choice of media for presenting outcomes of the learning contracts is seen by both students and teachers as a very positive element. At Ballarat, students in the program have first degrees in a wide range of disciplines (eg visual arts, media studies, social sciences, humanities, maths and science). They can choose to work from their strengths by producing a portfolio, an essay or a research report or challenge themselves to master a new communication medium such as a video production.

Everingham also cites the opportunity for students to master one or more methods of communication different from traditional academic writing as potentially a real benefit of the contract. Early experience at Sydney showed, however, that students were reluctant to take the risk involved in presenting their evidence of learning in an unfamiliar format. To help overcome this resistance, the School has produced assessment criteria for a range of reporting formats, so that students are clear as to what good communication in each format would look like. Students are encouraged to use these criteria as a base line and discuss and modify them in consultation with their supervisor.

Concerns about learning contracts tend to focus on three aspects - the time which may be necessary in supporting students as they negotiate their contract, difficulties in making comparable (reliable) assessments of very different products, and potential problems with self assessment.

Both Hayes and Everingham acknowledge that negotiating learning contracts can be slow in the initial stages. They speak of students' lack of experience and consequent lack of confidence in taking any responsibility for their own learning and students' distrust of self assessment. Both of the programs described here devote class time to discussing the requirements of the program, the nature of assessment criteria and what might constitute valid evidence of learning. Contracts may not be finalised until as late as week 10 of the semester when students have had time to do extensive reading and explore the topic. Contracts are negotiated in individual interviews with students. Hayes points out that while these interviews can be time consuming, they are effective in convincing students of the seriousness with which the School views the process.

Both programs attempt to ensure maximum reliability or consistency among assessments with the use of explicit criteria. In the Sydney University program two types of criteria are provided - general criteria applicable to all contracts, which differentiate the kinds of performance expected at 5 different grade levels and sample criteria for a range of different reporting formats. These criteria have been developed, not only to assist markers and improve reliability of marking (see Glossary) but also to encourage students to take up the self assessment option. Having the criteria available to students makes the task of self assessment less daunting, while at the same time making it clear to students that the process must be carried out with sufficient rigour to have academic credibility.

In both of these programs in cases where the student opts for self assessment, the program coordinator also marks the work. Any significant discrepancy between the two marks is then negotiated.

Although both of these programs grade student results, the assessment is criterion-referenced. That is, each student is graded according to how well he or she has performed relative to specific criteria and independently of how others have performed in the subject (see index and Glossary for more on criterion-referenced assessment).

The triple jump

Another method for assessing students' ability to plan and manage their own learning is the triple jump exercise, first introduced at McMaster University in Canada to assess medical students' problem solving strategies. Unlike the learning contract which usually involves one or more major projects which constitute much of the significant learning throughout a semester, the triple jump can be scheduled at the end of a course as a final test of the students' abilities in this area. The triple jump consists of three stages (hence the name).

- In the first stage students are presented with trigger materials which are usually closely based on real situations. The material might take the form of documents and reports or a case study. In this stage students must individually identify problems or issues in need of investigation from the source material. Results are assessed to evaluate the students' ability to identify problems and their significance.

- In the second stage students are assigned to groups and asked to consolidate and perhaps prioritise their lists of issues. They must then negotiate within the group to determine who will investigate and report on each of the issues which are agreed to be most important. The second stage provides an opportunity to assess the students' ability to work in groups.

- In the third stage students must research and write a report on their issue. They usually have several days to do this and are encouraged to tap a wide range of sources. Their reports are evaluated for their findings as well as for the students' ability to plan and manage a learning project.

19

Case study 19
The triple jump

Case study from Community Health
Grahame Feletti, University of Hawaii and Greg Ryan, University of New South Wales

The material presented here is drawn from an article provided to the project by the authors (Feletti & Ryan, 1994) and also incorporates additional comments they made after seeing an earlier version of the case study.

Context

This case study shows the triple jump exercise being used in a graduate course in holistic health studies at the University of Newcastle in which 43 students were enrolled. The course focused on identification of community health issues, problem solving and developing strategies for change, and the majority of the students enrolled were employed as health and social welfare professionals. Course philosophy emphasised inquiry-based and collaborative learning. The examination at the end of the first semester took the form of a triple jump.

The assessment

In the first stage students were shown a 15 minute video consisting of extracts from a current affairs documentary on an outback mining community. Students were asked to list the health problems that they could identify in the video. Students were then told to join a randomly assigned group of 7-8 students to discuss the issues they had identified and produce a consolidated list of key questions/health issues. Before the end of the 60 minute discussion period each student had to negotiate with their group and identify the key health issue that he or she would pursue as a self directed learning task. Students were required to hand in their initial list of issues, the consolidated group list and their issue for further research at the end of this second stage. (Also required was an evaluation of how well their group had worked, which is discussed later in this module, in the section on assessing collaborative work.)

For the third stage, students had ten days to research and write a four page report on their health issue. Reports of the research could take the form either of a literature review or of a plan for action. Students were expected to access a wide range of resources for this purpose. These reports were assessed on 6 criteria previously discussed with the students. Criteria were varied according to the form of the report (literature review or plan for action).

➤

The criteria were:

For the literature review:

- generation of key questions
- appraisal of information
- reliability of information collected
- outline of unresolved issues
- conclusions drawn from the study
- evaluation of relevance of your study

For the action plan:

- generation of key questions
- appraisal of information
- reliability of information collected
- outline of strategies
- resources you would draw upon
- outline for evaluating the plan

Strengths and limitations

The students who took this particular exam had been carefully prepared for it. They had been given a practice triple jump exercise 3 weeks previously and provided with written and verbal feedback. They regularly worked in groups throughout the course. As the contributors point out, "as graduate students already employed, they were capable of making group situations work". They valued the group discussions of the exam topics and found that 10 days to complete the individual reports provided sufficient time to search computer data bases, find material in libraries and access resource people. In general they found the exam stimulating and performed well.

One of the issues of concern with this particular application of the triple jump proved to be consistency between the two academics who marked the students' final reports (inter-rater reliability). Although each of the markers was internally consistent and produced similar overall score distributions, on closer analysis they differed in the value they gave to students' responses on the criteria concerning unresolved issues, conclusions drawn and outlines of strategies. Feletti and Ryan (1994) attribute this to the differences in values resulting from their different professional backgrounds (health and education respectively). Such lack of consistency between markers is far from uncommon and is by no means restricted to exercises like the triple jump. It does, however, reinforce Feletti and Ryan's recommendation that markers of such work should either meet beforehand to discuss and agree on their understanding of specific criteria and what kinds of responses will be considered acceptable or that dual marking should be used consistently.

■

Section 2

Assessing the ability to evaluate one's own learning

20

Case study 20
Learning evaluation exercises

Case study from Mathematics
Malcolm Roberts, University of Newcastle

This account is drawn from the original written materials provided by Malcolm Roberts and subsequent e-mail conversations in which he commented on early drafts and provided further information.

Context

Malcolm Roberts teaches mathematics to undergraduate students enrolled in the Bachelor of Education (Maths) - a four year degree for prospective secondary school maths teachers. The students take subjects in education, syllabus, pedagogy (teaching methods) and mathematics concurrently in each year of their course. Mathematics subjects are usually one semester long with a contact time of 2 hours per week. Class sizes are typically 20-35. Students are provided with printed lecture notes and study guides. The time spent in class is usually structured so that the first hour is spent with the lecturer discussing and explaining the key concepts in that week's work and the second hour in small group work where students work on solving problems related to those concepts.

The assessment method

Rather than have students hand in the worked problems which they have completed in their groups, or have them do more similar problems as homework, students must make an individual assessment of what they have learned and hand it in at the next class. Students carry out the self assessment by answering the following questions:

- What have I learned by doing this problem?
- What level of thinking is involved in doing this problem?
- Are there connections with previous work in this or other subjects?
- Do I have any other questions or comments?

Students are required to hand in their responses to this exercise every week. This homework is marked on a scale of 0-5 and ultimately contributes 20% to final marks for the subject.

The material which follows is an extract from a handout from Roberts' mathematics course. It helps to explain to students the different levels of mathematical thinking which might be involved in different kinds of questions. Examples of mathematical questions at each of the different levels are also provided to students.

➤

Why are exercise questions set?

Indeed! Why is this particular question set for me to do? If you make the effort to think about this each time you attempt a question of an exercise set then it is likely that you will learn more from doing the question than otherwise might be the case. The general philosophy is simple: students learn by doing, they need to get involved and need to attempt problems on their own. Unfortunately it is not quite that simple. Probably we should have a lecture on the theory of education here. Instead, we have just listed in Table I some of the possible reasons that we have thought of and made some accompanying comments. Following Table 1 we give examples of questions from each of our categories.

Table 1

Reason	Comments
1. To learn a formula. Practise manipulation. Become familiar with notation.	Not much mathematical thinking going on here, just practising routine procedures. These are basic skills that are a means to an end but not really an end in themselves.
2. To practise a new procedure for which an example has been provided	This is the view most students have of mathematics. Really, this is a low level of mathematics.
3. To practise a new procedure but set in a more general context	More difficult than category 2 questions since the students have to work out for themselves the specifics of the question.
4. To apply the new concept/theory to a new kind of problem in order to illustrate various applications of the ideas	This is usually done to give the students an idea of how and where the new ideas can be applied.
5. To apply the new concept/theory to a new kind of problem in order to develop a deeper understanding	This requires a greater understanding since students must be able to apply their knowledge to a new situation. Weaker students find this difficult.
6. To extend a concept or to prepare for the development of a new concept	Harder, since the students have to think on their own.
7. To reflect on results	Good students do this naturally. Most students don't; they look to see if they got it right and leave it at that. Actually thinking back on what you have done is one of the most important aspects in learning.
8. To draw conclusions, generalise results or make conjectures.	This is high level mathematical thinking. This is the kind of thinking a mathematician does. This level of thinking is what is necessary to do mathematics (to be original, to be creative).

Figure 4.1

Course handout
Malcolm Roberts

A given question doesn't necessarily fit neatly into one of the above categories. In multi-part questions it is possible for each part to fall into completely different categories. The above categories are given as a guide to the kinds of reasons why questions would be set. You may be able to think of others.

Notice that the categories are hierarchical. The early categories require only basic manipulation skills without much understanding, linking of ideas, or original thinking necessary. Questions from the later categories need more and more of these higher order mathematical skills. Clearly, to be successful with the latter a good mastery of the former is needed.

The initial questions in an exercise set are usually from categories 1, 2 and 3. This allows the student to become familiar with the new work and gives them some confidence. Questions of this type seem to be a very necessary first step in learning new material. Toward the end of exercise sets the questions are more likely to be from categories 4, 5 and 6. Our observations are that not many category 7 and 8 type questions appear in exercise sets, particularly in older textbooks. In our view these should be an important part in any exercise set. Reflecting on results definitely helps the learning process and category 8 type questions really are the heart of the subject.

Strengths and limitations

According to Roberts these assessment tasks are successful in getting students to think beyond just "getting the right answer" and contribute to his goal of helping students develop the ability to learn independently. The problems with copying which sometimes occur with conventional maths homework are avoided, as all responses must be individual. Apart from the weekly marking the only problem with this assessment task is the difficulty students have in adjusting to a very different set of expectations, and in helping them to do better than say, "I learned how to do this kind of problem." Once they have the idea of what is expected, students tend to do well and therefore this form of assessment is not particularly useful in discriminating among students where the system demands that only a certain percentage of students can be awarded specific grades.

■

For those who are interested in learning evaluation exercises like this, *Classroom Assessment Techniques* by Patricia Cross and Thomas Angelo (1988) contains other examples.

Portfolios

All assessment requires students to present evidence of their learning. In traditional university assessment the teacher decides what form that evidence will take - typically a lengthy essay or a set of responses to a series of exam questions.

John Biggs tries to connect assessment practice with what is currently known about how learning occurs, by pointing out that the most widely accepted theory of learning is some form or another of **constructivism** - that it is the student who constructs knowledge for himself or herself not the teacher who imparts it. The theories, concepts, data and evidence that students are offered by teachers and other sources are rejected, modified or accepted on the basis of their previous knowledge and experience. Students find some ideas, information and experiences to be so valuable that they incorporate them into their own repertoire and call upon them regularly to explain and order the world they encounter daily. Others are recognised only to have value in terms of satisfying the teacher's requirements and are retained briefly and used for that purpose only. Still others are rejected out of hand as flying in the face of what they already know from their own experience or from sources in which they trust.

As Biggs points out in the case study which follows "If we are to take constructivism seriously, then it follows that the student is the appropriate person to select the evidence for learning, not the teacher."

Portfolio assessment requires students to assemble a portfolio of evidence to show what learning has taken place. The portfolio can be used to demonstrate the student's knowledge and skills and his or her ability to apply these to real problems and situations. Whichever kinds of learnings the portfolio is intended to demonstrate, the student must make an evaluation of his or her own learning in order to decide what kinds of evidence can or should be provided.

21

Case study 21
Portfolios

Case study from Psychology
John Biggs, University of Hong Kong

Using his own words as much as possible we combine the written materials which John Biggs provided to the project and the extensive comments he made after reading an earlier draft of the module.

Context

Students in the psychology units described here are both pre-service and in-service teachers studying at the University of Hong Kong. The main aim in these units is not primarily to get students to learn about psychology, but to get them to reflect on their own classroom teaching in the light of concepts dealt with in this and a previous unit, in order to enrich the way they conceive of teaching and learning and the way they enact classroom decisions.

Assessment method

Students are provided with suggestions as to the forms that the evidence for their portfolio might take but are encouraged to go beyond that list if desired. The student must be prepared to explain why a particular package of components has been selected - whether the student is aiming to demonstrate coverage of the course content, or to make an integrated case that the student sees as important for his/her own purposes, or for reaching conclusions that go beyond the unit itself.

Below is Biggs' list of items which might be included in a student's portfolio. He suggests that the number of items can either be fixed, say four or five, or left to the student with a maximum word limit for all items.

➤

Some possible items for portfolio assessment

- a self-set essay, in note form

- a few objective test items, explaining the correct answers and why each item was selected

- an applied outcome of the unit; eg a lesson plan or test item or whatever suits the objectives

- a one or two page letter to a friend who is thinking about taking this unit next year, describing the unit and offering advice

- a concept map of the unit

- a list of questions that could be used to assess the unit

- a summary of a highly relevant book or article (not mentioned in the unit itself)

- a taped interview with a child, parent, teacher, another student, concerning the application of relevant content

- a case study

- a self directed seminar on a relevant topic with some fellow students, each describing how their understandings changed with group interaction

- design and carry out a small project, analyse and interpret the data, either alone or with a group of students

- a self assessment of any of the above, explaining clearly why it was graded the way it was. Self assessment should show awareness of one's academic strengths and weaknesses

- anything the student thinks is appropriate (important for gauging originality).

Figure 4.2
Items for portfolio
John Biggs

Criteria and grading

Each portfolio is assessed by the teacher to determine how well the evidence provided by the student matches the aims of the course.

In this unit, Biggs particularly looks for:

- evidence of how well the student has understood the topics taught and particularly their relevance to teaching and
- how far the student has actually 'taken on board' the course material in his/her own view of teaching and teaching practices.

Portfolios are graded, using the five point letter grade system: A, B, C, D, F. Each category reflects how well the aims of the course have been met.

A: Good evidence of reflection on practice using the concepts dealt with, changed conceptions of teaching, good and original illustrations of changed classroom decision making. A personal theory of teaching developing, as seen in the justifications for selected evidence.

B: Appreciates the general thrust of the course, clear understanding of major concepts and ability to see applications in the classroom: an A but less personal involvement and less originality: "Teachers should do this...." rather than "I did this....."

C: Emphasis on good understanding of concepts dealt with, but applications not thought out, reflection minimal.

D: Items isolated, addressing only one or a few aspects of the unit. Some serious problems but failure would be too drastic.

F: Items irrelevant or plagiarised.

Strengths and limitations

In Biggs' assessment, the portfolio system worked well for both pre- and in-service teachers, but best for the latter as they could obtain day-to-day examples of their reflections and classroom decision making. At first, the 82 students in the class for in-service teachers reacted particularly negatively, as this was an entirely new form of assessment to them. They also perceived four items and a compulsory diary (to note reflections on learning -related incidents) for the portfolio as an unacceptably heavy workload. However, a trial run of an item, and much explanation got them to accept the idea. Biggs reports:

The results were astonishing: over one third achieved As, showing high degrees of reflection and changed classroom practice (and this in the rigid Hong Kong system); 40% got Bs, and the rest Cs except for one D. Sample comments from students illustrate the congruence between course objectives, learning processes, and assessment that appears to have been achieved:

the portfolio is the highlight of this unit ... students have to reflect on what they have learned.

...now I do not see the portfolio as an assignment to be handed in, it's rather a powerful learning tool for the learner himself.

I found lots of fun (in making my portfolio)... and it led me to think about many questions that I never think of...

A few students reacted negatively, wishing to the end to be lectured to and assessed by exam or set essay assignment.

In Biggs' words,

The strengths of portfolio assessment derive from three features. First, it practises what is preached about the nature of student learning. Second, it reflects real world situations involving assessment, namely that one must provide evidence to convince others that one is the most deserving person for the job, for the research grant, etc. Practising teachers in particular, came to see the face validity of the portfolio quite quickly, once they realised what was required. Third, it allows students a great deal of freedom for originality, while remaining relevant to the course aims.

The limitations include the work involved, although this is adjustable. I put in far more hours in assessing than usual, but I mostly enjoyed this time; it was exciting seeing what students kept coming up with! This corresponds to the better students' reactions - one (who moaned loudest at the beginning about workload) commented, "the portfolio wasn't long enough, I kept wanting to keep adding more and more items!" Second, grading needs to be kept holistic, the portfolio being assessed as a whole package; so many marks for this and so many for that is a nonsense. Students and teachers reared on quantitative assessment find this hard to understand. Thus, the categories for grading, reflecting how well the aims of the course have been achieved, need to be quite clear from the beginning. Third, some students see it as "unfair" that they are not all evaluated on the same tasks; this is a hangover from competitive, norm-referenced grading, and needs re-education to combat it. One problem is that some students put in items of marginal relevance, but if the wording is clear ("...evidence for your learning in this unit ...") together with their justifications, there should be no problem on this ground. Now I think of it, none of these are what I'd call 'limitations'.

■

Whereas self evaluation of learning is a necessary but in some cases an incidental aspect of portfolio assessment, in the following case study, the ability to assess one's own learning and performance is a major focus of the unit.

Case study 22
Practising self evaluation

22

Case study from Resource and Environmental Management
Chris Trevitt, Australian National University

Chris Trevitt provided us with an initial written description of his assessment scheme and an invited paper he had presented to an international e-mail conference for further information. Follow-up phone conversations helped to clarify some of the points in the original draft.

Context

The subject under discussion is "Fire Science and Management", a compulsory third year subject for the professional forestry management degree which is also taken as an elective by students in other BSc programs including the BSc (Resource and Environmental Management). The subject generally enrols around 50 students.

According to Trevitt the goals of the subject include:
• helping students understand the central role in learning and on-going professional development played by criteria in assessment, and
• encouraging students to think in terms of criteria as determining factors when evaluating a piece of work, and specifically, their own work.

Assessment method

A number of assessment exercises all based on the content material of the course are intended to give students the opportunity to practise this approach.

• **Short answer written test**

    The first assessment task is a short answer written test, conducted at the end of the first term. Students assess their own work during class time, using model answers provided. Class discussion focuses on the criteria which are implicit in the model answers and on the need for honest self appraisal. This test contributes 30% of the final marks for the subject. Students are reminded that test results will be reviewed as part of the final oral debrief and if less than honest appraisal shows up at that time it will result in loss of marks.

• **The District Fire Committee simulation**

    The second assessment task takes the form of a simulation of the operations of a District Fire Committee. Students take on a role as a representative of one of the regional organisations involved in bush fire management. Representatives meet on a number of occasions as a committee to prepare a proposal for a District Fire Management Plan. The Fire Management Plan should include a written assessment of the fire weather history of the selected area; fire management priorities and issues; recommendations for action and timescale.

➤

A further part of the simulation exercise requires each student to make a written and oral report to the 'boss' of the organisation they represent on the District Fire Committee. Oral reports are presented in the group and the written account takes the form of a one page memo summarising the student's appraisal of the Fire Management Plan proposal from the point of view of criteria that are important to their own organisation. This assessment task also contributes 30% of the marks - 15% for the group work on the Fire Management Plan and 15% for the written and oral debrief. Initially an attempt was made to use peer evaluation to moderate the overall group mark, but the students did not respond well. Trevitt is now of the opinion that careful orientation to the process is necessary if students are to engage successfully in new experiences of this kind. With students having to cope with the many 'different' assessment experiences already included in this course, he has put peer assessment of the group work on hold for the time being.

- **Job application and interview**

The next and final assessment task requires students to prepare a job application for a fictitious job in fire science and management. This is modelled on an actual position recently advertised and filled by the Tasmanian Department of Environment and Land Management. Students present a written assessment of their knowledge, skills and experience against the selection criteria in the job advertisement. The written application is worth 15%.

Finally, students compile and organise their notes for the course in a way that makes sense to them and present themselves for interview. Students may use their notes in responding to interview questions and in defending the claims they made in their letter of application. The interview is used as a forum for students to demonstrate their ability to work with the subject matter and to exercise a range of interpretation and negotiation skills which they have been developing throughout the unit.

To help them prepare for the interview, students are provided with a package of materials from the Tasmanian Department of Environment and Land Management which provides detailed information relating to the job, the interview procedure, selection criteria and weightings, and examples of the kinds of reports written on applicants which highlight common weaknesses. Performance at the interview counts for 25% of total marks, but discussion of an appropriate final grade and the reasons for this form part of the interview agenda.

This comprehensive and innovative assessment package provides many occasions for students to develop and practise their self evaluation skills, as well as to provide evidence of their knowledge of fire science and management. In terms of the allocation of marks, only 30 % of the total marks are available through self assessment but self evaluation remains a strong theme in all assessment activities.

■

Implementing student self assessment: Some guidance from the research literature
Based on Falchikov & Boud (1989) ; Boud & Falchikov (1989) ; Boud (1989) ; Williams (1992)

Can student self assessment be trusted?

Analyses of the many studies of student self assessment that have been undertaken show that there is no general tendency for students to either overestimate or underestimate their own performance, although both have occurred in different studies. A tendency to over or underestimate performance is more likely to result from the students' understanding or lack of understanding of the assessment criteria or from the kind of rating instrument which is used than from any general student characteristics.

On the other hand, able students and students who have considerable experience of the subject matter have been shown to make more accurate judgments of their own performance than inexperienced, beginning students and less able students. In general, the less able students are, the more likely they are optimistically to over-estimate their own performance. Able and/or experienced students can and do produce highly accurate estimations of their own strengths and weaknesses.

What factors help to make student self assessment more trustworthy?

- **Provision of explicit criteria:**

    Asking students to make global judgments without specific criteria (eg. "Give your essay a mark out of 100 according to what you think it is worth" without providing any further guidance) has been shown to produce poor agreement between student and teacher assessors. Where students are provided with explicit criteria which distinguish satisfactory from unsatisfactory performance, and which distinguish different levels of performance if grades are required, there is much more likely to be a high level of student/teacher agreement in marking. There is some evidence which suggests that when students are involved in setting and negotiating the assessment criteria their understanding and ability to apply the criteria accurately are further increased.

- **Opportunities to develop and practise assessment skills:**

    Agreement between student and expert assessors is increased where students have the opportunity to practise assessing one or two pieces of work, and then discuss differences which arise in applying the criteria. With discussion, consensus can be reached about what each criterion means in practice. Such opportunities may be particularly important for students inexperienced in the subject area.

- **Avoiding the use of complicated and lengthy rating instruments:**

    Some rating instruments require the user to make hundreds of different discriminations which are difficult to perform and even more difficult to justify (for example - asking assessors to evaluate each of 10 different skill areas on a hundred point scale.) Teachers and researchers who design such instruments must keep in mind the number of different skill areas which can reasonably be assessed on one occasion or through one piece of evidence and the number of different levels of performance which could reliably be distinguished by expert assessors. Overcomplicated and lengthy instruments create confusion in the minds of assessors - particularly inexperienced ones.

- **Use of a second marker to moderate individual self assessment:**

    Where the results of self assessment are to contribute to the final assessment of the student, many teachers and students will feel more comfortable if the self assessment marks are balanced by those of a second marker. This could be a peer - another student - or the teacher. Where the marks differ by more than an agreed interval, the two judgments must be compared and negotiated until agreement is reached (or perhaps a third marker is called in as the final judge). This process of negotiation can also be a valuable learning experience for the student involved - an extension of the opportunities to develop and apply assessment skills.

    The research literature shows that the majority of students welcome the opportunity to become involved in assessment - both of their own work and that of their peers - provided that they have been given sufficient guidance to feel that they can do a good job.

Section 3

The ability to understand and manage one's own feelings and be sensitive to the feelings of others

Developing self-awareness is a life long task - its goal being that through accurately identifying our feelings and motivations we gain some level of choice and control in our personal lives rather than finding ourselves at the mercy of our emotions. Awareness of our own feelings and a greater degree of control both help us to manage our individual work more effectively and facilitate our interactions with others. It is equally important to our interactions with others if we can understand and acknowledge our biases and preconceptions about other groups in society. To provide just one example of how personal values influence professional practice - a manager in any field may or may not have heard of McGregor's theory X and theory Y (McGregor, 1960), but he or she will manage very differently according to whether they believe that workers inherently avoid work and can only be motivated to do it with extrinsic rewards and punishments or whether they believe that most people have the potential to enjoy their work providing they have some control of their working environment and the opportunity to learn and develop.

Theorists are divided as to whether one is more likely to develop an understanding of other peoples' feelings by first recognising one's own or whether one comes to self awareness through vicariously experiencing and identifying the emotions of others. It is safe to say that self awareness and empathy are to some degree linked, although individuals may show one attribute more strongly than the other. Psychotherapy of course is based on the proposition that self awareness is not an innate trait but can be learned. Similarly, Spencer (1984) has claimed that accurate empathy can also be learned (see Introduction to this module). Part of the experience of developing empathy - understanding of other's feelings and concerns - is acquiring the communication skills which enable one to find out what the other person is thinking and feeling as well as being able to express one's understanding. This may involve being able to make fine distinctions in everyday language so that one shows that one understands, while not being pushed into agreeing with the other person's position. Discussion of the assessment of such interpersonal communication skills will be found in Module 8, Section 2; Case Studies 8 and 9 in Module 2 are also relevant.

23

Case study 23
Autobiography

Case study from Town Planning
Robert Zehner, University of New South Wales and Michael Bounds, University of Western Sydney

The following case study is based on a draft of an article sent to the project by Zehner and Bounds. Quoted passages are from the draft.

Context

The course described here is a 5 year Bachelor of Town Planning degree taught at the University of New South Wales. According to Bounds and Zehner, urban and regional planners are increasingly caught between the conflicting demands of different community interest groups and competition for scarce resources. In their experience, students of town planning often do not appreciate the extent to which their own backgrounds (predominantly middle class, suburban and white) are likely to influence the way they approach their role and the decisions they make.

Assessment method

As part of their third year subject, Urban Society and Sociology, students are asked to write a paper which describes specific incidents from their own life which were significant in forming and confirming their values and sense of identity. They are asked to develop this into a broader discussion of what they consider to be their place in the community and finally to consider in what ways their particular collection of characteristics, values and opinions are likely to be an advantage or a disadvantage in a planning career.

The lecturers point out that while the content of the subject addresses concepts of socialisation, class, power and relationships between the professions and the structure of society, in the paper students are asked to apply their understanding of these topics to themselves as potential agents of community influence and control. Students are explicitly asked to work with their own experiences and not to use references to scholarly works to turn this into a conventional academic essay.

In helping prepare students for this assignment, class time is devoted to analysing one of the required readings for the course, Jill Ker Conway's autobiography, *The Road From Coorain*. (1989). The assignment has a ten week 'gestation period' to allow students adequate time for reflection. Zehner and Bounds report that initially students believe that this assignment will be easier than a 'real' paper, but the more time they spend trying to identify key experiences and explore their values, the more challenging they find it. According to student evaluations of the course, many students find that they end up putting more time and care into this piece of work than into anything they have previously written.

Marking

The autobiographical papers produced in this urban planning class are graded and contribute 40% percent to the final marks for the subject. Zehner and Bounds report that in one sense it is not difficult to distinguish different levels of performance as there are discernible differences in writing skills, the ability to structure papers and to communicate clearly. "What makes assessment difficult," they say, "is a recognition of the extraordinary level of personal commitment and disclosure most students put into these papers. The student's effort calls for a commensurate commitment from the reader, particularly when a student's life experiences have led him or her to reveal strong prejudicial feelings about other groups in society which the student knows (or suspects) are not shared by the lecturer. In practical terms, this tends to mean reading each paper at least twice and generally three times and a major challenge to provide appropriate, and frequently very extensive comments on the students' writings." ∎

Case studies 24 and 25
Autobiography

Two Case studies from Higher Education and Health Education
Susan Toohey, University of New South Wales
Barbara Pamphilon and Antoinette Ackermann, University of Canberra

The description of autobiography as used by Pamphilon and Ackermann is drawn from written materials provided to the project. Toohey is one of the authors of this package and includes her own use of of this assessment method because it offers another way of dealing with one of the central issues in using autobiography - the extent to which life stories should remain confidential.

Context

At the University of New South Wales, Toohey uses an autobiographical exercise in helping students identify the values that they hold about assessment in education and how they arrived at these; Pamphilon and Ackermann, from the University of Canberra, use autobiography in a course on adult learning in the Health Education degree.

At UNSW, students in the postgraduate program in higher education are asked to describe their personal beliefs and values about assessment, relate these to their own history with assessment, re-evaluate their current beliefs and make an argument for how they would now like to be assessed.

Students are provided with general criteria for all written work in the course and the paper is marked on a satisfactory/unsatisfactory basis. Indeed, this is the option that most students end up choosing for their other assessable work in the course. Toohey believes that the ability to examine one's own experience with a degree of detachment is dependent on many factors including personality and maturity. Levels of ability vary widely and establishing common grade standards for this type of personal writing is difficult. Precisely because the writing is so personal, failure to achieve a desired grade may be even more devastating for some students than lack of success in other areas of academic work. Extensive written feedback is usually provided and this takes the form of conversation rather than corrections where the lecturer offers similar experiences or alternative interpretations.

In the Health Education Degree at the University of Canberra, students are asked to take an autobiographical incident or evolution, describe it, analyse it from a personal perspective and then link it to macro issues through the relevant literature. Four weeks of tutorial time are devoted to preparing for the autobiographical paper - students work in small groups to discuss and analyse their personal experiences, help each other achieve insights and understandings and find relevant literature. The resulting paper is marked and graded and contributes 35% to the final grade. Criteria for assessment include clarity of argument, ability to think critically and ability to link personal ideas to the relevant literature.

Strengths and limitations

All three contributors point to the impact on students as one of the great strengths of using autobiography. Identifying the origins of their own values and beliefs often allows students to question them with a freedom not previously possible. In course evaluations students frequently point to the autobiography as a very significant learning experience for them.

■

Comments

Questions about the difficulty and desirability of grading such personal writing have been discussed earlier. Another issue that causes considerable debate concerns the desirability of confidentiality for this kind of writing. The three contributors handle this in very different ways. Zehner and Bounds in urban planning believe strongly that the autobiography ought to be confidential to the student and the lecturer. They believe that privacy is essential if students are to be able to discuss honestly their perceptions of other groups in society and bring up personal or family crises which have shaped their lives but which deserve to be kept private. In support they cite Stoddart's experience in using autobiography, where students spent much of the semester trying to pick up clues to match autobiographies to classmates after papers were circulated anonymously (Stoddart 1991).

Pamphilon and Ackermann's approach falls at the other end of the spectrum. They make the autobiography the focus of four weeks small group work. As they explain, "A very strong emphasis is placed throughout the course on peer support and the creation of a safe environment for people attempting to explore what have sometimes been painful and traumatic learnings. In the first weeks, students are guided to choose an issue that has been resolved to the extent that they will feel comfortable sharing it with peers. Further, through the process of linking autobiographical experiences to larger social issues, students are able to move beyond an analysis that locates the problem solely within the individual. They develop an awareness of the mechanics of victim blaming and move to a more socially critical perspective."

Toohey takes a position between the other contributors. The autobiography in her class is essentially an individual exercise, but a class discussion takes place after the work has been handed in where students discuss what has been learned from the exercise. Students compare their reactions to similar assessment experiences and the conclusions they draw for their own practice. The choice of whether to contribute to the discussion or not, and what kinds of experiences they wish to contribute, are left to them.

Zehner and Bounds point out that occasionally this exercise produces more than the usual amount of term paper anxiety for some individuals. While most people overcome such attacks, it may be worthwhile suggesting that a visit to student counselling services to talk through troubling issues may be helpful.

Using journals to develop and assess empathy

Probably the best known method for helping students reflect on their personal and professional values is the journal. In the following case study a journal is used for this purpose with second year occupational therapy students. As well as providing an opportunity for students to clarify values, the journal helps students document their clinical reasoning and develop empathy with clients.

Case study 26
Journal

Case study from Occupational Therapy
Penny Westhorp, University of South Australia

This case study is drawn from a published report of action research projects undertaken at the University of South Australia (Westhorp, 1994) Penny Westhorp provided her own report of her action research into the use of journals to the assessment project and the following account is adapted from that material.

Context

The second year subject in paediatric practice for occupational therapists is built around three major case studies involving real patients (confidentiality protected). Students work through a mass of materials including video tapes of the client and the assessment process, assessment reports from medical specialists and other therapists, a fabricated social history, input about the client's condition and a considerable amount of small group research on the diagnosis, functional problems, assessment method, treatment agencies and roles of the occupational therapist.

Assessment method

As well as producing initial and final reports on the case, students keep a journal throughout on their reactions to the client and family and their own growth as therapists. In Westhorp's words, "Through personal feedback on each journal entry, students are encouraged to identify their own values, attitudes and beliefs underlying their reactions and to reflect further about where these came from, how valid those past engendering situations were to current therapeutic situations, and how those values, beliefs and attitudes might affect their work as a professional therapist and their interactions with clients, families, other staff and administrators."

Marking

The journal for each case study is worth 10% or 15% depending on where the student wants to allocate marks. Grades only are reported to students although marks and grades are recorded for academic purposes. Criteria for assessment include the depth of reflection, indicated by a willingness to recognise and explore one's own issues; to question the status quo and to imagine the impact of their beliefs, attitudes and values in future therapy. Detailed comments were fed back to students on each of three entries in their journals, identifying issues and themes in their approach to the client and family. These might include comments on professionalism or the assumptions which have been made about economic circumstances or gender roles.

According to Westhorp, "The issue of grading reflective journals is a thorny one. The major rationale was that I considered it an integral part of the process toward the goal of empathic reasoning. If it was left ungraded, it seemed likely that only a small number of the students would complete the activity in their own time and thus many would not undertake the process of empathic development. Grading meant that all would at least undertake the process, even if all did not achieve the goal."

Strengths and limitations

Grading journals is extremely time-consuming in Westhorp's experience, but she reports that it is also fascinating and that on the evidence of the journals, students do make progress in empathy. They can see the impact on their practice and positively value this kind of learning. The following comment is typical of many students who documented their change in attitude: "At the start of semester my responses to the client, family and therapist were rigid and some-times unemotional, but over time I began to think about how they feel and how I would react in a particular situation."

As Westhorp commented, "The decision about whether to grade journals or not was a diffi-cult one. Some students commented that because all work was to be graded, they were initially inhibited about speaking (writing) freely about issues because of concern about 'what the lec-turer wanted to hear'. This problem tended to resolve itself once students came to understand and believe that what the lecturer wanted to hear was open and reflective thinking on any issue." Westhorp helped this process by keeping her own journal throughout the class and sharing entries with students.

As contributors described in the case studies on using autobiography to develop self awareness, progress in developing empathy is highly individual. Westhorp identifies what she considers to be some of the factors that affect students' success: their predisposition (or otherwise) to this type of thinking; willingness to be open and trust the lecturer; non-judgmental responses in detail from the marker; responsiveness to feedback; maturity and life experience. In her experience, the progress that students make is so variable that no starting point or finishing point could be prescribed.

■

Comment

Universities usually select students on the basis of their performance in tests which measure logical/mathematical reasoning and language abilities. They do not usually make personal and interpersonal understanding and ability part of their selection criteria. (Although a few, such as the medical program at the University of Newcastle have done so.) It is not surpris-ing then, that there is such a wide range of performance among university students when it comes to this particular set of abilities.

Section 4

Making ethical judgments

While there may be almost universal agreement that commitment to practising one's discipline or profession in an ethical manner is a desirable outcome for all graduates, there appears to be no consensus on whether questions of professional ethics are best explored in dedicated subjects taught by specialists or whether they can be more effectively dealt with as part of core units. In either case students may be expected to identify ethical issues in everyday practice, to propose ways of dealing with them and be expected to justify their responses in terms of personal, community and professional values. While it is far from universal, it is becoming increasingly likely that a student will be expected to demonstrate understanding of ethical behaviour in the professional context before being allowed to graduate.

27

Case study 27
The case study examination

Case study from Business
Margaret Blackburn, Auckland Institute of Technology

This case study is constructed from the extensive subject documentation which is given to students in the Business Degree at AIT and from Margaret Blackburn's comments on her use of the case study examination.

Context

Ethics, Business and Society is a compulsory unit in the Bachelor of Business degree. Students usually take the subject in their fourth semester of the four year program. The subject aims to enable students to identify ethical problems in business; to critically analyse approaches to ethical issues and to make and evaluate judgments using ethical frameworks, decision making models and professional codes.

Assessment method

Assessment in the subject typically consists of four items:
- a group project and presentation in which students are required to research an ethical theory and formulate a coherent response. Responses might include the relevance and practicality of the theory and how it accords with the personal values of group members. (30%)
- an essay in which students must investigate a particular ethical question, describing various responses to it, evaluating those responses and finally devising their personal response to the issue and their reasons for choosing that approach (30%)
- class participation involving both self assessment and tutor assessment of preparation and contribution to classes (10%)
- a case study examination requiring students to identify ethical issues in a case study and to devise and evaluate alternative courses of action (30%)

The case study on which the exam is based is given to the students a week beforehand. They are given the case descriptions only and not the questions which must be answered so as to encourage them to think as widely as possible about the issues raised. In the example provided by Blackburn, the particular case study is closely based on a recent New Zealand situation. Students are asked to consider the position of a manager of a printing company which is experiencing problems in its handling of dangerous chemicals. Reducing risks to workers will involve greater capital investment. However, the company is only marginally profitable and is under considerable pressure from overseas competitors. The community from which workers are drawn is already hard hit by recession and unemployment.

In analysing the case study students are asked to:

- identify each of the ethical issues which the case study raises;
- devise and describe in detail two alternative strategies which the manager could undertake to address the situation;
- choose the strategy which they would personally follow, identifying the personal values, the legal, professional or community obligations or duties and the possible consequences which they would take into consideration in reaching their decision.

Marking

In marking the responses to the case study, marks are given for well thought out and clearly articulated strategies, both of which should be practicable. Answers should indicate how the ethical issues which have been identified in the case study are addressed by each of the proposed strategies. In justifying their choice of strategies, students may call on the ethical theories that they have studied but may also cite principles such as justice and fairness, loyalty or professionalism or belief systems such as Maori spiritual values. In general, assessors are looking for rational, thoughtful and coherent justifications for the choice of a particular strategy, although Blackburn points out that 'rationality' is itself value-laden and it is important to acknowledge other ways of viewing the world.

Strengths and limitations

The strengths of this particular approach to assessing ethical decision-making obviously lies in its relevance to real situations, similar to those that students will experience in practice. Case studies can also be designed to bring in elements from different disciplines (an advantage in a multi-disciplinary program). Students can focus on those aspects according to their expertise and interests.

In discussing difficulties with designing case study exams Blackburn says,

> *Case studies can be time-consuming and difficult to research and write. It is a challenge to learn how much detailed information to include: too little means students will side-step definitive answers by claiming that they don't have enough data to make a decision, and too much may result in paralysis and confusion between 'wood' and 'trees'.*

> *Sometimes a particular case study may not be sufficiently flexible to enable an assessor to pose questions in all the areas he/she wishes to test. To stretch a case study in order to accommodate all one wants to examine can result in a loss of realism which is after all the advantage of this type of assessment instrument.*

■

Section 5

Working collaboratively

Working collaboratively may be limited to working with one other person or may involve the greater complexities of working with a group of people. In professional disciplines, such as engineering, nursing, medicine and business, many teachers are introducing group work as a preparation for professional practice which increasingly requires graduates to work in teams and to make teams work. In general education some teachers and students have come to value the richness and variety of data and interpretation that a group project can generate, while feminist theory points to group work as a more natural and comfortable way of working for women students.

Difficulties arise of course, when group work must be assessed by and for a system of higher education which predominantly recognises and values individual achievement. High achieving students, even those who enjoy and value group work, are likely to be concerned that the distinctiveness of their contribution will be lost when it comes to assigning marks for a group project and that they will be outstripped in the race for grades.

Broadly speaking, there have been three approaches taken to the assessment of group work. One is to assess only the product or outcome of the group work. The assumption is made that if the product is of high quality the group must have worked well together and group processes for allocating tasks and handling conflicts are at least adequate. Marks for the product are divided equally between all the students in the group (or all students are given the same mark).

The second method acknowledges that a good outcome may in some cases be the result of varying degrees of effort and quality of input on the part of group members. With this method, a total mark is allocated for the product or outcome of the group work. However, the mark is not divided evenly among all students in the group - total marks are divided and allocated to individual students on the basis of their contribution. Sometimes it is left to each group to determine how the marks should be divided; in other cases, students are given a rating schedule and asked to identify the nature and quality of other group members' contributions - marks are then divided according to the group's assessment of each of its members. Some quite elaborate formulae have been developed to make this process as fair as possible.

A third possibility is for an observer (usually the class teacher) to observe each group, noting for example, the extent to which each group member is involved and the way the tasks are planned and allocated. Group functioning is then rated by the observer, either on a satisfactory/unsatisfactory basis or on a limited scale.

Case studies 28 and 29
Group Projects

28

29

Two case studies from Education
Helen Hayes, University of Ballarat and John Woods, Edith Cowan University

These two case studies are brought together here because they have many similarities, but also some interesting differences. Helen Hayes' account combines the materials which she originally supplied to the project and comments from subsequent correspondence; John Woods provided us with a conference paper (1994) on his use of group projects and the information in this was supplemented by a telephone interview.

Context

Both Hayes and Woods assign a group project in curriculum design to their students. Hayes' students are enroled in the Graduate Diploma of Education; since primary and secondary curricula are usually the products of curriculum teams, Hayes feels that it is pointless trying to teach students the conceptual skills involved in curriculum design without also encompassing the skills for the necessary teamwork.

Assessment method *(Hayes)*

Students in the course face a number of requirements when it comes to the assessment task - they must research a topic and prepare a curriculum design as a group; present a group workshop on their topic; participate fully in all aspects of the group's activities and carry out an evaluation of how effectively the group worked together.

Marking *(Hayes)*

Early in the life of the project each group develops a set of assessment criteria by which their curriculum design and their group work will be judged. Each group also prepares evaluation/feedback sheets for the other students to complete at the end of their workshop presentation. The students in the group which presented the workshop collate these evaluation sheets and they contribute to the final grade for the presentation. The curriculum design project is marked by the lecturer on the basis of the aims of the project (specified in advance by the lecturer) and the assessment criteria developed by each group. In addition, each group prepares a group statement describing and reflecting on the ways in which they learned to work together as a group. Students also submit an individual evaluation of the way their group functioned and their part in it. These are marked by Hayes with 10% of marks available for the group report and 20% for the individual report.

Assessment method *(Woods)*

Another example of group work in curriculum development presents some interesting variations. John Woods at Edith Cowan University also requires students to work in groups on a curriculum design project. Groups are formed on the basis of their preference for a particular philosophical approach to curriculum design. As they work on their project week by week, each group must keep a group diary, documenting what decisions were made, how decisions were made, how tasks were allocated and how disagreements were resolved. The task of record keeping is usually assigned to one member who regularly feeds his or her perceptions back to the group.

➤

Together with their completed curriculum design project, each group must submit a report, based on the group diary, reflecting on how they worked as a group. They are specifically asked to compare their group dynamics with the way of working suggested by the curriculum philosophy which they were supposed to be following (for instance - did they take a linear approach to decision making? or in practice did the decision making turn out to be cyclical?).

Marking *(Woods)*

The project and the report on group processes are together worth 30% of the final grade for the subject. Each group member gets the same mark because Woods is concerned that this aspect of the project should mirror the real world as far as possible. Students understand from the beginning of the project that is up to them to negotiate their way through difficulties.

Strengths and limitations

Both Woods and Hayes report that the students see the relevance of the group tasks in the context of curriculum development and are interested in reflecting on the ways in which they negotiate the task sharing and the group relationships. Hayes says that, on the other hand, when things do not go well they may become angry at the constraints put upon their achievements by group members who don't do their share. Problems like this are always referred back to the group to solve. This may be less of a problem in Woods' group where the group project accounts for only 30% of the marks. (An individual assignment and an exam count for 30% and 40% respectively.) The additional assessment items in Woods' program also produce a much greater spread of marks than the group project alone would do. The group project alone is not useful for discriminating among students as most students tend to do reasonably well. By incorporating the additional assessment events a spread of grades is produced which satisfies the university's expectations.

An unrelated problem which Hayes encounters is that students find it difficult to decide on and formulate criteria for assessment. (In the program at Edith Cowan the assessment criteria are supplied by the teaching staff.) However, because this is such an important learning experience in itself for student teachers it has been retained as part of the project.

■

Case study 30
Group work in the triple jump

Case study from Community Health
Grahame Feletti, University of Hawaii and Greg Ryan, University of New South Wales

The material presented here is drawn from an article provided to the project by the authors (Feletti & Ryan, 1994) and also incorporates additional comments they made after seeing an earlier version of the case study

Context

In Case Study 19, the "Triple Jump" exercise used in assessing a course on community health at the University of Newcastle was described. The second stage of the triple jump exercise consists of group work and this group work is carried out and assessed under exam conditions.

Assessment method

As described in greater detail earlier, the triple jump consists of three stages. In the first stage students are shown a fifteen minute video consisting of extracts from a current affairs documentary. Students must individually list the health problems that they could identify in the video. Students were then told to join a randomly assigned group of 7-8 students to discuss the issues they had identified and produce a consolidated list of key questions/health issues. Before the end of the 60 minute discussion period each person must negotiate with their group and have documented the key health issue that he or she will pursue as a self directed learning task. The third stage involves the individual research and writing of the report on their chosen health issue.

Criteria

Group work in the second stage of the exercise was evaluated using the Group Process Evaluation form developed at the University of Newcastle (see below). It has three sections - one assesses the degree of involvement of all members of the group and its methods of handling conflict; the second section looks at the way the group organises itself and manages its tasks; the third section looks at the quality of reasoning and critical thinking that takes place during the group work (Murphy & McPherson, 1988).

The Group Process Evaluation Form

GROUP TASK: SUMMATIVE ASSESSMENT

GROUP PROCESS AND GROUP REASONING

Each criterion, listed below, is specified as a pair: the first behaviour is that which is considered appropriate; the second, that which is considered inappropriate.

In assessing the group in respect of each attribute, the presence of the appropriate behaviour or the absence of the inappropriate behaviour is considered "satisfactory". Only if the inappropriate behaviour is evident is the group considered to be "not satisfactory" in that dimension.

Mark each item S or NS for the group: cross out whichever is not applicable.

1. Structural/Functional/Dynamic aspects of group process

1.1	all members included/involved: members isolated/excluded	S/NS
1.2	all members attentive in posture: some members inattentive in posture	S/NS
1.3	widespread interaction between members: discussion limited to few members	S/NS
1.4	freedom to express ideas/thoughts: group rejection of non-conforming ideas	S/NS
1.5	evenly distributed discussion: domination of group by 1 or 2 members	S/NS
1.6	ability to resolve conflict/disagreement: conflict/ disagreement disrupt or interfere with progress	S/NS
1.7	critical consideration of all ideas: uncritical acceptance and/or rejection of ideas	S/NS

2. Organisational/Maintenance aspects of group process

2.1	group limits discussion of peripheral issues: group readily diverts from main line of problem	S/NS
2.2	group demonstrates ability to review progress towards objective: group unable to ascertain whether making progress	S/NS

Figure 4.3

Group process evaluation form
Murphy & McPherson, 1988

2.3	group demonstrates coherence of approach: group appears to have conflicting approaches to problem	S/NS
2.4	group consciously works towards making decision: decisions arise by default/disinterest	S/NS
2.5	tasks clearly allocated/accepted with group: no clear division of labour or allocation/acceptance of task responsibility	S/NS
2.6	ability to adopt alternative route to solution if one is blocked: able to proceed along only one route	S/NS

3. Procedural/Reasoning/Critical Thinking aspects of group process

3.1.	recognition of appropriate cues in problem presentation: failure to recognise important cues	S/NS
3.2.	development of broad-based hypotheses: hypothesis generation limited in scope	S/NS
3.3.	hypothesis generation using all available relevant data: hypotheses do not take into account all relevant data available	S/NS
3.4.	hypotheses well grouped or organised: no apparent organisation of hypotheses developed	S/NS
3.5	group attempts to identify an order of probability for hypotheses: no evaluation of hypotheses in order of probability	S/NS
3.6.	frequent re-formulation: absence of re-formulation	S/NS
3.7.	linking between data requested and hypotheses: seeking of data without clear reason	S/NS
3.8.	group identifies/specifies appropriate learning topics: group fails to identify/specify learning topics	S/NS

General Comments:

_____

_____

_____

_____

_____

ASSESSOR NAME: SIGNATURE

Figure 4.3 *(cont)*

Group process evaluation form
Murphy & McPherson, 1988

Marking

This instrument was developed for assessment of problem based learning in the Bachelor of Medicine degree at the University of Newcastle and in that context, it is used for summative assessment. Students working in groups are observed and rated for two hours by tutors in the program. The raters then agree on a composite assessment. Groups which are rated as unsatisfactory on two or more dimensions within the three areas are considered to be not satisfactory overall. They are required to undertake remediation and re-sit the exam satisfactorily in order to pass the course.

In the Community Health course, the group process evaluation was used for formative purposes only. The assessment was not done by observers but by the students themselves. All members of the group were required to complete the group process evaluation at the end of the group work stage of the triple jump. Results were compiled and returned to students with their marks for the other stages of the exercise.

➤

Comment

The use of an instrument such as this with one or more observers is obviously an expensive form of assessment. Murphy and McPherson have justified its use in the medical degree on the grounds that it emphasises the importance which the faculty places on process skills such as the ability to work in groups and to reason logically through medical problems. It also provides a method of quality control in a relatively new and radical problem-based curriculum, which assured faculty and stakeholders that the goals of the program were being met. Feletti & Ryan (1994) argue that the way it is used in this case study - being completed by students themselves rather than by an observer - may be more appropriate for postgraduate courses such as this and more realistic for large groups.

Peer tutoring in a Business course

A different approach in helping students develop the ability to work collaboratively is that employed in the following case study where students taking the human resource management specialisation in a business degree are offered an elective in Peer Tutoring in Business.

Case study 31
Peer tutoring

31

Case study from Business
Phil Ker, Bryce Mason and Fe Day, Auckland Institute of Technology.

The information on which this case study is based was collected during a series of interviews with Ker, one of the course designers.

Context

The developers of this new subjec, believe that peer teaching can be a powerful vehicle for developing the skills of reflection and critical analysis which they see as an essential outcome for professional education.

The subject aims to prepare students for practising in a professional context through:
- developing students' understanding of the principles of teaching and learning and their application to a chosen discipline
- helping students develop a greater awareness of their own learning processes
- developing students' skills at communicating the concepts associated with their chosen discipline area
- developing students' coaching skills as a basis for mentoring/training others in a work situation
- helping students develop professional skills such as reflection and self evaluation.

The program differs from many other peer tutoring programs in the emphasis that is placed on developing understanding of the learning process and tutoring skills rather than on the content of the subject being taught.

➤

The subject runs for 13 weeks and is structured with four hours of instruction in the first three weeks, when students develop a conceptual framework and some basic skills in tutoring, followed by an eight week practicum during which they tutor individuals or small groups of students. During the practicum students meet weekly with their own teacher in one-to-one or small group sessions to reflect on their progress, follow up gaps in their knowledge and report on the self-directed study that they undertake in learning issues. In the last two weeks students meet for group reflection and feedback sessions in which they present a critical review and analysis of one of their cases.

Students may find their own 'tutees' or be allocated students in need of assistance through the Student Learning Centre. They may tutor in any subject related to their degree including areas such as language and mathematics. The students whom they tutor may be junior to them or at the same level in their degree program.

Criteria

Criteria for good practice as a peer tutor are developed with the students and are returned to and re-worked over the whole period of the subject. As a result, students have a deep understanding of what they mean and spontaneously refer to them when making their own informal assessments.

The criteria include - being an active learner oneself; being a critical thinker; establishing rapport; exercising good judgment; communicating effectively and organising oneself. Each of these broad criteria are further specified. For example, being a critical thinker is broken down as - seeing different points of view, questioning effectively and being able to recontextualise problem areas.

Assessment method

Five assessment events are used to assess students. The primary one is the assessment of effectiveness as a tutor. This is carried out by the subject teacher on the basis of student self appraisal, feedback from the learners being assisted, and feedback from the subject teacher and other teachers who may have observed tutoring sessions. At present, a session is scheduled in which the subject teacher observes the student tutor. This is likely to be discontinued in future, as Ker feels that having the lecturer present changes the usual atmosphere and interactions to such an extent that the teacher observation does not make a particularly reliable contribution to the assessment. This assessment of effectiveness as a tutor is not graded but students must be judged satisfactory in order to pass the course.

Grading is undertaken on the basis of four additional assessments:
* preparation of a learning resource package
* written reports on two students with whom the tutor has worked. The two reports include diagnosis of the original learning needs, choice of strategies and analysis of success.
* an oral report of a critical incident or issue arising from the practicum. The oral report is included as a way of assisting students who are stronger in oral communication skills than written.

Strengths and limitations

Ker comments that the faculty is very happy with the success of this unit which was run for the first time in 1994. He believes that the assessment offers a good balance between practical, oral and written forms of assessment. Having the class collaboratively determine the assessment criteria with the lecturers was a powerful learning strategy in itself, he reports, and the fact that the criteria were developed in conjunction with class work, literature reviews and practical experiences meant that the student input into criteria setting was an informed input.

Comment

Many teachers in higher education recognise the desirability of students learning to work effectively with others but are discouraged from setting group projects by the resistance they anticipate from students who want their individual contributions recognised in their grade and the difficulty in finding a marking system which can deliver such recognition. As can be seen from the cases described above, many of these difficulties can be reduced or eliminated by practices like the following:

- making the assessment criteria as clear and explicit as possible. It is helpful if students are involved in developing the criteria because of the greater depth of understanding this is likely to bring.

- requiring students to keep a log of the activities which they undertook as part of a group project. These lists of tasks can form the basis for a group discussion on how marks for a project might be divided.

- setting an additional piece of written work in which students analyse how their group worked, what they contributed to it and how its effectiveness might have been increased.

- asking group members to evaluate their own and others' contributions to the group effort. These should include tasks, ideas and group management functions. The combined evaluation of each individual's performance can be used to moderate the mark for the project, if desired.

In short, the experience of being involved in the assessment of group work can make a significant contribution to the learning achieved through the project itself.

Conclusion

The abilities we've been talking about here - developing understanding of oneself and others; taking responsibility for one's own learning and work; making realistic self assessments; working efectively with others - might be considered as aspects of personal effectiveness. While such personal effectiveness has always been valued, its development has often been left to chance. Students who learned these kinds of skills often did so unconsciously. If they were fortunate, they found good role models. But as it became clearer that success in the profession or discipline often depended as much on personal effectiveness as on knowledge and technical skills, it began to be suggested that this kind of learning should be planned for, supported and assessed.

Developing and assessing personal effectiveness has not proved a particularly easy task. Teachers have had few effective models to work from in developing these kinds of skills and the issues that arise in assessing personal effectiveness are often complex. We believe that the examples of current practice in this module will make a substantial contribution to this emerging area and provide inspiration and support for teachers who are aiming to help students develop the full range of their abilities.

References

Boud, D. (1989). The role of self-assessment in student grading. *Assessment and Evaluation in Higher Education,* 14(1), 20-30.

Boud, D., & Falchikov, N. (1989). Quantitive studies of student self-assessment in higher education: a critical analysis of findings. *Higher Education,* 18, 529-549.

Boud, D., Keogh, R., & Walker, D., eds (1985). *Reflection: Turning Experience into Learning.* London: Kogan Page.

Brookfield, S. D. (1987). *Developing Critical Thinkers: Challenging Adults to Explore Alternative Ways of Thinking and Acting.* San Francisco: Jossey-Bass.

Conway, J.K. (1989). *The Road from Coorain.* London: Heinemann/Mandarin

Candy, P. C. (1991). *Self Direction for Lifelong Learning: A Comprehensive Guide to Theory and Practice.* San Francisco: Jossey-Bass.

Cross, K. P., & Angelo, T. A. (1988). *Classroom Assessment Techniques: A handbook for faculty.* Ann Arbor, Michigan: National Center for Research to Improve Postsecondary Teaching and Learning.

Falchikov, N., & Boud, D. (1989). Student self-assessment in higher education: a meta-analysis. *Review of Educational Research,* 59(4), 395-430.

Feletti, G., & Ryan, G. (1994). The triple jump exercise in inquiry based learning: a case study showing directions for further research. *Assessment and Evaluation in Higher Education,* 19(3), 225-234.

Gardner, H. (1993). *Frames of Mind: The Theory of Multiple Intelligences.* (2nd ed.). London: Fontana.

Higher Education Council (1992). *Higher Education: Achieving Quality.* Canberra, A.C.T.: Australian Government Publishing Service.

McGregor, D. (1960) *The Human Side of Enterprise.* New York: McGraw Hill.

Mezirow, J. D. (1990). *Fostering Critical Reflection in Adulthood: A Guide to Transformative and Emancipatory Learning.* San Francisco: Jossey-Bass.

Murphy, B., & McPherson, J. (1988). The group assessment task: a real time test of small group, problem based learning. In B. Wallis (Ed.), *Problem Based Learning - The Newcastle Workshop, held as part of the conference - Ten Years of Innovative Medical Education 1978*-1988. University of Newcastle. pp137-8.

Ramsden, P. (1992). *Learning to Teach in Higher Education.* London: Routledge.

Spencer, L. M. (1984). *Soft Skill Competencies - their identification, measurement and development for professional, managerial and human service jobs.* Edinburgh: Scottish Council for Research in Education.

Stoddart, K. (1991). Life Story: a device for dispersing authority in the introductory course. *Teaching Sociology,* 19, 70-73.

Westhorp, P. (1994). The experience and outcomes of action research and reflective teaching in occupational therapy. In B. Smith (Ed.), *The experience of reflective university teachers addressing quality in teaching and learning: The CUTL action research project.* Adelaide: University of South Australia. pp33-62.

Williams, E. (1992). Student attitudes towards approaches to learning and assessment. *Assessment and Evaluation in Higher Education,* 17(1), 45-58.

Woods, J. D. (1994). Bridging the gap between curriculum theory and curriculum practice. In *Quality in Teaching and Learning - Making it Happen: Teaching Learning Forum 94,* . Claremont, W.A.: Edith Cowan University.

MODULE 5

ACCESSING AND MANAGING
INFORMATION

PEGGY NIGHTINGALE

Module 5
Accessing and managing information

This module covers assessment of tasks which are primarily of the "research a topic" type. These tasks usually involve finding information and organising it into some sort of presentation, but the teacher is more interested in the process of accessing and sorting and sifting than in the presentation at the end. Accessing information may include tasks of interpretation like reading a map or a plan or a diagram, or collecting data in the field.

This module covers broad abilities such as:
- researching
- investigating
- finding appropriate information
- interpreting (eg. a plan, diagram, aerial pictures)
- organising information
- reviewing and paraphrasing information
- collecting data
- searching and managing information sources
- observing and interpreting

Themes
- Developing search and synthesis skills
- Purpose of the presentation
- Pressure on resources
- Impact of new technology
- Assessment in context of teaching

Techniques
- Library research assignment
- Self-assessment schedule
- Brief for markers
- Developing a data base
- Peer assessment
- Multiple tasks associated with one research assignment

Case studies
32. Research assignment, Law
33. Developing a database, Design

Module 5

Accessing and Managing Information

Peggy Nightingale

Back in the good old days - not all that long ago - teachers taught students how to use library card catalogues and printed bibliographies, huge books in many-volumed series. We taught students to be systematic, keeping their references on file cards, one per card for ease of sorting, and we taught them to take notes as they read, again encouraging them to identify key topics and sort their notes on (larger) file cards with topic headings for ease of sorting and access and with some sort of numbering system to cross-reference the bibliography card to the information cards.

Although they may use bibliographic software instead of file cards, students still need to learn where to look for the information of their discipline, how to search, and how to organise and use that information once they find it. In this module, we will look at the tasks teachers are setting students which help them learn these skills. In demonstrating their research skills, students are also asked to demonstrate abilities covered in other modules, such as thinking critically and communicating, but the two case studies which follow put an emphasis on accessing and managing information.

The first case study is from law, a discipline and a profession where research skills are integral to success (at least until one reaches an exalted level where someone else does the searching!). The assignment is "traditional". The second case study comes from design. The assignment task is one of the most innovative we have collected as part of this project.

Case study 32
Research assignment

32

Case study from Law
Enid Campbell, Monash University

The following case study is an edited version of information provided to us by Enid Campbell. We use her own words as much as possible.

Context

Administrative Law is one of the required subjects for the LL.B. It is taught at the rate of 2 lecture hours and one tutorial hour per week over two semesters. Most students enrol for the subject in year 4 or year 5 of the five year degree course.

The number of students currently enrolled in the subject is approximately 400. There are four lecture groups, each with an enrolment of approximately 100. The enrolment in each tutorial group is approximately 25.

Assessment method

For several years now, students have been required to submit a research assignment of 2500 to 3000 words on one of several set topics (25% of total marks in subject; there is also an examination). The research involved is mainly library-based research and involves search for and use of relevant primary and secondary sources.

A different set of assignment topics is prepared for each lecture stream and a maximum of 15 students are allowed to choose any one topic. This practice is adopted to reduce pressures on the law library and to facilitate detection of cases in which there has been excessive collaboration between students. Assignments on a particular topic will all be marked by the same person.

The nature of the assignment topics varies. Some assignments involve the giving of legal advice to a hypothetical client. Some are exercises in law reform. Some involve the preparation of a paper destined (hypothetically) for presentation at a conference or for publication in a learned journal.

Administrative Law is considered to be a subject which lends itself to development of the research skills which are required of lawyers in the performance of their professional work. The reasons are that investigation of questions of Administrative Law frequently involves reference to a wide range of legal materials and also presents a researcher with special difficulties in identifying relevant source materials.

Students are supplied with a manual which is designed to assist them in finding relevant sources - *Administrative Law: Finding Aids.* In addition, staff of the Law Library conduct l-hour tutorials for small groups of students on computer-aided research.

➤

Specifying the criteria

The following two sections , "Advice on Writing" and "Objectives and Criteria for Assessment" are extracted from the course handout given to students.

Advice on Writing

Some references on legal writing are listed at the end of the *Guide to Preparation and Presentation of Written Work in the Law School.* Pamela Samuelson's article "Good Legal Writing" (1984) 46 *U. Pittsburgh LR* 149 and S. Murumba's article "Good Legal Writing: A Guide for the Perplexed" (1991) 17 *Monash ULR* 93 are especially recommended.

In writing your assignment, have regard to the stated purpose for which the assignment is meant to be written and the audience to which it is to be addressed. You are meant to be writing as a lawyer who is well-informed about the subject of the assignment, but how you present your assignment may be affected by considerations such as:

- whether the paper is designed to provide advice on a specific legal problem to another lawyer;
- whether the paper is designed to educate persons who are not lawyers;
- whether the paper is designed to assist the deliberations of a law reform agency;
- whether the paper is designed to stimulate thought about a particular subject, among persons attending a conference/seminar or among readers of a journal.

Before you submit your assignment, you might appraise it according to the following self-assessment schedule. This schedule is a modified version of a self-assessment scheme developed by teachers at the University of Sydney Law School (Shirley Rawson and Alan L Tyree, 'Self and Peer Assessment in Legal Education' (1989) 1 *Legal Education Review* 135 at 143).

Goals, Relevance of Material
- aims and objectives defined
- target audience identified
- stays within the boundaries of the question(s)
- all points covered
- each point clearly related to main thrust of assignment

Research
- overall knowledge of the subject
- quantity, quality, depth of research
- appropriate number of sources and authorities used
- use of primary as well as secondary sources
- alternative views (if any) noted
- comparative research where appropriate

Synthesis, Innovation
- originality of ideas (where there is scope for originality)
- innovation in application of theory
- own ideas formulated
- suggestion for change where appropriate

Style, Structure
- clarity, conciseness of expression
- direct and assertive
- consistent theme(s)
- interesting
- use of correct legal language

Figure 5.1

Course handout
Enid Campbell

- grammar, syntax, spelling correct
- good use of section headings, paragraphs etc.

Arguments and Analysis
- arguments logical and well organised
- clear exposition of the problem(s)
- issues and sub-issues clearly identified
- sources analysed, not just quoted
- well reasoned conclusions
- no loose ends in conclusions
- sources well organised
- no plagiarism

Presentation
- good typing (or handwriting), general presentation
- thorough and accurate citation of references
- interesting to read.

Objectives and Criteria for Assessment

The aim of the research is not the regurgitation of material set out in basic texts. What is sought is demonstration of a capacity not only to locate relevant material but also to synthesise information from a range of sources and to develop reasoned analysis and argument.

The following matters will be considered in assessing the research papers:

- evidence of thorough and wide-ranging research, beyond the materials referred to in lectures and tutorials, and in reading guides for the course;
- understanding of issues discussed;
- analytical thought and critical evaluation;
- the quality and clarity of expression, and order and style of presentation;
- how well the paper serves the purpose for which it is written;
- accuracy in spelling, punctuation and citation of references;
- conforming with the conventions of citation indicated in Campbell and Fox, *Guide to Preparation and Presentation of Written Work in the Law School.*

Figure 5.1 *(cont)*
Course handout
Enid Campbell

Procedures for assessing

(a) The teacher who has composed an assignment topic prepares a written brief for the marker of assignments on that topic. Preparation of the brief itself involves research. It will indicate what source materials students ought to have located and will identify issues to be considered.

(b) Markers are reminded of factors to be taken into account in assessing the submissions.

(c) Markers are reminded of what they need to do when they suspect plagiarism.

(d) Markers are reminded of the need to provide constructive comment on individual submissions.

(e) Markers attach to each submission a typed statement about expectations and about common mistakes and shortcomings in the submissions.

(f) Students are not given an opportunity to up-grade the mark for the assignment by re-writing. (Staff resources are not sufficient for this purpose!) On the other hand, the assessable work of all students whose aggregate mark in a subject is below the pass mark must, under University Examination Regulations, be reassessed by a second examiner.

➤

Strengths

The research assignment component of Administrative Law has proved to be worthwhile for several reasons. They are, briefly, as follows:

(i)   The assignment is an occasion for students to learn in a way many find very conducive to learning, ie. by actually doing a task of a kind which they can recognise as one which they might be called upon to do in the capacity of a professional lawyer.

(ii) The assignment is also an occasion for reinforcement and development of the most elementary legal research skills which were introduced in first year.

(iii) Students are given an opportunity to perform well in a task other than an examination. Many students earn marks for their research assignments which will, when added to the marks awarded for their performance in a time-limited examination, secure them an overall pass mark or a credit (or higher grade).

Limitations and problems

i)   The demands made on the time of staff involved in the setting and assessment of the assignments is considerable, and far in excess of that involved in the setting and assessment of work to be examined by time limited class tests and examinations.

(ii) A distinct research component in a law subject in which 300 to 400 students are enrolled can impose extraordinary strains upon the law library system. The reasons are: Over certain periods of time, law library staff encounter special demands on their time by students who seek their assistance. It is virtually impossible to set research assignments in law which do not involve reference to some central reference materials in the nature of indexes, digests and other aids to finding relevant documentary material. Much legal material is now produced in loose-leaf editions which are periodically up-dated, rather than in bound editions; the library system cannot control or prevent excision of pages in these loose-leaf editions.

Comments

The criteria for assessment in the case study above include those we find in tasks where the emphasis is on skills in analysis, critical thinking, and communication (see Modules 1 and 8), but the task is primarily designed to require significant research so that students become familiar with a wide range of key resources available to lawyers. The emphasis in advice to students is on finding and using correctly the necessary reference material. The material provided to students to assist them with the task includes a great deal of detailed information about those resources and about how to cite them, and the criteria for assessment emphasise thoroughness in the research and accuracy in citation.

The materials submitted to us did not, however, provide any advice or models for students about how to organise the material they collected during the process of conducting the research, nor was this phase of the research assessed in any way. Perhaps how to read and interpret legal texts and how to identify and summarise key points were covered in class exercises or possibly in an introductory subject. It did occur to the project team, however, that asking students to access and manage information without help in developing these skills makes it very difficult for students who are novices within disciplines.

The next case study offers an example of how students may be assisted with developing the skills of managing information as well as accessing it, and how they may be assessed on their success in this part of the research process as well.

Case study 33
Developing a database

33

Case study from Design

Dean Bruton and Alan Barnes, University of South Australia

The following case study was developed from materials provided to us by Bruton and Barnes and after telephone conversations with Bruton. A published account of their innovation is available (Bruton & Barnes, 1993).

Context

The School of Design offers a Bachelor of Design (BDes) degree consisting of eight semesters. The assessment exercise described here occurs in the third year of study.

This exercise is a project which requires students to contribute information on three 20th century designers to a CDROM database.

The traditional understanding of design as an arts and crafts manual training has hindered the development of a design research discipline. Australian designers have traditionally not been known for their ability to talk or write about design. Design History in the BDes course comprises 12% of the curriculum while in the UK it usually comprises 20% of the course. The Design History course has been operating within a limited timeslot, on a conservative lecture/tutorial basis, and with limited resources, making it impossible to cover many areas adequately. Since the subject is in its infancy, the problem has been to engender research skills in students who have a bias for practical skills. The utility of this assigned project is that an appreciation for a vital research culture in design may be fostered within the undergraduate program.

In addition, the introduction of computer technology has changed the role of designers from single-focused manual skills to multi-functional design managers; for example, specialists like graphic designers who used to concentrate on layout of print materials now work in multimedia dealing with audio, video and design of material to appear on computer screens.

It was decided to require students to present their research assignments using multimedia. These technologies allow designer related materials in text, image, sound and video to be brought together in an archive immensely more accessible and more manipulable than the physical materials themselves. Such new technologies can foster new understandings of the importance of design, designing and design research.

The construction of this database has facilitated the presentation and storage of information collected by students, which had been lost in previous years.

The tasks

Students were required to research three 20th century designers (two international and one local). They presented their research, which could include slides, illustrations, video clips, and their own text commentaries, using hypertext, in a specified format, fully referenced and suitable for inclusion in a CDROM database. With technical assistance, these materials were incorporated into the database, and students were then required to give, in a seminar presentation, a comparative study of the designers they had researched, using the database for visual displays. They also submitted an essay.

➤

In the first stage of the process students were to prepare on disc a chronology of the chosen designer's work, a summary of her/his philosophy and design processes, a description of the products of her/his work, the student's evaluation of the designer's influence, and a list of images and sources. Students were expected to use the software package EndNote to collect the resources and they were required to find the international copyright address that applied to the materials. In this first stage students worked independently.

In the second stage of the process, after Bruton checked the content, Barnes assisted the students with the design of the database. In this stage students were working collaboratively, assisting each other to design the interface and logo etc which would be used for their seminar presentation. The seminar presentation (third stage) used the database for illustrations.

Finally students submitted an essay in which they compared the work of their chosen designers.

Abilities being assessed

Abilities that were given assessment priority were:

- critical and analytical writing skills
- oral presentation skills
- visual presentation for group discussion
- research skills
- social interaction, teamwork skills
- technical competence, computer literacy

Procedures for assessing

a) Critical and analytical writing skills were assessed by the students' academic supervisor. Students were expected to provide on disc, research on design and designers in a specified format, fully referenced.

   Essays were assessed using a weighted feedback form, that included a comments section. Attention was drawn to traditional academic writing issues as well as a need for originality and vitality.

b) Oral presentations were assessed by the group using criteria agreed upon after initial discussions with the academic supervisor. Each student filled in a form with comment on the merits of the presentation. These were collated, recorded and returned to the student presenter in the following two weeks. These student assessments were used as a guide for the teacher who finally determined the grade.

c) Social interaction and teamwork skills were assessed by the students in conjunction with the academic supervisor and the technical assistant. They jointly determined the degree of each student's contribution to their presentation team.

Strengths, limitations and problems

This assessment required students to carry out the required research and increased their knowledge and appreciation of the history and theory of design. In addition, it presented a real design task in preparing the materials for presentation via the database.

After some initial computer-phobic reluctance, students worked with committed zeal on their project. Their enthusiasm was evident in the sense of discovery and excitement that pervaded their presentations. Responses indicated that the electronic mode of presentation was superior to the traditional forms of tutorial and seminar; the data base allowed quick comparisons of the designers, their philosophies and their works which greatly enhanced the comparative studies and the discussion following each presentation.

➤

Strengths

1. The Design History and Theory subject became an exciting pioneering prototype project. For the first time student research could be reused and built upon from year to year with the CDROM facility.

2. Students extended their awareness and capabilities in the areas of history, theory and presentation technology, through hands-on design linked to critical research techniques.

3. Editing skills became an important addition to the students' toolkit as restraints imposed by the medium and the timetable demanded efficiency in the presentations.

Problems

1. Time was limited and often prevented extended exploration of interesting topics and issues raised.

2. Technical assistance was necessary and became an essential feature of the program (academic staff plus 2 students from previous groups who were employed to help). The Library also assisted with scanning of visual images though some students chose to scan their own materials.

3. Increased participation beyond information provision requires curiosity and persistence.

Use of results

The results were used as a compulsory component of the BDes program. Feedback assignment report sheets provided a guide for future improvement of writing ability and research and presentation competence. Results were used to select student assistants for further development of a design database facility suitable for a library resource in future years.

Peer assessment

In Bruton and Barnes' case study, we learn almost as an aside that students engaged in peer assessment of the oral presentations and of the social interaction and teamwork skills needed in developing the design of the presentation. Peer assessment is an element in other case studies (see Index) but has not been discussed in any detail in other modules.

There have been many studies of the validity and reliability of peer assessment. One of the most recent is Falchikov (1995). She overviews the literature and offers the following points in summary:

*   The majority of studies attempt to assess the 'accuracy' of peer assessment by means of comparisons between the ratings of an 'expert' (usually the lecturer) and the mean peer mark.

*   The overwhelming view is that peer assessment is generally a useful, reliable and valid exercise. However, in some circumstances student over-marking occurs.

*   Comparison between studies is difficult... A wide variety of measuring instruments have been used to meet the requirements of a wide variety of situations.

- Studies focus on either a product or performance. Performance assessment studies greatly outnumber product assessment ones.

- Peer assessment of supervised performance at work takes place in locations such as hospitals or schools, whereas peer assessment of educational products takes place in university classrooms.

- Classroom studies tend to focus on interpersonal skills or group dynamics.

- Few student evaluations of peer assessment are reported. Those that are available suggest more benefits than reservations.

- In some circumstances students appear to experience difficulty or reluctance in awarding marks to their peers.

Brown and Knight (1994) stress problems of over-marking or worse, collusion or retribution in peer marking, as well as students' lack of sophistication in not being able to discriminate between the showy student and the quiet achiever. Nevertheless, they encourage the use of peer assessment as an important step towards learning to assess oneself (see Module 4 which emphasises skills of self-assessment).

Brown and Knight (1994, p58) offer an exercise by which peer assessment may be introduced: Students are asked in small groups to make a container to carry an egg which can be dropped from a height without the egg breaking. Before students are allowed to start work, they must prepare the criteria on which they are to be assessed. They are asked further to decide on the weighting to be attached to each criterion: how many marks out of 20? They are asked to consider whether they are assessing the product or the process. They are also asked to decide who will do the assessing: the teacher? self? peers in their own group? peers in other groups? Throughout this preparation and the actual construction of the containers, the teacher maintains a list of issues as they come up. Finally, the containers are tested and graded and the whole process is discussed, giving an opportunity to raise issues such as collusion, fairness, and validity.

For those concerned about the impact of ethnic/cultural differences on peer assessment, Oldfield and Macalpine (1995) report similar findings to those summarised by Falchikov (above) in implementing peer assessment in Hong Kong with students almost exclusively of Chinese cultural origin. Obviously, this is only a beginning of cross-cultural comparisons.

The best way to avoid the predictable problems seems to be to ensure that the process is carefully introduced and that the criteria to be used are negotiated and tried out by the group before expecting them to apply the criteria to each others' work. Falchikov (1995) reports few problems with implementing Peer Feedback Marking of an oral presentation (a summary and critique of a journal article by third year students in human developmental psychology in a Scottish university) when

1) criteria were developed by students' recalling the characteristics of good presentations and bad ones at which they had been present;

2) students were reminded of marking bands and of a likely pattern of ultimate degree classifications (ie, not many firsts and thirds, distribution over upper and lower second range);

3) marks out of 20 corresponding to the groupings were calculated and noted by all students; and

4) a peer assessment form, asking students to note the best feature and a weakness of each presentation as well as a mark out of 20, was distributed.

Students evaluated the system as fair, an aid to learning, and as challenging (made them think about own work as well as learn to critique others) even though it made them a bit uncomfortable in that they had to judge their friends.

Encouraging deep learning

Throughout this package we have emphasised that assessment plays an important role in encouraging students to engage in "deep" (or meaning-making) learning as opposed to "surface" learning (or superficial rote memorisation). Samuelowicz. (1994) reports on research which reveals that it is not the assessment task itself which is of critical importance but the context in which it is set. That is, teachers may set tasks that seem very similar - for instance, to describe how one would diagnose and manage a particular type of injury - but if one teacher has covered the expected answer in a lecture and in practical classes and the other has offered strategies for reaching a diagnosis and deciding on a therapy but not covered this particular type of injury in detail, then students of the second teacher will be required to integrate knowledge and techniques and engage in decision-making while those of the first teacher can get by on recall.

When we think of tasks which involve accessing and managing information, we can easily imagine many that do not really ask students to do much more than collect references or facts. In the examples above, the information is being collected for a purpose. The law students must use it to do something which they can recognise as a task lawyers actually do in practice. The design students are asked to compare the work of eminent designers, but they are also asked to perform as designers themselves in placing material in the database and using it to make their seminar presentations. We encourage our readers to consider carefully the context of their assessment strategies; as we have said before, there may be occasions where 'simple' fact-finding is what is important and exactly what you wish to occur, but there may be other times when the re-design of an assessment task can promote deeper learning or acquisition of other skills as well.

References

Brown, S., & Knight, P. (1994). *Assessing Learners in Higher Education*. London: Kogan Page.

Bruton, D., & Barnes, A. (1993). Design Theory hypermedia studio. In *EcoDesign 2 Conference*, Powerhouse Museum, Sydney.

Falchikov, N. (1995). Peer feedback marking: developing peer assessment. *Innovations in Education and Training International*, 32(2), 81-93.

Oldfield, K., & Macalpine, M. (1995). Peer and self-assessment at tertiary level - an experiential report. *Assessment and Evaluation in Higher Education*, 20(1), 125-32.

Samuelowicz, K. (1994). Teaching conceptions and teaching practice: a case of assessment. In *Phenomenography - Philosophy and Practice*. Brisbane: Queensland University of Technology. (pp. 343-54)

MODULE 6

DEMONSTRATING KNOWLEDGE
AND UNDERSTANDING

CHRIS HUGHES AND DOUG MAGIN

Module 6
Demonstrating knowledge and understanding

In this module the focus is on the assessment of the student's ability to demonstrate knowledge and understanding of the subject matter, usually in isolation from other abilities.

This module covers broad abilities such as:
- recalling
- describing
- reporting
- recounting
- recognising
- identifying
- relating (interrelating)

Section 1: Demonstrating understanding

Themes
- Using assessment to encourage learning, including:
  - Reworking traditional tutorial questions
  - Linking visualisation and representation abilities
  - Encouraging students to reason from principles
- Authentic assessments

Techniques
- Modified tutorial questions
- Diagram sheets
- Reasoning exercises
- Projects
- Portfolios

Case studies

34. Modifying traditional questions, Physics
35. Diagram sheets, Chemistry
36. Reasoning testlets, Engineering
37. Authentic tasks, Physical Oceanography
38. Project report, Commerce Information Systems
39. Project essay, English Literature

Section 2: Defining and assessing essential knowledge

Themes
- Defining essential knowledge requirements
- Using schemata to communicate knowledge structures
- Objective testing
- Assessing prerequisite knowledge in laboratory contexts
- Writing and reviewing tests

Techniques
- Schemata
- Algorithms
- Multiple Choice testing
- Tests and Quizzes
- Practical exams

Case studies

40. Self study questions with algorithms, Chemistry
41. Computer-Administered MCQs, Physiology and Pharmacology
42. Minitests, Biomedical Science

Module 6

Demonstrating Knowledge and Understanding

Chris Hughes and Doug Magin

Introduction

Assessing content knowledge and understanding is often assumed to be far less problematic than assessing higher order skills and abilities. Academic staff have a long familiarity with conventional methods of assessing knowledge and understanding, and comprehensive texts on how to assess knowledge in its different guises in different fields of study have been in existence for many years (Ebel, 1972; Gronlund, 1976; Heywood, 1989; McIntosh, 1974).

However, several contemporary researchers of student learning (Dahlgren, 1984; Marton & Saljo, 1984; Ramsden, 1984) have identified an alarming phenomenon whereby numerous students who have done well in examinations intended to test understanding, have been found to still harbour fundamental misconceptions about the most basic underlying principles and concepts on which they were supposed to have been tested.

> *Some of the most profoundly depressing research on learning in higher education has demonstrated that successful performance in examinations does not even indicate that students have a good grasp of the very concepts which staff members believed the examinations to be testing.*
>
> *(Boud, 1990, p103)*

Thus, while considerable familiarity with techniques for assessing knowledge and understanding may be presumed to exist in the higher education community, there is clearly room for improvement in practice.

Recently, work on how the development of knowledge and understanding in a subject area occurs has led to changes in our view of assessing knowledge and understanding. For example, John Biggs (1991, p12) has proposed that as students work with unfamiliar material their understanding grows through five stages of ascending structural complexity.

Prestructural	a stage characterised by the lack of any coherent grasp of the material: isolated facts or skill elements may be acquired.
Unistructural	a stage in which a single relevant aspect of the material or skill may be mastered
Multistructural	a stage in which several relevant aspects of the material or skills are mastered separately
Relational	a stage in which the several relevant aspects of the material or skills which have been mastered are integrated into a theoretical structure
Extended Abstract	the stage of 'expertise' in which the material is mastered both within its integrated structure, and in relation to other knowledge domains, thus enabling the student to theorise about the domain

Note that as mastery develops the character of the knowledge acquired changes:

*The first three stages are concerned with the progressive growth of knowledge or skill
in a quantitative sense, the last two with qualitative changes in the structure and nature
of what is learned.*

(Biggs, 1991, p12)

From this point of view, the development of knowledge and understanding takes place along
a continuum from incompetence to expertise:

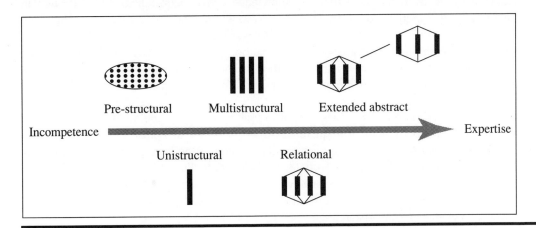

Figure 6.1
Motif based on Briggs
(1991, p13)

At one end of the continuum lie fragments of knowledge relatively unconnected with other
fragments; towards the middle we find fragments in several unstructured groups which are
unrelated to each other; towards the right hand end these groups gain structure and the relationships between them begin to be articulated; and at the far right, the now structured
knowledge domain is in sharp focus and is related to other areas of knowledge. Knowledge
and understanding at the left end are simple, unstructured, unsophisticated and of only
narrow use as supports for higher order abilities, while at the far right end, they are complex,
structured, sophisticated and provide the basis for expert performance.

Biggs further proposes that the focus of student learning changes as the student's mastery
develops:

*Thus, in the sequence from pre- through uni- to multistructural, student learning is
focused on the accrual of knowledge; in the move from multistructural to relational,
with the organization and structuring of knowledge; and in the shift from relational to
extended abstract, with how knowledge may be theorised and generalised.*

(Biggs, 1991, pp12-13)

Thus, the complexity of student responses to assessments of knowledge and understanding,
analysed by stages such as those proposed above, can be used as an indicator of the student's
progress towards the development of competence.

In the light of this view, we can regard the assessment of isolated fragments of knowledge as,
at best, appropriate at the earlier stages (perhaps the first two or three) of Biggs scheme. This
should not be taken to mean in the earlier years of a course etc. as the scheme can be applied
to any discrete knowledge domain, such as 'ohms law', 'rhetorical devices', which may in
fact be addressed within a single subject or unit. Assessing factual knowledge fragments at
the end of a unit of work may not differentiate between those students who are still in the
early stages of mastery in relation to the subject matter, from those with a more structured
and integrated grasp of the material. Only the assessment of higher order abilities, including

more complex demonstrations of knowledge and understanding, will bring out these differences. Perhaps the most graphic illustration of the use of such higher order assessments is provided by the problem-based learning assessment methods, such as OSCEs, as described in Module 2, "Solving problems and developing plans."

Such developments in our conception of the processes by which growth in understanding and mastery proceed provide one reason for the current interest in the assessment of higher order abilities. This increased interest has been accompanied by a reduction of interest in 'traditional' approaches to the assessment of knowledge and understanding. This reduction in interest has been influenced by a reaction to assessment practices in previous eras, in which it is generally perceived that too much emphasis was placed on assessing low level abilities such as the memorisation of a body of information. This reaction has perhaps been given added impetus by the recognition that information technologies now provide rapid and efficient means for retrieving requisite knowledge in most professional and work settings.

It is clear that in the practice of assessment in higher education, the ability to demonstrate knowledge and understanding is frequently assessed. This module contains published material and cases describing a broad range of circumstances and methods in and by which practising teachers assess the ability to demonstrate, in their words 'knowledge and understanding'. Some focus on the assessment of relatively isolated fragments of knowledge; others demand much more complex demonstrations. In doing so, they reveal the emerging ambiguity in the terms 'knowledge and understanding'.

Some teachers use 'knowledge and understanding' in a way which encompasses a broad and developing sense of the growth of mastery - from incompetence to expertise - and consequently they seek to assess the students' development towards competence in the area of concern. These teachers are also often concerned to use teaching and assessment to encourage the development of competence. Cases submitted by these contributors are grouped together in the first section entitled "Assessing students' knowledge and understanding".

However, others use the terms in a narrower sense to refer to the ability to state facts or definitions or to explain straightforward processes, and yet others to differentiate the independent demonstration of knowledge or understanding from the exercise of other, higher order abilities. These contributors are also aware of the effect that their assessments have on student learning, and are trying to ensure that this effect is as positive as possible. We have grouped the cases where the assessment of knowledge and understanding is primarily understood in these two more restricted senses, in the second section entitled "Defining and assessing essential knowledge".

What unites the published material and cases presented in this module is the articulated goal of assessing knowledge and/or understanding, interpreted in one of the three senses just introduced. In response to this generic goal the cases present a wide range of assessment methods from the traditional to the very innovative.

Section 1

Assessing students' knowledge and understanding

Using assessment to help students in their learning is a consistent theme in these modules. A number of examples in which traditional tutorial or examination questions calling for the recall of factual material are being modified to instead assess and encourage the development of students' understanding of principles and concepts were brought to the attention of the project team. The following case looks at how traditional 'factual recall' tutorial questions can be modified to both assist student learning and to better assess the students' progress towards understanding.

34

Case study 34
Modifying traditional questions

Case study from Physics
Judith Pollard, University of Adelaide

This case has been developed from a published paper (Pollard, 1993).

Pollard has reported on some simple changes made to the way in which physics questions were structured so that the assessment method could reveal the students' level of understanding of basic concepts (Pollard, 1993) .

Context

Pollard is involved in teaching first year undergraduate Physics. The students are taught in a lecture/tutorial format, with tutorial question sheets forming the basis of tutorial discussions. Expert solutions to all questions are made available to students towards the end of each tutorial so that students can compare their responses with the suggested solutions.

Assessment method

Working from a framework that regards the way students organise their knowledge of physics as an important factor in learning, Pollard and her colleagues modified the tutorial questions to "provide explicit guidance to the students in constructing their knowledge of physics by requiring them to:

• identify the important concepts in the topic;

• establish for themselves the relationships between the concepts, making use of lecture notes and textbooks;

• confront common misconceptions..." (Pollard, 1993: 358)

Students were also required to work a range of exercises to become familiar with the concepts, and to solve problems using higher order problem solving skills.

➤

Pollard worked with her colleagues to identify what the students could do or think about in relation to the lecture content. The possible responses identified included: stating a definition or principle; understanding the logical connection between concepts or principles; recognising situations in which a particular principle applies; and applying a principle or method in problem solving.

Pollard shows how the tutorial questions were rewritten to encourage such responses:

The new approach is illustrated by Examples 1 and 2, an old-style question about Gauss's law and its replacement. Gauss's law states that the net electric flux emerging from any closed surface is equal to the total charge enclosed by the surface divided by ϵ_0. It can always be used to find the average electric field over a surface, but its real value is that, in situations with appropriate symmetry, it provides a simple way of finding the electric field at a point.

Example 1: Old-style question

(a)   State Gauss's law.

(b)   Use Gauss's law to find the electric field just outside a conducting surface carrying charge per unit area 3.0 x 10-6C m-2.

It was common for students to answer part (b) of this question by looking up or remembering a formula and inserting numbers into it, or perhaps by 'deriving' the formula using the following lines of algebra, with no indication of the logical argument in which they belong:

$$\phi E \quad = \quad q/\epsilon_0$$
$$= \quad \sigma A/\epsilon_0$$
$$\therefore EA \quad = \quad \sigma A/\epsilon_0$$
$$\therefore E \quad = \quad \sigma/\epsilon_0$$

To encourage the students to appreciate the logical argument by which Gauss's law can be used to find the electric field at a point, in situations with appropriate symmetry, this question was replaced by Example 2.

Example 2: New-style question

(a)   Describe the Gaussian surface used in lectures to derive the electric field near a flat charged plate. Describe two other Gaussian surfaces which could be used instead. Be careful in specifying their position and orientation.

(b)   In response to the question: "Use Gauss's law to find the electric field just outside a conducting surface carrying charge per unit area s, the following student answer was given:

$$\phi \quad = \quad q/\epsilon_0$$
$$= \quad \sigma A/\epsilon_0$$
$$\therefore EA \quad = \quad \sigma A/\epsilon_0$$
$$\therefore E \quad = \quad \sigma/\epsilon_0$$

Comment on whether this answer is satisfactory, and make any improvements you think necessary. (Pollard, 1993, p359-60)

Strengths

Pollard reports that student responses to a question of the type shown in Example 2 above more clearly indicated the level of Physics understanding at which the students were operating, and that "even when students do not produce a complete answer to this question, the subsequent discussion in tutorials encourages them to examine and appreciate the logic in a way which is rarely encouraged by standard textbook problems" (Pollard, 1993, p361).

■

Developing visual models

Encouraging students to develop an understanding of how abstract representations actually relate to processes in the real world is a challenge faced by many teachers. In the following case study the students' inability to develop visual models of what is happening at the molecular level is seen as a major source of misunderstanding of chemistry fundamentals. The response of this teacher is to try to develop students' visualisation skills as a way of helping them to improve their understanding of fundamental chemical processes.

35

Case study 35
Diagram sheets

Case study from Chemistry
Roy Tasker, the University of Western Sydney

This case study is based on materials submitted to the project.

Context

In his submission, Tasker states that:

> *A 'deep' understanding of chemistry involves being able to link what one sees substances doing in the laboratory to what one imagines is happening at the invisible molecular/ionic level. Only then can these ideas be communicated using abstract symbolism (eg. chemical formulas), terminology and mathematics... Our proposition is that many of the misconceptions that students develop result from poorly developed visual models (or images) at the molecular level.*

Tasker is working with first year students of applied chemistry in a program which includes business studies and occupational health and safety as core subjects. The program aims to produce graduates who are problem solvers as well as being 'good at the bench'. Many of the lecture, laboratory and tutorial sessions focus on the drawing of molecular representations of chemical processes. This focus aims to improve student skills at visualising structures and processes at the molecular level and at representing those structures and processes diagrammatically.

Assessment method

These visualisation and representation skills are assessed by asking questions of the following type, 'under exam conditions':

In the top box provided on the Diagram Sheet [see over] write an equation representation for the reaction that occurs when a few drops of ammonia solution are added to the cobalt (II) nitrate solution.

In the large box provided draw a labelled molecular/ionic representation of the products of this reaction. Two water molecules and an ammonia molecule are shown for scale.

Figure 6.2
Assessment method
Roy Tasker

➤

In the lower large box provided draw a labelled molecular/ionic representation of the products of the reaction that occurs when excess ammonia is added to cobalt (II) nitrate solution. Two water molecules and an ammonia molecule are shown for scale.

In the bottom box write an equation representation for the reaction in [question above].

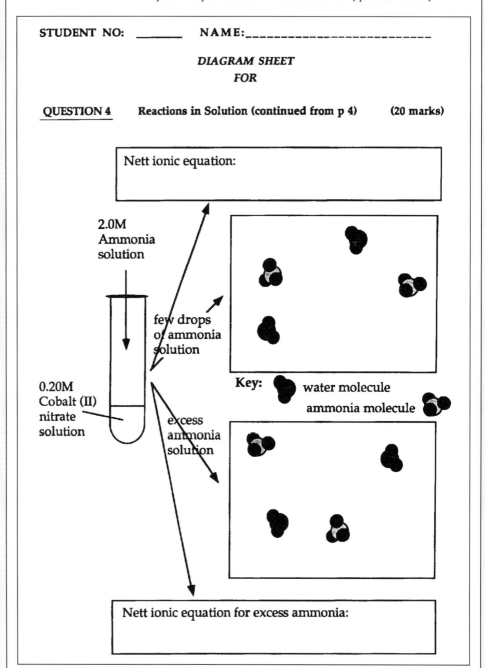

STUDENT NO: _____   NAME:_____

DIAGRAM SHEET
FOR

QUESTION 4   Reactions in Solution (continued from p 4)   (20 marks)

Nett ionic equation:

2.0M Ammonia solution

few drops of ammonia solution

0.20M Cobalt (II) nitrate solution

excess ammonia solution

Key: water molecule
        ammonia molecule

Nett ionic equation for excess ammonia:

Figure 6.2 *(cont)*
Assessment method
Roy Tasker

Tasker provides an illustration of what a good answer to this question would look like:

Figure 6.2 *(cont)*
Assessment method
Roy Tasker

Marking

Marking of these molecular diagrams is based on specific criteria (eg. are molecules oriented appropriately to one another, etc.). Tasker notes that by correlating results from these molecular model drawing exercises with students' work on equations and writing formulae for ions, misconceptions are easily diagnosed. He finds a direct correlation between improvements in students' molecular model diagrams and their problem solving and equation writing performance.

Reasoning as ability to understand processes

University teachers are universally concerned to develop their students' reasoning abilities. What this means in practice varies considerably from discipline to discipline. Often it means something like being able to 'understand and explain what might happen in a given set of circumstances', at other times it is used to indicate a requirement to solve problems. In the following case the challenge to assess reasoning is taken up, again with an assessment process designed to both assess the ability while encouraging its development.

Case study 36
Reasoning testlets

Case study from Engineering
Richard Harman, University of Canterbury, New Zealand

In this case study Harman presents a novel approach to assessing students' reasoning via a series of short in-class tests, called 'reasoning testlets'. For reasons which will become obvious as you read this example, we have taken the term 'reasoning' here as meaning, essentially, 'understanding of processes'. This case study was developed from a published paper (Harman, 1992).

The paper describes the introduction of brief in-class tests, called 'testlets', within an engineering subject. These are designed to assess students' understanding of fundamental principles and their ability to reason from them.

Context

The objectives of the reasoning testlets were to (i) reduce the workload by containing the entire course activity within the timetabled lecture periods, (ii) make the learning process more active by requiring all students, rather than the usual handful, to respond (in class), and (iii) develop the students' reasoning powers.

The assessments were given in a twenty lecture section on gas turbine engines as part of an optional course for final year students in mechanical engineering.

Assessment method

On seven occasions throughout the subject, classes were cut short to accommodate the 10-15 minute 'testlets'. Each testlet was "carried out with the seriousness appropriate to a formal examination. It was open-book to the extent that they had access to their lecture notes but were to have no outside sources of information" (p97). The required answer "did not involve writing what was remembered of material presented earlier in that period or during a previous lecture. It required the student to look at and use previous material to reason."

➤

A typical question

A single shaft jet engine is caused to accelerate by increasing the fuel flow rate above that required at steady speed. If the fuel flow is suddenly increased from, say, the point marked on the compressor characteristic, what are likely to be the most immediate significant effects on shaft speed, turbine entry temperature, turbine output torque, final nozzle area and compressor surge margin?

Marking

The seven testlets comprised 75% of the total mark for the subject (with 25% given for an assignment). For these reasoning testlets, 60% of each test was given for the 'reasoning' shown in arriving at answers for each sub-question, with the remaining 40% given for the correctness of the answers themselves. The tests were marked in time for return and discussion at the next lecture.

Strengths, limitations

Harman describes two positive outcomes from this innovation.

First, it was effective in allowing students to detect conceptual misunderstandings at an early stage.

> *The error often lay in the misunderstanding of a basic physical principle ... Whether the responsibility for the more extreme form of errors should be ascribed to the lecturer, the student, or the previous year of study, the process was extremely good at finding misunderstandings.*
>
> *(Harman, 1992, p97)*

Second, following each testlet "the class became lively and vociferous and an active learning process was achieved. Productive discussion reinforced the grasp of fundamentals and the understanding of the machine's behaviour."

One concern expressed by Harman's colleagues was that the introduction of these in-class tests significantly reduced the amount of time in lectures for coverage of the subject matter. Harman concedes that "some material was indeed omitted which had normally been included in the past". The learning process was seen as "more important in this case than the detailed material. The gas turbine engine was merely the framework on which to hang the reasoning process, and could be replaced by many other types of hardware or system." (Harman, 1992, p97)

■

Authentic assessment tasks

Many teachers are concerned to ensure that the assessments they set are as authentic as possible, in part to help students gain skills that will be applicable in their professional careers, and in part to give them a real context for what they are learning. The teachers who submitted the following two cases have attempted to bring as much of the real world into their assessments as is possible.

Case study 37
Authentic tasks

Case study from Physical Oceanography
Matthias Tomczak, Flinders University

The idea of studying Oceanography in a classroom naturally raises issues of authenticity. In this case study, which was submitted to the project, Tomczak has attempted to give the skills and techniques being addressed as much authenticity as is possible in a paper-based assessment.

Context

In a second year course in physical oceanography the assessment of the practical component of the course is designed to address "students' understanding of the physical processes at work behind observations." During the subject students attend lectures followed by weekly tutorials. The tutorials focus on the material covered in the previous lecture.

Assessment method

In each tutorial students work through a number of 'authentic' tasks under the supervision of a tutor. The tasks usually require the students to interpret real-life data (including oceanographic readings, maps and charts), make assumptions, calculate variables and graph or chart 'currents and water masses formed under different force balances'. One such task begins:

> *The year is 1964. You are chief scientist of a cruise on the Australian research vessel H.M.A.S. Gascoyne. The purpose of your cruise is to survey the East Australian Current and identify possible eddies that might exist in the Tasman Sea. The ship departs from Sydney and is due in Brisbane nine days later...*

The task then gives some background information and assumptions, and several charts and tables listing the work done at each of the 32 'stations', the station positions, a range of surface observations, and temperature readings at 200m depth at each station.

Students are then asked to complete a number of tasks normally completed during such a voyage:

- plot the stations on a chart
- plot the distribution of sea surface temperature over the region
- plot the distribution of 200m depth temperature over the region and to make a number of observations on the basis of the data and the plots:
- explain what can be said about the East Australian Current on the basis of 200m distribution
- explain how eddies are identified from the 200m distribution
- explain why the surface temperature distribution does not allow conclusions to be drawn with the same degree of certainty.

The tutorial task sheets include an outline of the suggested method, necessary formulae, constants, maps, background information and worksheets, and questions and comments to guide the student's attention.

Grading

Tutorials are marked and returned one week after the submission date. Each tutorial counts as 4%, the combined tutorial marks counting as 40% of the final mark in the subject. ∎

Sometimes it is possible to make assessments more relevant and authentic by going beyond the classroom or laboratory. Project work, in which students investigate and report on examples or situations in the real world, is one way of increasing the authenticity of assessment. In the following case study, students visit an organisation to examine and analyse its information systems.

Case study 38
Project report

38

Case study from Commerce Information Systems
Cherry Randolph, the University of Western Australia

Teaching students whose primary interest is in another discipline is often difficult. In this case study, which was submitted to the project, Randolph has chosen a project report, a task which should be familiar to most of her management and marketing students, in order to encourage them to understand the real world applications of the computer science theory they are studying.

Context

Randolph teaches the second/third year unit, Introduction to Information Systems. Most students are finance, management or marketing majors, although some are from the Department of Computer Science. The unit is designed "to cover basic terminology", "to give a working overview of the field," and "to give relevance to the material of the unit." The specific objectives being addressed under the heading of the assessment of knowledge and understanding were:

...to recognise the real world application of what they had been studying.

...to state the subject matter and then use their experience from their organisation [the focus of the project] to illustrate the theory.

Assessment method

The project required the students to "investigate an information system within an organisation of their choice." The final report must contain the following sections:

1. A brief description of the company and the industry in which it operates, including the size, market and product etc.

2. The stated objectives of an information system within the organization chosen.

3. A description of the information system chosen, including hardware, software and personnel involved. The description must cover the integration of the system into the overall system of the organization, how it was developed, tested and installed, and how successful it has been.

4. A comparison of reality with theory. Students must relate the results of their investigations to the specific sections of the course, categorising and discussing the system chosen in the terms used in the course and in the main text book. They must also review the literature for this type of information system and comment on the similarity and/or dissonance between theory and practice.

➤

This last two sections of the report enable an assessment of the students' understanding of the key categories and concepts used in the course to be made by looking at how the students are able to employ them in the process of analysing and reporting on a real-world example.

Some students work in small teams of three on this project, some individually. Students are encouraged to submit a proposal for the project which is discussed with them before the project starts. An advanced draft is also requested for comment before the final report is handed in. In addition to comments on this draft, a preliminary grade is indicated, together with suggestions as to how this grade might be improved in the final report.

Grading

The marking scheme used awarded the marks to: the descriptive sections covering the organisation, industry and the information system chosen (60/200 marks); and the discussion and analysis of the chosen information system under the categories and in the terms used in the course (120/200 marks). The remaining marks were awarded for the presentation of the final report (10/200 marks) and the executive summary (10/200marks). Randolph notes that the feedback given on proposals and drafts resulted in all final reports being acceptable in terms of their presentation.

Strengths

Students seemed to appreciate the opportunity to gain feedback on draft work, and the feedback given resulted in improved performances in most cases.

■

Essay topics which assess knowledge and understanding

It is common to find essays used to assess a number of different objectives, including that of 'demonstrating knowledge and understanding'. Essays often call for description, analysis and argument. In the following case project work is used to encourage and assess the development of the student's understanding of the structure of a play and its performance implications. In focusing on more or less real-world tasks, this case continues the theme of authenticity which united the previous two cases. While the report received from students taking the first option below may resemble a traditional essay, the second will not, and both options encourage students to approach the material in a very practical way.

Case study 39
Project report

39

Case study from English Literature
Mary Chan, University of New South Wales

English Literature is perhaps the traditional home of the essay question, but in this case study, which was submitted to the project, Chan offers her students unconventional ways of demonstrating their understanding.

Context

Chan teaches Eighteenth Century Theatre as a 3 credit point second/third year subject. The subject is taught by a one and a half hour seminar each week for one session. The seminar usually consists of about 45 minutes of lecture and explanation, and 45 minutes of general discussion of the material by students, who are expected to have read and thought about the topics before the class.

The subject aims to introduce students to the literature and the stage conditions and conventions of early to mid eighteenth-century London and to draw particular attention to the relationship in the plays of this period between character and action. The major assignment in the subject is an essay which aims to assess the students ability to 'draw together ideas and concepts discussed throughout the session and to bring these to bear on the explication of any one of the works discussed in the subject'.

Assessment method

In addition to this major assignment a project-based assignment is set and due a little over half-way through the session. The project assesses a number of different abilities, depending on the options chosen, but aims to 'encourage students to think of their work in this subject in ways other than simply the production of an essay'. Two of the options provided to students for the minor project demonstrate interesting approaches to the assessment of the student's understanding of the structure and purpose of a play and of the conditions of its original performance.

Option 1

Take a scene, or an act, and describe how you would produce it on a stage similar to that of its first production.

This option assessed the students' ability to read a play as a theatrical script, one written for production rather than as a literary text. It requires students to develop (through their reading) an understanding of the conditions of various London theatres in the period and of the theatrical conditions such as lighting, scenery, costumes and acting methods, and to produce a non-anachronistic reading of a scene linking this to the whole play.

Option 2

Produce a cut, or edited version of a play for a performance taking approximately half the time of the original. You need not reproduce the text (a note of scenes, speeches, pages, lines, to be cut is sufficient). The major part of your exercise will consist of a justification of your version.

This option assessed the student's ability to understand a play's basic structure and to make some assessment of its main focus or theme.

Grading

Students are encouraged to seek discussion and feedback on these projects before they are finally submitted in mid session, and are given feedback on their performance well before the final essay is due. The project options contribute 40% of the final mark, the remaining 60% being awarded for a major essay assessment.

Strengths, limitations

Chan sees these projects as both learning and assessment tasks. Feedback from some of her classes indicates that this dual nature of the tasks needs to be communicated clearly to students. ■

Using portfolios to assess understanding

The cases considered so far in this module all involve a high degree of specification by the teacher of what the student is to produce. Whether it be exam questions, reasoning exercises or the development of a plan for staging a play, all the techniques used so far require the student to respond to specific demands in order to demonstrate their knowledge and understanding.

It is possible, however, to grant the student considerable freedom to decide how best to demonstrate their mastery of an area without sacrificing reliability to an unreasonable extent. One technique which allows such freedom is the use of student-developed portfolios for assessing understanding.

Originally used to assess students' growth as writers (see also Section 1 of Module 8, "Communicating"), portfolios are now employed in a much wider range of disciplines and for wider purposes. Courts and McInerney (1993) report on their own experiences with portfolio assessment, and in doing so note a range of portfolio types and disciplines in which they are used, including: English, business, social science, history, science, and mathematics. Some uses of portfolios require students to submit all significant work produced, some to select work which meets a range of criteria.

In Module 4, focusing on the ability to develop and manage oneself, a case study by John Biggs on the use of portfolios to assess, in part, students' understanding in an educational psychology course is presented. It is placed there rather than in this module because of its focus on the student gathering and presenting evidence of his/her own learning. However, it provides a good example of the use of a portfolio for the assessment of a student's growth in competence in a subject area.

One of the major benefits of portfolios is the way they involve students in gathering and reflecting on evidence for their own growth in understanding and mastery. In fact most of the aims of portfolio assessment listed by Courts and McInerney involve the effect that this form of assessment can have on students' learning and growth in metacognition (Courts & McInerney, 1993, p100-101). Readers interested in the use of portfolios to assess understanding should consult Case study 21 and Section 1 of Module 8.

Section 2

Defining and assessing essential knowledge

Despite concern to develop alternative ways of assessing knowledge and understanding, teachers still need to acquaint themselves with best practice in setting and marking conventional examinations. There are many readily available texts which provide a comprehensive coverage of model practice in these conventional forms of assessing knowledge and understanding. While some submitted case studies illustrated such practice, very few of the case studies submitted provide any detailed information on how the validity or reliability of the highlighted assessment practices and mark outcomes are evaluated. Despite the existence of long-established techniques for determining the validity and reliability of different assessment methods and marking procedures, it appears that it is still uncommon for teachers to use these techniques to investigate their assessment procedures.

Basic accounts of validity and reliability will be found in the Glossary; however, the reader is advised to consult the Annotated Bibliography for sources which provide more detailed coverage and which explain how the associated procedures are undertaken. (See for example Ebel, 1972.)

Defining essential knowledge

The revolution in information technology, with the ability rapidly to access and retrieve information from specific purpose databases, poses a major challenge to traditional thinking about what knowledge a student needs to underpin the development of conceptual understanding and higher order abilities. A vast array of information can be contained in any one unit of study, and deciding on which parts of the knowledge domain within a discipline need to be committed to long-term memory has to be regularly reviewed. Thus, a central issue for some teachers is: what knowledge needs to be acquired and organised in long-term memory, and how is this to be assessed?

Some teachers and schools approach this issue by investigating what the core knowledge, concepts and understandings required by practitioners in the field are, and by determining how these are organised. Glaser (1991) emphasises the way in which key knowledge and understanding elements are organised and stored in the long term memory of experts as a key to conceptualising what needs to be learnt by novices:

> *The precision of expert performance results from specialized schemata that drive performance… Experts develop the ability to perceive large meaningful patterns. Pattern recognition occurs so rapidly that it appears to take on the character of 'intuitions'... the extraordinary representational ability of experts appears to depend upon the organization of knowledge existing in memory.*

> *(Glaser, 1991)*

This has two implications for teachers and assessors: that of deciding on (i) what knowledge is essential for students to commit to long-term memory, to, for example, enable algorithms to be generated, and (ii) what kinds of schemata are to be developed and committed to 'pattern memory' as algorithms guiding problem solving or performance within a discipline or profession.

Using schemata in neuroscience

One approach to deciding what is required to be memorised is to examine the details of schemata or hierarchies which are utilised within the field or discipline. An illustration of this is taken from material submitted by Jim Taylor at the University of Southern Queensland using what is described as 'Novex' analysis (which compares the ways in which novices and experts employ knowledge schemata). This approach allows the teacher to identify what the essential item-specific knowledge elements are, to define the conceptual understandings required to perform a specific task, and to specify how such knowledge needs to be organised into a hierarchical schema.

The example opposite is based on an algorithm developed by Lev Landa for medical diagnosis. (Landa, 1974)

Taylor refers to this as an 'example of strategic knowledge in neuroscience, represented as an algorithm', and suggests it illustrates how knowledge and understanding are made 'relational'. Representations such as these enable the teacher to identify what knowledge students must possess in order to be able to carry out higher order skills and problem solving tasks.

This algorithm shows the sequence of tests needed to differentiate between two possible sites of damage in the spinal cord. Reading from left to right each test produces evidence in support of the possibility of damage at either site T4 or site T6.

In some disciplines, the factual knowledge base required to be committed to long- term memory (and recall) may be much more detailed than in others. It appears that chemistry, for example, requires much more detailed factual knowledge on 'instant call' for solving problems and 'practising' chemistry, than would, say, physics. The challenge in fields such as chemistry and the life sciences is threefold: how to determine what factual knowledge is absolutely essential; how to find ways to organise the large knowledge base so that it is learnable and so that it relates to problem solving and professional practice; and how to communicate to students which parts of the huge knowledge domain they must commit to memory?

Using schemata in polymer chemistry

The following case study in the field of polymer chemistry illustrates how students can be led through a series of self-assessment questions in which they are supplied with a hierarchical decision model or schema to enable a problem to be solved. Through these experiences in employing the schemata for problem solving, students become able to identify the key knowledge elements (contained in course notes and text) which are required for problem solving in the particular unit of study.

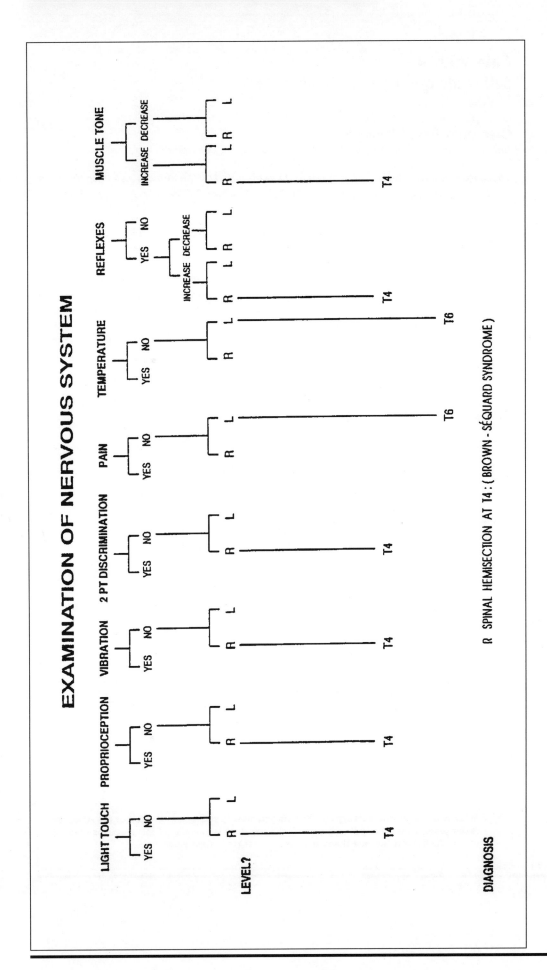

Figure 6.3
*Strategic knowledge
in neuroscience
represented as an
algorithm*
(Landa, 1974)

Case study 40
Self study questions with algorithms

Case study from Chemistry
Jim Taylor and Michael Morgan, University of Southern Queensland>

This case study was developed from materials submitted by the authors and from the study book they have produced for students in the Engineering Materials course at USQ.

Context

The context of this material is a 'Bachelor of Engineering degree which is taught both on-campus and off-campus, the latter via distance education mode.' The specific context is a module within this course titled 'polymer chemistry'.

Assessment method

An example of a self-study question is illustrated below, together with an algorithm for how the student is to proceed in order to provide a 'description' of the polymer.

---

7. SAMPLE ASSESSMENT QUESTIONS

7.1 Worked Examples of Typical Assessment Questions

Question

- Describe the polymer whose structure is depicted schematically below.

Solution

- When confronted with this type of problem you must first determine whether the structure is composed of just one type of mer, or if the structure is made up of more than one type of mer. If the latter is the case then the structure is that of a copolymer.

Figure 6.4

Sample assessment questions
Jim Taylor & Michael Morgan

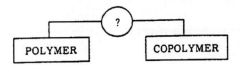

- *In this case* the structure contains two distinct types of mer; these are

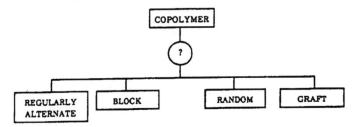

So we have a copolymer.

- If we have a copolymer, we must next classify the particular type of copolymer. Copolymers are described by reference to the relative positions of the different types of mers of which they are composed.

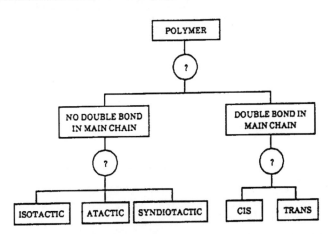

- *In this case* the polyethylene has been grafted onto the main chain of polyvinyl chloride.

- We would now proceed to try to describe each component of the copolymer as for an individual polymer. This may be difficult to do for some regularly alternate and random copolymers but should be attempted.

- Polymers are initially differentiated on the basis of the nature of the bonding in the main chain. If the main chain contains only single covalent bonds we classify the polymer by reference to the position of any side group present. If the main chain contains double covalent bonds, the relevant position of the side groups at the site of the double bond determines the nomenclature of the polymer.

- *In this case* neither the main chain nor the grafted chains contain any double bonds. The main chain has a chlorine atom as a side group. The chlorine atom always lies on the same side of the chain and this arrangement is referred to as isotatic. In the grafted chains there is no side group and no further description is warranted.

- *In this case* the answer is a graft copolymer of isotactic polyvinylchloride with side chains of polyethylene.

The complete strategic model for solving this type of problem and the particular path used to find the solution *in this case* are shown below.

Figure 6.4 *(cont)*

Sample assessment questions

Jim Taylor & Michael Morgan

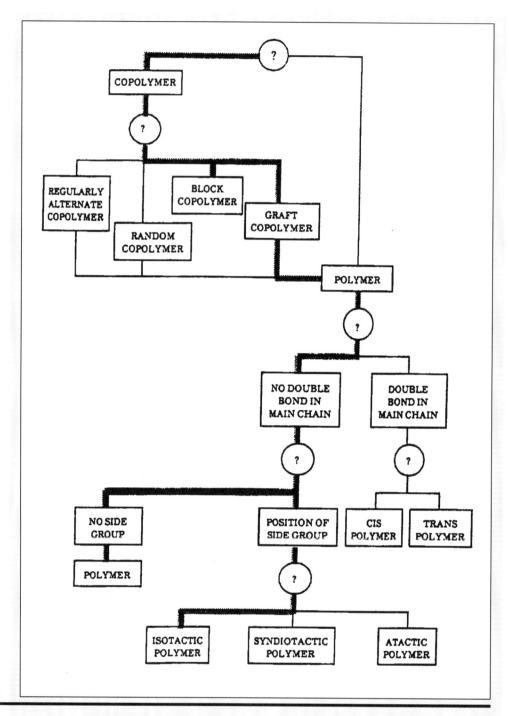

Figure 6.4 *(cont)*

Sample assessment questions
Jim Taylor & Michael Morgan

This example comes from a Study Book made available to students for self study purposes. The book contains an introduction to the subject area and the above worked example, which provides the suggested solution algorithm.

In the final examination in this subject students are presented with similar questions and expected to use the appropriate algorithm in developing their responses.

Comment

The retention of algorithms within long-term memory provides a support for the development of an understanding of the relationships between structural properties (item specific knowledge) and functions (relational knowledge).

The examples discussed above illustrate how teachers have addressed the question of determining what knowledge is essential to a specific unit of study, and how such knowledge can be ordered into schema to achieve 'relational knowledge' and understanding. The use of self-study questions and the provision of appropriate algorithms suggests an approach to communicating to students the kinds of knowledge which are essential to understanding and application.

Assessing a knowledge base

Given that in many disciplines the essential knowledge base is likely to be extensive, another major issue often arises: how to select and develop appropriate assessment methods which can adequately and independently test students' knowledge?

Current understanding of effective pedagogy has emphasised the need for 'authentic' assessment. That is, assessment tasks which, as far as possible, mirror the kinds of situations in which a professional or practitioner is required to perform competently, and which are similar or related to those which professionals perform. In so far as specific knowledge and understandings are required to meet an adequate level of the performance, these can be assessed through the 'authentic' assessment tasks.

A difficulty that can sometimes arise here is that assessments which embed the testing of knowledge within tasks assessing higher order skills and abilities (such as authentic tasks) can sometimes be ineffective at comprehensively testing a large domain of knowledge (although they may be quite effective in the testing of the specific aspects of knowledge domain required to perform those tasks successfully).

In situations where it is necessary to assess students' command of a substantial essential knowledge base together with its accompanying concepts and understandings, a range of objective testing methods can be used to ensure adequate sampling of the core knowledge domain.

Objective tests

Tests are said to be 'objective' to the extent that each student's answer to a question can be marked objectively. Such tests have three advantages: they can be marked quickly (often by automatic means); when hand marked by staff, no training in marking is required other than familiarisation with the answer marking code; and test scores can be highly reliable (see the entry on reliability in the Glossary for an explanation of this term). Graham Gibbs (1992) has identified the main disadvantage of such tests: they are "often used to test superficial learning outcomes involving factual knowledge, and that they do not provide students with feedback" (p31). However, in the same place he argues that this disadvantage is not inherent in the tests in that "it is possible to devise objective tests which involve analysis, computation, interpretation and understanding and yet which are still easily marked." He also points out that when used in very large classes, "students knowing how they have done on a multiple choice test can provide more feedback than is otherwise available ... and that it is also possible to provide computerised tutorial feedback for students when they give incorrect answers to multiple choice questions" (p31).

The main question types used in objective tests are:

right/wrong or true/false	multiple choice
short answer	matching
completion	best answer

Gold illustrates these six types of questions:

Types of Objective Test

Short answer

Q. Name three of the 'first generation' New Towns that were designated in Great Britain between 1946 and 1950:

1. ....
2. ....
3. ....

Completion

Q. Central Place Theory was originally formulated by _____ in Germany in the 1930s.

True / False

1. Modern crofting was founded by the 1886 Crofters Holdings Act. ....TRUE / FALSE
2. The run-rig system was introduced by Jethro Tull ....TRUE / FALSE
3. Kelping was widely practised in the interior parts of Highland Scotland ....TRUE / FALSE

Matching

Match each of the writers in List Y with one of the books in List X by filling in the boxes below the lists. Do not use any of the boxes more than once.

LIST X		List Y	
1	Towards a New Architecture	A	Herman Mutheslus
2	Yesterday: A Peaceful Path to Real Reform	B	Lewis Mumford
3	When Democracy Builds	C	Patrick Geddes
4	The Culture of Cities	D	Frank Lloyd Wright
5	The English House	E	Ebenezer Howard
		F	Walter Gropius
		G	Le Corbusier

List X 1 2 3 4 5
List Y [] [] [] [] []

Multiple Choice

Q. In a test with a mean of 100 and a standard deviation of 12, a raw score of 124 is equal to a standard score of:

A +24
B -2
C +2
D 84%
E 124%

Best Answer

Q. What does the term 'teleological' mean when applied to the early attempts of geographers to study the relationship between people and of the environment?

1. the view that the earth has been designed for human purposes by a supreme being.
2. the argument that human beings are an integral part of their environment.
3. that people are at the mercy of their physical environment.
4. that people should always seek to change their environment to suit their own ends.
5. that the environment never changes.

(Gold et al., 1991, cited in Gibbs, 1992)

Figure 6.5

Types of objective test
(Gold et al, in Gibbs, 1992)

Multiple choice questionnaires

Multiple choice questionnaires (MCQs) have been the most developed of all objective tests. There is a long history of their use in medicine (Freeman & Byrne, 1976), and they continue to be used extensively for national testing as part of registration examinations in surgery and other medical areas. In undergraduate education they are generally used within formal examination settings in which a large number of questions (which can often exceed 100 items) are used. They also tend to be used in classes where enrolments are large.

The applicability of MCQs to a wide range of disciplines is discussed in detail by Gronlund who gives extensive examples of how items can be constructed (Gronlund, 1976). In addition to supplying illustrations of questions testing item-specific knowledge, Gronlund also provides a range of examples which cover the testing of broader abilities such as those mentioned above by Gibbs, namely "analysis, computation, interpretation and understanding".

One set of examples given by Gronlund illustrates the use of questions directed at assessing 'understanding':

EXAMPLES

Bread will not become mouldy as rapidly if placed in a refrigerator because

A   cooling retards the growth of fungi.
B   darkness retards the growth of mould.
C   cooling prevents the bread from drying out so rapidly.
D   mold requires both heat and light for best growth.

There is an increased quantity of carbon monoxide produced when fuel is burned in a limited supply of oxygen because

A   carbon reacts with carbon monoxide.
B   carbon reacts with carbon dioxide.
C   carbon monoxide is an effective reducing agent.
D   greater oxidation takes place.

Investing money in common stock provides protection against loss of assets during inflation because common stock

A   pays higher rates of interest during inflation.
B   provides a steady but dependable income despite economic conditions.
C   is protected by the Federal Reserve System.
D   increases in value as the value of a business increases.

(Gronlund, 1976, p195)

Writing and reviewing multiple choice tests

Writing or reviewing multiple choice tests is not always easy. The following information and advice is based on material supplied to the project by Jim Tognolini of the Educational Testing Centre at the University of New South Wales.

Standard terminology for multiple-choice questionnaires

Multiple-choice questions have their own terminology.

Item:	the term for the whole multiple-choice question, including all answer choices.
Stimulus material:	the text, diagram, table, graph etc. on which the item is based.
The stem:	either a question or an incomplete statement presenting the problem for which a response is required.
Options or alternatives:	all the choices in an item.
The key:	the correct answer or best option.
The distractors:	the incorrect options (or the responses for which no mark is awarded).
Item set:	a number of items all of which are based around the same stimulus material.

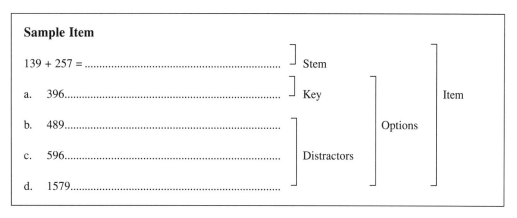

Sample Item

139 + 257 = ...] Stem

a.   396...] Key

b.   489...

c.   596... Distractors

d.   1579...

Options

Item

For best results when writing or reviewing multiple choice items, you should ensure that the following guidelines are followed.

The item as a whole

- The item should test one or more important learning outcomes, processes or skills.
- The item should actually test the outcome(s), process(es) or skill(s) it is supposed to test.

The above two guidelines may appear self-evident and somewhat patronising. However, the commonest faults found in MCQ items are 'irrelevance and triviality' (McIntosh, 1974, p300). McIntosh suggests that both of these faults can be avoided only through a process of ensuring that all questions are related to previously established learning objectives, and that the answering of each question requires application of knowledge, understanding or other abilities which have been identified as important course outcomes.

- The item should be structured around the one central idea presented in the stem.
- The item should be written in simple, direct and clear language. Avoid negatively stated items, and avoid double negatives. The item itself should not be a test of reading ability.
- The item should be independent of other items in the test: one item should not help students answer another item.
- Any complexity in the item should be caused by the complexity of the reasoning required or concepts being tested and not by the obscurity of the question. Never write 'trick questions'.

- The item should be free of sexual, cultural, racial and/or ethnic stereotyping.
- The item should be free of spelling, punctuation, grammatical and other editorial faults.

Finally, attention needs to be given to how difficult answering the question is likely to be. Item difficulty depends largely on how fine the distinctions are between the options: the finer the distinctions that must be made, the more difficult the item. However care must be taken to avoid using options in which the distinctions are too fine. See the discussion below on deriving an index of difficulty for an item.

The stem

- The stem should present a single, clearly formulated problem, question or issue which indicates the response required.
- State the stem in a positive form wherever possible.
- Include in the stem any words that would otherwise be repeated in the options.
- The stem may be stated as a question, or as an incomplete statement which the options make complete.

The options

- There should be one and only one clearly correct or best response. Write the correct or best response first, then the distractors.
- Make the distractors plausible and attractive, yet clearly incorrect or inadequate.
- Make the optional responses grammatically consistent with the stem, and punctuate them accordingly.
- Make the options the same length, wherever possible.
- Avoid similarity of wording in both the stem and the correct or best answer. Avoid giving inadvertent clues to the correct or best response. Avoid using technical terms in the key as this might provide a clue.
- Make sure the options are not overlapping, inclusive or synonymous with one another. They should not present opposite cases to each other.
- The options should be as homogeneous as possible.
- Present the options in some logical or systematic order (numerical, chronological, alphabetical, length, etc.).
- Avoid words like 'always' or 'never' in the options.
- Use 'all of the above' or 'none of the above' with great caution.
- If two options are similar to each other, one is likely to be the key. Therefore the other two options should also have some similarity to each other.

The test as a whole

- Related item types may be grouped together with instructions that apply to the group.
- The number of items relating to a topic area or ability should reflect the relative importance of that area or skill in the course or subject.
- Vary the position of the correct answer in a random manner across the items.
- The difficulty level of the test should be suitable to the students. See the discussion below on deriving an index of difficulty for individual items.
- The material and tasks should be interesting and varied.
- The directions should be clear.
- The allowed time should permit 90-95% of candidates to complete the test.
- There should be a reasonable balance between reading time and thinking time in the test.

Constructing a Test

When constructing a test, begin with a statement of the abilities or competencies to be assessed. Learning outcomes and performance criteria can then be developed to describe, in behavioural terms, the appropriate knowledge, understanding and application skills at the required standard of performance for each ability. A test specification may then be prepared in a form such as:

For the purposes of this multiple choice test Ability **A**, is defined to consist of:
- knowledge of terminology about…
- knowledge of criteria for…
- recognition of sequences in…
- ecognition of strategies for…
- understanding of principles for…
- understanding of the processes used in…
- ability to distinguish between…
- ability to make valid judgements about…

When detailing performance criteria and learning outcomes, you should ensure that they are appropriately worded. Criteria such as:
- Recognise…
- Identify…
- Select…
- Calculate…
- Discriminate between…

can be assessed by means of multiple choice questions, while criteria such as:
- Explain why…
- List…
- Rewrite…
- Recall…
- Negotiate…

are more appropriately assessed by other means.

MCQ items which exemplify the application of the above guidelines and principles can be found in Gronlund (1976) and in McIntosh (1974).

Monitoring the effectiveness of an item

Once the items have been written it is advisable to collect data on the candidates' responses before the items are finally accepted into a test or item bank. This is best done by trial testing, but it can be done by monitoring the performance of the item in a series of tests. There are two critical issues in the development of good tests: reliability (the degree of consistency between two measures of the same thing) and validity (the extent to which the test measures what it purports to measure). (See the Glossary for a fuller explanation of these terms.)

All test scores will be liable to some variation due to a range of sources such as the student's comprehension of the instructions, health, fatigue, motivation and the testing conditions. In measuring a student's performance, steps should be taken to increase reliability by minimising variance due to factors such as these. The guidelines on writing and reviewing test items above should, if followed, help to produce reliable and valid items.

Two simple measures enable a judgment as to whether an item is usefully discriminating between those who have mastered the topic and those who have not—the Difficulty Index and the Discrimination Index.

The essential components of these indices are based on the following records of performance on an item:

1.   The total score on the test for each person.

2.   The option selected as the correct answer by each person.

To derive these indices it is necessary to divide the candidates into three equal groups or thirds: the higher third (h), the middle third (m), and the lower third (l) performers, based on **total test scores**.

Consider the following table of results for an item in a test given to 540 students:

Options							
	A	**B***	**C**	**D**	**Omitted**	**% Correct**	**# in group**
Highest third of performers in test	2	176	-	2	-	98	180
Middle third of performers in test	18	135	10	16	1	75	180
Lowest third of performers in test	31	90	24	32	3	50	180

* Option B is the key for this item

Note: the groups in the above table are decided on the basis of the **total test score**, and **then** their responses on this item are analysed. Hence some people in the high performing third chose a distractor as a response to this item, even though nearly 75% of the candidates chose the correct option.

This item is performing well (ie. it is discriminating clearly between high and low performers in the test). 176 (98%) of high performers chose the correct alternative, compared to 90 (50%) of low performers, and the distractors attracted few of the high performers. If items do not perform in this way then the distractors and perhaps even the item as a whole needs closer examination and perhaps revision or rejection.

Item difficulty

Item difficulty is not an absolute property of an item, but rather a guide to the performance of the candidates to whom the item was given, provided the item is a valid and reliable item.

$$\text{Difficulty} = \frac{H + L}{N}$$

where   H   is the number in the high performing group getting the item right

L   is the number in the lower group getting it right

N   is $2/3$ of the total number of candidates who sat the test

(N = the total number of candidates in the high and low performing groups).

In the above example, Difficulty = $\dfrac{176 + 90}{360}$ = .74

The lower the Difficulty Index, the more difficult the item, so this is a relatively easy item. If all candidates choose the key on an item, the Difficulty Index works out to be 1, indicating a very easy item.

A test which is made up of items with a difficulty range from .30-.80 (calculated from the results of a trial or previous tests) should produce a spread of results across candidates.

Item discrimination

The extent to which the item discriminates between the high and low performances is regarded as an indicator of the validity of the item. An index of item discrimination may be obtained as follows:

$$\text{Discrimination} = \frac{H - L}{n}$$

where   H   is the number in the high performing group getting the item right
          L   is the number in the lower group getting it right
          n   is $1/3$ of the total number of candidates who sat the test.

In the above example, $\text{Discrimination} = \dfrac{176 - 90}{180} = .48$

The higher the Discrimination Index, the better the item is at discriminating between the high and low performers. The maximum is 1 and the minimum is -1. Therefore this item is a good discriminator.

Items with a Discrimination Index of .4 or higher are regarded as good discriminators, while those with an Index between .3 and .39 may need improvement. Items with an Index between .2 and .29 usually need improvement, while those with an Index below .19 (including negative values) may be rejected or radically revised.

In selecting items for a test, the higher the Discrimination Index the better, but this should not be the sole criterion for the exclusion of items which are measuring important learning outcomes. If the distractors seem to be working reasonably well in discriminating between the candidates, if the item is measuring an important outcome, and if the Discrimination Index in not too low, the item may be retained.

Further guidance on measuring item effectiveness and question validation can be found in chapter 4 of McIntosh (1974).

Case study 41
Computer-administered multiple choice questions

Case Study from Physiology and Pharmacology
Catherine Dallemagne, Queensland University of Technology

This case study, developed from materials submitted to the project, describes how Dallemagne and her colleagues were able to use MCQ assessment procedures to promote student learning in addition to their use in examining students.

Context

Catherine Dallemane, who teaches clinical physiology and pharmacology to students of nursing at the Queensland University of Technology, uses computer based testing using MCQs to try to make up for the lack of tutorials and resulting lack of direct feedback to students' questions.

Dallemagne and her colleagues teach 400 students in a lecture series (with one repeat) without tutorial support. She needs to assess the students' knowledge of physiology and pharmacology and their understanding of pathophysiology. The main method of assessment is two traditional MCQ examinations, conducted in week 8 and at the end of semester.

Assessment method

The computer based project has been developed to support students in their learning. Students answer each computer administered MCQ and are given a feedback screen on their answer. There are nine lessons on various topics. The students get a print out of the questions in a booklet, but not of the feedback screens. The only way to get feedback on their answers is to work through the questions on the computer.

Students may attempt the computer based project lessons as many times as they like providing that each lesson is completed within two weeks of the relevant lecture. They are encouraged to try different answers to check up on the logic of their answers, and feedback is given on every answer entered.

The computer based (CB) project component is allocated 15% of the total mark, with equal weight given to attendance and to successful completion of the computer administered MCQ's. The computer logs the time each student spends on each CB lesson. Students are expected to devote a minimum of 30 minutes interaction time at each lesson, and the attendance mark is calculated on this basis. The remaining 85% is distributed between a mid-semester MCQ examination (35%), and an end-of-semester MCQ (50%). Grades on a 7-point scale are then determined from the totals for the three assessments.

Strengths and limitations

Dallemagne and her colleagues claim that this use of multiple choice questions in the computer based project results in students learning how to answer MCQs, how to reason to eliminate incorrect alternatives and to accept correct ones. This should lead to a lower level of stress when confronted with MCQs in the examinations. They also hope that the feedback screens in the computer based project will foster deep learning.

The main limitation seen by Dallemagne is the high level of resources required to implement the system. A further limitation is that it is possible that a small number of students could circumvent the system and 'cheat' by obtaining answers from other students' screens during work on the CB component. Given that students can attempt the same lessson as many times as they like to maximise marks, and that the CB assessment is a small percentage of the total (7.5%), there is little incentive to engage in this practice. Dallemagne views the overall learning benefits accruing from use of the CB project as outweighing the effects of occasional abuses. ∎

Comment

Each CB project lesson requires students to spend at least 30 minutes considering alternatives, making choices, and studying feedback. This is likely to overcome to a large extent the propensity to memorise and 'spot' the correct answer. However, it should be emphasised that the outcome of promoting understanding is contingent on the demands made on the student by each item. This requires attention not only to the question being posed, but to the quality of the distractors used. In particular, the distractors need to function in a way that requires students to understand and apply concepts, and engage in reasoning, in order to consider and eliminate alternatives before choosing an answer.

Assessing knowledge in laboratory contexts

It is usual to think of laboratory work as developing procedural skills which (it is hoped) will eventually become routine. Examples include: microscopy; common pathology tests; procedures used to demonstrate phenomena; and basic experimentation skills. In order to be able to successfully complete a laboratory task the student must use task specific and discipline specific knowledge. They may also need to become familiar with the procedural steps involved in the task.

In many laboratory-based tasks, the requisite knowledge is not assessed directly, but is inferred from the finished laboratory task report. There are examples, however, where the knowledge required to conduct a laboratory task is assessed before the laboratory work is attempted.

Assessing prerequisite knowledge in physics laboratories

In a contribution provided by Ian Dunn from the University of New South Wales (described in greater detail in Module 3, Case stude 16), the knowledge necessary for the completion of first year physics experiments is assessed before the students carry out the related experimental procedures. Laboratory work in this subject has three learning objectives: (i) the development of technical skills (ii) the development of knowledge of certain topics in physics, and (iii) an understanding of the process of scientific inquiry. Before students begin their experimental work, they must complete 'exploratory exercises' to test their knowledge. These are then subject to a 'check test' by the demonstrator, and marked on a pass/resubmit basis. Once a student has demonstrated that the requisite knowledge to undertake the experiment has been mastered, he or she can proceed to the experiment itself.

Another example of testing knowledge in a laboratory context is contained in the following case study.

Case study 42
Minitests

Case study from Biomedical Science
Dianne Budd, Curtin University of Technology

This case study was developed from material submitted to the project.; a published version (Budd, 1994) is available.

Context

This case study is drawn from a Medical Laboratory Science subject taken by all first year students enrolled in the Bachelor of Science (Medical Science) and Associate Diploma (Medical Laboratory Techniques) within the School of Biomedical Sciences. The subject has a large practical component which is designed to "familiarise students with a wide range of basic laboratory skills and to reinforce theoretical concepts introduced during the formal lecture sessions".

Assessment method

A series of 'minitests' was introduced, consisting of five questions based on both the theoretical and practical aspects of the laboratory exercises. The specific ability being tested by these minitests is described as "the ability to tie theoretical concepts in with a particular application in the laboratory". Budd describes these minitests as follows:

> *Minitests are short written tests consisting of five questions based on both theoretical and practical aspects of the practical exercises. The information assessed by these minitests is contained within a written introduction to each practical. Students are presented with a minitest at the beginning of a practical session and allowed a maximum of ten minutes to complete the paper. A range of different types of questions are set, including true/false, sentence completion, and requests to provide relevant definitions and equations. No single question requires more than a one sentence answer.*

Grading

The papers are collected and a brief prelab is held, during which the answers to the minitest questions are given and discussed within the context of the practical exercise to come. Students are tested on 10 of the 20 practicals in a random fashion. The ten minitests comprise a total of 10% for the unit.

Strengths and limitations

The minitests had been introduced because it was found that previously "students were not gaining the maximum benefit from the practical sessions. Teaching staff were spending much time going over basic background material". The majority of students were not making sufficient preparation for undertaking laboratory work, and were consequently "disorganised and unfocused when performing the required exercises".

Budd claims that the introduction of the minitests has caused a number of changes: ➤

(i) an improvement in student performance. "Most importantly, the students have developed a greater understanding of the concepts behind the various practical exercises. This in turn has led to a notable improvement in the manner in which the students tackle these exercises and a higher number of students gaining a satisfactory grade for the practical component of the unit."

(ii) the new program "frees up tutors to lead the students forward instead of going over ground they should have already covered."

(iii) it provides a form of continuous assessment and feedback: "constant monitoring of a student's performance via the minitests makes it a simple matter to give the student immediate feedback and to clarify any problems that the student may be experiencing with a particular topic."

Conclusion

In this module we have looked at a wide range of methods aimed at the assessment of the student's ability to demonstrate knowledge and understanding. Contributors have produced some innovative and impressive examples of practice - some aimed at the earlier stages identified by Biggs in the development of understanding and mastery, some at the later stages (see the introduction to this module for a fuller explanation of Biggs' developmental model).

One aspect of the case studies and other material that has been presented which is especially worthy of comment is the almost universal concern shown by teachers for supporting the learning of their students. Teachers appear to be keenly aware of the effect that assessment can have on student learning, and have risen to the challenge of developing stimulating and valid assessment approaches. The phenomenon noted in the introduction, whereby students who have done well in examinations intended to test understanding, have been found to harbour fundamental misconceptions about the underlying principles and concepts on which they were supposed to have been tested, is being seriously addressed in the cases presented.

Teachers are using their assessments of the ability to demonstrate knowledge and understanding to encourage and support their students in many ways—to support the development of an appropriately structured knowledge base, to increase the relevance of material by the use of authentic tasks, to encourage the development of a deep understanding of the material, to improve feedback on performance, and to ensure that students have developed a sufficient grasp of prerequisite material to enable them to take on the development of higher order abilities with good prospects of success—whatever the strategy chosen, the attention to this aspect of assessment should be encouraged.

References

Biggs, J. (1991). Student learning in the context of school. In J. Biggs (Ed.), *Teaching for Learning: the view from cognitive psychology*. Hawthorn, Victoria: Australian Council for Educational Research. pp7-29.

Boud, D. (1990). Assessment and the promotion of academic values. *Studies in Higher Education,* 15(11), 101-111.

Budd, D. (1994). Minitests in medical science: maximum gain, minimum pain. In L. Summers (Ed.), *Quality in Teaching and Learning: 'Making It Happen'* . Perth, WA: Educational Development Unit, Edith Cowan University.

Courts, P. L., & McInerney, K. H. (1993). *Assessment in Higher Education: Politics, Pedagogy, and Portfolios.* Westport, CT: Praeger Publishers.

Dahlgren, L. (1984). Outcomes of learning. In F. Marton, D. Hounsell, & N. Entwistle (Eds.), *The Experience of Learning.* Edinburgh: Scottish Academic Press.

Ebel, R. (1972). E*ssentials of Educational Measurement.* New York: Prentice Hall.

Freeman, J., & Byrne, P. (1976). *The Assessment of Postgraduate Training in General Practice* (2nd ed). Surrey: SRHE.

Gibbs, G. (1992). *Assessing More Students.* Oxford: The Oxford Centre for Staff Development.

Glaser, R. (1991). Expertise and assessment. In M. Wittrock & E. Baker (Eds.), *Testing and Cognition* (pp. 17-28). Engelwood Cliffs NJ: Prentice Hall.

Gronlund, N. E. (1976). *Measurement and Evaluation in Teaching* (3rd ed). New York: Macmillan.

Harman, R. (1992). The reasoning testlet. *Australasian Journal of Engineering Education,* 3(1), 95-100.

Heywood, J. (1989). *Assessment in Higher Education.* London: Kogan Page.

Landa, L. N. (1974). *Algorithmization in learning and instruction.* Englewood Cliffs: Educational Technology Publications.

Marton, F., & Saljo, R. (1984). Approaches to learning. In F. Marton, D. Hounsell, & N. Entwistle (Eds.), *The Experience of Learning.* Edinburgh: Scottish Academic Press. pp36-55.

McIntosh, H. (1974). *Techniques and Problems of Assessment.* London: Edward Arnold.

Pollard, J. (1993). Developing physics understanding through guided study. In J. Bain, E. Lietzow, & B. Ross (Eds.), *Promoting Teaching in Higher Education.* Brisbane: Griffith Institute for Higher Education. pp 355-370

Ramsden, P. (1984). The context of learning. In F. Marton, D. Hounsell, & N. Entwistle (Eds.), *The Experience of Learning.* Edinburgh: Scottish Academic Press. pp144-64.

MODULE 7

DESIGNING, CREATING, PERFORMING

PEGGY NIGHTINGALE AND DOUG MAGIN

Module 7
Designing, creating, performing

This module covers tasks in which interpretation and synthesis lead to the creation of a product or a performance which is assessed with an emphasis on its creative or innovative qualities. Tasks often require analysis and problem solving but the essential feature of the abilities being assessed is creativity. Many disciplines other than the fine arts include tasks of this type: sport and leisure studies, engineering and architecture, drama, dance, music. Assessment of these abilities is possibly the most subjective of all types of assessment but case studies include carefully articulated criteria ranging from functionality and manufacturability to aesthetic value and originality.

Abilities encompassed in this module include:
- imagining
- visualising
- designing
- producing
- creating
- innovating
- performing

Section 1: Designing

Themes
- A wide variety of criteria
- Assessing technical skill or creativity/artistry
- Assessing process as well as product
- Differences of opinion on what constitutes quality

Techniques
- Design projects
- Design and build projects
- Group projects
- Assessment by panel
- Authentic assessment tasks
- Participating in competitions

Case Studies
43. Design projects, Architecture
44. Design and build project, Mechanical Engineering
45. Design and build competition, Mechanical Engineering

Section 2: Creating

Themes
- Judging creativity
- Emphasising progress and development of abilities
- Assessment by jury or panel, authenticity vs trauma
- Possibilities of gender bias in assessment

Techniques
- Sequence of tasks which build on developing expertise
- Contracts
- Portfolios
- Assessment by panel, including external members

Case studies
46. Process to product, Media Art
47. Portfolio, Visual Arts

Section 3: Performing

Themes
- Trying to quantify qualitative judgments
- Rewarding progress
- Establishing descriptive criteria
- Conflation of results
- Profiles rather than numbers

Techniques
- Performance examinations
- Multiple assessors
- Profile of achievement

Case studies
48. Assessing performance - improvement and achievement, Dance
49. Assessing performance - descriptive criteria, music
50. Profiling achievement, design

Module 7

Designing, creating, performing

Peggy Nightingale and Doug Magin

This module encompasses tasks in which interpretation and synthesis lead to the creation of a product or a performance. These may include the production of such things as: design drawings and supporting documentation, fabrications and models, computer system design, art works, musical and drama performances, musical compositions and choreographies.

While the various assessment tasks included in this module span a wide range of different disciplines, all of the tasks have two distinctive features in common:

- there is an essential assessment core demanding creativity and synthesis. Many of these tasks may also involve substantial research, analysis and problem solving. While some of these components (eg. quantitative analysis and calculations) can be assessed in ways described in other modules, the assessment of the completed work as a creative product or performance raises issues and approaches to assessment quite distinct from those described in other modules.

- the outcomes of students' work where creativity and synthesis are required cannot be gauged against a 'correct solution' template. Assessments usually involve judgments of the creative or innovative qualities of the product or performance. In many instances these judgments incorporate a wide range of apparently disparate criteria such as function, manufacturability, aesthetic value and/or artistic merit.

In this module we see educators grappling with Schön's (1990) key question:

> *how education for artistry can be made coherent with the professional curriculum's core of applied science and technology (p14).*

Schön argues that professionals, or "practitioners," in many disciplines need "artistry" in order to deal with the messy problems which crop up constantly in professional practice.

> *"Technical rationality" is sufficient for managing tidy problems, but complex, unpredictable, unusual problems need more than "familiar rules, theories and techniques" (pp34-5).*

The dilemma for educators in a system which requires assessment is how to judge both the technical competence and the artistry of students. Schön bases his approach to educating practitioners on the following premises:

- Inherent in the practice of the professionals we recognise as unusually competent is a core of artistry.
- Artistry is an exercise of intelligence, a kind of knowing, though different in crucial respects from our standard model of professional knowledge. It is not inherently mysterious; it is rigorous in its own terms; and we can learn a great deal about it - within what limits, we should treat as an open question - by carefully studying the performance of unusually competent performers.

In the terrain of professional practice, applied science and research-based technique occupy a critically important though limited territory, bounded on several sides by artistry. There are an art of problem framing, and art of implementation, and an art of improvisation - all necessary to mediate the use in practice of applied science and technique.

(Schön, 1990, p13)

While Schön has a great deal to offer on techniques for educating the type of practioners he believes will lead their professions, he does not take up the issues of formally assessing student work. There is no doubt that when one is imagining what it means to coach students rather than to teach them (as in a design studio in architecture or fine arts) and what it means to ask students to attempt to practice artistry before they even really know what it looks like, there are significant difficulties in constructing assessment tasks and criteria for judging students' work. The case studies and discussion which follow in this module attempt to address some of these difficulties; some of the solutions exemplify their own artistry in practice.

Section 1

Designing
(Magin and Nightingale)

In some instances, design tasks may be set which do not require the application of complex, multiple criteria for assessing students' work (eg. design of a simple electronic circuit to meet set performance specifications). However, even in basic design exercises of this kind, there will be a range of different configurations or design solutions which could be 'correct' in the sense of fulfiling the primary specifications set. Often, additional criteria are built into such exercises (eg. cost, reliability) which enable judgments to be made about the relative merits of different designs.

In other instances, the task set may require a large number of varied criteria, employing quite different methods of assessment. A good illustration of the latter, which echoes Schön (1990, see module introduction) is contained in an article by Kingsland and Cowdroy (1991, p166) with reference to architecture:

> *Architectural design is an activity where complex multiple criteria, often conflicting, are used to create a solution. Many individual aspects of a design solution can be considered using an objective scale but the overall combination should rise above the level of a technical assembly of parts. In assessing the design solutions proposed the total package must be assessed subjectively by design experts who have an intimate knowledge of the problem and possible solutions.*

In this section, we look at assessing design tasks typical of architecture and engineering. However, issues raised in this section frequently apply to assessing other types of design tasks: for instance, the interplay between criteria of utility, practicality, functionality and aesthetic appeal, and the use of external professionals on assessment panels. Other case studies from design disciplines are included in Module 5 (Case study 33) and in Section 2 of this module.

Case study 43
Design projects

Case study from Architecture
Arthur Kingsland, University of Newcastle

How assessments have been designed and implemented to meet the challenge of coping with complex multiple criteria is first illustrated from a study presented by Arthur Kingsland at the Problem Based Learning Workshop at the University of Newcastle in 1988 (Kingsland, 1989). Quoted material is from this report.

Context

The course consists of two sequential degrees: the Bachelor of Science (Architecture) in years 1-3, followed by the Bachelor of Architecture in years 4 and 5. The course has a problem-based learning approach "loosely based on the University of Newcastle Medical School model".

Each year of the course is broken into Phases: each Phase requiring the student to undertake a project. These projects are sequenced from small, single user designs at the beginning of first year, to multi-storey developments combined with studies of the effects of these developments on the surrounding urban fabric in fourth year. In fifth year, each student chooses a separate project and accompanying research topic, and studies these in great depth.

> *... Each Phase commands a student's complete study attention for a period of weeks. Typically, in first year, a Phase is five weeks.*

Formative assessment

In each Phase a Consultant (teaching member of staff) is appointed to small groups of students to assess new skills introduced during the Phase.

> *To aid a student's understanding of new skills, a Consultant may give exercises which are assessed and handed back with comments aimed at improving a student's work.... The consultant assesses whether or not the skill has been correctly applied in a student's Phase submission. Phase Assessment Sheets identify the part of the submission (eg. two-point perspective) and the quality which is being assessed (eg. accurate set-up). Each of these criteria is assessed as being 'OK' or 'Not OK'. ... A comment on the Phase Assessment Sheet can identify why a submission is 'Not OK'. ... For each Phase, for each Study area an overall grade is given as a guide to progress for the student.*

Summative assessment

Summative assessment occurs at the 'End-of-Phase' on the developed design. Here a Design Panel (consisting of teaching staff) is formed to "assess the integration of these skills" developed through the Phase project. In support of a student, the relevant Group Tutor will indicate progress through the Phase. The Design Panel uses a list of criteria (provided to the students at the start of the Phase) to assess the work submitted. The Phase assessment checklist used to assess the developed design by the panel is illustrated over page.

➤

Department of Architecture
University of Newcastle

ARCHITECTURE 1 1988

PHASE ASSESSMENT - Design Integration   Phase 3 : The Envelope

Student :

ASSESSMENT BY GROUP TUTORS   Group Tutor

Intermediate Submissions	Guide Grade	Comments
Preliminary Design		
Attendance during Phase	/	

ASSESSMENT BY DESIGN PANEL   Panel

ASSESSMENT CRITERIA	Submission OK	Not OK	Comments
Process (Intermediate Submissions)			
Presentation Qualities			
Functional response to brief			
Siting			
Use of Site			
Evidence of framework of ideas			
Design Concept development			
Quality of Design - Plan			
- Spatial			
- Circulation			
- Envelope			
Integration of Structure			
Fabric			
Services			
Environmental Control			
Cost Control			

End-of-Phase Submission :   **Developed Design**   Grade   Mark

Notes :

Figure 7.1

*Phase assessment
sheet – Design Integration*
(Kingsland, 1989)

The Design Panel is formed to "assess design integration work to ensure a consistency of marking. Although labour intensive, this generally guards against superficial marking and the effect of preconceptions about a student's work, and enables different viewpoints to appreciate subtleties within the presented work."

The development of the checklist was seen as a way of: making the Design Panel assessment more objective; providing a guard against omission of relevant assessment criteria; and allowing more consistency in the method of marking widely different designs.

Comment

An additional rationale for the introduction of a Design Panel, consisting of other teaching staff, and, in some Phases, outside professionals, is further elaborated by Kingsland and Cowdroy (1991) in a HERDSA conference paper:

> *There is a view that, in a professional course, assessment should mirror the method of assessment used in practice. In the 'real-world' groups of partners in practice and design committees judge schemes presented for assessment. This occurs with competitions for design solutions for major building works, where a corporation requires a number of feasibility studies to be performed before choosing their building team. We also find that in the real-world specialist consultants give expert comment on architectural design and make modifications necessary for their particular discipline. (p166)*

See Section 3 for a discussion of panel or jury assessment.

Another example of criteria for judging design

Another study, from the U.K., provides details of an assessment scheme and marking schedule which have been developed to grade students' project work at the Glasgow School of Art and University of Glasgow. This assessment scheme, described by McNally (1993), is used to mark a major project task (in Product Design Engineering) in which assessment criteria spanning various kinds of analysis (such as ergonomic, technical, economic and market need) and a further set of criteria related to creativity and imagination are included in the total assessment of the project (see checklist over page).

PDE Assessment 1992 / 93

UNIVERSITY OF GLASGOW		Student Signatures			Date	
GLASGOW SCHOOL OF ART						
PRODUCT DESIGN ENGINEERING						
Student				Session		
Project				Year		

GLASGOW SHOOL OF ART								
		A	B	C	D	E	Weight	Weight
		100-70	69-60	59-50	49-40	< 40	Factor	Mark
Summary							1	0
Design Criteria							1	0
Design Methods							1	0
Ergonomic Analysis							1	0
Technical Analysis							1	0
Economic Analysis							1	0
Aesthetic Analysis							1	0
Design Communication							1	0
						Average Mark		0

Design Activity - Progress and Development Assessment								
		A	B	C	D	E	Weight	Weight
		100-70	69-60	59-50	49-40	< 40	Factor	Mark
Research and Analysis								
Interpreting the Project Brief							1	0
Understanding Market Needs							1	0
Problem Analysis							1	0
Creative and Imaginative Development								
Concept Generation							1	0
Concept Development							1	0
Critical and Decision Making Skills							1	0
Synthesis and Detail							1	0
Aesthetic / Formal Ability							1	0
Professional and Executive Abilities								
Presentation 2D							1	0
Technological Understanding							1	0
Project Management							1	0
Ability to Apply Engineering Theory							1	0
Presentation Viva							1	0
Tutorial Assessments							1	0
Staff					Average Mark			0
Date					Total Assessment Mark			0

Figure 7.2

Assessment checklist
(McNally, 1993)

Comment

The context in which the project assessment task is conducted is in sharp contrast to that described in architecture at the University of Newcastle. First, the major task is the same for all students (eg. design development of a 13 to 15 metre rigid inflatable raft accompanied by a specific design brief); and second, the task is not attempted as an individual project, but is undertaken by project teams (of five students each) who are 'multidisciplinary', being drawn from Product Design students at the Glasgow School of Arts, and Product Design engineers from the University of Glasgow.

More features of assessing design

While not necessarily unique to assessment tasks in this module, there are two other features which are commonly found in assessment in this area.

- There is an increasing trend to use substantial projects as the major vehicle for assessment. Assessments often take place throughout different stages of student work on the project, as well as at the end when the final product or performance is assessed. This usually places a considerable burden on teaching staff in providing both informal and formal assessments of students' work.

- There is often tension between very different kinds of criteria and interpretations which are brought to bear on the same work or performance being assessed. This tension takes a number of forms.

Tensions in assessing design

First, as Schön also emphasises (1990, see Module introduction) a hiatus is sometimes seen between the technical and the aesthetic. Boysen (1994, p249) characterises the ideal industrial designer as a 'hybrid with connections to both engineering and the arts'.

> If the engineer is involved with the application of science, then the designer is involved with humanising these applications. The designer must stand between the mechanical and the sensual, between the rational and the emotional, and between the digital and the intuitive.

Redmond (1986, p133) echoes a similar sentiment in relation to the need for closer integration of the 'art' and 'science' of design:

> It would seem that many engineering students, either by temperament or training, tend to selectively see certain aspects of a product/problem. These are often aspects of what they refer to as the product's function: the interface between the product and 'work' it is required to do. There is a tendency to discount the human, social, or cultural aspects of a product and sometimes even production efficiency as a primary objective. This may be because they do not see the product's existence as a marketable commodity, but rather as an aspect of science. The design they develop must be scientifically correct and therefore the resultant production cost must be inevitable. This perceptual problem combined with a lack of conceptual and visualisation skills is a cause of the limited success engineers have with product design. For engineers to rediscover these skills and capacities there will have to be re-balancing of the priorities of engineering education in which the art of engineering is promoted in conjunction with the science of engineering.

The study by McNally (1993) described above illustrates how the multidisciplinary nature of the project team and the marking schemes used at Glasgow attempt to overcome this hiatus within a course in Product Design Engineering. Similar concerns can be found in the expressive arts in which both the mastery of technical skills and the demonstration of creativity and artistic expression are assessed in the same task. Another case study, by Mann, (see Case study 46 in Section 2 of this module) outlines how, within courses conducted in the School of Visual and Performing Arts at the University of Ballarat, assessments shift from the weighting of 'practical and competency elements' to that of 'creative, innovative and unique elements' through the stages of student project work.

A second source of tension that can arise is through misunderstanding or ignorance of the criteria which are being used to judge the merit of a student's work. This is often a complaint in many other areas of assessment. However, there can be difficulties in implementing the usual ways in which this is remedied (e.g. development of explicit and detailed assessment schedules, communication of these to students, formative assessments and feedback on students' work). As described in some of case studies (eg 46 in section 2 or 48 in section 3), the assessments conducted throughout the process of producing the final work often do incorporate these procedures, and give substantial weighting based on explicit criteria. The major difficulty is seen to reside in the judging of the finished product or work. This arises from the subjective nature of the assessor's response to creative or artistic expression - a response which Boysen (1994) has referred to as being based in the "emotional", "sensual" and "intuitive" feelings of the individuals who are called on to appraise the work.

Finally, a third source of tension can arise through strong differences in opinion, values, and understandings of 'quality'. Often these are associated with allegiances to different styles of expression or schools of thought. They also arise in students' lack of experience in or appreciation of what is required to achieve 'quality' in a product. Both Redmond (1986) and Boysen (1994) have identified the latter as a major deficiency in engineering students engaged in developing product design skills. These students are seen typically to view the task of designing a product as virtually finalised when they have completed all the 'hard engineering' design and documentation required to meet the technical specifications set, and often show little appreciation of the human aspect - that of customer needs relating to usage and appeal. In reinforcing the point on the need for engineering designers to realise the importance of refinements and design modifications based on human needs and aesthetics, Boysen draws on a quotation from Picasso:

> *When you make a thing, a thing that is new, it is so complicated making it that it is bound to be ugly. But those who make it after you, they don't have to worry about making it. And they can make it pretty.*

Design-and-build projects

The studies we are considering in this module have one further feature in common:

> *Students are often required to spend a great deal of time in completing major assessment tasks which culminate in a finished design, product or performance. The processes and stages of development undertaken to reach this end point are seen as producing powerful learning outcomes before final formal assessments are made.*

Although projects requiring students not only to design but also to build their products may be even more time-consuming, they address concerns of employers who have complained that students are ill-prepared if they have not learned to consider production realities as they design. That is, there is little totally conceptual design done in most industrial settings. Once again, we see teachers seeking authenticity in assessment in the following case studies (see Glossary and Index for further discussion of authentic assessment tasks).

West, Flowers, & Gilmore (1990, p563) refer to this pedagogical feature in the context of projects which require students to both design and build a working device for assessment:

> *The goal becomes not to produce the best machine, but the optimal machine that can be manufactured in reasonable time and with reasonable confidence. Students learn experientially the value of considering how to make a part as they design it. The frustration experienced by some students of finding that it is impossible to make a part as it was originally designed drives this point home. Even the most elementary hands-on experience teaches a profound lesson: the difference between what you can conceive and what you can build... Success demands that they design, test, measure, model, analyse, estimate, communicate, visualise and fabricate.*

Assessment projects which require progression through a number of stages to the completion of a product are becoming increasingly common in many disciplines. Perhaps the most well-known are the design-and-build projects now found in most engineering design courses. While there is little disagreement on the pedagogical value of these projects, substantial differences (even within the same discipline) exist on how such projects should be formulated and assessed.

These differences are illustrated through two case studies on design-and-build projects within the same field (mechanical engineering design). The two case studies, by Davey and Wheway (1986) at Wollongong University, and by Churches (1989) at The University of New South Wales, provide contrasting approaches, both in the formulation of such projects, and in the methods of assessment which are appropriate to each. In the first case study, student teams are required to choose a 'real life' engineering design problem for which no known device exists to solve the problem. Students were evaluated on two products: 1) the design and prototype; 2) their report and presentation. The design, together with the prototype, was judged in terms of the "quality of the engineering work evidenced"; and each student group's design report and presentation were judged according to "evidence of imagination and creativity as well as the quality of the students' analytical and critical abilities".

Case study 44
Design and build project

Case study from Mechanical Engineering
R.J. Davey and R.T. Wheway, University of Wollongong

A published article (Davey and Wheway, 1986) provides a case study of the way in which a major 'design-and-build' project is assessed within engineering at the University.

Abilities being assessed

- ability to design and build a quality prototype
- ability to use imagination, be creative
- ability to analyse and critique

Context

This is a first year mechanical engineering design course of one semester duration. Students are organised into groups of four in which they compete with other teams in tackling a 'real life' engineering design problem for which no known device exists as a solution. They are encouraged to define a problem of their own choice, although a range of design problems are available to select from. The project forms a major part of their course over the semester.

Task

Each student group is required to identify a problem, outline a proposed design solution in a preliminary report, generate an optimum design solution, build and test a prototype, and submit a final design report. In addition, they make a 10 minute oral presentation explaining the design need and demonstrating the quality of the design they have produced.

Two types of assessment criteria were used. The major criterion was the quality of the engineering work as evidenced by the design and the prototype. A second group of criteria was related to "evidence of imagination and creativity as well as the quality of the students' analytical and critical abilities". This assessment was based on each student groups' design reports and presentations. Assessment was carried out by a panel of design staff in the department.

∎

Case study 45
Design and build competition

45

Case study from Mechanical Engineering
Alex Churches, University of New South Wales

In the second case study (Churches, 1989), student teams engaged in a 'design and build competition'. While all teams were set a common task, a diverse range of design solutions and devices were produced. The criterion for assessment was based on how well the device performed, that is, on 'function'. Quotations are from the published report.

The abilities being assessed

Author's words:

> *...The most important criterion on which each each report is judged is the quality of the engineering work which it evidences.*

> *...look for evidence of imagination and creativity as well as the quality of the students' analytical and critical abilities.*

> *...if after thorough review a group recommends further development of specific aspects of the problem, or a complete abandonment of the project, it is quite possible that the group may win the final design competition if its members have shown the required evidence of creativity and objectivity.*

Context

Students are in their second year in mechanical engineering design courses at 18 campuses in Australia. Each of the participating Engineering Schools require their students to undertake the design-and-build project as part of the requirements for the second year design course. Competitions are held at each campus and finalists attend a national competition. All campuses employ national assessment criteria at local level, but some variation exists in local assessment practices (weighting given, and employment of additional criteria).

The task

A common task is set. In 1988 the task required students (in groups of 4) to "design and build a device to climb 5 metres up a vertically hanging rope, carrying a payload comprising a table-tennis ball resting unsecured in a plastic saucer". While a diverse range of devices were built, based on different conceptual designs, the competition assessment was restricted to performance of the device.

Assessment

Assessment for the competition consisted of:
(i)   achieving the 5 metre ascent with the table-tennis ball remaining intact
(ii) time taken for the ascent.

Even at national finals, some of the devices do not succeed in keeping the ball intact during rapid ascent. Placings are determined on the basis of minimum time to successfully complete the device's mission.   ➤

At the local level, 9 campuses also required students to prepare a formal report. The combined mark allocation for device performance and report quality varied from 10-25% of the total subject mark. Nine other campuses did not require a formal report, allocating up to 15% for design-and-build construction and performance.

Why the task is set

As a national competition: The design and build competition was seen

> to have benefits in involving many more engineering students in a new and worthwhile design experience, in increasing the visibility and status of engineering design in students' eyes and in increasing student interaction on campuses, between campuses and with the engineering profession.

As part of local assessment within second year design subjects: The competition was seen by a large majority of subject co-ordinators at local campuses as "contributing to students' understanding of design relative to their design course objectives". It was also seen to increase student interaction at several levels, including "how to work in a group". Other sources (publications on this design competition) stress the crucial role of understanding design through the experience of building and subjecting the prototype to rigorous testing and performance trials.

Issues

One of the major issues with an assessment task of this type is the artificial nature of the design task, with competition criteria restricted to the competitive performance of device. Failure can occur with a 'good design' through faulty construction. Although this does create awareness and learning opportunities unlikely to be found elsewhere in a second year course, there can be some conflict with central course objectives which stress the development of creative design per se. Additional assessment criteria at local level may have a correcting effect on this 'performance' bias. The common design task can also lead to one group 'taking over' some of the design ideas of another group, with rewards then going to the best performing prototype. Finally, some groups spend excessive amounts of time in completing the design-and-build task. ∎

Changing needs: challenges to traditional assessment

Despite the quite different approaches in the above two case studies, both of these design-and-build formats have arisen out of an identification of shortcomings in more traditional approaches to design teaching and assessment. An expression of these shortcoming has been made by spokespersons from the Boeing Corporation in America (McMasters & Ford, 1990, p527-8), who have written:

> *...we are no longer satisfied customers of the products of many colleges of engineering. None of the students we encountered had been prepared by their education to deal with the open-ended design-related problems we posed, nor did they seem to have much experience working in groups to solve problems collectively...*

Conceptual design, which is the bread and butter of most university capstone airplane design curricula, is practiced by very few people professionally; we do a disservice to our students if we offer it as a viable career option for the majority. It is this lack of understanding of how, when, and why we conduct the various stages in the design of a product that, more than any other factor, tends to confuse discussions of appropriate design education even among those who wish to provide it.

The integration of the processes of design, manufacturing and commercial planning to meet aims of cost-effective design and manufacture, short lead times, and quality-assured market-appropriate products is now generally referred to as 'concurrent engineering'. Crucial to change in engineering practice towards concurrent engineering is the introduction of effective multi-disciplinary design teams.

As we shall see in the next section of this module, the so-called creative arts also face dilemmas in teaching and assessing practical skills along with imagination and aesthetic qualities.

Section 2

Creating
(Nightingale)

When we picture the tasks students are expected to do for assessment in higher education, most of us do not think first of the creative work of painters, sculptors, jewellers, photographers, creative writers, and theatrical designers.

Assessing work of this type shares many issues with assessing design as covered in Section 1 of this module. There is the problem of the disjunction between the "technical" and the "artistic"; there are the inevitable subjectivity of the assessment of the final product and the strong differences of opinion about the appeal of a work of art.

In the creative arts we are likely to encounter portfolio-based assessment (other discussion of portfolios in Modules 4 and 8, see Index) as opposed to assessment of a single assignment task and to find judgments being made by panels of people rather than by individuals.

One of the common themes in the following cases is that early in students' programs the emphasis of assessment may be on acquisition of practical skills - such as being able to use equipment effectively, while the emphasis shifts to students' success as creative artists later.

Where staff in many disciplines strive for objectivity teachers in these disciplines may not even attempt to avoid subjectivity when they are judging the 'art'. Allan Mann from Ballarat's School of Arts wrote to us that assessing in some subjects where there is a "functional product" is amenable to criteria, "correct or incorrect responses… to specified… questions", but that "this applies hardly at all to the Creative Arts [where] it is the word CREATIVE which concerns us most." He went on to say that he must assess

> *in terms of a student's ability to handle the medium and material to achieve their goal whatever that might be.*

> *But then that is only a portion of the assessment, what about the finished result…their goal. How do I/we assess an attempt at conveying a feeling or an emotion which is a uniquely personal statement and response by an individual?*

Mann also emphasised to us the importance of staff who assess creative works being in touch with a wide range of work in their field and the standards by which it is judged so as to be able to make fair and comparable assessments of students' achievements.

46

Case study 46
Process to product

Case study from Media Art
Lynne Roberts-Goodwin, UNSW

This case study was developed from subject handouts and comments provided by the educator.

Abilities being assessed
(quoted from subject description)

> *Imaginative translation of thought and experience into two-dimensional and other 'image' forms*
>
> *Generation of imagery from a wide range of stimuli*
>
> *Working photographically and with associated processes*
>
> *Development of personal visual languages in relation to contemporary visual arts photographic practice*
>
> *Conceptualisation and realisation of work in the context of photographic and media related production*

Assessment method

There are four assignments over the half year subject - due in weeks 4, 7, 10, and 15. Three are weighted 30%, and one 10%. This is a first year subject, and the important thing in deciding whether students pass or fail any element or the whole subject is whether they were showing evidence of growth in skills and the ability to conceptualise their work. Hence, the final exhibition (see below) is worth only 10% of the grade; a student could pass the subject with a good grade even if the selected best work was not judged to be very successful as a final creative product.

The assigned work in one year was as follows:

Assignment 1 - Experimentations

A series of tasks are required of the student.
1. Produce one grey scale. Students use the enlarger and the timer to produce shades of grey on a sheet of photographic paper.
2. Produce two photograms. Students arrange objects on photographic paper, expose, develop, stop, fix and wash their prints. They experiment with different arrangements of objects, objects of varying opacity, and exposure times.
3. Produce two photographs by painting with developer. Students expose the paper in the usual fashion but they select what parts are to be developed by applying developer to that part only.
4. Produce two photographs by shooting blind. Students use an instamatic camera or one set on automatic, point in selected and random directions, holding the camera still and moving it, and shoot. Images may be cropped for final prints. Filters may be used to adjust print contrast. Burning and dodging may be used to lighten and darken portions of the print.

➤

5. Produce one photograph - an abstract image. Students concentrate on the background of the photograph rather than the subject as they manually use the exposure meter trying to think of the view-finder as a framing device, a way of composing things so that shapes, lines, angles, and tones achieve significance to make an abstract image.

Assignment 2 - Presence in Absence

Describe a subject without representing the subject itself in the image frame. Consider other ways of providing information about, giving a sense of, representing a trace of..., that subject's presence and/or absence in the image space.

For this assignment the students' mission is to extend how the image in a photograph might operate and open up ways of describing a subject (representing and providing information about it) in an image instead of the predictable photograph of the subject itself.

The teacher suggests experimenting with techniques from assignment 1.

Assignment 3

Produce a minimum of 4 final photographs as well as a selection of work in progress - the results of the second assignment. The selected work is to be prepared for presentation to the group. It is to reflect students' response to the assignment and demonstrate their consideration of the ideas and possibilities it raises.

Assignment 4 - Media Art Foundation Assignment Presentation

This is an exhibition of work done during the term for the assignments above. Students choose what to display, title their work, and set up the exhibition.

Criteria

The criteria in Figure 1 are provided to all students in Photographic Studies. Note that the department says these are "some factors" and that they take on different degrees of importance at different levels within the course.

Students are also required to participate actively in lectures, discussions, critiques, seminars and gallery visits. Full and punctual attendance is required and students are expected to maintain regular contact with the lecturer to obtain feedback and critique.

Strengths

- It is progressive in that each task builds on the one(s) before.
- It seeks "evidence of the individual's activities in developing and completing assignments".
- It seeks "evidence of working methodology and conceptual development".
- It requires "the development of students' own ideas and working method towards the semester assessment and presentation".

THE UNIVERSITY OF N. S. W.

COLLEGE OF FINE ARTS

PHOTOGRAPHIC STUDIES

CRITERIA OF ASSESSMENT

1993

Some factors brought to bear upon assessment, bearing in mind that all these factors are necessarily overlapping and that in identifying them in relationship to the work produced, a comparative scale of weighting is used relative to the course level.

LEVEL OF COMMITMENT AND MOTIVATION

The level of application, the ability to persevere, the level of involvement and degree of participation in the subject or course and the developing professional attitude, ie. that the work produced be autonomous enough to function without undue 'good will'.

SATISFACTION OF REQUIREMENTS

As determined by staff in conjunction with the student, as agreed to in collaboration with staff or other students, or a combination as mutually understood prior to the work undertaken.

RECOGNITION OF INDIVIDUAL RESPONSIBILITY

The ability to be self-directed, in determining objectives and the appropriateness of resources, and in the evaluation of progress.

EVIDENCE OF CRITICAL PROCESS

Within the work, the willingness to instigate research and the apparent analysis of experience and information, and the evidence of synthesised hypotheses.

DEVELOPMENT

The ability to develop contextually appropriate work using existing models and to develop a palpable 'content'.

CONTRIBUTION TO STUDIO FUNCTIONING

The maintenance of a responsible attitude to: the needs of the other community members, to the use of the space and equipment, and a contribution to the working dialogue.

CRAFT / SKILL APPROPRIATE TO THE WORK UNDERTAKEN

The effective control and use of the selected media relative to the result. The appropriateness of 'means', vis a vis 'form' of realisation , its context and content.

Figure 7.3
Criteria of assessment
Lynne Roberts-Goodwin

Case study 47
Portfolio

Case study from Visual Arts
Allan Mann, University of Ballarat

In the next case study we have a description of the assessment process common to all studio subjects in a program of study in the visual arts.

The following is a slightly edited version of the case description provided by Allan Mann.

Context

The BA (Visual Arts) is a six semester program. It is predominantly a practical studio-based program, which also includes theory related to a specific major - Ceramics, Drawing, Graphic Design, Painting, Printmaking and Sculpture.

Compulsory units include Art Theory and Support Drawing for 5 semesters.

Three elective units are studied during semesters 2 -5.

A student enters a studio major in semester 1. Major program studies involve specific set tasks within each major studio from semester 1. They become less prescriptive as the student matures. By semester 5 when they begin a full year unit, students provide a contract of work aims and expected outcomes which is negotiated with the supervising lecturing staff before being approved as appropriate.

Abilities being assessed

The students are assessed on their practical abilities to undertake work/projects for specific disciplines and units and for their ability to conceptualise ideas and articulate these.

They are further assessed upon their knowledge of the history and theory of visual arts.

Procedures

All subjects in the School are assessed as follows.

Semester 1-4 Major Studio, Support Drawing and Electives:

Students are required to present a portfolio of completed set tasks and self-initiated projects during the assessment period at the semester end. They offer both works which are professionally presented and notes and sketchbooks. During the semester they also offer a seminar or submit a written assignment.

The Lecturer with whom they have been principally associated and normally at least one other lecturer from within the same discipline, will assess students' work and may require students to provide an oral commentary or explanation of the rationale behind the complete or part submission. The staff will be seeking assurances that students clearly understand the media and processes, the manner by which their figurative or abstracted outcomes have been reached and the conceptual notions upon which the work is based. The emphasis shifts as students progress, from weighting towards the practical and competency elements to weighting towards the conceptual, creative, innovative and unique elements of the individual's work.

The final one year unit in semesters 5-6 differs only in so far as an external advisor is brought in to each studio discipline and independently forms her/his own judgments and opinion.

School staff and the external advisors liaise and arrive at a final arbitrated result for each student.

The work is judged on criteria which include:
- Evidence of practical ability to handle the media being utilised;
- Evidence that knowledge has been acquired about how to use the materials to achieve an end result which 'works' in the sense that it does not fall to bits before it is hung on a wall, presented to a client as a model or whatever;
- The student's ability to discuss the work in terms of the materials and manner of production;
- The student's ability to talk about the finished work and how the creative idea or concept was formulated and how they developed their ideas (in some instances what the work represents, what it is about, why they decided to interpret visually a particular theme and the relevance of that, their motivation or lack of it);
- Reasoning about the research undertaken, the background material and information sought out for use and reference;
- The student's ability to relate their idea or notion orally and to demonstrate that what they set out to accomplish has been successfully achieved.

Graphic Design stands somewhat apart from this process only in-so-far as it follows the graphics industry practice of working briefs for set projects, giving precise parameters within which to tackle each project and within given time constraints. Each project is assessed and graded and the accumulative grade aggregated to provide a final assessment in conjunction with an overall final complete folio presentation.

Strengths and limitations

The strengths of these processes were:
- flexibility within the course structure to allow for freedom to work within and across disciplines, discover and explore ideas;
- teamwork among staff and between disciplines whereby comment and views can be garnered and expressed freely;
- interaction between student levels, again involving feedback and response to work in progress;
- promotion of independence and self confidence critical for a visual arts professional; and
- the review process offers individualised feedback about the work and conceptual directions.

The limitations and our concerns are that:
- perhaps too much emphasis is placed upon the final 'polished' image or portfolio presentation; possibly we should put more emphasis on nurturing students to create and conceptualise unique ideas;
- the external advisor may not be completely familiar with the expectations of the academic program; the industry or profession is the ultimate assessor but may not share our perspectives;
- there is some concern about different staff using different criteria to reach a grade for students in units which are common to all majors;
- we question whether attendance and participation should be weighted against the final outcomes (should an 'A' student be penalised for irregular attendance?).

Marks, grades

Grades are:
A   excellent performance
B   very good performance
C   good pass standard
D   moderate pass standard
E   marginally below pass standard
F   considerably below pass standard

Students must have passed all prescribed units with a minimum D grade to achieve their BA.

■

Comments

The meeting with assessors to "defend" one's work can be a very intimidating process and it is important to allow students to practice it. (See discussion of assessment by jury/ panel below.) Mann emphasised that there is a mid-semester formative assessment. A portfolio is presented and discussed and students receive a written report advising them of their current standing.

At the end of term the final assessment result for the portfolio is reached by consensus; agreement is negotiated between the internal and external examiners of the work. Mann describes the assessors reaching an "arbitrated result" rather than one which is calculated by assigning numerical marks and averaging them. (See discussion of conflation and the meaning of marks in the following Section of this module.) He also emphasised the quite remarkable degree of agreement in most cases. The panelists view students' work, talk with them, and assign a provisional grade (A-F) independently, but when they meet to reach final grades, usually they have reached very similar conclusions.

Assessment by jury or panel

Like visual arts students, architecture students spend a lot of their time in design studios. They, too, execute projects of increasing complexity as they progress through their courses. Most of these are done individually but the studio does provide a place for interaction and discussion of work-in-progress. Also like Mann's visual arts students (and the dance and music students in the following section of this module), most projects are assessed by a panel or jury. The number of members varies but usually includes at least one external assessor, a practicing architect, in addition to staff of the school. The architecture student usually presents the design orally to the jury and engages in discussion with the jury, answering members' questions and explaining the design decisions taken in executing the project. Sometimes there is a presentation of work-in-progress; more often it is presented when the project is completed.

Schools of architecture - and indeed other design disciplines - believe that jury assessment prepares students for professional practice in that it requires students to learn to make an oral presentation, to explain their design and "sell" it. It also ensures that students get a variety of opinions on their work including those of practitioners.

On the face of it, having a grade determined by several people rather than one, allowing the student to present and defend the work, and creating a situation at least similar to one students will have to face after graduation seems like good assessment practice. It does seem that schools using these assessment methods have thought about the abilities students must develop - both as designers and as communicators of design - and are creating an assessment situation which actually assesses those abilities.

On the other hand, jury assessment is not without its problems which are recognised by teachers of architecture (see Anthony, 1987; Frederickson, 1993). In particular, this is an opportunity to raise issues of gender bias in assessment which have come up in some other discussions (see Index) but which have been specifically studied in relation to jury assessment in architecture.

What happens to women

Frederickson (1993) filmed 112 juries in three design schools in the United States. On only 9 were there more women than men, and on a further 5 there was equal male-female balance; on 52 panels there was not one woman. Unless a woman was leading the jury, the female jurors spoke less and were interrupted more than their male colleagues.

At all three schools female students' presentations were interrupted more frequently and their juries were shorter than the average duration of all juries. Frederickson's observations suggest female students appear more acquiescent to critical remarks; they do not defend themselves and their work as do the male students.

Frederickson observes some interesting differences in atmosphere between the schools. In School 3 there are no female staff, no female jurors and an atmosphere Frederickson describes as condescending. Female students were given less time, interrupted more often, asked more rhetorical questions, and there was less "idea building" during their sessions.

One of the behaviours tallied was incidences of a staff member, usually the student's teacher, interceding to "protect" the student from hostile questioning or from criticism. In School 3 incidence of protectionism was 0.53 times less for female students. In School 2, on the other hand, they were protected by the jurors 0.60 times more frequently, and Frederickson describes the jury environment as at times overly nurturing.

School 1, which had 4 females out of 19 full-time staff and which always had at least one female juror, "was as consistently disrespectful of male students as of female ones except on two measures: Female students were protected 1.25 times more frequently than male and female students were asked 0.65 times fewer rhetorical questions" (Frederickson, 1993, p42).

Let us compare these observations of a specific assessment situation with some other observations of gender differences.

Simple bias

The general tendency to devalue women and their work is illustrated by a well-known series of related studies in which two groups of people were asked to evaluate particular items, such as articles, paintings, resumes and the like. The names attached to the items given to each group of evaluators were clearly either male or female, but reversed for each group - that is, what one group believed was originated by a man, the other believed was originated by a woman. Regardless of the items, when they were ascribed to a man they were rated higher than when they were ascribed to a woman. In all of these studies, women evaluators were as likely as men to downgrade those items ascribed to women.

(Hall & Sandler, 1982, p4)

One extraordinary omission from Frederickson's report was data on the distribution of grades awarded to female and male students. However, we see the devaluing of women's efforts in both the condescension of School 3 and the protectionism of Schools 1 and 2.

Getting trapped by stereotypes

It has become a truism that behaviour which is acceptable as assertive in a male is characterised as aggressive and unacceptable behaviour in a female. So women are encouraged not to exhibit self-confident behaviours. Note that the female students described above do not defend their work or themselves in the jury setting.

But, in addition, much of what happens to them in educational settings works to undermine what self-confidence they are already covering up in order to be well-regarded. Valerie Walkerdyne has demonstrated through studies of school records that when a boy does well, teachers say it is because he is talented but when a girl does well, teachers say it is because she is a hard worker (keynote address, Conference on Thinking, Townsville 1992 and Walkerdyne & Unit, 1989) .

Thomas's study (1990) of male and female physics and English students revealed an astonishing lack of self-confidence in the female students in both fields, women who were extremely well-qualified and successful students. They even discussed with Thomas the change in their self-perception between school and university and their loss of confidence. Male students, whether in a numerical majority or in a minority, were supremely self-confident and even boasted about dominating discussions where there was a majority of women present.

How can the women facing those juries avoid a loss of self-confidence? It is true that Anthony's study (1987) of students' responses to jury assessment shows both male and female students to be heavily stressed - often seriously traumatised - by the experience, but other work, including Thomas's suggests that the males recover better. Is this because the self-esteem of males is not eroded as continuously as that of females?

It can be very difficult for a teacher not to be influenced by a student's expressions of uncertainty (whether they are explicit or covert); many of us can remember someone about whom we were concerned surprising us with a brilliant essay or examination. But if the essay or examination submitted by the person lacking confidence is ordinary, do we value it as highly in our grading as the ordinary work of a self-confident person?

Staff consistently spoke of male high-fliers in both fields studied by Thomas and wondered why women did not do as well. Thomas points out the unequal distribution of first-class honours with 9.1 per cent of male graduates but only 5.1 percent of female graduates gaining firsts. As she points out,

> The anxieties [the female students] voiced were genuine feelings of inadequacy resulting from a social situation (finding themselves with a group of people who were superficially intellectual and articulate) in which they feel at a disadvantage. Women's sense of inferiority is heightened and re-created through a seminar system which rates articulacy and even aggression more than thoughtfulness.

> *(Thomas, 1990, p158)*

Thomas recommends blind marking of degree results. Blind marking is desirable in all situations where it is possible, even if there is a degree of inconvenience associated with it. However, it is not possible in a jury, so the best that one may suggest is a conscious awareness of the potential for devaluing women's work, a review of grade distributions, and reappraisal if things seem inequitable. It may help to have women on the panels, preferably in equal numbers since Frederickson (1993) observed a changed dynamic when women led the group and were well-represented. On the other hand, there is evidence that women also undervalue contributions by female students.

Both Anthony (1987) and Frederickson (1993) described juries in which the members of the panel entered into lengthy theoretical discussions with each other and seemed virtually to forget the student's work. In architecture, as in any other discipline, there are different ways of conceptualising design, different trends in design which are more or less "fashionable" and possibly more or less "masculine". It seems likely that in a discipline so dominated by men, both as teachers and as assessors of student work, female students may be mis-matched with their assessors.

In raising these issues about potential gender bias in assessment, we do not intend to suggest that any of our contributors or our colleagues in higher education intends to be anything other than scrupulously fair and unbiased. The difficulty is that it is sometimes so hard to see the things which may unintentionally disadvantage one group in relation to another, especially in a system which so often emphasises competition and relies on norm-referencing and rank-ordering to determine grades (see also Nightingale & Sohler, 1994) .

Section 3

Performing
(Nightingale)

In this final section of this module we focus on issues relating to attempts to describe students' achievement by attaching quantitative values to qualitative judgments. The difficulties of trying to "weight" one task more heavily than another so as to indicate which abilities a teacher most values are common to all disciplines, but for us on the project team, they were highlighted when we looked at assessment practice of the ability to perform. Our contributors from performance disciplines, such as music and dance, also shared the concerns of contributors to the other two sections of this module: concerns about the differences of opinion between assessors and the need to judge students" progress as well as the standard they reach at the end of a subject or program of study. The final case study in this section brings us back to practice in design where a contributor has found a way of avoiding some of the problems of conflation of marks (see discussion below and Glossary).

Case study 48
Assessing performance - improvement and achievement

°48

Case study from Dance
David Roche, University of Adelaide

Just when the project team was about to despair of finding case studies from the performing arts, a colleague suggested we contact David Roche. He generously took a number of phone calls and reviewed our draft descriptions of practice in his department to provide the following glimpse of assessment in a dance studio.

Context

This example is located in the context of a Bachelor of Arts (Dance). The three year program requires students to take "Modern Dance Technique 1," MDT2, MDT3, MDT4, MDT5 and MDT6.

The technique classes are conducted at three different levels, and students are placed into an appropriate level when they enter the degree program. For example, a first year student may go to a Level 2 or 3 class rather than starting at Level 1. Students go through 6 semesters of Technique no matter what level they start on. There is no requirement that students reach Level 3 in order to graduate.

This subject is undertaken each semester, but is split into 2 halves. That is, 2 different teachers instruct the students, each for half a semester.

The assessment program has two strands (described in detail below). Students are assessed on their progress or improvement after each half semester, and they are assessed on the standard they attain at the end of each semester.

There are 17-25 students in each class. There are 7-1/2 contact hours per week.

➤

Assessment method

Midway through the teaching program (ie about 3 weeks) the teacher notifies students of the timing and "content" of the assessment class. They have previously been given the criteria on which they will be assessed. During the actual assessment, the teacher gives both oral and physical directions to the students; students perform the particular movements (which have been learned and practiced in class), and the teacher assesses them according to the criteria (see below).

There are two strands in the assessment program:

1) **Progress assessment - which considers the (quality of) progress the student has made from the time they entered the class to the time they exit (ie is over a 13 week period)**

    The teachers are the sole assessors for this assessment procedure. Each of the half semester progress marks is combined and averaged, then combined with the assessment mark for the standard achieved at the end of the term (see below) to arrive at a final grade for the student. Using two teachers (ie multiple assessors) for the progress assessment is an attempt to remove individual bias from the assessment procedure.

    The students' skill level at entry is compared with that at the end of the half semester and they must make make some progress in order to pass. In an effort to record what that initial skill was like at entry, video taping has been tried but was not found to be particularly useful. Instead the teachers "hold in their heads" what the skill of each student was like at entry and compare that with the end of "session" performance; long contact hours and relatively small groups make this possible, but the contributor of this case study is still considering other ways of addressing this situation.

2) **Product or Standard assessment - which is concerned with the level the student has reached at the end of each semester.**

    This assessment is undertaken at the end of the semester. Students are assessed by four assessors (three external, ie teachers from other classes or performers from outside of the university, and the class teacher). Once again, using multiple assessors is an attempt to reduce bias in the assessment.

    For an hour and a half the group of students perform the routines that they have practiced in class over the semester for the assessors. Students wear numbers back and front to ensure correct identification. No instructions or directions are given by the teacher. The judges both sit and move around the studio in order to assess each student.

    Each of the criteria is given a mark, and all marks are aggregated and converted into a grade of either HD, D, CR, P1, P2, F.

Criteria

Assessment criteria for each of these strands are as follows:

Progress assessment

*   Attendance
*   Ability to focus attention on training of the body
*   Overall increase in ability to move with clarity
*   Ability to hear and implement teacher's suggestions and/or corrections
*   Ability to maintain teacher's suggestions or corrections for an appreciable time
*   Ability to give graciously through movement projection
*   Space - clarity in the use of space in technique study
*   Dynamics - ability to move in various tempi, with various appropriate tensions
*   Time - clarity of rhythms in technique study

- Independence - ability to focus and work responsibly when not receiving individual instruction
- Sociability - ability to dance with and around others
- Imagination - ability to extend movement creatively beyond what has been asked for

Product (standard) assessment

- Clarity of execution (an amalgamation of some of the progress assessment criteria) - mainly concerned with alignment and placement
- Focus of performer - concentration and awareness
- Accuracy of detail - sequences, tempi, rhythms, tensions

Grades

The weighting of each of the assessment strands (ie progress or standard) is determined by each teacher and class at each of the different levels. For example while Level 1 may be weighted at 20% for the progress assessment and 80% for the product assessment, it is possible for Level 2 to have the reverse weighting. Any student who misses more than 25% of classes of a practical nature automatically fails the subject. Any student failing the course, with a mark of 47-49% is offered a supplementary assessment, which is judged once again by four assessors.

Strengths and limitations

The educator who provided this case study commented on the major limitation as being the inherent difficulty in assessing qualitative differences in performance, and the doubts that assessors have as to how well they are doing this, how biased they might be for certain aspects of performance. Using a number of different assessors (ie external and internal) helps reduce this bias.

The students appear to be "happy" with the system of assessment, and wherever difficulties arise these are addressed in an open fashion.

■

Comments

It has been interesting in collecting case studies from so many disciplines to see that except when they are trying to assess "creative" abilities, such as those covered in this module, few educators are trying to reward the progress students make rather than only the final standard of their performance. The balance between progress and performance standard is negotiated in the case described above, though Roche tells us that the students tend to accept the teachers' views about what balance between improvement and achievement is most appropriate. (As one might predict, when the class is taught by someone who is primarily a professional performer and not on the full-time staff of the University, the emphasis is usually on the final performance, while the full-time University staff tend to take more interest in the progress.) In other cases, e.g. in Case study 46 in the preceding section of this module, the emphasis is on the progress and the student could pass even if the final exhibition were not considered to be very successful.

Because of our awareness of some of the unwanted side-effects of adding and averaging marks to determine grades (see "Conflation" below), we asked Roche whether the Department of Dance had ever considered not quantifying the assessment of the two aspects of the students' work and simply asking the various assessors to give a general descriptive rating to the performance and using those to determine final grades. He advised that students are given verbal feedback on their performance but the practice of quantifying the assessment so as to arrive at a grade has not been questioned to date.

Case study 49
Assessing performance - descriptive criteria

Case study from Music
David Lockett, University of Adelaide

A CAUT Teaching Development project gave us the lead to this case study. We saw materials produced by the Advisory Centre for University Education (ACUE) at the University of Adelaide which described workshops on assessment and criteria-setting; included were criteria for judging a musical performance and we managed to track down David Lockett who provided materials from the Elder Conservatorium of Music. Most of the material below is taken from handouts provided to students.

Context
In a 3-year Bachelors degree in Music, the Performance subject constitutes half of the year's load for students (12 points out of 24).

Abilities
Performance criteria are distributed to the students. They are told:

> *In considering the matter of performance assessment, the Department has devised the following list of specific criteria. This should be a useful guide to students as a general indication of the main elements to which they should be directing their attention in their daily practice. Assessment will be based on a combination of all appropriate elements.*

Technical proficiency
- articulation
- tonal quality
- accuracy
- agility
- posture
- memorisation
- intonation
- diction (if applicable)

Musicianship
- sense of style
- use of colour
- phrasing
- line
- dynamic differentiation
- rhythm
- tonal balance
- improvisation (if applicable)

Musical character / temperament
- sense of individual personality
- interpretive qualities
- ability to communicate emotion
- sense of involvement
- personal presentation

Overall impact

Assessment method

Assessment in performance comprises three areas:

1. Teacher's report (based on standard of achievement, progress and technical development, punctuality and attendance).
2. Performance class assessment (one or more performances during the course of the year of a duration equal to half that of the end-of-year examination).
3. End-of-year examination. Students must pass this in order to pass the subject for the year.

As students progress through the three years, the teacher's report (item 1 above) decreases in weight from 25% to 15% to 0%, and the final performance (item 3) gets longer and counts more (50% to 60% to 75%). The class assessment (item 2) stays at 25%

End of year examination/recital

Choice of programme

The student has the choice of his/her programme, subject to approval by staff members in the appropriate instrument or vocal panel. Students are encouraged, as far as practicable, to study a range of pieces from different periods. Examination programmes are to be submitted well before the examination period. It is essential that students conform to the required length of time for their examinations.

Assessment criteria

Practical examinations are conducted by a panel of examiners who will take into account the following criteria:
- Technical mastery of music
- Appreciation of style
- Interpretation
- General presentation

The examiners in marking will pay attention not only to accuracy of notes and time, but also to other things inherent in a good performance, for example, quality of touch, variety and gradation of tone, choice of tempo, observance of marks of expression, rhythm, phrasing and accent.

Membership of examination panels

First and second year students have a panel of three examiners for the end of year recital/ examination.

Third year performance students, Graduate Diploma and Honours students have a panel of four examiners, including a non-voting chair. In the event of controversy, the chair will exercise a casting vote.

A student's teacher is not a member of the assessment panel.

Examination procedures

At the conclusion of the examination, each examiner will without discussion write down their percentage mark and hand it to the chair. The aggregate percentage will be the provisional score. Acceptance of this mark by the panel will then be confirmed by mutual consent. Discussion will ensue only if there is controversy over the mark.

➤

In first and second year examinations, one report will be submitted which will consist of the balanced view of all the examiners. The aggregate mark will be on this report which will be signed by each examiner.

In third year, Graduate Diploma and Honours examinations, signed individual reports from each of the three voting members of the panel will be submitted. All reports should be submitted within 48 hours of the examination and copies will be made available to students (for whom the report is written) upon request.

Other relevant information

All results are to be regarded as provisional until they have been ratified at examiners' meetings. A student's teacher will not be a member of the assessment panel, but may be present during the examination and available afterwards for comment. The teacher does not have speaking or voting rights but may contribute to the discussion if invited to do so by the examiners.

Students must be allowed to play their whole programme provided that it remains within the specified playing time.

In the event of a public recital, members of panels should be present at least five minutes before they are required to examine and should report to the chair before taking their seat in the auditorium. If the chair or any member of a specific panel is concerned that irregularities have occurred, or that the marking standards of one panel within an instrumental category are considerably different from another panel and cannot amicably achieve co-operation, he/she should raise the issue with the Board of Examiners at the end of the examination period. In the (unavoidable) event that there is not the full constitution of panel members, the student has the option of proceeding or not. The student may opt to reschedule the examination or continue it by giving written consent.

One copy of the music to be played must be made available to the examiners in first and second year examinations. For third year and above, two copies of the music are to be provided.

Criteria and grading

Assessment guidelines for performance subjects

High Distinction (85% - 100%)

This category is reserved for those performances which show exceptional achievement in all aspects. They demonstrate flair, individuality and maturity of the highest order.

Distinction (75% - 84%)

Performances at this level will show an outstanding technical and musical achievement, combined with flair, imagination and an individual musical personality. All sections of the programme will be of a consistently high standard. In particular, the following characteristics will be evident:
- A consistently high level of accuracy and technical facility
- A highly developed structural understanding, evidenced by excellence in phrasing and an effective organisation of dynamics
- A well-developed sense of line and musical momentum
- A thoroughly reliable rhythmic sense, including consistent pulse and accurate subdivisions
- Excellent quality and range of tone
- A high level of concentration and musical involvement

- Well developed sense of style, combining historical knowledge with convincing communication of character and emotion.

Credit (65% - 74%)

Performances at this level will show an above average technical and musical achievement. Compared with the distinction category, there may not be the same flair or imagination but other elements will be present to a substantial degree. In particular, the following characteristics will be evident:

- A high level of accuracy and a well developed technical facility
- A good understanding of musical structure, evidenced by suitable phrasing and appropriate treatment of dynamics
- A good sense of line and musical momentum
- A reliable rhythmic sense, including consistent pulse and accurate subdivisions
- Good quality and range of tone
- Good concentration and musical involvement
- Good sense of style, combining historical knowledge with an ability to communicate character and emotion

Pass Division 1 (55% - 64%)

This category represents an average level of achievement. The programme is well known technically, but may appear untidy at times and may not be completely consistent from one work to another. It shows evidence of sincere effort and solid musical understanding but does not have the polish or control found in the higher categories.

The playing could well demonstrate the following characteristics:
- Generally secure technique but perhaps lacking in polish and consistency
- An adequate understanding of phrasing
- Limited variety in dynamics and colour
- Limitations in tonal quality
- Some sense of style but lacking a confident projection of mood and character

Pass Division 2 (50% - 54%)

Playing in this category is only barely acceptable. It will normally demonstrate serious technical limitations together with a lack of musical understanding and involvement.

Fail (0% - 49%)

This grade is awarded when the performance shows a serious lack of basic technical and musical achievement. The playing will be marred by technical insecurity and there will be little evidence of coherent musical projection. A supplementary examination will be offered when the result is in the 45% - 49% range.

Strengths and limitations

The procedures are well-established and working satisfactorily. There are some inconsistencies between different examiners but these are normally resolved through discussion.

The documentation for students needs to be clarified from time to time. It is difficult to set out such a large amount of detail in a clear, simple format.

Detailed reports are made available to students as a source of feedback.

■

Comment

In this case study we see well-defined descriptive criteria for a performance. As in the case study from Dance, assessors give a mark as a percentage and those marks are averaged to determine a grade. In the case of the Music panels, discussion may follow if there is some concern about the grade.

The following discussion raises some concerns about such processes which apply equally to all attempts to quantify students' achievement and determine an overall mark by simple averaging of results expressed numerically.

Conflation

Quantifying the evaluation of students' work is common throughout the case studies we collected. In most institutions educators are required to attach a number to a grade even if there was no numerical rating used to determine the grade. That is, for instance, at the University of New South Wales if a teacher grades a term project and decides it is an HD (High Distinction) and that is the only piece of assessable work in the subject, the teacher still has to enter on the official grade sheets a numerical grade between 85 and 100, as well as the HD. This enables a calculation of an average grade over the session, year or degree program. This is not the place to get into a discussion of the administrative practices which press academics into doing things which might not be really desirable, but we do want to raise just a few of the possible problems with attempts to quantify and combine results of assessments.

When we are combining results of different assessments, one of the things we should review is the *spread of the marks* given to different tasks or to the same task by different markers. This is important because where there is a wide range of marks, they will have a greater impact on final grades than a narrow range of marks.

Consider an exaggerated example: In an English literature course, there are two essay assignments. Lecturer A marks the first and Lecturer B marks the second. Marks are given out of 20. Lecturer A's marks range from 3 to 19, but Lecturer B awards 15 to everyone on the second assignment. While the two assignments are meant to be equally weighted in calculating the final result, the second will have no impact at all on the rank order of students.

Similarly, two markers assessing the same task may not have equal impact on the outcomes if they do not use the same range of marks. There are, however, both relatively simple and quite complex ways of "stretching" the range of one set of marks to match the other.

We shall borrow an example from Rowntree (1987, pp221-224) . Four students sit two examinations which are marked out of 100 and meant to have equal weight; here are their scores and ranks:

Student	A	B	C	D
Exam 1 score	10	21	38	50
Rank	4	3	2	1
Exam 2 score	100	95	85	80
Rank	1	2	3	4

Add the scores and we get the following:

Student	A	B	C	D
Total score	110	116	123	130
Rank	4	3	2	1

The ranking is exactly the same as on Exam 1, though the scores are closer together after Exam 2.

A crude way to adjust Exam 2 marks to match the spread of Exam 1 marks is the nomogram: one draws lines connecting the two highest scores and the two lowest scores; then one uses the point of intersection to determine a line from the second highest score on Exam 1 to the scaled second highest score for Exam 2.

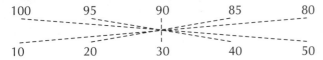

Once the marks are scaled in this way, the new results are as follows:

Student	A	B	C	D
Score Exam 1	10	21	38	50
Scaled score Exam 2	50	40	20	10
Total	60	61	58	60
Rank	2.5	1	4	2.5

Rowntree reminds us that real-life results are unlikely to be this dramatic. Students who do well on one task or question - or with one marker - tend to do well on other tasks or with other markers. However, we do need to be aware of the possibility of such outcomes.

The other point to make here is that the nomogram is a very crude way of scaling marks. It is better practice to calculate standard deviation and mean and standardise all marks to a common mean and standard deviation. Many standard texts take up the statistical issues: see, for instance, Ebel and Frisbie (1986), Oosterhof (1987), Theobald (1974).

When are conflation problems really a problem?

The simple answer is that when one is using a norm-referenced grading system (see Glossary and Index for further discussions), one needs to know the range of marks and understand the differential impact if the ranges are not similar. In a norm-referenced system the students are compared with each other and their rank order determines the grade they are awarded. If, as is often the case, there is an expectation that only a small percentage of students will be awarded an HD, a slightly larger percentage will get a D, and so on, then the rank order is indeed very important to the students near the "cut-off points".

If, however, one is using a criterion-referenced system in which one specifies that a particular grade is achieved when a student achieves a certain number of objectives, it may make perfectly good sense simply to add percentages:

> *...if Billy has reached 80% of the organic chemistry objectives and 60% of the inorganic objectives, it means something to say he has reached 70% of the chemistry objectives; he can be compared directly with students who have attained, say, 77% or 64%. The fact that his 80% was almost the poorest achievement in his group because all did very well and at much the same level of performance, while his 60% attainment put him well out in front on 'inorganic' which seemed to spread people out more, is neither here nor there.*

> *(Rowntree, 1987, pp225-6)*

On the other hand, in a criterion-referenced system, one may specify that students must attain 7 out of 10 of the objectives for each of the two areas of study. In that case Billy's performance would not be acceptable, and averaging of marks is pointless. The issue is being sure one knows what the implications of following different procedures really are and whether one is reaching conclusions which really mean what one thinks they do.

What do marks mean anyway?

Rowntree (1987, pp227-40) suggests that marks like "75" or grades like "Credit" do not really contain much information regardless of how carefully we arrive at them. We only know that Jane is better than Joe or possibly that she is good at the majority of things she was expected to attain, but we do not know whether she excels at retention of facts but is not so good at synthesis, or whether she is wonderful in a clinical situation but falls apart under the pressure of a classroom written examination.

One solution is profiling.

Profiles

We have, in fact, seen many profiles throughout these modules. A checklist is a type of profile; it tells a student on which aspects of an assignment they have done well and on which they may need to make more effort (see Index for examples and more discussion).

A transcript of grades provided to a student on graduation is a very simple profile. A dentist seeking a graduate to join her practice would be likely to value the student with high grades in clinical subjects rather than one with high grades in research methodology, while a university department looking for a young researcher and supervisor of research students might prefer the second student.

However, profiles usually are more complex, detailed reports, often with some narrative element in which the assessor comments on the attainment of particular goals of the subject or program of study. In the case study above, each of the many assessors involved in judging students' technique might have contributed a brief comment highlighting what was most and least impressive about each students' performance. Rowntree (1987, p235-6) argues that such commentaries are:

> *revealed quite transparently as opinion, especially if different assessors produce different opinions of the student. It can be seen to be describing the student through the assessor's human, perhaps fallible responses. Hence those responses, and the perhaps debatable criteria on which they are based, are no longer shielded by the objective-seeming grade to which they would otherwise have been reduced.*

Profiles are:

> *formats for the more manifest (more explained and more fully displayed) portrayal of students. To the extent that they are more manifest they are also more accountable - more likely, for example, to be challenged by students*
>
> *(Law, 1984, p2).*

Of course it may be uncomfortable to have to explain your judgments in detail to students, but obviously those judgments are more likely to encourage the desired learning outcomes if students understand their strengths and weaknesses. Profiles certainly serve formative purposes of assessment; they also serve summative purposes in better communicating to those who use summative evaluations of student achievement such things as exactly what it is students can and cannot do, what attitudes they have displayed and so on.

Broadfoot (1987) highlights the many decisions to be made if one wishes to move to use of profiles:

- Purpose - summative or formative or both? To enable negotiation of learning contract, for diagnosis, for pastoral purposes, for external use?
- Who is being profiled? Students in particular programs only? All students?
- Who contributes to the profile? Teacher? Panel of assessors? Student?
- Who uses it? Student only? Other teachers? Institution? External people?
- Who owns it? Student? Institution? Higher education system?
- What does it cover? Aspects of subject achievement? Cross-curricular skills? Personal qualities? Work skills? Extra-curricular activities?
- What recording techniques are used? Student reflections? Record of student-teacher negotiation? Teachers' comments? Comment bank? Grid?
- How is process to be managed? How often? How reported? Where stored?
- How is the record validated? External accreditation? Moderation?

All of the above is more difficult if one is thinking of changing a system for a program of study or an institution (as has been done in many schools). But it is worth thinking hard about what goes on a simple checklist as well.

In the case study which follows, as in the ones above, we see attempts to be specific about criteria, give students detailed information in advance of assessment, and provide meaningful feedback as well as meeting the institutions' demands for traditional grades. What is different is the method of quantifying the judgments.

Case study 50
Profiling achievement

50

Case study from Design (Visual Communication)
Jenny Wilson, University of Technology Sydney

In the following case study we highlight the use of a type of profiling to report on students' achievement. The case is presented as given to us by Wilson.

Context

The Bachelor of Design (Visual Communication) is a full time course offered over eight semesters. In 1991 a Problem Based Learning curriculum was introduced which aimed to offer a realistic model of design practice. The learning objectives of all separate subjects were integrated and reconceptualised to offer a holistic learning experience. Each semester, students enrol in a single subject. Theory lectures and tutorials establish the context for the project activity of the design studio which involves students in creative problem solving, and the design process of visualising, evaluating and refining ideas. Practical experience gained in technical workshops and media laboratories supports the development and realisation of design solutions.

➤

The integrated PBL strategy provides the ideal framework for study in 3rd and 4th years which must be flexible to accommodate the learning needs of students aiming to enter the diverse arena of professional practice. Senior students undertake personally directed, professionally demanding design projects negotiated through a learning contract with a supervising lecturer. By this stage students have gained the necessary understanding, processing ability and technical competence to apply theory to practice and visualise design solutions through the skillful manipulation of media and visual production technologies. Project work can be assessed effectively using criterion referencing and can involve students in the process by using peer and self assessment strategies.

This is not the situation in the earlier 1st and 2nd years. Students enrol in the study of visual communication with little knowledge of design as a field of practice or experience of designing as a methodology. Each student presents a very different profile of motivation, awareness, understanding, visual literacy and technical skill. At this early stage overall group and individual performance is very erratic as each student must learn unfamiliar content, experience unaccustomed methods of teaching and acquire many new skills. Consistent levels of performance are rarely achieved across all learning objectives. This makes it impossible to adhere faithfully to the criterion referenced strategy of assessment used in later years as few if any would achieve more than a pass and the pressure to scale and spread the range of marks would exacerbate the mystification of an already complex and contentious process.

Teaching in the single subject must accommodate this diversity of competencies, knowledge and skills. The numerous learning objectives must be assessed by individual members of the design project team responsible for teaching each specialised study component. As students are enrolled in one subject, summative assessment consists of one grade and percentage mark (the mark is a requirement of the university which was unsuccessfully challenged). The production and receipt of a single grade and mark has created real problems for students, teaching staff, coordinating examiners, and ultimately the assessment appeals committee.

Initially the assessment grade and mark was an aggregation of individually assessed components. This final grade was not only subject to problems of conflation [see discussion above] but also failed to reveal a student's strengths and weaknesses or offer any formally documented recognition of performance in any one study component. The percentage mark demanded by the university could not be statistically (or ideologically) defended.

The assessment process became a nightmare of explanations and justifications to informal queries and formal appeals. Angry frustration was expressed by both the student body and members of the teaching teams as the outcome of assessment had become a "meaningless mark". In order to offer students a clear indication of performance in each learning objective and ensure the accountability of all contributing to assessment, alternative strategies were researched and tested.

Evaluation revealed a number of issues. In our study field which promotes idiosyncratic creative solutions to "ill-structured" problems requiring the production of visual work, the qualitative assessment of learning outcomes is easily open to accusations of subjective bias. We identified that opinions were often at variance when assessing levels of achievement as good (credit) or very good (distinction) but proved to be relatively consistent at the extreme levels of fail, pass and high distinction.

The degree of accuracy and accountability of all the strategies we trialed seemed to bear a direct relationship to their complexity and cumbersome nature. Over 60% of the teaching is offered and assessed by sessional staff accustomed to using a personally devised system. The burden on the subject co-ordinating examiners to initiate a new assessment strategy requiring consistent implementation by all staff was identified as a potential problem. To achieve all objectives, the solution had to be perceived by staff and students as better than current practice, simpler to understand, easier to use and a more effective piece of communication.

➤

Criteria

The solution that evolved required the learning objectives to be very precisely detailed. Equally valued assessment criteria were devised. This increased the number of criteria but required each to be assessed at one of only three levels of achievement described as:

EXCELLENT, SATISFACTORY, UNSATISFACTORY.

It was agreed to establish a minimum of 10 criteria (which could be expanded) to reflect the primary learning objectives progressively developed each semester. These are summarised as follows:

1. Depth and breadth of library research
2. Evidence of visual research and experimentation
3. Investigation of phenomenological characteristics
4. Commitment to sourcing external suppliers and expertise
5. Design processing and critical reflection
6. Clarity of communication and practicality of form
7. Innovation and appropriateness of concept applied to solution
8. Quality of detailing and refinement
9. Ability to communicate visually and personally present concepts and solutions
10. Impact and engagement with user/ viewer

The assessment document that resulted indicates all assessment criteria and the level achieved in all learning objectives. It is straightforward to understand and use and provides students with detailed written feedback. It also offers a good visual guide which at a glance indicates overall performance, degree of consistency, strengths and weaknesses, high levels of achievement and areas of concern. The basic format is applicable to all stages of study as it is ideally designed for criterion referenced assessment. To assess students in Years 1 and 2 the criteria are expanded to provide greater detail and the system can be subverted for use as a numerical chart by placing values for the three standards as follows:

2 = Excellent level of achievement/ performance
1 = Satisfactory level of achievement/ performance
0 = Not yet achieved a satisfactory level
X = No evidence made available (this alerts students and assessor to missing work)

Grades

The following table gives a basic guide to implementation:

10 criteria assessed @ 2	=	20/20	100%	
9 criteria assessed @ 2 and 1 @ 1	=	19/20	95%	
8 criteria assessed @ 2 and 2 @ 1	=	18/20	90%	
7 criteria assessed @ 2 and 3 @ 1	=	17/20	85%	HIGH DISTINCTION
6 criteria assessed @ 2 and 4 @ 1	=	16/20	80%	
5 criteria assessed @ 2 and 5 @ 1	=	15/20	75%	DISTINCTION
4 criteria assessed @ 2 and 6 @ 1	=	14/20	70%	
3 criteria assessed @ 2 and 7 @ 1	=	13/20	65%	CREDIT
2 criteria assessed @ 2 and 8 @ 1	=	12/20	60%	
1 criteria assessed @ 2 and 9 @ 1	=	11/20	55%	
10 criteria assessed @ 1	=	10/20	50%	PASS
9 criteria assessed @ 1 and 1 @ 0	=	9/20	45%	FAIL
8 criteria assessed @ 1 and 2 @ 0	=	8/20	40%	(and so on)

By simple addition a mark is achieved which falls into a band that equates to a grade. A typical assessment document for students in Years 1 and 2 is expanded to include 20 criteria each numerically valued at half of those given above. Achievement in each is assessed by the lecturer responsible for the teaching input. Selected criteria may be assessed by the student group, by the individual student or by invitation (eg. a client or visiting designer). This is decided at the outset of project briefing and may be initiated by staff or students. The subject co-ordinating examiner overviews the assessment process at mid-semester and end of semester. At both times the matrix of marks is also reviewed by the full-time staff on the design project team who assist with advice on handling issues such as idiosyncratic marking standards (which become clearly exposed), medical certificates, poor attendance and resubmitted work.

At a personal interview each student receives a copy of the assessment document which may include additional written advice. This is mailed to students who do not attend interviews. Students either providing insufficient evidence for assessment or failing in one or more criteria but passing on aggregate are required to negotiate the submission of additional work through a learning contract.

Strengths and limitations

Although the process remains time consuming to organise, it is a vast improvement on any previous strategy. It easily accommodates various inputs according to the demands of the problem and the stage of learner autonomy. Excellence can be acknowledged and strengths and weaknesses can be clearly identified by staff and students. The introduction of the strategy has been well received by students and most sessional staff but less enthusiastically by those who are reluctant to demystify their approach. An improved level of equity in marking standards and feedback quality has been achieved. The integration of summative and formative assessment has, in particular, insured open communication. This avoids confusion between what is said and what is meant by the grade and mark that is finally awarded. (The design project team's emphasis). ■

Comment

This procedure avoids an attempt to make fine distinctions between levels of achievement on each of the criteria (53 or 55? 76 or 79?) and also avoids the problems associated with different markers using a different range of marks. At the same time, it is possible for the teaching team to provide the grade required by the University.

Conclusion

This module has highlighted the assessment of abilities related to designing, creating, and performing. While these abilities tend to be associated with 'artistic' disciplines, it is worth remembering, as Schön frequently reminds us in his many writings on professional practice (see Annotated Bibliography), that there are elements of artistry in the practice of management and in clinical settings and, indeed, in just about any activity. The issues which have surfaced in discussions of the case studies - whether to emphasise technical skills or artistry in assessment, how to establish criteria when people do not necessarily agree on what constitutes 'quality', whether to assess improvement or achievement, possibilities of gender bias, whether and how to quantify results - have come up in other modules as well. We hope the cases in this module will be relevant to educators in a wide variety of disciplines and prompt them to think about the ways their students might demonstrate the abilities associated with designing, creating and performing.

References

Anthony, K. (1987). Private reactions to public criticism; students, faculty and practicing architects state their views on design juries in architectural education. *Journal of Architectural Education*, 40(3), 2-11.

Boysen, O. (1994). Integration of engineering and design. In P.J. Parr & S.F. Johnston (Eds.), *Proceedings 6th Annual Australasian Association for Engineering Education Conference* (pp.247-51). Sydney: University of Technology Sydney.

Broadfoot, P. (1987). *Introducing Profiling: A Practical Manual*. London: Macmillan Education Ltd.

Churches, A. (1989). A national design-and-build competition. In *Proc. World Conference on Engineering Education for Advancing Technology* (pp.535-539.). Sydney: IEAust.

Davey, R., & Wheway, R. (1986). Creative design competitions as means of teaching design in first year. In *Proc. Conference on Teaching Engineering Designers for the 21st Century* (pp.46-53). Sydney: School of Mechanical & Industrial Engineering, University of New South Wales.

Ebel, R. L., & Frisbie, D. A. (1986). *Essentials of Educational Measurement*. Englewood Cliffs, NJ: Prentice-Hall.

Frederickson, M. P. (1993). Gender and racial bias in design juries. *Journal of Architectural Education*, 47(1), 38-48.

Hall, R. M., & Sandler, B. R. (1982). *The Classroom Climate: A Chilly One for Women?* Association of American Colleges, Project on the Status and Education of Women.

Kingsland, A. (1989). The assessment process in architecture at Newcastle. In B. Wallis (Eds.), *Problem-based Learning, The Newcastle Workshop* (pp.121-30). Newcastle, NSW: Faculty of Medicine, University of Newcastle.

Kingsland, A., & Cowdroy, R. (1991). Assessment of multiple criteria: focus on skills. In B.Ross (Ed.), *Research and Development in Higher Education* (pp.163-167). Sydney: HERDSA (Higher Education Research and Development Society of Australasia).

Law (1984). *Uses and Abuses of Profiling: a Handbook on Reviewing and Recording Student Experience and Achievement*. London: Paul Chapman Publishing Ltd (1988 reprint).

McMasters, J., & Ford, S. (1990). An industry view of enhancing design education. *Engineering Education,* 80, 526-529.

McNally, N. (1993). Integrating two design cultures. *International Journal of Mechanical Engineering Education*, 21(3), 283-296.

Nightingale, P., & Sohler, C. (1994). *Considering Gender*. Sydney: Higher Education Research and Development Society of Australasia.

Oosterhof, A. C. (1987). Obtaining intended weights when combining scores. *Educational Measurement: Issues and Practice,* 6(4), 29-37.

Redmond, J. (1986). Product design and education for the art of engineering. In *Proceedings Conference on Teaching Engineering Designers for the 21st Century* (pp.130-33). Sydney: School of Mechanical and Industrial Engineering, University of New South Wales.

Rowntree, D. (1987). *Assessing Students: How Shall We Know Them?* (2nd ed.). London: Kogan Page.

Schön, D. (1990) *Educating the Reflective Practitioner: Toward a New Design for Teaching and Learning in the Professions*. San Francisco: Jossey-Bass.

Theobald, J. (1974). *Classroom Testing: Principles and Practice*. Hawthorn, VIC: Longman.

Thomas, K. (1990). *Gender and Subject in Higher Education*. Buckingham: SRHE and Open University Press.

Walkerdyne, V., & the Girls and Mathematics Unit, (1989). *Counting Girls Out*. London: Virago Press.

West, H., Flowers, W., & Gilmore, D. (1990). Hands-on design in engineering education: learning by doing what? *Engineering Education,* 80, 560-564.

MODULE 8

COMMUNICATING

PEGGY NIGHTINGALE

Module 8
Communicating

The cases considered in this module are ones in which the teacher is primarily interested in assessing students' ability to communicate. Obviously, students must communicate something and the assessment cannot ignore the content but the emphasis is on effective communication. The teacher may be interested in oral, written or visual forms of communication. In addition to the common presentation-to-others types of communication, this module addresses the assessment of one-to-one communications and interpersonal communication.

This module covers broad abilities such as:
- arguing
- describing
- advocating
- interviewing
- negotiating
- presenting

Section 1: Communicating in writing

Themes

- Content or style
- Establishing marking criteria
- Criteria-referenced or norm-referenced?
- Scoring guides
- Grades, feedback and learning
- Relationship between content and communication
- Personal vs academic
- Setting questions
- Code words
- How much to expect when time is limited

Techniques

- Checklists and forms for feedback
- Holistic scoring
- Scoring guides
- Self-evaluation
- Portfolios

Case studies

51. Essay - critical review, Sociology
52. Using checklists, Philosophy
53. Peer reading and self-evaluation, Political Science
54. Portfolio, Mathematics Education

Section 2: Communicating orally

Themes

- Importance of context
- Interpersonal communication
- Importance of clear criteria
- Possible bias by gender or language background

Techniques

- Assessing class participation
- Negotiating criteria with class
- Self-assessment
- Assessing a formal presentation
- Checklists

Case Studies

55. Reporting on interviews, Psychology
56. Assessing class participation, Law
57. Self-assessment of class participation, Law
58. In-class presentations, Geography
59. Formal presentation, Commerce

Section 3: Communicating information visually

Themes

- Alternative modes of communication
- Matching content to communication style

Techniques

- Posters
- Public displays

Case studies

60. Poster presentations, Pharmacy
61. Poster exercise, Geography
62. The Installation Project, Sociology

Module 8

Communicating

Peggy Nightingale

This module will cover tasks where the teacher is primarily interested in assessing students' ability to communicate. Obviously, students must be communicating something and the assessment cannot ignore the content but the emphasis is on effective communication. The module addresses written and oral communication, and those visual forms of communication which are aimed at getting across information (as in a poster). Other, primarily creative, visual forms are covered in Module 7 "Designing, creating, performing".

Section 1

Communicating in writing

The content or the communication?

A writing task appears in each module of this package. Teachers attempt to assess students' abilities to do almost everything by asking them to write about the process or the knowledge required. It seems odd, then, that in Australian higher education, it is extremely rare to find a task set with the explicit and sole purpose of assessing students' ability to communicate effectively in writing. (Lacking local case studies, in this module we use White's account of his teaching in a writing course in an American university (White, 1994) to make compar isons with common Australian practice.) Teachers' objectives almost invariably include developing skills in written communication - by which they usually mean written communication within the conventions of academic style in general and the conventions of their own discipline in particular. However, their assessment tasks and the important criteria by which students' success is judged put the emphasis on the subject content; teachers will even say explicitly, "The chemistry/ anthropology/ mechanics/ literature was right, so I could not fail her/him even though the paper itself was all over the shop." The following case study illustrates this point.

Case study 51
Essay - critical review

51

Case study from Sociology
Patricia Duncan, University of Newcastle

Writing a critical review of assessment practice in a number of subjects under revision at the University of Newcastle, Patricia Duncan described the assessment strategies of a subject known as Health Sociology. The following case study is an edited version of a section of a paper she submitted when she was studying with Sue Toohey in Assessment and Feedback, a Graduate Diploma subject in the UNSW Postgraduate Program in Higher Education.

Context

Health Sociology was one of two first year sociology subjects; it was offered to students in the health sciences, including nursing, medical radiography, occupational therapy, nutrition and dietetics.

Abilities

The objectives for this subject concentrated on knowledge acquisition, rather than skills or attitudes; the basic aim was to provide the students with sociological information from a health perspective.

From the subject handout:

Subject aim:

The aim of this subject is to introduce the student to a sociological perspective with a particular focus on health sociology. This will provide the student with the ability to understand basic sociological concepts and apply them to the health area in the Australian context.

These concepts will then be built on and broadened in subsequent years.

Subject objectives:

At the end of this unit, students will be able to:

- Describe the sociological perspectives and differentiate between the major traditions within the broad perspective (eg. Conflict, Functionalism, Interactionist).
- Understand the key concepts and theories that underpin an analysis of the distribution of health and illness in Australian Society.
- Identify social, economic, political and cultural factors which constitute the context for individual life chances and the distribution of resources - including health.
- Explain the way that the conflict tradition in health sociology provides a foundation for and an explanation of social process and social change.
- Critically assess the assumptions, methods and findings of key selected readings within the research literature.

Figure 8.1

Aims and objectives
Patricia Duncan

➤

Assessment methods and criteria

Assessment consists of two essays, each 30%, and one end-of-year examination (40%).

The first essay is an attempt to foster correct presentation, although it also emphasises critical review of reading material:

> This review (maximum length 800 words) will ask students to critically review one key selected reading. This will provide early assessment and feedback of student skills in written expression and knowledge of fundamental sociological concepts.

The student is given an open choice as to topic, within a broad range of provided readings. This type of question relates to the cognitive nature of the objectives, and can provide both summative and formative assessment. It could be argued that concentration on format at this stage may suggest to the student that those factors are more important than the material being studied since students adapt their learning style to meet the requirements of the test situation. However, it does fulfil three basic functions:

- to aid in student learning;
- to provide a means of communication for student and tutor; and
- to assess the student.

The second assignment is of a broader nature and focuses on both description and analysis. The question is left somewhat ambiguous in the handout and therefore open to student interpretation:

> This essay (maximum length 1500 words) will focus upon the social distribution of health in Australian society, and will assess student skills in research, description **and** analysis.

This may lead to complexity of marking and confusion for the student. However, sample marking criteria are provided at the beginning of the year:

Sample marking criteria

Unacceptable. This grade will only be given if the work does not represent an acceptable effort (including non completion) and if the assignment consists of extensive copying or paraphrasing from readings and/or from the work of other students.

Unsatisfactory. Students will receive this grade if the work done is clearly inadequate. That is, the writer has not understood the basic principles of the subject matter and/or has been unable to express his/her understandings in a comprehensible way.

Marginal. The work is borderline. The writer has made a fair attempt at addressing the question, but has shown an inadequate understanding of the basic principles of the subject-matter and/or unsatisfactory comprehension.

Sufficient. The assignment shows some grasp of the basic principles of the subject-matter and a passing knowledge of the required reading. The work is adequately referenced and shows some coherence.

Good. The assignment shows clear understanding of the basic principles. The ability to integrate the material is clearly evident. There is evidence of additional reading and/or research. The work is coherent and accurate. A deficiency in any of the above may be compensated to some extent by evidence of independent thought.

Figure 8.2
Criteria
Patricia Duncan

> **Excellent.** The assignment shows a thorough understanding of the subject-matter and additional reading and/or research. The work reflects a high level of independent thought, presents an insightful and informed discussion of the topic, is well organised and clearly expressed. The assignment shows that the writer can critically evaluate the subject-matter.

Figure 8.2 *(cont)*
Criteria
Patricia Duncan

We see that these approach Bloom's taxonomy at the upper levels, requiring a high level of evaluation, understanding and independent thought. However, the other levels from "Unacceptable" to "Good" predominantly reflect basic knowledge.

The examination in Health Sociology utilises essay and short answer questions. It is assumed that the same marking criteria are adopted here.

Overall the assessment procedures meet Andresen's tests of honesty, validity and strategic rationality (Andresen, 1993).

Apart from the initial focus on presentation in assignment one, the student is being led toward an understanding of sociological concepts and an ability to review them critically as stated in the objectives.

■

Comment

Duncan calls attention to the fact that criteria for lower levels of achievement emphasise basic knowledge. It is interesting to look again at the criteria for "marginal" and "sufficient" achievement: these grades are determined by the student's ability to persuade the marker that s/he has a grasp of the basic principles of the content. At the "marginal" level, there is no mention of criteria relating to communication skills, style or presentation; at the "sufficient" level, referencing is emphasised and "some coherence" is expected.

The communication intertwined with the content

The problem with trying to separate assessment of content from assessment of communication skills is that it fails to recognise just how deeply intertwined are the effectiveness of communication and a students' understanding of the content. At a very simple level, we can observe basic mechanical errors multiplying when a student is having trouble expressing complex concepts: sentences merge or get terribly tangled; subjects and verbs do not agree in number; tenses get mixed, etc. The student knows, and applies, the "rules" in one section of a paper and somehow forgets them in another.

Example A

Topic: Did the English lower classes have a separate culture in the Eighteenth century?

> I will approach the topic of separate culture by investigating the extent to which the lower classes had a separate culture. Due to commercialisation of sport, literature and arts, culture enjoyed by the lower classes was also shared by the upper classes. Popular culture was one where "everyone participates because it's very idea embraces all the people", including the rich and the poor. Therefore, the lower classes did not have a separate culture. However, I wish to argue that they did in fact have a separate culture which was distinguished by riots and festivals.

Example B

A common form of festival was the wake. Wakes were annual feasts celebrating the erection of a parish church. When a church was built it was named after a saint. That very night the community would remain at the church with candles, hence the name 'wake'. As day broke, the festivity began. All thought of reverence and devotion was forgotten. It was a holiday atmosphere. Feasting and drinking characterized these wakes.

These wakes were also characterized by acts of cruelty. Reid sees this as 'crudely functional' as it was a chance to release violent feelings and transfer it from men to animals.

These two typical passages were written by the same student in the same essay. The first, as you would guess, is the opening section. It shows all of the typical first draft problems of a student floundering around trying to figure out what she really thinks. The result is self-contradictory, confused, simple poor writing. But the second passage, while not particularly profound, is of an acceptable standard of communication skill; it is clear, succinct, and grammatically correct.

Example C

Thompson has pointed out the problems of the use of "Vulgar Marxism" when he says:

What I am calling in question is...that it is possible to describe a mode of production in "economic" terms, leaving aside as secondary ("less real") the norms, the culture, the critical concepts around which this mode of production is orgaised...it is an argurment in the head.

In this sense, Burgmann has described 'racism'. which is a sociological concept, as a 'supersrutural manifestation' which,as Thompson protests, is placed in the 'base' as an element of also of 'workdiscipline'. Thus, as Anderson has commented, that by dismissing alternates as 'unimportant' is 'highly questionable' because it ignors the need to present

...the views of of the situation and substituting our own concepts and linking machanisms in their place....but only a satisfactory interpretation of an individual event in as far as the analysis can satisfactorily demonstrate that the actors involved perceived their actions in Marxian class-based terms.

As I will show below, Burgmann's historical account is exposed as 'mechanistic' and reductionist'. Before looking at these problems of Burgmann's article I will deal with the an alalysis of Burgmann's tools of analysis.

Example D

The establishment of a long range weapons program came as a request from the British Prime Minister: on the 3rd of July 1946, the Australian Cabinet approved the joint weapons programme. The program was based on proposals and recommendations by a British expert group called the 'Evatts Committee'. This Committee suggested that Australia would provide the facilities for "...research and development work on guided missiles and supersonic pilotless aircraft." The laboratory was to be located at Salisbury, while the range was to take up an area of huge dimensions (Appendix 2). The Cabinet was assisted in its deliberations by maps of the area displayed on Cabinet walls, which assured them that the white populations were in no danger. Compensation was paid to whire pastoralists; anagnu peoples would be moved out by state government legislation already in place. Nothing was too much trouble, and since Britain was contributing financially to the project, money was not a difficulty.

These two extracts from student work were also written by one student. The first was written in his third year of (successful) university study; the second was written in his first year. The first exhibits an extraordinary level of grammatical and mechanical error as well as failing to make sense. The second is certainly acceptable. Had the student completely forgotten all the rules? We think not. We believe that in struggling to write "good academic" prose he imitated some of the worst characteristics of material he had been reading. We also believe that he had been struggling with very complex political concepts - some of which raised personal and emotional conflicts for him - and that he simply did not know what he was trying to say. It is an extreme case of what happened in the introduction (Example A) above. (See Taylor, Ballard, Beasley, Bock, Clanchy, & Nightingale, 1988 for extended discussion of these examples and the issues they raise.)

52

Case study 52
Using checklists

Case study from Philosophy
John Ozolins, Australian Catholic University

The following case study offers an example of a teacher who is combining the teaching of subject content with the teaching of the discourse of the discipline. Using his own words as much as possible, we merge Ozolins' original submission with additional comments he offered after reading the draft module. Ozolins' checklist or assessment guide has been revised several times; we present the most recent version.

Context

The Department of Theology and Philosophy offers a BA major in Philosophy which may be taken by students in other courses; the major is relatively new so in 1994 the students enrolled in this third year subject were the first to attempt it. At least two previous units of philosophy would have been successfully completed by all students.

The major is designed to develop students' skills in philosophical discourse so that they can critically explore their own beliefs and the beliefs of others. The subject also introduces them to new ideas and general philosophical problems. The background of the students is diverse and they have a range of abilities. The class is small - only 10 students.

Abilities being assessed

Students should be able to:
1) Identify and describe the key issues involved in the question;
2) Argue effectively, using clear, logical and philosophical arguments;
3) Advocate a philosophical position on a question, thereby showing evidence of creative and independent thought;
4) Investigate a question by applying the methods of philosophical research;
5) Present their arguments in a cogent, fluent manner, observing the canons of philosophical writing.

Assessment

The five areas above are assessed through the presentation of two minor papers (1000 words and 25% each) and a major essay (2000 words and 50%). The students are given a choice of topics.

➤

Feedback

A detailed checklist is filled out for each student for each assignment. This checklist is used to guide the preparation of comprehensive written comments. I have used the checklist at several levels from 1st year to 4th year, though it was initially designed for use with advanced undergraduates where there was an emphasis on written assignment work and where detailed feedback seemed to be required.

AUSTRALIAN CATHOLIC UNIVERSITY
Theology and Philosophy Department

ESSAY ASSESSMENT SHEET

Student's name...Assignment Grade.....................

Rating Scale

Argument	5	4	3	2	1	Comments
Accurate exposition of material						
Discussion of key issues/relevance of facts						
Logical development of argument						
Depth and complexity of argument						
Evidence of creative thought/articulation of own ideas						
Structure						
Essay contains Introduction and conclusion						
Paragraphs are linked						
Consistent thread of argument						
Fluent writing						
Succinct writing						
Style						
Accurate spelling, grammatical sentences, correct punctuation						
Presentation (neatness, legibility, layout, general appearance)						
Referencing (correct citation, adequate acknowledgement of sources, consistent use of referencing style)						
Bibliography						
Length						

General comments _____

_____

_____

_____

Figure 8.3
Essay assessment sheet
John Ozolins

➤

The checklist has undergone some changes as a result of lack of specificity in one of the criteria. The area of "general content" has been dropped for this reason and replaced with a criterion under the Argument section called "depth and complexity of argument". This criterion has been included because in the original assessment sheet there did not seem to be any place for giving credit for handling complex and difficult argument.

In designing the structure, I found Bertola and Murphy's (1994) checklist layouts useful and they were also helpful in refining my own checklist.

Marking

The assignment is assessed by giving each criterion a rating and then adding these numerical ratings to arrive at a rough grade for the assignment. Generally, this method works quite well, though sometimes the result is too high or too low when the assignment is considered globally. It is true to say that it is not the only means of determining the grade; sometimes, usually when a grade is borderline, some adjustment of the grade is made. For example, if a student is on the border between a "D" and a "C", other factors may come into play, such as comparison with other similar standard pieces of work by other students.

In coming to write some general comments on the essay a global assessment is made and a judgment made whether the numbers accurately reflect the grade the assignment should receive. Mostly I would say that the assessment seems to fit closely the judgment I would give if a global assessment only were used, but this may mean that I make the judgment first and allocate the ratings accordingly. I am sure the global assessment and the ratings are linked and it is not easy to say definitively how much they influence each other.

There is a weighting of the assessment toward the Argument section and to the Structure section as there are five criteria under each of these two major headings, giving 50 out of a potential 75 points to these two areas. The criteria under the Argument section are weighed up as far as possible independently of each other and although this is not made explicit, probably carry the most weight in determining whether the assignment is satisfactory or not overall.

The Structure section is also important as I regard the structure of the essay as being linked very much to the ability to organise and present the argument in a cogent manner. In actual marking, however, although each of the criteria in the Argument section is clearly distinguishable, this is not always so easy to do in the Structure section. For example, "linkage of paragraphs" and "consistent thread of argument" are sometimes somewhat similar. If a student has good linkage of paragraphs there is often a consistent thread of argument. "Fluent writing" and "succinct writing" are also difficult to separate on many occasions.

The remaining criteria are all used in the assessment, though with perhaps not quite the same weight as the other two major sections. Students are definitely penalised for poor spelling, grammar and punctuation. Presentation is usually satisfactory or higher, rarely poor. As a criterion in the overall assessment it does not carry the same weight as the Style criterion.

Correct referencing and citation of sources to support argument is very important. In the extreme case, this criterion could result in a student failing for plagiarism. Generally, however, if students have referenced correctly and acknowledged sources, this criterion is not as important as the others. It is, as it were, a part of the general understanding of what is to count as an academic piece of work.

An adequate bibliography, using a consistent style, is important. A bibliography of one or two items, depending on the question, would be inadequate. However, by itself this would not mean that the essay is failed. Length of essay is generally not important as a criterion, but is certainly part of a satisfactory piece of work. If the assignment falls short of the required number of words by more than 25%, it will usually fail. This is generally because there are other inadequacies as well. Although a student will be penalised if an assignment is more than 25% longer than required, usually the student will not fail. ➤

Strengths, limitations and problems

In using this checklist I want to develop the skills of students to higher levels of sophistication by providing more detailed feedback about where they need to improve their skills. Certainly student evaluation of the checklist indicates a very high level of appreciation of the feedback they are given. They are also more aware of what is expected of them.

The use of the checklist sheet in the first instance helps in the preparation of comments, but it also helps in consistency of the marking. One of the difficulties in marking essays which may vary greatly in both content and style is the maintenance of consistent marking, especially when all the essays cannot be marked at one sitting. This also reduces the level of subjectivity of the marking.

The limitations of the process are that the amount of time required to do this thoroughly with a large group would perhaps be somewhat prohibitive and secondly, the students need to get the marked essay back fairly promptly so that they can incorporate any suggestions into their next piece of work.

There is probably still room for refinement of the checklist; as I have said, the 15 items are not equally important and the checklist does not make that clear.

Comments

We have not often managed to persuade case study contributors to give us so much detailed thought about the relative importance of various criteria in deciding on an essay grade. We suspect that Ozolins is not unusual in what he values and we know others will find it useful to match their values and assumptions against his. He commented, "I found it a very useful, not to mention challenging exercise going through my checklist to work out exactly how I did the assessment." A special thanks to him.

While Ozolins' class is small and he wondered whether his process would be too time-consuming for large classes, teachers of larger classes have also developed checklists as an aid to more efficient marking, using them to save time in commenting on papers' strengths and weaknesses and to assist several markers to be more consistent in their grading standards.

Ozolins does not say whether the checklist is distributed prior to the first assignment, but he does use it three times in the session. Assuming that such checklists are available to students at the time the assignment is given to them, they also help to clarify teachers' expectations.

As Ozolins notes, the 15 areas covered by the checklist are not equally weighted and this can lead to some confusion and even argument with students when students do well in the minor areas, such as getting the referencing right, but fail to achieve in a key content area, such as "discussion of key issues" or a key communication area, such as "consistent thread of argument". In fact, most teachers seem to use the checklists as a feedback tool but determine the grade through a holistic judgment plus some sort of comparison with the achievement of others in the group. It is interesting that Ozolins describes a process of analytic scoring (adding marks for different criteria) which he checks against a holistic judgment of the quality of the essay. (See Glossary for "holistic" and "analytic".) In a following section we will consider how to make these holistic expectations clearer as well, but for a moment let us consider the reference point for assessment.

Establishing marking criteria

Branthwaite, Trueman and Hartley (1980) established that students and their tutors do not necessarily share the same views about what counts as most important in successful essay writing. Norton (1990) collected information on their strategies in essay-writing from 98 1st year psychology students in a British institute of higher education; the research also obtained interview data from 6 tutors on their marking strategies. Finally, the essays were analysed. While questionnaires suggested students were more concerned with content, tutors claimed to be concerned with argument. Nevertheless, the essays which showed a higher proportion of research based content and a larger number of references got higher marks. Norton does not raise the possibility that tutors' criteria were more content-oriented than they themselves were aware.

Regardless of whether this is the case or not - and our case materials lead us to believe it may well be so, it is absolutely essential to good assessment practice and to improving student learning that criteria are carefully established, adequately communicated to all - students and markers, and adhered to in the marking. Just as the students in the Norton study may have understood the criteria better than the markers, clever students rapidly learn to distinguish between espoused values and those which are actually in use. If the espoused criteria are that quality of written communication is important, but students continue to pass when the content is considered adequate even though it is poorly expressed, students will not put in the effort to edit and polish their written text. The other side of this coin is that the poor expression may well be a symptom of poor understanding of the content and teachers may be finding what they hope is in the paper rather than what is really there.

Probably most of the time teachers establish criteria for grading by themselves; they are solely responsible for the design and administration of their subject. Sometimes there are other markers involved and they may or may not be briefed on the criteria for marking a specific assignment. One workshop exercise we have used many times involves having participants assign a grade of 1-5 to six short essays and then compare their judgments. As everyone fears, there is virtually no inter-marker reliability. But after a very short briefing on criteria - both relating to content and to presentation - the agreement between markers improves dramatically (see Nightingale, 1986).

Anyone who has been involved in mass marking of state or national examinations has had the experience of working with a group to reach agreement on the expectations for a set of papers, and has been impressed with how few substantial disagreements occur when papers are double- or even triple-marked. White (1994) covers at length issues of large-scale testing and establishing the shared criteria for collaborative marking, but this sort of work is not common to most academics in higher education. What we can learn from such programs is the importance of thinking through the criteria by which an assignment is to be marked at the time of designing the question and of finalising criteria by trial marking some papers.

As we noted previously, few courses in Australian higher education are designed solely to teach writing skills; in fact, a number of us have argued that higher level academic writing skills are better taught within subject discipline contexts. This does place a demand on the subject teachers to become specific about outcomes in the communication sphere as well as in the content knowledge areas. Perhaps the goals of an advanced general education writing course in an American college, (White's, 1994) practice which we mentioned at the beginning of this section) will help teachers in other disciplines clarify their expectations.

Goals: Advanced Writing Course

The goals for the course were defined as follows: 'to develop students' writing skills, not necessarily knowledge of any specific subject matter, at a higher level of competence and sophistication than in freshman composition.' The goals were then clarified by the following specifications:

Students should learn to:

1. Develop awareness of audience, control of tone, and appropriate use of individual style in various modes of discourse.

2. Define their intentions in a given rhetorical situation and organize and express ideas according to their purpose.

3. Use sources properly to support their ideas; synthesize source material, incorporate it into their writing, and document sources.

4. Demonstrate competence in recognizing and using conventions of edited American English.

5. Express and develop complex ideas in coherent, logical fashion.

6. Revise as well as edit their work, through regular rewriting of assignments.

Figure 8.4
Goals: advanced writing course
(White, 1994, pp221-2)

Criteria-referenced assessment or norm-referenced?

In a paper in the *Journal of Geography in Higher Education*, Iain Hay (Flinders University) and Edward Delaney (University of Colorado) describe having students use writing groups to give each other feedback on a final draft paper prior to submitting it (Hay & Delaney, 1994). One section of the paper makes the point that students are unaccustomed to working together in this way partly because of the competition engendered by "common curve-related assessment strategies" (which are norm-referenced). Hay and Delaney moved towards criterion-referenced assessment as an alternative. (See also Index and Glossary for discussion of norm- and criteria-referencing.)

Reflecting on our own practice, that of many people with whom we have worked, and that described in case materials submitted to this project, we have come to the conclusion that even where criteria are specified as in Ozolins' checklist - or indeed, the very similar checklist used by Hay and Delaney and their students (see following page) - it is common practice to use some sort of norm-referencing at the stage of determining the final mark. That is, the best papers in the batch still get 'A' or 'High Distinction' even if they were a bit disappointing to us - maybe 'A-' or 'Distinction'; the majority get 'C' or 'Pass'; and a few fail. There is often considerable pressure from school or faculty or university assessment review committees to meet expectations of a distribution of grades pretty much like that just described. If we are genuine about establishing clear criteria and then using them to determine grades, we may have to defend ourselves and our students when an "unacceptable" number of high, or low, grades are given.

Hay and Delaney suggest that if one is using a checklist of criteria, those which are considered essential or most important could be italicised.

Student grades may be determined by identifying a number of objectives as most important or essential and coupling those variables with less important others to establish minimum performance levels associated with each grade. An example of one possible assessment scale is shown [below]:

Grade Requirements to achieve grade

A All essential criteria at satisfactory standard; > 75% of other criteria satisfactory.

B All essential criteria at satisfactory standard; > 60% of other criteria satisfactory.

C All essential criteria at satisfactory standard; > 50% of other criteria satisfactory.

D Fewer than 6 out of 10 essential criteria at satisfactory standard; 40% or more of other criteria at least satisfactory.

F Fewer than 6 out of 10 essential criteria at satisfactory standard

Figure 8.5
Assessment scale
Ian Hay and Edward Delaney

Hay has recently been involved in a CAUT-funded teaching development project and has offered the project team a manuscript copy of a paper expected to appear in the *Journal of Geography in Higher Education* (Hay, forthcoming). In it he describes a retreat from a commitment to attempting totally criterion-referenced assessment. The reasons are varied and include its inflexibility and the inability to reward effort and progress rather than outright achievement; the possible stifling of creativity and experimentation; difficulties with weightings of criteria; difficulties in attaining inter-marker reliability; and losing sight of the forest in trying to assess each of the trees. However, being clear about what is valued remains an essential element of communication between teacher and student.

Holistic scoring

The checklist (see Case study 52) is an attempt to judge the important subskills of writing. If weightings were attached to each of the subskills and the scores granted were multiplied by those weightings, and then added together to give a score, we would have an example of analytical scoring. In large-scale testing situations, it has proved difficult to get reliability from analytical scoring and it is time-consuming and expensive as well (White, 1994, p233). The alternative is to determine a grade on a holistic basis.

Holistic scoring tries to make a judgment about the overall quality of the work; it is predicated on the argument that a piece of writing is more than the sum of its parts and recognises that there are many subjective elements in judging quality of writing. This does not necessarily mean, however, that one has to be as vague as the marker who said, "I know one (a first-class Honours thesis) when I read one." The following Sample Holistic Scoring Guide was prepared by committees in the California State University English departments in 1988; the source is White (1994).

Sample Holistic Scoring Guide

Score of 6: Superior

- Addresses the question fully and explores the issues thoughtfully
- Shows substantial depth, fullness, and complexity of thought
- Demonstrates clear, focused, unified, and coherent organization
- Is fully developed and detailed
- Evidences superior control of diction, syntactic variety, and transition; may have a few minor flaws

Score of 5: Strong

- Clearly addresses the question and explores the issues
- Shows some depth and complexity of thought
- Is effectively organized
- Demonstrates control of diction, syntactic variety, and transition; may have a few flaws

Score of 4: Competent

- Adequately addresses the question and explores the issues
- Shows clarity of thought but may lack complexity
- Is organized
- Is adequately developed, with some detail
- Demonstrates competent writing; may have some flaws

Score of 3: Weak

- May distort or neglect parts of the question
- May be simplistic or stereotyped in thought
- May demonstrate problems in organization
- May have generalizations without supporting detail or detail without generalizations; may be undeveloped
- May show patterns of flaws in language, syntax, or mechanics

Score of 2: Inadequate

- Will demonstrate serious inadequacy in one or more of the areas specified for the 3 paper

Score of 1: Incompetent

- Fails in its attempt to discuss the topic
- May be deliberately off-topic
- Is so incompletely developed as to suggest or demonstrate incompetence
- Is wholly incompetent mechanically

Figure 8.6

Sample holistic scoring guide
(White, 1994)

This scoring guide may be compared with one offered to teachers of geography in higher education by Unwin (1990, pp34-5) ; note that the grading is the system common in England and Wales:

1st: is a well argued response to the question, providing clear references to relevant literature and examples; shows independence of thought and some originality; includes references to material not mentioned in lectures or on reading lists; shows a clear ability to distinguish between different ideas and arguments, and is able to form an independent opinion based on an evaluation of the evidence; is well written and interesting to read.

2.i: is well argued, showing clear signs of reading through reference to particular authors; uses a range of examples to support the student's own arguments; reveals clear logic and is well structured; shows a reasonable breadth of knowledge; has an ability to write good English; can weigh up and evaluate different arguments.

Figure 8.7

Scoring guide
Unwin, 1990)

2.ii: provides a reasonable response to the question; shows some knowledge of the literature and examples, but rarely cites specific references; can distinguish between relevant and irrelevant material; provides a reasonably structured account, but includes some signs of confusion.

3rd: a bare response to the question set; some knowledge of relevant material; poorly organised and structured; poor written style; usually along the lines of 'All I know about...'

Pass: reveals a limited knowledge of what the question is about; shows no real knowledge of relevant material; is poorly organised and structured; has poor grammar and spelling; shows no real sign of thought.

Fail: `does not answer the question; is short and irrelevant; shows no sign of reading, or even of knowledge of the relevant literature; is unstructured; has bad grammar and spelling.

Figure 8.7 *(cont)*
Scoring guide
Unwin, 1990)

Developing scoring guides

Note that the first scoring guide was devised by committees in the California State University English departments; most of us would find it hard simply to take either guide and apply it to any marking task. If we were not involved in the discussions that developed a guide, we would at least need some training, involving reading sample papers at each level and discussing them with colleagues, before we could begin to use it well. A guide is only generic, it does not give us the specifics about, for example, what constitutes thoughtful exploration of the issues raised by a specific question.

The general rubric could be made specific in classroom discussion with the students prior to grading the assignment. One way to do this is to offer a sample paper and ask students to work out what grade it should receive and to use that discussion to reach some statements describing papers at each level. As an example, White's first assignment for his writing students was:

Describe as clearly as you can a person you knew well when you were a child. Your object is to use enough detail so that we as readers can picture him or her clearly from the child's perspective. At the same time, try to make your readers understand from the tone of your description the way you felt about the person you describe. (White, 1994, p28)

In discussion students first established characteristics of an upper-half (5) paper and a lower-half (2) paper - after reading a sample that was eventually determined to be a 5. The preliminary guide was:

Score of 5: These papers give enough detail so that the reader can visualize the character. They also describe the narrator and give enough interaction between the two to allow the reader to understand an aspect of their relationship. Writing errors do not distract the reader.

Score of 2: These papers give little or no detail, telling us about a person instead of describing one. The focus may be almost entirely on the narrator or a situation, the language may be vague, and there may be more than an occasional spelling or grammatical error.

(White, 1994, pp32-3)

Subsequently, they elaborated the guide for the other grades, and then they engaged in peer marking of each other's work in clusters of 3 or 4 students. Grades were compared and differences reconciled in discussions in the cluster. White circulates and listens to the clusters and decides whether he will need to collect and grade the papers himself on the basis of how capable and responsible the groups are.

When Hay and Delaney (1994) used writing groups to give students feedback on final drafts (see above), they were a bit disappointed with the quality of the feedback offered. The main problem was that students tended to be too generous with each other, and negative feedback was avoided; students did not revise their work and were upset when teachers were less rewarding. Hay comments in a personal communication: "We have gone some way to overcoming this by letting all peer reviewers know that 'being kind is being cruel'...The result is more honest reviews. And as yet, no fisticuffs!!" (See also discussions of peer assessment, especially Module 5; refer to Index.)

Gibbs (1981,pp38-9) describes a similar workshop on establishing criteria. Students are asked to mark an essay and write comments on it. Then in small groups they compare their marks and comments and try to arrive at some general criteria. Finally, in a plenary these general criteria are pooled. Gibbs comments that the "idiosyncratic and misconceived criteria" tend to drop out as the students work together. The other outcomes are greater appreciation for the work done by markers and students' resolving to pay more attention to the comments they receive on their own work in future. Students are also moving toward being able to engage in more meaningful self-evaluation. Gibbs advises that teachers choose "an ordinary essay which is perhaps patchy in quality with both good and poor characteristics"; terrific essays put ordinary students off, and terrible ones are just too hard to deal with. Students need to be familiar with the subject matter.

An in-class exercise on criteria-setting is a necessary preliminary to using either peer assessment or self-assessment strategies. (Check Index for discussions of self-assessment, see especially Module 4.)

A similar process could be employed with a group of tutors when a large class is to be assessed on an essay assignment. It has become painfully obvious to many of us who have been involved in teaching subjects assessed by a number of people that it is not safe to assume that everyone shares the same standards and understanding of what a particular grade means in a particular subject, course, department, or university. It is too late to discover at the end of term that one of your colleagues has given 90% of her students grades of 'A' or 'B' on the three essays assigned over the term; when their exams are double-marked by other people and the majority of them get 'C' and the department demands that the assignment grades be adjusted to bring them into line with others, students have reason to be upset.

Grades, feedback and learning

Assessing and examining student work is not most teachers' favourite task, and yet it is the key element in encouraging meaningful student learning. Some of the case materials we have collected suggest ways to reduce the drudgery while students learn more about the abilities we hope to foster - such as students assessing each other's work collaboratively or using a checklist to provide systematic feedback to all students. Many of us wonder whether the effort we put into commenting on essays is worthwhile - do students even read the comments? Hounsell's study of student writers (1984) suggested that students do not transfer the feedback on one essay to the task demands of the next very well. That is, they seem to assume that a disappointing result was caused by not getting the answer to the question right rather than by some more general failure to understand how to approach the task of writing an essay in history or psychology.

Michael Jackson offered us the following description of a strategy to encourage students to think about their own work and understand the demands of their disciplines.

Case study 53
Peer reading and self-evaluation

Case study from Political Science
Michael Jackson, University of Sydney

The case study below is an edited version, retaining his own words as much as possible, of a longer account of this strategy provided to the project team by Jackson.

Concerned to concentrate the attention of students on formative comments, I have adopted the following practice in marking essays in political science classes, ranging from first year courses with 150+ students to honours seminars with 90, and postgraduate courses with 60.

Essays are returned at the end of a class with evaluative comments but no grade on them. I have read and assigned grades to the essays and recorded them, but this summative evaluation is withheld from students for the time being.

The assigned grade will not count until each student completes a self-evaluation. I require that each student read the essay of two peers from the class and then write a three paragraph (one page) appraisal of her/his own paper in light of the other two. The first two paragraphs evaluate the work of the peers and the last is a reflective evaluation of the student's own work.

Peer reading is a powerful tactic. It enlarges students' experience in the same way as it enlarges our own as scholars. Students have no idea of the range of work that teachers see, and partly as a consequence, do not understand why grades are distributed as they are.

If we really want peer reading to be done, it has to be built into the requirements. If time is not set aside in class and if it is not explicitly required, students will not take the task seriously. I suggest that teachers announce this requirement before returning the papers and allow class time for the necessary contacts to be made. This will work even better if once or twice earlier in the term some class time has been used for students to establish social networks to support each other when the going gets tough in the cough and cold season and at the end of semester.

I have done the self-evaluation in other ways. I have asked students to complete a self-evaluation questionnaire designed to focus attention on the process and form of essay writing. I have also asked for a short self-evaluation essay of 3 pages or less due 7 to 10 days after the return of the essays. Even these limited tactics pay off. Students are motivated to re-read their own work, something that they almost never do. I have also asked them to nominate a grade for themselves after completing the self-evaluation exercise.

When these self-analyses are submitted, some of the students do such a good job that I revise the grades assigned earlier. The revisions are marginal, but they reward learning. A good reflective evaluation deserving of such reward is one that is honest and has some insight into the process and outcome of essay writing.

The self-analyses may also be used as the key to re-writing . In my experience re-writing never seemed to work until I added the reflective step.

Other elements which will contribute to developing independence and the ability to evaluate their own work are:

• Spell out the criteria the essay must meet when it is assigned and repeat them before the self-analysis.

• Require self-analysis before granting an interview to any student to discuss their work.

➤

- Keep some copies of very good work to show to those students who cannot recognise the flaws in their own work.
- Before revealing the grades, offer formative comment to the class as a whole.
- Use class time to teach the process of writing through offering examples of drafts and good revisions, etc.

One of the advantages to working this way is efficiency. Try not to over-mark the essays. Limit marginalia to a few important points which are explained to the whole class. In the concluding remarks make no more than two comments, the strongest and the weakest quality of the essay. This can be done because the students are going to get plenty of time to think about their work and class time is devoted to going over the assignment with them.

■

Teaching writing independent of discipline

We noted earlier that writing courses are rare in Australia. In the United States, where many courses in writing are offered and where mass testing of writing skills occurs at entry and exit from higher education, assignments like the following (which we quoted earlier) are common; this is the first in a first-year university expository writing course:

> *Describe as clearly as you can a person you knew well when you were a child. Your object is to use enough detail so that we as readers can picture him or her clearly from the child's perspective. At the same time, try to make your readers understand from the tone of your description the way you felt about the person you describe.*
>
> *(White, 1994, p28)*

A teacher setting an assignment like this will emphasise the importance of concrete detail in description and relate this to the use of evidence to support conclusions - a skill very necessary in more "academic" writing as well. The assignment also requires students to understand "tone" and how it is affected by choice of words, and again, learning to choose the right language for the audience and the subject is important to academic writers. Finally, the assignment requires the writer to reveal reactions to the other without stating them explicitly; it teaches students to "control the 'I' in their writing, using it when appropriate but not turning the writing into simple subjectivism" (White, 1994, p29) .

The second assignment in this course would normally combine description and analysis:

> *Describe and analyze an institution or a group that you knew well as a child: a school, a school group, a scout troop, a dancing class, a summer camp, a club, a Sunday school - any group with an internally consistent set of values. You have two specific jobs to accomplish: a clear description of what it was like to be a member of the group at the time, and an assessment from your mature perspective of the meaning of the group's values.* *(White, 1994, p35)*

This assignment is much closer to one we would expect in Australian higher education, in a sociology class or teacher education, perhaps. It requires students to locate the group and its members in time and place, to evaluate its meaning to the writer, and to evaluate the group and its values from a different perspective. White comments, "...I am convinced that one valuable benefit of writing about personal experience is to gain an understanding of it - through the kind of organization and evaluation this assignment demands. The students also learn the most important skills for writing expository papers: to think systematically about aspects of their topic and relate careful description to a central controlling idea." (p42) (See also Case studies 1, 2, 6, 23, 24, 25, 26 which refer to journal writing or the use of autobiography in assessing various abilities.)

Personal experience and academic writing

We can see why learning to organise and evaluate personal experience, to gain control of it so that it does not intrude inappropriately in "academic" writing is so important. In a very perceptive discussion Shay, Bond and Hughes (1994) analyse student responses to the following question, set in a first-year Political Studies course in a leading South African university:

> *In practice the institutions of liberal democracy fail to protect and promote the principal ideals of liberal democratic ideology. Analyze and evaluate this claim.*

One of the students they describe is "a mature student who matriculated some years ago from a Catholic private school of sound academic standing - since then [Dumisani] has pursued self- and distance-studies, some of which took place during a period of political imprisonment" (p2). Later in the paper the authors comment:

> *Dumisani highlights the most pertinent tensions which emerge when personal identity attempts to blend with the social identities of the institution and the discipline as manifest in the academic task. ....On one hand, he had particular difficulty locating his own biography of political commitment within the course's assumption of dispassionate, analytical political theory. On the other hand, he found little means to articulate his own ideological perspective in this particular essay. Although the essay topic suggests the possibility of a socialist critique of liberal democracy, there is little in the readings or the lectures which presents such a first-hand critique. Dumisani is thus forced to tackle the topic, about which he has strong and developed views (particularly regarding liberalism and democracy) by means of texts which seem to close off the topic. So his strategy is - to stand aloof from the topic at times; to draw on in an unconvincing and sometimes inappropriate manner the writing of a number of profound exponents of liberalism; and to support his position, as opposed to arguing, with examples from his own background knowledge.*   *(Shay, et al., 1994, p5)*

Dumisani knew a lot about this topic, but he knew it from a deeply involved personal perspective and found it very difficult to use the set texts and imitate their tone and style, but he knew that he should attempt to do so if he wanted to pass.

One of the other students, Susan, has never been called upon to examine the political assumptions underlying her experience in an independent, fee-paying school steeped in "liberal democratic" ideology. She does not recognise that she may well have lived out the conflict between the institutions and the ideals which the question asks her to examine. When teachers are counselled to help students learn to draw on personal experience, to relate what they are learning to what they already know, the point is to try to resolve some of these problems, and in the resolution, make it possible for students to communicate effectively as well as "get the content right".

In order to assess, and improve, the effectiveness of written communication, we need to understand the causes of students' difficulties with academic writing - such as the problems of personal experience, and we have an obligation to assist students to overcome those difficulties before they submit the work for a grade.

For fledgling academic writers, the majority of problems are caused by the very fact that they are novices - novices within the disciplines they are studying and novices as academic writers. As high school students they may be extremely successful producing text which is much less analytical than university students are called upon to write, and they have not yet had to deal with a multitude of sometimes contradictory opinions in their source materials. (No, this does not mean the schools are failing, simply that young people progress gradually through a number of stages to reach sophisticated adult capabilities. Helping students learn to write academic text is the universities' job.)

If we consider the Political Studies question above, it actually expects students to know a great deal and to see one of the fundamental paradoxes of institutions which seek to encourage ideals of freedom while still preserving the culture within which they exist. White's (1994) first year exposition students face a similar question as they progress from description to exposition:

> *Write a short essay examining what the anthropologist Jules Henry means in the following passage and showing the extent to which the passage applies to your own schooling.*
>
> *Another learning problem inherent in the human condition is the fact that we must conserve culture while changing it; that we must always be more sure of surviving than of adapting - as we see it. Whenever a new idea appears our first concern as animals must be that it does not kill us; then, and only then, can we look at it from other points of view....In general, primitive people solved this problem simply by walling their children off from new possibilities by educational methods that, largely through fear (including beating, ridicule and mutilation), so narrowed the perceptual sphere that other than traditional ways of viewing the world became unthinkable....*
>
> *The function of education has never been to free the mind and the spirit of man, but to bind them....Schools have therefore never been places for the stimulation of young minds"* (Henry, 1963, pp284-288). *(White, 1994, p43)*

To answer either question, students need to understand the statement or passage first, then discuss it in the light of personal experience and prior knowledge, and in the Political Studies class, in the light of academic reading and the subject lectures. The biggest difference is how much personal experience is *expected* to be used, but as we have seen, it may intrude where it is not expected.

Demands of discipline vocabularies

The next difference to note between White's assignment and one in the Political Studies is the substantial demand on a novice made by using a phrase like "liberal democracy" in the question. One of the students interviewed by Shay *et al* (1994), a very successful and confident high school student, commented:

> *'It's because when you look at liberal democracy there's no clear-cut definition...you find a variety of concepts, but they were saying roughly the same thing not exactly the same thing, so it's just that in politics I found that you can't say democracy is this, this and this, you just can't...sometimes I would want a nailed down definition because then you're certain that you know what you're talking about, but when you don't have the background...it's difficult.'* *(Shay, et al., 1994, p8)*

Here is a clear example of the novice recognising her lack of sufficient knowledge of the subject; a later comment was that she just "'had to get on and do it'" so she takes some gambles and pretends she knows what she is talking about in order to do the essay. In fact, she did not do badly, but at the level where she tried to move beyond analysis to evaluation, her conceptual uncertainty revealed itself. There had been in-class discussion and pre-writing exercises in this case but it was not enough to resolve all problems.

In a personal communication Bond writes about questions that were raised about whether the assignment itself was inappropriate in a first year subject with students of varying levels of preparation: "I am increasingly uncertain about how much/just what type of classroom preparation for essays is fruitful and how much writing development must come through grappling with demanding tasks as well. By the end of last year I began to wonder whether we were in danger of suggesting that no task should be set which we weren't sure all students could cope with."

Discipline conventions and plagiarism

In the example above we see a novice struggling with the language of the discipline. This is a common problem in all disciplines. Words which are used comfortably in everyday speech and writing have special and very specific definitions within disciplines. Colleagues in Commerce faculties tell us that "finance" is a problematic word, as is "mass" in Physics. But it is not only the words of the discipline which novices must master. There are also conventions about sentence structures - is a passive construction the preferred way to report empirical results, or may a writer use a first person singular or plural construction? There are conventions about how and where in the text to include summary of data presented in figures and tables. There are conventions about where to include reference to authorities in the field - in a literature review at the beginning of a paper or interpolated in the body of the paper? These conventions vary from discipline to discipline and rarely are clearly articulated to novices - probably because we, as experts, have so deeply internalised them that we do not even recognise them.

The result of all of the above is often something which looks suspiciously like plagiarism - and probably technically it is. On the other hand, if we appreciate the dilemma of novice academics, we may see "not a cheater, but rather a student trying to become an 'insider'. If students feel they have nothing to say, or know they have something to say but do not know how to say it, what better way to try to communicate than to mimic - mimic the 'voices' of those they know have authority" (Shay, et al., 1994, p8). Shay et *al* refer to a compassionate and perceptive discussion of plagiarism - Hull and Rose (1990) - which may be more easily located than their own paper.

The other side of the plagiarism coin is that for a novice, every substantial idea needs to be referenced, but the models of good writing they are trying to emulate do not do so. Students are told that they must "synthesise" or "evaluate" for themselves, and they have learned that a cut-and-paste essay is not what is wanted, but they are also questioned if an idea is not referenced, so they are often between the proverbial rock and hard place.

Finally, students are told that if something is "common knowledge", a specific reference is not necessary. One student we know, writing in a health sciences discipline, read many texts on pronation of the foot; they all said the same thing about one aspect of the topic, so she assumed that made it "common knowledge" and, in fact, had internalised the information by the time she went to write the paper; she was severely criticised and penalised for not referencing that item though she had been scrupulously careful about referencing throughout the paper.

Setting questions

In this section, we will consider some of the issues in setting essay questions; this is of special importance in setting examinations, when students cannot seek further information or advice from teachers about what is wanted. In a preceding section we looked at two questions which are quite similar in some aspects:

> Write a short essay examining what the anthropologist Jules Henry means in the following passage and showing the extent to which the passage applies to your own schooling.
>
> Another learning problem inherent in the human condition is the fact that we must conserve culture while changing it; that we must always be more sure of surviving than of adapting - as we see it. Whenever a new idea appears our first concern as animals must be that it does not kill us; then, and only then, can we look at it from other points of view....In general, primitive people solved this problem simply by walling their children off from new possibilities by educational methods that, largely through fear (including beating, ridicule and mutilation), so narrowed the perceptual sphere that other than traditional ways of viewing the world became unthinkable....
>
> The function of education has never been to free the mind and the spirit of man, but to bind them....Schools have therefore never been places for the stimulation of young minds" (Henry, 1963, pp284-288).   (White, 1994, p43)

> In practice the institutions of liberal democracy fail to protect and promote the principal ideals of liberal democratic ideology. Analyze and evaluate this claim.
>
> (Shay, et al., 1994)

Two things are especially noticeable when we consider the differences in these questions: the length of the quote or statement which students are expected to address and the choice of instructional words. Teachers often ask whether it is good practice to use a quote from an important text to give students something from which to work. Of course, there is no simple answer to the question. However, it is certain that if one is going to use a quote - or statement, it must be very carefully chosen, taking into account the stage of study students have reached. As an expert, a teacher has a wealth of background knowledge and a sentence or two, taken out of context, may call up many concepts, but the novice, even at the end of a term, has not yet achieved that richness. The two topics above were both given to first year university students. The quote from Jules Henry is long enough to give students something to work from, even if they have not studied human culture or institutions previously, but the statement offered to the Political Studies students is brief to the point of being cryptic and contains a paradox without any elaboration. In the latter case, if the teacher were to engage in substantial pre-writing discussion and classroom exercises to help students deal with the topic, the question might not pose a big problem, but if that question were to appear on an examination, it could elicit answers that disappointed the teacher.

The Political Studies question is typical of many questions we have seen in case materials in that it uses two code words - 'analyse' and 'evaluate'. The problem with these code words is two-fold: 1) conscientious students seek help from manuals on essay-writing which offer definitions of these code words, 2) teachers do not read the manuals. The code words do not have fixed meanings despite what the manuals say to try to help students: for example, 'compare' may be used to elicit a discussion of both similarities and differences, but most manuals will say it is asking for similarities and 'contrast' asks for differences.

Words like 'discuss,' 'analyse,' and even 'describe' are often used interchangeably; one teacher in a workshop we conducted commented that she simply tried to make her papers sound more interesting by not using the same instructional word over and over. As White (1994, pp71-2) reminds us, what we often get is a file dump of an answer where students just write everything they know about a topic, and markers complain about lack of focus and organisational skills. White suggests slightly more "cumbersome" instructions that do not require so much de-coding; a question like the following could well be used in cultural studies, communications, teacher education, possibly even sociology:

> *Choose an advertisement from a popular magazine for careful analysis. An ad is, of course, designed to urge hasty readers to buy a product. Your concern, however, is not with the ad's selling power but with its concealed message. What does it assume and imply about its readers? What does it suggest about their needs, desires, motives, and so on? How does the ad define the self and the world for its readers?*
>
> *(White, 1994, p45)*

Rowntree (1987, pp154-56) cautions that setting a question which is too specific, too highly structured may reward "convergent" thinkers over "divergent" ones. He demonstrates rewriting a question on the same topic to become more and more specific about what the teacher is really expecting (p155):

> *What aspects of the political system of modern Sweden seem to you most worthy of comment?*
>
> *Comment on the political stability of modern Sweden.*
>
> *Explain the political stability of modern Sweden.*
>
> *Identify and discuss three factors that might help explain modern Sweden's political stability.*
>
> *Identify and discuss three factors that might help explain the emergence of a stable political system in Sweden despite the massive social and economic changes engendered by processes of modernization.*

Rowntree comments that while we gain comparability of answers and are in a better position to rank order the quality of response and get inter-marker reliability, we lose the chance to discover whether some students could formulate the question for themselves, identifying key issues, possibly even some their teachers had not thought of. So we may reward the convergent regurgitators and disadvantage the divergent creative thinkers. This Rowntree identifies with "Macnamara's Fallacy... - making the measurable important rather than the important measurable" (p156).

Related to the issue of writing a question that offers students specific information about what the teacher really wants (but without completely cutting off their options as creative, critical and analytical thinkers), is the issue of freedom to choose among topics. We assume students will have a better chance to demonstrate their knowledge if they can pick a congenial question. However, it is almost impossible to write several questions on different topics which make equal demands on students.

> *I used to ask students completing my course in the eighteenth-century English novel to choose from among three questions, each question referring to one of three novels: Moll Flanders, Tom Jones, and Tristram Shandy. Only recently have I realized how*

unfair that choice of questions was to my class. The best students often chose to write about Tristram Shandy, a quite difficult book, demanding great skill of a writer. I should not have been surprised that my good students often wrote poor examinations. Those selecting the Moll Flanders question, however, almost always received a higher grade than those choosing the others. I now ask a single question, on a larger topic (focusing specifically on the relationship of the characters in the novels to their worlds, for example, or on the relationship between the rise of the novel and notions of money), and require frequent references to the novels in the response. The students are just as free to demonstrate what they know - more free, in fact - and the test is much more fair.

(White, 1994, p59)

This brings us back to the theme running through these modules on assessment, that teachers should be examining their own assessing and examining in order to learn about what works and what doesn't, and in order to make adjustments, if necessary, to the results to achieve fair outcomes.

Few of us ever have the luxury of being able to trial our essay questions with a test group before we give them "for real", but as White (1994, p66) reminds us, a teaching career offers opportunities constantly to develop and refine our assignment and examination topics. What is needed is careful attention to the results we get as well as to the process of setting the work, so we continue to improve the clarity, validity, reliability, and interest (for both writers and markers) of the work we set.

One last point about how much to expect in exam conditions: again this is an issue we can learn about from experience and giving careful attention to the papers we receive. It can be very revealing to spend some time after the marking is finished looking at the range of work received; the numbers of students turning in excellent, good, acceptable, and poor papers; which questions seemed to encourage success and which, failure; and common errors and misconceptions. The following rough rules of thumb are adapted from White (1994, pp79-82); teachers may find them of some help as they try to work out whether the question they are setting is possible in the time available:

- If one uses "short essays", say, to be completed in about 20 minutes, one should not expect more than two or three paragraphs on a fairly limited and very clearly defined topic. Students simply do not have enough time to interpret a complex question or produce an answer of much profundity.

- A 30 minute essay test will allow for an organised and coherent essay but of limited complexity. Students do have time to give some thought to the question, find a focus for the essay, write three or four paragraphs and do a quick proof-reading. The question should not demand much synthesis or analysis at a level which has not been done during the term.

- A 45 minute essay can be more thoughtful, organised and even somewhat creative. It may fit the classic five-paragraph theme model of an opening paragraph, three paragraphs of development, elaboration etc, and a solid conclusion.

- Long essay examinations - an hour up to 3 hours - can become quite complex and are typically open-book exams, where students can use the time to refer to material already studied in some detail. White [1994, p82] comments that in his experience with nation-wide mass testing programs the writing does not seem to improve in quality over that found in the 45 minute test, but students are able to include more detailed analysis and development of a single controlling idea.

See also Gibbs and Habeshaw (1992), pages 100-106, for a very useful summary of typical questions and students' approaches, what these questions really elicit, and which type one might choose depending on one's goals as a teacher.

Portfolios

In previous modules (see Index) we have seen examples of assessment based on portfolios of work. However, once again, we turn to American experience (White 1994, see especially Chapter 6) for information about using portfolios of students' writing to determine grades for communication skills. White says several times that portfolio assessment is still very new territory and that it is very time-consuming and expensive and difficult to achieve reliability on a large-scale. On the other hand, since we know that students do not respond equally well to all tasks - that some find one task difficult but another relatively easy (often when their teachers would have said the first was less demanding) and that some do well writing in one subject but dreadfully in another, portfolio assessment of writing abilities would appear to be a more fair practice. Especially if a program of study aimed to judge whether its graduates had achieved a level of competence in written work within the discipline, a portfolio of work produced over the last year of study, or even longer, would seem the appropriate material to assess.

The sort of assessment suggested above would require many decisions: about the content of the portfolio, whether to insist on 'clean' copies (without teachers' comments), scoring procedures, criteria for scoring reliably, and appeals procedures - especially important if, for instance, a pass were required before a student could graduate.

On the other hand, the portfolio could be used not as a barrier to student progress but as a way of evaluating the program of study itself. In the following case study, Angelo and Cross (1993, pp208-12) stress the richness of information teachers get about their own work when they collect portfolios.

Case study 54
Portfolio

Case study from Mathematics Education
Anon (Angelo & Cross, 1993, pp209-10)

"The professor leading this practicum, herself a longtime mathematics teacher, required her student teachers to make annotated portfolios of lessons and materials they had created. Specifically, each student teacher was to put together a folder containing original lesson plans and materials from three related lessons, along with an explanation of the pedagogical and mathematical principles applied in those plans and materials.

The professor was impressed by the amount of work and level of creativity evident in many of the lesson plans, and she found that most of her student teachers were able to articulate the pedagogical principles underlying the lessons. There were two common areas of weakness in their portfolios, however. First, many of the lessons were at inappropriate levels of difficulty for the students they addressed; second, many of the students did a poor job of identifying or explaining the mathematical principles their lessons were meant to illustrate. Since most of the student teachers were not math majors, the professor was not surprised that this task was difficult for them, but the level of their responses did shock her. As a result, she decided to spend much more meeting time on reviewing the fundamental mathematical principles to be taught and learned in elementary school and on assessing readiness and skill - and less time discussing lesson design and teaching techniques."

■

White (1994, p300) offers "Submission Guidelines and Scoring Guide for Portfolios" as a resource in his appendices. This material was prepared at Miami University in Ohio and is used to collect and assess in-coming freshman students' writing skills for placement in freshman composition classes or possibly exemption from the requirement. Students select and submit no more than 12 typed double-spaced pages of work from their high school efforts; the portfolio must include a story or description, an explanatory, exploratory or persuasive essay, and a response to a written text. It must also include a reflective letter about the portfolio - a sort of self-assessment, and it must include the drafts of the work chosen for submission (drafts are not included in the 12 page limit). A teacher from the school and the student sign a form attesting to the work being that of the student.

A typical portfolio presented to a teacher for assessment in one subject contains a variety of work including pieces written in class as well as assignment writing. Portfolios usually include drafts as well as the final piece. One of the important messages of preparing a portfolio is to convey to students that writing is a process and that mastering the stages is as important as turning out an acceptable final product if one is to continue to grow as a writer. Students are also usually asked to prepare a self-assessment. This combination of material is a pretty good guarantee that the work in the portfolio is genuinely that of the student and discourages plagiarism.

In a conference presentation encouraging the use of portfolios at the ISETA (International Society for Exploring Teaching Alternatives) conference in Tempe, Arizona, in October 1994, Virginia Hartman emphasised the importance of being able to see evidence of:

- Evolution and change [through inclusion of drafts and work done over a period of time],
- Accomplishment [through best work], and
- Integration [through reference to various subjects].

She also emphasised the importance of having students write reflective statements on the materials included in a portfolio and suggested using prompts such as:

- Evolution and change: What were your initial reactions to the instructor's comments? What were the weaknesses in the first draft? What steps were taken to improve the draft? What comments do you wish to make about your final draft?
- Accomplishment: Why are you proud of/satisfied with this assignment? What factors contributed to the successful development of this assignment?
- Integration and application: Describe how this course is connected to previous courses in curriculum. Describe how this course is connected to future plans in the major or career area.

White recommends some reference materials on portfolio assessment:

Belanoff, P. and Dickson, M. (eds) (1991) *Portfolios: Process and Product.* Portsmouth, NH: Boynton Cook.

Yancey, K. (1992) *Portfolios in the Writing Classroom.* Urbana, IL: National Council of Teachers of English.

Hamp-Lyons, L. and Condon, W. (1993) Questioning assumptions about portfolio-based assessment, *College Composition and Communication*, 44 (2), 176-90.

Names to look for in a literature search could include the following whom White identifies as having most experience at the time he was writing:

- William Condon, University of Michigan
- Donald Daiker, Miami University of Ohio
- Chris Burnham, New Mexico State University
- Russell Durst, University of Cincinnati
- Joan K. Waters, University of Alaska - Southeast
- Marcia Mentkowski, Alverno College

Section 2

Communicating orally

Just as we started the first section of this module by noting that students cannot write about nothing, so we must remember that content knowledge will affect their success in oral communication and our evaluation of it. We also noted that some students excel in one type of writing and have problems with another. An interesting report of oral communications skills testing conducted by the Royal New Zealand College of General Practitioners (Thomson, 1992) showed that oral communication skills are also highly context-dependent.

Oral communication - interpersonal

The Royal New Zealand College of General Practitioners tests applicants for membership on their interpersonal communication skills. Concerned that lack of knowledge about a particular case might interfere with valid assessment of communication skills, the College provided candidates with knowledge necessary to deal with the situation in the simulated patient interview prior to testing. Candidates were required to conduct two interviews: they had to deal with at least one "confrontational" situation (eg. where a patient is unwilling to accept the doctor's advice) and either a second confrontation or a situation requiring the doctor to break bad news to a patient. The correlations between results on two confrontational situations were "modest" but the correlation on two unlike situations was virtually non-existent. Thomson (1992, pp366-7) concludes:

> It can be seen that if an examination is to be both a valid and a reliable assessment of clinical competence a number of prerequisites exist:
>
> (1) The domain of the competence that is to be assessed should be clearly specified. An examination should not be based on vague notions of assessing global traits. Critical competencies should be defined, an approach well suited to summative assessment conducted at the end of training.
>
> (2) Even where critical issues are defined it is essential to test these in a number of ways, since it is not possible to divorce context completely from the skill (at least not in a meaningful way at postgraduate level).
>
> (3) Resource limitations will always require that examinations test only a sample of the critical competencies.

Case Study 55
Reporting on interviews

Case study from Psychology
Patricia Duncan, University of Newcastle

The material in this case study came to us through Duncan's participation in the UNSW Postgraduate Program in Higher Education. In an assignment she outlined her intention to use, in a new subject she was planning, an assessment task on interpersonal communication, which she had already used successfully. Quoted material is from Duncan's paper

Context

The new subject is introductory general psychology for students who will not major in psychology. It provides "a broad introduction to the psychology of the individual with the emphasis placed on the development of the individual within the environment".

Ability being assessed

Included in the five draft objectives for the new subject were the following two:

- "knowledge of the processes associated with interpersonal communication"

- "the ability to apply the principles of interpersonal communication"

Assessment method

"In teaching communication skills within psychology subjects I have found that one of the most effective methods is to allow the students to evaluate their own ability by utilising a simple practical task. I have developed a unit which has been successful in raising students' awareness of communication principles and in developing associated skills. It has also been designed in such a way as to relate to the various stages of human development, thus tying in with the lecture content overall.

"In essence, the student interviews four people of varying ages (approximately 5-7, 12-18, 35-55 and 65+), using set tasks such as Piaget's conservation, or Kohlberg's moral dilemma concepts.... During this process the student then observes differences and/or similarities in the communication process for both themselves and the respondent. This is then explored through both class discussion and written report. Observation sheets [see below] are provided to facilitate their observation, and these are modified according to specific concepts under review.

"Students write an essay of 1500 words. Their aim is to consider the experiences they had, especially with relation to differences (or lack of them) between the four age groups, and to attempt to explain these experiences by relating to the literature on both communication and lifespan development. The emphasis is on the former. The observation sheets are included in their appendices and are mainly for their own benefit and reflection."

"This type of assessment not only examines their knowledge of the processes of interpersonal communication, and their ability to apply appropriate principles, but also relates this material to the theories of human development. This method of assessment is directly related to the objectives of the subject, provides for both formative and summative assessment, and fulfils the criteria set down by Andresen (1993) of honesty, validity, and strategic rationality."

➤

Task Observation Sheet

1. What was your first impression of the respondent?

2. How did this change during the course of the interview?

3. How did you open the conversation?

4. What percentage of time did you spend i) speaking, and ii) listening?

5. How did the age of the respondent influence your behaviour?

6. Was the immediate environment already set up, or did you arrange it? Draw a diagram of the setting and explain the advantages and disadvantages of using it for an interview.

7. Describe the overall impression given by the respondent's non-verbal communication?

8. What facial expressions did you observe through the interview?

9. What verbal comments did these facial expressions accompany?

10. Was the amount of eye contact a) too much; b) too little; c) just right? Explain why.

11. What did you find to be your "personal distance"? and why?

12. Was there any instance of touch? Who did it originate with? Under what circumstance?

13. What colours was the respondent wearing? How did they make you feel?

14. What types of "noise" were evident?

15. List the emotions displayed by the respondent through the course of the interview.

16. What was the strongest emotional response shown by the respondent? What verbal communication did it relate to?

17. How did it make you feel?

18. How did you respond?

19. What particular facial expression appeared to indicate how the respondent was feeling at this time?

20. How did you demonstrate empathy with the respondent?

21. How was silence used in the interview? What did it achieve?

22. Give an example of i) a positive comment, and ii) a negative comment, made by the respondent about themselves.

23. Describe how you felt at the following times:

    a) When arranging the interview appointment,

    b) When you arrived prior to commencing the interview,

    c) Halfway through the interview

    d) Immediately after it had finished.

24. Describe the feedback you gave - was it effective? How do you know?

25. What non-verbal behaviours did you use to signal that the interview was coming to its conclusion?

26. What non-verbal behaviours did you observe in the respondent when you were closing the interview?

27. How did you close the interview?

28. What was the best feature of your performance?

29. What was the worst feature of your performance?

Figure 8.8

Task observation sheet
Patricia Duncan

Marking

While students do engage in evaluation of their own performance as they write their report, there is no element of self-evaluation in the determination of the grade for the work.

As for criteria by which the report is judged by the teacher, Duncan writes, "What I am looking for is their awareness of the *principles* of communication and their *understanding* of how these *could* have affected the *interaction.* "

Strengths and weaknesses

This task is worth 15% of the grade for the subject. When we asked if this was a lot of work for a small proportion of the grade, Duncan commented, "It is a reasonable amount of work but most feel that it is worthwhile. Every effort is made to ensure that the practical applied nature of the materials is focused upon and the students seem to appreciate this and learn a great deal from it. I don't believe it is excessive in the way it is done. Students are encouraged to be familiar with the content and questions *before* attempting the task. The interviews only last about 15 minutes and students fill in the sheets as soon as possible. We have discussed the question thoroughly in class beforehand."

Duncan has used essentially the same task for first year students and for Honours classes. She advised us that for the junior students her expectations in relation to the written work are not as high. However, "the basic principles still have to be understood and their effects on interaction considered."

Assessing class participation

In disciplines like law where a professional must be able to communicate orally with a high degree of skill, teachers have frequently included assessment of class participation as a fraction, usually less than 20%, of subject grades. While we must recognise that the context of a classroom is very different from that of a courtroom or an office consultation with a client, and there must, therefore, be some doubt about the validity of this as an assessment of students' abilities in settings other than classrooms, the practice does, at least, communicate to students the importance placed on these skills.

The following case study addresses a number of issues which need careful consideration if class participation is to be assessed; it also suggests very strongly that this means of assessment may encourage deep student learning and so could be good practice regardless of its effects on communication skills.

Case study 56
Assessing class participation

Case study from Law
Annette Marfording, University of New South Wales

The following is an edited version of an unpublished paper provided by Marfording to the project team. The words are her own.

Improving Student Learning by Assessing Class Participation

> *Just as our choice of teaching methods should be informed by the nature of the subject matter we are teaching, so our choice of assessment methods should be conditioned by our goals for student learning.*
>
> (Ramsden, 1992 p190)

The reasons generally put forward for assessing class participation include the development of oral communication skills, the encouragement of preparation for class and the need for a variety of assessment methods (Armstrong & Boud, 1983 pp34-5). In the context of legal education, commentators have pointed out the need for lawyers to be able to develop and present an argument under pressure. A further reason suggested for assessing class participation is therefore that it could be a means of developing these lawyerly skills at law school. So far, no one seems to have considered this form of assessment as a means of improving student learning. Yet, for me, that seems to be the best reason for using it.

The rationale for assessing class participation

The assessment of class participation can potentially improve student learning for the following reasons. Firstly, class participation involves some form of interaction in class. In order to be able to assess class participation, the teacher would therefore need to employ interactive teaching methods of some kind. Interactive teaching can be a very powerful strategy to induce deep student learning in which students seek to make sense of the learning material, relating the content of new information to a larger context, examining the logic of an argument and generally thinking about and engaging with the subject material rather than focussing on memorisation and reproduction of knowledge.

Secondly, assessment and students' perceptions of assessment have been found to be the most critical factors influencing their approaches to learning (see, for instance, Gibbs, 1992, pp17-18; Ramsden, 1992 p186). If class participation is assessed, it seems logical therefore to assume that students will endeavour to contribute to the discussion in class with a view to gaining a good mark. If a teacher uses appropriate criteria for assessing class participation and informs the students what the criteria for assessment are, students may gear their learning accordingly and may thereby develop a deep approach to learning.

Thirdly, the assessment of class participation can be a continuous process throughout the course and therefore seems to fit in well with what Gibbs suggests as a useful assessment strategy to influence student learning: "integrating the assessment into the learning process so that what is assessed is the total learning experience rather than a separate performance after learning has finished" (Gibbs, 1992, p17).

Lastly, and perhaps most importantly, the importance of feedback in assessment must be emphasised. If assessment is used, as it should be, as a means of helping students to learn rather than mainly as a means of certifying competency to future employers and professional bodies and of maintaining standards, then effective feedback to students is a crucial element of assessment (see, for instance, Rowntree, 1987 pp16-24). Feedback on class participation can be given in every class throughout the course and is therefore potentially a very useful means of influencing student learning.

Students' views on assessing class participation

In 1992, I surveyed two groups of first year law students about their perceptions of the benefits of assessing class participation. They listed all the benefits normally advanced by other commentators, namely the encouragement of preparation for class, the development of oral communication and professional skills, and to have a balance with written assessment. A number also said it would encourage less confident students to be more active. Significantly, many of the benefits suggested by the students are factors associated with deep learning:

- it makes you think about the reading,
- it encourages work throughout the year and discourages cramming,
- class discussion is a good way of learning,
- better understanding as a result of active participation,
- students learn to express their opinion,
- the discussion is more informed and more stimulating,
- it brings in new ideas,
- classes are more interesting and personal,
- you get instant feedback from the teacher,
- the teacher gets feedback that the students understand the material.

Abilities assessed with class participation

The abilities assessed with class participation can encompass a very broad range. Some class activities will require students to demonstrate knowledge and understanding of the subject matter. Here abilities such as the recall, reporting, and recounting of the facts, legal issues and legal principles of a case will be assessed. In this context, development of the ability to relate a new case and the legal principles established therein to previous cases is important.

Other class activities focus on the development of students' abilities to think critically and to justify their ideas. For instance, the impact of a particular decision on society might be discussed, or recommendations of a law reform commission be evaluated, or the students might be asked to suggest ways of reforming the law themselves. In such activities, students' abilities to develop arguments, to apply ethical values, to determine criteria for assessment or evaluation, to reflect, to evaluate, to assess and to judge will be assessed.

In addition, many law teachers will employ problem-solving activities, such as presenting students with a hypothetical or real life situation and asking them to solve the problem by applying the law to the situation. This will develop problem-solving abilities in students, namely to define the issues, to review and analyse the relevant case law and to apply it to the problem at hand. Since there is often not just one possible solution to the problem, such activities will also foster skills to create an innovative legal argument using judges' reasoning in case law as a base.

Last, but not least, the assessment of class participation will foster general oral communication and professional skills. Students will learn to argue, to advocate a case, to present their opinion and in specific class activities they may learn interviewing and negotiation skills.

I believe that no other assessment task could achieve the encouragement of such a broad range of abilities in combination. This is an additional factor which makes the assessment of class participation particularly useful.

➤

Criteria for the assessment of class participation

Armstrong and Boud (1983, p38) have referred to the lack of attention that seems to be given to the establishment of criteria for the evaluation of students' work generally and of class participation specifically. I surveyed colleagues as well as students in 1992. Twenty-nine responses led to thirty-two different though partly related criteria, even though no one listed more than six criteria. One colleague's answer was "guess work", whereas others differed widely in what they professed to value. For illustration I include two very different responses here:

- Good preparation, thoughtful discussion, helpful to the class members (ie. not showing off), sensitivity to others in the class
- Regularity of attendance, quantity of participation, quality (subjective)

Only one colleague indicated that s/he discussed with the class in advance what criteria the assessment of class participation would be based on. If teachers are not using the same criteria and if students are not informed which criteria their teacher is going to employ, they do not know what is expected of them and a valuable opportunity to influence student learning is lost.

The survey of staff also raised the issue of using quantity of contributions as a criterion for the assessment of class participation. Seven colleagues listed it whereas others specifically emphasised their rejection of quantity as an appropriate criterion. I agree with the latter group because the use of this criterion may undermine efforts to foster deep learning. Its use may encourage students to concentrate on making many 'correct' contributions, ie. focussing on accurate reproduction of facts of cases studied and of legal principles, a characteristic of the surface approach. Assessing quantity may also result in a few students dominating the class discussion, which may have a negative impact on the group climate.

Students themselves do not regard quantity as an appropriate criterion for assessment either. When I surveyed students, I asked one group to list and rank up to five criteria and the other group to rank a given list of thirteen criteria: quantity was not ranked highly by either group. I have also given final year students in an elective course the opportunity in the first class meeting of the course to establish criteria for me to use when assessing their class participation. Employing the nominal group technique, a list of criteria including quantity was written on the board. The next step was to ask students whether they thought any of the criteria should be struck out as inappropriate. One student commented that she thought quantity and no domineering were mutually exclusive and the others agreed with her, deciding unanimously to strike out quantity and leave no domineering.

Another issue is whether to use attendance as a criterion. Minorities of both the student groups and the staff groups favoured including it. I agree with Armstrong and Boud (1983 p39), however, who point out that "attendance in class is a necessary prerequisite for class participation but the measurement of attendance has nothing to do with the quality of participation." In the University of New South Wales Law School there is an 80% attendance requirement anyway, so I vetoed attendance as a criterion. On the other hand, I do consider it proper to reward a positive attitude to the subject in the form of demonstrated interest, motivation and attentiveness in class. Attendance may be one indicator for these.

When criteria are made explicit to students, they will attempt to gear their learning towards these criteria. In any assessment task, the teacher should therefore link the criteria with the abilities which s/he seeks to develop. As discussed before, the assessment of class participation can encompass a broad range of abilities, which can be listed for students and assessed in terms of quality of contribution.

To facilitate the free flow of ideas in class discussion and to help create a non-threatening and supportive atmosphere in the classroom, criteria such as preparedness to listen to others, respect for other people's ideas, constructive criticism, no domineering and helping other students may be useful.

➤

Since student preparation for class is vital, it should be considered to reward evidence of reading, analysis and understanding, and consistency of such preparation.

My students receive a handout which lists the criteria for class participation. Below are examples of a handout for my first year students and of one for my final year students with whom I negotiate criteria.

Assessment of Class Participation
Legal System-Torts
Annette Marfording

Abilities   I am seeking to develop further include

Knowledge and	{ .	recall, report, recount
understanding of	{ .	relate new information to previous knowledge
subject matter		

Ability to think	{ .	develop an argument
critically and to	{ .	apply ethical values
justify one's ideas	{ .	determine criteria for assessment or evaluation
	{ .	reflect, evaluate, assess, judge

Problem solving	{ .	identify problems/issues
skills	{ .	review, analyse, apply relevant law
	{ .	be creative, innovative

Oral communication	{ .	argue, advocate, present personal opinion
skills	{ .	be articulate, concise

Criteria for Assessment

Quality of Contribution
Demonstrated ability in four areas listed above

Quality of preparation for class
- Evidence of reading, analysis and understanding
- Consistency of preparation
- Indication of reading outside set materials

Contribution to group climate
- Preparedness to listen to others
- Respect for other people's ideas
- Constructive criticism
- No domineering
- Helping other students

Attitude to learning and the subject
- Interest and motivation
- Attentiveness in class
- Willingness to contribute
- Progress in participation for those with initial difficulty

Figure 8.9

Method of assessing class participation
Annette Marfording

➤

AGREED CRITERIA FOR CLASS PARTICIPATION

JAPANESE LAW

Annette Marfording

Quality of contribution

- Relevance

- Contributing to understanding

- Critical analysis

- Clarity of contribution

- Originality

- Comparative insight

- Consistency of valuable contribution

- Facilitation of further discussion

- Evidence of learning in the subject

Quality of preparation for class

- Evidence of reading, analysis and understanding

- Indication of reading outside set

Contribution to group climate

- No domineering / brevity

- Courtesy and tact

Attitude to learning and the subject

- Interest

- Attentiveness in class (instead of mere attendance)

- Contributions based on current topics

Figure 8.10
*Method of assessing
class participation*
Annette Marfording

Method of assessing class participation

The questionnaire survey conducted among my colleagues showed that opinions are divided about assessing after each class or giving an overall assessment at the end of the course. Reasons for the latter are partly due to concerns about students, such as each class giving only a limited picture and some students not 'clicking' with the subject immediately. Other reasons are teacher related, namely its expediency, its value in terms of cost/benefit analysis, the fact that assessing after every class may distract too much from concentrating on teaching and the time it takes to learn students' names.

Reasons given for an assessment after each class involve fairness to students: it is seen as precise, fairer, providing an objective record, assisting in monitoring a student's progress, can otherwise not be remembered nor can consistency of preparation and quality be judged in another way. However, my students told me that my practice of assessing every class meeting contributed to their anxiety.

I now give each student detailed feedback on the criteria listed above about five weeks into the course. I particularly comment on areas where improvement is needed. About five weeks later students are asked to evaluate their own performance on the basis of the same criteria and I provide them with feedback on the extent of my agreement with their self-evaluation. At the end of the course they receive more feedback and a formal mark.

The distribution of marks is generally quite high as a result of achieving everyone's involvement in class (see below about how). The lowest mark is almost always a credit (65%), the highest always a high distinction (85%-95%). The average mark is usually around 75%. This may appear high, but seems justified on account of students putting a lot of work and thought into class participation throughout the whole session.

The individual mark is arrived at through a combination of adding up and holistic judging. Every five weeks I give each student a provisional mark on each of the clusters of criteria (eg. quality of contribution; quality of preparation for class; etc.), each of the four clusters counting for 1/4 of the mark. If the mark for quality of contribution is higher or lower than the provisional mark, I mark the provisional mark 10% up or down, since the quality of contribution is the most important cluster. Then I work out an aggregate mark for the whole session, marking it up if the student's quality of class participation has improved over the session. Lastly, I do some holistic judging by comparing the provisional marks of all students against each other's marks.

The process may sound extremely complicated and time-consuming but it is not really. Of course, it requires more time than sitting down and giving each student a mark based on holistic judging for the whole session, but I feel students deserve a more careful and individual assessment. The time commitment involved in the process is still substantially less onerous than marking an assignment or exam.

Problems with assessing class participation - and some solutions

1) Possible side-effects on student learning: Assessing class participation may induce anxiety which may inhibit some students' participation and/or lead them to adopt a surface approach to learning. Others may feel the urge to make as many contributions as possible which may undermine a supportive group climate and reduce the fruitful exchange of ideas among students. My survey of students confirmed that these concerns need to be addressed.

On the other hand, it is not quite clear whether these students would experience these feelings regardless. It may be important for these students' personal development to get the chance of building up more confidence in a supportive small group. In addition, many students including some of those expressing anxiety noted the professional benefits of practicing public speaking and arguing under pressure.

➤

Some of the student anxiety may have been due to my initial method of assessing class participation after each class. I have now changed this method in favour of assessing every few weeks only on the basis of the criteria listed on the handout. One of those criteria is especially directed at the more anxious students, namely, 'progress in participation for those with initial difficulty.' I think this is a valid criterion because the process of learning, developing self-confidence and oral skills is itself important; this also helps students with English language problems. In addition, anxiety can be reduced by creating a safe and relaxed atmosphere and by employing small group exercises to enable the students to get to know each other better. Supportive feedback can also be used to encourage anxious students when they do participate. The students of mine who used to be very quiet in the first session now seem to be far more active in class discussion.

Competitiveness is another possible negative side-effect of assessing class participation, but this can be reduced by excluding quantity as a criterion and including no domineering instead. The teacher can also discourage domineering students and encourage the quiet ones in a supportive way. Directing questions to the latter - their own suggestion - has also helped to make them more confident to volunteer.

Overall, I believe the positive side-effects outweigh the negative.

2) Unreliability of interpretation: Reliability is concerned with consistency, ie. the agreement among several assessors as to the quality of a student's work. One of the major criticisms made of the assessment of class participation is its unreliability due to subjectivity and teacher bias. It is clear though that written work suffers from the same problem. Yet essays are widely used because they give students the opportunity to reflect, demonstrate understanding and critical analysis, all of which are aspects of deep learning. The most important use of assessment is as a means of helping students to learn and not simply to ensure reliable testing of knowledge. Therefore, assessment forms with a high educational relevance should be used and the unreliability factor be reduced as much as possible.

In the assessment of class participation this can be done by establishing clear criteria for assessment actually using these criteria, and informing students what they are. In addition, where possible, assessment by other colleagues on the basis of the same criteria can contribute to reliability (Armstrong & Boud, 1983 p36). Fellow students and the students themselves can be used in addition to or instead of other colleagues to assess every student's class participation. Particularly peer assessment tends to be fairly consistent with the teacher's assessment (Boud & Tyree, 1980 p70). Although self-assessment by students has been found to be fairly reliable, there seems to be a tendency for better students to under-rate themselves and for weaker students to rate themselves more favourably than they are rated by their teacher (Boud, 1989 p23).

Perceived unreliability of interpretation in the assessment of class participation is therefore no reason to reject this form of assessment as long as the problem is recognised and effective action to reduce the unreliability factor is taken.

3) Disproportionate impact on female and overseas students: Both female and overseas students may be particularly disadvantaged by the assessment of class participation. The relative silence of women in classroom discussions has been pointed out by many commentators (Nightingale & Sohler, 1994). Morgan has described her observation that when contributions to class discussion are controlled by the teacher, "women almost invariably lower their hands when someone else is speaking while men are much more likely to keep their hands raised" (Morgan, 1989 p158). Most of my female students behave in this way too.

As Wildman suggests, men's relative assertiveness and women's relative silence may be due to cultural conditioning (Wildman, 1988, p147). Teachers' behaviour patterns experienced at school may contribute to this. Spender showed that both female and male teachers paid far

➤

less attention to their female than their male students even though they had thought they focussed more on their female students (Spender, 1982). The resulting silence of women in the classroom would seem to put them at a disadvantage when participation is assessed.

The same would be true to an even greater extent for overseas students. Their English proficiency may be deficient; in particular, they may have trouble with spoken language. In addition, it seems that particularly Asian students may have experienced fundamentally different educational styles and philosophies.

Students themselves perceive the potential disadvantage to students of non-English speaking background but not to female students.

I feel there are a number of strategies that a teacher can employ to make sure that female students are not disadvantaged. The creation of a safe and supportive group climate is particularly important. Directing questions to female students has proved successful (they encouraged me to do so and it has worked). Since a female student may indicate her willingness to contribute in a less obvious and persistent manner than a male student, teachers must be very alert to the slightest indication that she wishes to speak - a frown, smile, raised eyebrow, shift in posture. Reflective writing tasks in class or small group work can be effective in giving women more self-confidence by giving them some preparation for speaking. My experience is that once someone gets started, she gradually increases her contributions.

In relation to overseas students, the problem is more difficult. To some extent the strategies above may go part of the way. Initially, it may be necessary to reward reproductive learning, but eventually the teacher will need to probe with encouraging questions, such as "Can you explain this concept in your own words?" "What kind of reasoning does the judge employ here?" "What will this principle mean for future cases?" The teacher should take care not to speak too fast, to use short sentences and to explain subject specific terminology. Visual aids and handouts will also make it easier for students with language problems. English language skills may need to be further developed in concurrent "English for academic purposes" courses and the teacher should find out to what extent s/he can cooperate with the English teacher. A criterion such as "progress in participation for those with initial difficulty" is of particular importance with respect to these students.

Case study 57
Self-assessment of class participation

Case study from Law
John Goldring, University of Wollongong

The case on the following pages is similar to that above, except that it uses more self-assessment and rationalises the practice in terms of students learning to judge themselves and to evaluate their own learning processes. It is reported in Goldring's own words.

Context

Since the introduction of methods of legal education which encourage student participation in the learning process (starting at the University of New South Wales in the early 1970s) progressive law teachers have encouraged assessment of class participation in order to

- encourage students to prepare for and contribute to seminars and problem-based learning sessions
- develop students' ability to listen and to communicate orally.

I have used the current procedure, or versions of it, since about 1984, with law students at all stages (from 1st to 5th year) at Macquarie University and at the University of Wollongong.

Abilities

- Ability of students to assess or evaluate their own learning processes
- Ability of students to recognise their own strengths and weaknesses
- Listening skills
- Oral presentation skills
- Working in groups

Assessment strategy

a) At the beginning of the session, students receive, as part of the subject outline, the document which is reproduced opposite.
b) Students are told that they will be asked to complete the form each four weeks.
c) I observe the students in classes and make my own assessment, based on the same criteria.

➤

APPENDIX "A"
A NOTE ON SELF-ASSESSMENT

You will be **required** to assess your own participation in class. This is not a cop-out by academic staff, as we will be making an evaluation of your participation. But one of the objectives of the law subjects at Wollongong is to enable you to develop your own learning skills. You will need to assess your own learning performance at various stages in your career, so in this subject, and in other subjects, you will receive assistance in developing your ability to assess your own performance.

Academic assessment is supposed to be a process by which the achievement of specified objectives is measured. The objectives of class participation are:

1. to provide an opportunity to get you to develop your **learning skills:**

   a. to **reinforce** your own learning (ie to see whether you have correctly learnt and understood the assigned material)
   b. to give an incentive for you to **plan, allocate** and **manage** your own time, including the development of techniques of selective reading and making judgements about the **priority** to be given to different tasks

2. to assist other members of the class to give and provide feedback on their learning

3. to indicate to academic staff that you either have understood the material or whether you need assistance

4. to assist you to develop skills of

   a. expressing arguments orally
   b. expressing abstract and complex ideas orally
   c. listening
   d. comprehension.

In this context, we have stated what we think the objectives of the process are. In real life, you will need to work out your own objectives and the way in which you measure them. For this purpose you will have to work out the criteria by which you assess whether or not you achieve the objectives.

Each four weeks, you will be asked to complete a form which will ask you to rate your achievement of each of the objectives listed above on a six point scale, and to give yourself an overall score. This form will also give you an opportunity to indicate any abnormal factors affecting your work. We will check your self-assessment against our assessment of your participation, and will discuss with you any different perception we may have of your participation. You may be aware of factors affecting your participation of which we a are unaware. The figure ultimately recorded will be agreed, though academic staff must reserve the final power of decision. When we have used this method previously, we find that initially students tend to *under*estimate their own participation, but by the end of the session, there is a good measure of agreement between staff and students.

A sample self-assessment form appears on the next page.

Figure 8.11
A note on self assessment
John Goldring

UNIVERSITY OF WOLLONGONG
FACULTY OF LAW

Self-Assessment Sheet No......

Student's name:...

Tutor/Lecturer's name:...

Subject: ....From ....../....../ 19... to ....../....../ 19...

During this period I assess my participation in each of the following areas as follows:

Note: F (0-44%). extremely poor
PC. (45-50%) poor;
P. (50-64%) acceptable/average
CR. (65-75%). above average; very good achievement in part
D. (75-85%). well above average; very good achievement overall
HD. (85-100%). outstanding in all respects.

TICK EACH ROW IN THE APPROPRIATE COLUMN

AREA OF ACTIVITY	HD	D	CR	P	PC	F
Learning and understanding material						
Planning study; coverage of assigned material						
Organisation of study and preparation						
Assisting other members of the class						
In full class groups						
In buzz-groups and syndicates						
Informally and outside class						
Expressing and countering arguments orally						
Understanding and expressing abstract and complex ideas orally						
Listening.						
Comprehension of class discussion.						

Special factors affecting me during this period were:

[NOTE: In making the next assessment, you must decide how much weight you give to each of the above factors in the light of the need to measure achievement of your learning objectives]

Overall, I assess my participation in class during this period at.........%.

Figure 8.11 *(cont)*
A note on self assessment
John Goldring

Marking

a) Students complete the forms, including the overall percentage grade, and return them to me.

b) I read the forms, compare them with my own evaluation, and write comments if I do not agree. If my perceptions are markedly different from those of the student, I have an individual discussion with the student.

c) At the end of the session, I average all the marks (mine and the students') and this mark becomes the mark for that component of the assessment for the subject.

d) The proportion of marks in the subject which Active Class Learning carries varies from 10% (in a first year subject) to 25% of the marks available in the subject.

The weight I give to each component of the assessment does vary. Primarily I am looking for comprehension of the material being discussed and critical ability, rather than oral presentation skills, so I would tend to weight the knowledge-based criteria more heavily than the others.

When the criteria are stated, I have found that students' evaluations are fairly close to mine. Differences arise because of the weightings given to different components. I do not state these because I want students to think about the relative weight to be given to various components. If there are differences about the assessment of the various components, it is more often because students consider that their achievement does not measure up to the criteria. Typically, weaker students are more likely to over-assess their performance.

Regardless of the stage of the course reached by the students, I am looking for the same qualities, although the level to which I expect students to have developed their abilities varies with the level of the subject.

Strengths and limitations

All strengths I think. The scheme seems to meet a number of objectives. It is quite time-consuming but no more so than other methods of assessing class participation.

When I started to assess class participation, I was diffident about how to do it. I decided that there were certain criteria, or performance indicators, to which I referred subconsciously. I decided to make these explicit and found this led to differences of opinion with students. I also encountered, as most teachers do, the problem of students who were reticent. I then decided to ask students to make their own assessment of their contribution and realised only after doing this that the process of self-evaluation could and should itself be an important part of the learning process.

My view is that a law degree may be a professional qualification but in any event it designates an ability for communication and the criteria for assessment relate to communication and understanding. I do not actually grade the students on their ability to assess themselves. However, as the law degree, in my view, is more than anything else a way of developing the students' own ability to learn independently for as long as they live, the ability to assess how well they are learning , or in other words, how well they are meeting the learning objectives they set themselves and achieving the learning outcomes they wish to achieve is very much a part of the learning experience which should be part of every law degree.

The process of discussing differences in perception is valuable formative assessment for students. Because students continually reflect on their own experience, they are providing their own feedback, which is reinforced by my regular comments three times each session.

Conclusion

Students are often very sceptical about this process initially, but later - sometimes years later, they have thanked me for assisting them to develop a method for evaluating their own performance in a variety of situations. ■

Comments

In both Marfording's discussion and Goldring's we see teachers using an assessment strategy to encourage students to develop a wide range of abilities, but, in fact, the assessment strategy itself does not actually evaluate the acquisition of all those abilities. This is not necessarily a problem but it is something teachers need to be aware of when they are trying to document learning outcomes for accountability purposes.

Assessing a formal presentation

Hay (1994) advocates including formal student presentations in the assessable work for courses. He argues that geographers and other social scientists, indeed most professional people, are required to present information, argue points and 'sell' themselves orally even more often than they are required to write, but there is little attention to teaching and assessing speaking skills in most university courses. He also notes that a side-effect may be promoting listening skills when students provide each other with an audience.

Case study 58
In-class presentations

Case study from Geography
Iain Hay, Flinders University

The following material describing student presentations in Hay's class is extracted from the article referred to above (Hay, 1994); it was provided to us by Hay.

"The time demands associated with oral presentations may cause some instructors to baulk at their application, despite their considerable worth. The argument could be put that class time might be better spent with lectures. However, if students are assigned topics which mesh closely with the course content..., some advantage may be obtained. Carefully researched and delivered student presentations may be used as an examinable supplement (or perhaps even a replacement) to other material presented by academic staff... This serves to heighten the attention of class members to the work of their peers, as well as providing a range of perspectives on material which one staff member may be unable to replicate. Instructors may monitor presentations and provide the class with material to supplement, complement, or correct that provided in the student talks. Thus, staff and students can be seen to be working collaboratively towards educational goals whilst students are provided with an opportunity to develop vital communication abilities. In practice, if a written paper to accompany an oral presentation is required, it is useful to ask it to be submitted some time before the talk is delivered so that any additional and corrective material may be prepared in advance.

"One problem encountered with the use of oral presentations in some classes has been small audience attendance!... students can be compelled to attend all or some proportion of presentations in order to satisfy course attendance requirements. Without provision of some good justification for this requirement, the strategy can, unfortunately seem somewhat Draconian to students. Alternatively, the subject matter of presentations may be connected closely with other course content and may be made examinable. ...

Another difficulty encountered with the application of presentations is that many students feel reluctant to ask their peers questions or to make public comments after a talk. This can lead to an embarrassing silence... Firstly, it might be made clear to students that you, as the teacher, will not lead the post-presentation discussion. Secondly, in the manner of some professional conferences, a number of discussants for each presentation can be appointed, with these people assigned the task of raising questions and initiating discussion. Thirdly, class members can be asked to note at least one comment or question for each presentation with these being solicited by the speaker during question time. ..."

Hay discusses using well-established criteria to assess oral presentations rather than a norm-referenced system. See discussion in first section of this module, page 214. He provides students with an evaluation schedule, reproduced on the next page, prior to preparation of their presentations. Students are also given extensive advice on preparing for a talk, delivering the talk and coping with questions.

It needs to be emphasised that this schedule is for the evaluation of presentation skills only and, as such, it includes no component for assessing the content of the talk.... In very small classes, such a schedule may also be used by students to assess their peers, thereby providing additional feedback to speakers as well as heightening the critical listening and observational capacities of student assessors.

"Satisfactory speaker achievement of the criteria ...is recorded by the assessor's checking of the appropriate box. Criteria which might be considered essential or most important to a successful presentation are italicised. Student grades may be determined by identifying a number of objectives as most important or essential and coupling those variables with less important others to establish minimum performance levels associated with each grade.

(Hay, 1994 pp49, 52-3)

See pp248-249 for an example of such an assessment scale.

➤

Oral Presentation Assessment Schedule

Objective: To successfully deliver a spoken presentation

Aspect 1.   **Speaker appearance and other first impressions**

	Pass	Fail

Dressed appropriately, tidy and free of distracting features
Relaxed and comfortable poise
Speaker appeared confident and purposeful before starting to speak
Speaker attracted audience's attention from the outset
Little or no fidgeting and few distracting mannerisms

Aspect 2.   **Presentation structure**

Introduction

Title/topic made clear
Purpose of the presentation clear
Organisational framework made known to audience
Unusual terms defined adequately

Body of presentation

Main points stated clearly
Sufficient information and detail provided
Sufficient periodic recapitulation
Appropriate and adequate use of examples/anecdotes
Correspondence of presentation content to introductory framework
Discussion flowed logically

Conclusion

Ending of presentation signalled adequately
Main points summarised adequately/ideas brought to fruition
Conclusion linked to opening
Final message clear and easy to remember

Figure 8.12
Oral presentation assessment schedule
Iain Hay

59

Aspect 3. Coping with questions

	Pass	Fail
Whole audience searched for questions		
Questions addressed in order		
Questions handled adeptly		
Full audience addressed with answers		
Speaker maintained control of discussion		

Aspect 4.   Delivery

	Pass	Fail
Speech clear and audible to entire audience		
Suitable vocabulary (few cliches, little jargon and repetition)		
Interesting variety in tone of voice		
Little false or excessive use of spoken emphasis		
Short, comprehensible sentences		
Few unfinished sentences		
Presentation directed to all parts of audience		
Eye contact held with audience throughout presentation		
Meaningful gestures appropriately used		
Full text not read		
Speaker kept to time limit		
Good use of time without rushing at end		
Pace neither too fast nor too slow		

Aspect 5.   Visual aids and handouts

	Pass	Fail
Visual aids clearly visible to entire audience		
Overhead and slide projectors etc. operated correctly		
Speaker familiar with own visual aids (e.g. OHPs, blackboard diagrams		
Visual aids well prepared		
Effective use made of handouts and/or visual aids		
Handouts well prepared and useful		

Aspect 6.   Target and audience

	Pass	Fail
Presentation met level of knowledge for audience		
Presentation met need for knowledge of audience		

Figure 8.12
*Oral presentation
assessment schedule*
Iain Hay

Comment

If the presentation is to form an integral part of the content of the course, it will be necessary to assess content at some stage, but that could be done when the written paper Hay mentions is received, leaving the emphasis of assessment of the presentation to be on the communication skills.

Case study 59
Formal presentation

Case study: Co-operative Education Programme
Meredith Caisley, Auckland Institute of Technology

The following description is based on: Caisley, Meredith (1994) Communication Skills - Key Capabilities, Dialogue: the AIT Journal of Adult and Higher Education, June, pp8-11. Ina TeWiata, who was the educational developer working on this cooperative education program (see also Case Study 1 p4, Module 1), provided additional information.

Context

Students are enrolled in a Bachelor of Business degree course. Students are placed in an organisation for a period of approximately three months. During this time they are closely monitored by both the host company and an academic supervisor.

In the Aims of the Cooperative Education programme it is stated:

> *The Cooperative Education programme is a key strategy for helping students develop each of the capabilities central to the degree programme, and is particularly strong in enabling students to extend and apply their learning beyond the educational institution. In is important to appreciate that the Co-operative Education programme is not simply work experience, but rather a strategy of applied learning.*

The capabilities referred to include:
- critical thinking
- problem solving
- effective teamwork
- technical competence in both subject discipline, eg. accounting; and in applying business tools, eg. computer software
- effective oral and written communication
- research
- reflective thinking
- problem posing
- independent learning

Learning contracts are signed by the student, the employer and the academic supervisor. On completion of the project there are four assessment events -
- written report
- oral presentation
- work performance evaluation
- critical thinking interview

This case study focuses on the oral presentation.

Abilities being assessed

Oral presentation skill appropriate to the business context in which students have been operating.

➤

Criteria are specifically indicated on grading sheets, pages following.

Procedures for assessing

Students had 30 minutes to give their presentation and to answer questions. The topic was their coop education experience; that is, the oral presentation is based on their written report, or aspects of it.

The written report is a critical analysis and reflection on their cooperative experience. Performance criteria include:

* analysis of theories that underlie the work they did;
* importance of their work to the organisation;
* analysis of what was successful;
* analysis of contribution to student's own learning and professional growth, etc.

The audience included members of the firm in which the students had worked, so there was a total of 4-8 people in the classroom used for the testing - which was rearranged to simulate a boardroom. An OHP and whiteboard was available as well as any other AV resources the student requested, eg. slide projector, video.

Caisley is a speech specialist and examiner for New Zealand's Speech Board. She conducted the assessments and graded students on presentation, while the academic supervisor graded on content (see grading sheets, pages following). One other member of the course team was also present and wrote comments about the presentation which were passed on to the assessor.

Strengths, limitations and problems

After the first year the major areas needing refinement were identified as:

* the degree of importance placed on the oral presentation module
* the minimum pass mark
* introduction of the concept to the students
* availability of training for the students
* time for students to prepare for their presentations
* presentation venue

One of the serious problems in the first semester was that only one student accepted the invitation to the first of two speech training sessions; after some word-of-mouth advertising by that student, nine (out of 20) attended the second session. It turned out that the students had felt very threatened by the written materials circulated at the beginning of the program and had decided the task was unachievable so they simply resolved not to waste time on it. In the second semester, after reflection and evaluation of the whole module (see also Case study 1 in Module 1) an obligatory pass in this task was introduced because it addressed key capabilities in respect to the overall degree program. Students were offered an opportunity for one resubmission. All 18 attended the first 1-1/2 hour session at which they all gave a 1 minute impromptu speech - with no feedback and much informality and laughter.

AUCKLAND INSTITUTE OF TECHNOLOGY
Faculty of Commerce

School of Integrated Business Studies

February 1993

THE CO-OPERATIVE EDUCATION PROGRAMME OF STUDY

MINIMUM COMPETENCY FOR ORAL PRESENTATIONS

The criteria listed below are those expected in any organisation in the commercial world.   A pass will indicate that the student is competent to represent that organisation in a public forum.

To this end the student will demonstrate the ability to:

. choose an appropriate standard of dress for the occasion;
. demonstrate eye contact with the audience;
. speak with impact;
. clarify specialist terms;
. appear pleased to be sharing time and expertise;
. greet all listeners courteously;
. commence the address at the time scheduled;
. conclude the address within the given time limit;
. use visual aids effectively;
. invite and conduct question time constructively;
. include appropriate content.

THIS SKILL REQUIRES TRAINING, PREPARATION AND PRACTICE.

Training is offered by AIT.
Preparation and practice are the responsibility of individual students.

Figure 8.13
Assessment sheets
Meredith Caisley

School of Integrated Business Studies

ASSESSMENT CRITERIA FOR ORAL PRESENTATION

Presentation Skills

Student ....

This presentation will be assessed holistically. It is the overall effect that your presentation has on the audience that is important.

The following feedback sheet will be used.

CRITERIA	COMMENTS
Physical Presence *Standard of dress for occasion . Stance/body language *Eye contact with audience . Hand and body gestures . Use of location in room . Audience rapport	
Vocal Skills *Projection *Clarity of communication *Clarity of pronunciation . Quality of pronunciation . Delivery rate . Modulation . Use of pauses *Use of explanatory language . Minimisation of jargon	

Figure 8.13 *(cont)*

Assessment sheets
Meredith Caisley

➤

CRITERIA	COMMENTS
Attitude . Acknowledgement of variations in audience understanding *Enthusiasm *Approachability . Residual impression	
Presentation *Time management . Introduction . Use of examples . Organisation . Unobtrusive use of notes . Conclusion	
* Visual Aids . Impact . Integration into presentation . Management	
Questioning *Approach to audience *Listening ability *Responses	
Overall Comments	

Presentation mark (out of 12) ....

Content mark (out of 3) ....

Final mark ....

Signed: .... (Communications Lecturer)

Figure 8.13 *(cont)*
Assessment sheets
Meredith Caisley

APPENDIX 9 (Continued)

Appropriateness of Content

Student ....

CRITERIA	COMMENTS
*Appropriateness of Content . To audience . To time available for explanation . To main focus of the written report	

Mark awarded out of 3 ....

Signed: .... (Academic Supervisor)

ANY MARK LESS THAN HALF WILL REQUIRE YOU TO RESUBMIT

Figure 8.13 *(cont)*
Assessment sheets
Meredith Caisley

Section 3

Communicating information visually

Academic conferences, overcrowded with paper presentations, often ask participants to consider offering their contribution in a poster instead of an oral presentation. Some of us react to this suggestion with horror, knowing we lack all "artistic" skills; some relish the prospect of making something eye-catching and interesting.

This difference in skills and pleasure in speaking and/or writing is one of the justifications for including visual presentation of information in the assessable tasks in some courses. Howenstine *et al* (1988, p139), describing an assignment which requires students to prepare a poster in an introductory geography course, argue that "requiring graphic expression (in contrast to purely written work)...acts as a 'leveller', allowing first-year students to compete with more advanced students whose technical writing skills are generally better developed."

Another argument in favour of poster presentations is that some professions require practitioners to engage in various sorts of educational activities which can demand creating public displays, sometimes simplifying or making accessible complex information needed by clients or customers or students.

Case study 60
Poster presentations

Case study from Pharmaceutical Microbiology
Ian Griffith, Monash University

The following case study is almost exactly as it was written for us by Ian Griffith.

Context

Pharmacy is a three year undergraduate course; it is a broadly based science course designed to train students in the nature, mode of action, use and dispensing of medication. Microbiology is taught as a 78 lecture/ 13 tutorial/ 60 practical hour course in the second year; it covers basic bacteriology, virology, mycology, parasitology, epidemiology, immunology, pathology and biotechnology with emphasis on the nature of infectious disease and its control and treatment.

It has been traditional in science-based courses to assess practical skills by, *inter alia*, requiring students to write detailed reports on practical exercises and submit these for marking. While excellent training for graduates intent on a career as a laboratory-based technician or research scientist, few graduates in pharmacy choose this path. The majority enter community pharmacy practice where skills such as accurate dispensing of drugs and effective communication with members of the public about their medication are of paramount importance.

As part of the Pharmaceutical Microbiology course in 1992 and 1993 students were given the option of additional training in laboratory report writing (already provided in other parts of the Pharmacy course) or instruction in communication; they opted for the latter. This was to involve

➤

presentation of a chosen topic in poster format. In 1992 students each prepared one poster on an infectious agent in Semester 1 and on a preventative or curative agent in Semester 2. In Semester 1 of 1993 students each prepared a poster on a different infectious disease. The class sizes were 131 in 1992 and 110 in 1993.

At the start of the year, students were provided with a list of texts and journals which might prove useful as sources of information. They were also issued with instructions on what was required in the poster and advice on effective presentation. A tutorial was given on how to write the text for, and design posters: an example of a poster (prepared by the chief instructor) was placed on display in the College. Students were also issued with a list of the criteria to be considered when posters were being assessed. Each poster comprised 4% of the marks for the year.

Abilities

Being assessed was ability in:
(a) acquiring information on a chosen topic
(b) presenting technical information
   (1) accurately
   (2) in a concise way
   (3) in a way meaningful for the lay public
   (4) in an interesting and stimulating manner
(c) following written instructions
(d) creativity and artistic flair.

Assessment methods and criteria

(a) Ability to acquire and present technical information in written form

Students were required to submit the text for their poster (including any Figures and Tables, with their legends and references) for marking by staff. As it was intended to place posters on public display (eg. for marking by the student body, for Open Days, for teaching purposes) students were asked to submit the text in a form they would be happy to see published.

The main criteria used for assessment of the text were:
(1) accuracy of the information included
(2) absence of spelling and grammatical errors
(3) proper use of punctuation
(4) avoidance of waffle and repetition
(5) accuracy of citation and use of the required convention for citations
(6) sentence construction and style
(7) avoidance of technical terms
(8) stimulus (presentation of content, style, and nature of illustrations)
(9) whether there was evidence of plagiarism
(10) complying with the word limit requirements

For each poster, the mark for the text comprised 2% of the year's mark (ie. half the marks for the poster *in toto*).

(b) Ability to communicate technical information in a stimulating format.

The other half of the marks for this assessment were awarded for the finished poster; marking was performed by the students themselves. Each student was assigned, on a random

➤

basis, ten posters to mark. A mark was to be given (out of 20) for each of five different aspects of the poster: these aspects were (with advice for the students in brackets)

(1) **Visual Impact.** [Was the poster attractive, easy to read and follow? Was the text too small, cramped, excessive? Did you like the layout, use of colour? Were you drawn to it? Did you feel like staying to read it all?]

(2) **Text.** [Did you detect errors of fact, spelling, grammar? Was the text stilted, or punchy (short sentences, simple words)? Did you feel the author was wordy, or adept at precis? Were technical terms over-used?]

(3) **Figures.** [Were all the Figures really needed? Would the data have been better presented in some other way? Did each Fig. stand alone? Was each readily understandable, readable?]

(4) **Balance.** [Did you feel there was unnecessary repetition? Was there too much, or not enough detail? Did part(s) of the text merit illustration with a Figure? Did you feel the author was communicating the important aspects of the material (ie. able to sort the wood from the trees)?]

(5) **Stimulus.** [Did the poster stimulate your interest? Did it readily prompt questions in your mind? Did you find it exciting, memorable?]

An average of the marks obtained (with, or without elimination of the highest and lowest, depending on Semester), reduced to 2% maximum, was used as the final mark for the poster presentation.

Strengths and limitations

Strengths included the strict word limit (400) on the body of the text forcing students to think deeply about how best to restrict their text to the essentials, and yet maintain the interest of the reader (because of the requirement to present the information in a stimulating format). The project also required them to read ahead of, and beyond, the formal lecture/ practical course and consider how best to communicate their new knowledge in a form understandable to the lay public, and in a format (the poster) which was informative yet visually stimulating and exciting. A major strength of the assessment procedure for the posters was to use the student body to mark each other's efforts: by using a panel of assessors, in view of the subjective nature of assessing posters, a fairer overall mark could thus be arrived at. In addition, by listing the criteria to be used in assessing the posters and issuing these early in the year, by reviewing these criteria, students were better able to examine critically their own efforts as they formulated them. Another advantage of using the student body as assessors was each individual had the opportunity to learn something about other topics, ie. those on posters assigned to her/ him to mark. The finding that a 1992 poster included in the 1993 batch of posters as a "control" received a virtually identical average mark from a different panel of ten students on the second occasion provides some evidence for consistency in the assessment process. The fact that the posters were to be placed on public display and subjected to peer review was another strength of the assessment procedure - the element of competition served to raise the standard of many of the posters to a very high level.

Limitations/ problems included those usually associated with the marking of written work (ie. it is often, to a greater or lesser degree, subjective) and this was compounded by the fact that each student had a different topic and some topics were more difficult to research than others. Thus more emphasis was placed, in the marking, on whether students had followed the written instructions and advice provided to them. Texts which were well below standard were marked, corrected, and then returned to the student concerned for resubmission (but not remarking). Problems associated with using the student body to assess each other's posters included, in some cases, bias (since posters included the author's name) and in some cases unethical practices (such as submitting mark sheets without actually viewing the posters "marked"). However, deleting the lowest and highest marks from the panel of marks submitted had such a marginal effect on the average final mark that adjustment was ultimately considered unnecessary. Another problem with the use of student assessors is the reluctance of students to fail another student; only one poster out of a total of 371 submitted failed on average mark.

Despite these problems, on the basis of feedback from the students, the use of student peer group assessment of posters has proved to be a very valuable teaching tool.

Marks and grades

As outlined above, students received a mark from the teaching staff for the written text of their poster, to a maximum of 2% of the year's mark and marks on each of five criteria for their poster from a panel of fellow students (selected at random) reduced to a maximum of 2% of the year's mark.

For each poster the aggregate mark contributed 4% of the total mark for the year's work. Students were not required to pass this component of the course, but had to pass Pharmaceutical Microbiology as a whole before proceeding to the third year of their Pharmacy course. ∎

Comments

There is an interesting separation of content and communication in this case study, reinforced by having different assessors making the judgments.

Case study 61
Poster exercise

61

Case study from Geography
(Howenstine, Hay, Delaney, Bell, Norris, Whelan, et al., 1988)

The poster exercise described by Howenstine et al (1988) was more heavily weighted.

Course assessment comprises two 50-minute multiple choice examinations worth 50% of the final grade with the remainder of the grade being based on assignments provided by the TAs (teaching assistants at the University of Washington). Although additional requirements vary from quarter to quarter, the poster exercise has become the most heavily weighted of teaching assistants' assignments. (p140)

In this case the poster exercise actually comprises three separate assignments:

(1) an abstract of the key ideas and graphic layout adopted for the poster, which is due two weeks before the poster, (2) the poster itself, and (3) a two-to three-page poster write-up, which is due one week after the poster's due date.

➤

The intention of the abstract is to stimulate the student to think about a topic of interest and to formulate a focus of research, and to direct later work. It is also useful for flagging projects that are ill-conceived, or otherwise unworkable. The abstract requires the following: a title, a topic of study, explanation or argument within that topic, a description of specific content, and a brief illustration of the graphic design and organisation of the poster material. The poster is intended to have the student analyse a spatial phenomenon and display this study in graphic form. Although the short paper augments the poster by adding further detail, the poster itself is expected to be a "unified coherent statement requiring no further explanation". Students are warned not to stop with simple description; they are directed to *explain* why certain phenomena exist, or to explore the *relationships* between phenomena.

To assist the student with concept formation, examples of possible poster topics are listed on the assignment handout, such as:

(1) environmental factors influencing the location of microbreweries in Washington State;
(2) the relationship between income levels and the provision of private music teaching in Seattle suburbs;
(3) factors explaining why pornographic bookstores are located where they are.

(p141)

Howenstine *et al* emphasise, as does Griffith, the value of having students express complex ideas succinctly. However, the University of Washington TAs found that students had great difficulty moving past simple description to achieving some original analysis or formulating judgments; this was true of students at various stages of their university careers. Although this is an introductory course, it is open to all students and is even taken by some postgraduate students.

While Griffith employed peer assessment, at the University of Washington, each poster was graded independently by two TAs on the following criteria:

(1) How clearly does the poster make a case and how thorough is the explanation?
(2) How well does the poster stand alone? Is it self-explanatory?
(3) How well is the poster organised?
(4) Does the poster display original thought?
(5) How professional is the presentation, in terms of neatness, spelling, appropriate use of graphics, etc.?
(6) What is the degree of difficulty - how complex is the issue or topic?

(p144)

There was no problem with agreement in the grading between the TAs.

Howenstine *et al* report that their students found the assignment difficult and stressful. They seemed to be uncomfortable with both the "level of analysis requested by the exercise and ... the medium of presentation" (p144). On a five-point scale with 3 representing "fair" and 2 "weak", students rated the value of the poster exercise as a teaching tool at 2.9.

Finally, Howenstine *et al* discuss the value of the posters in promoting discussion, interest and unity among the students in the course and within the department when they are displayed. They also advocate displaying selected posters publicly on or off-campus to promote the subject itself and better understanding of what a geographer actually studies.

∎

The next case study also emphasises the importance and challenge of public display.

Case study 62
The installation project

Case study from Sociology
Michael Bounds, University of Western Sydney, Macarthur

We have reorganised material provided by Bounds but have used his own words as much as possible.

Context

"The Installation Project" is an assessment task in a second year undergraduate sociology subject, Class and Social Stratification. The subject is taken by BA and BSocSci students. Average enrolment is 80.

Groups of 4-6 students mount displays in public areas of the university. These are intended to demonstrate a grasp of the theoretical content of the course thus far and the relation of theory to evidence of social inequality in the world around us, as expressed through class status or some other measure of social stratification, the choice is left up to the students. It is thus particularly important that the completed project stands as coherent evidence of the process of learning that students have worked through or that they are able to argue the rationale for their choice of presentation.

Abilities being assessed

*   Application of sociological theory of Class and Social Stratification to the observable processes and structures of everyday life in Australian Society.

*   Assessing grasp of theory, grasp of the contingent nature of forms of stratification and their manifestation.

*   Capacity to represent understanding of the practical relevance of the subject.

*   Capacity to critically assess some of the more dubious claims of the theory through the failure to discover examples of the practices and relations portrayed in the literature.

*   Skills at group working complex theoretical positions to represent them to passing traffic.

*   Analysis of the symbolic order of everyday life to deconstruct its relation to the maintenance of class relations and a stratified social order.

The assignment as given to the students

Rationale

The installation is intended to provide a visual depiction of the social life and situation of comparative class and status groups (two of either) in Australian society. The object is to provide you with the opportunity to actively apply the theory of C&SS regarding inequality to an understanding of the real lives of people today. If the theory works you should be able to find real groups that correspond to the categories of class and status you are discussing. It is

➤

anticipated that this will be a contemporary observation but you may wish to make it historical by comparing one group at different times in history (for example, working class women in 1890 and 1990).

Information

The installation is to be established as a public display in the university in the semester week 10 by work groups of 4-6 students (you will have the tutorial of week 9 free to organise yourselves for preparation during the break). The display should be mounted during week 10 and dismantled and removed at the end of week 10. I have arranged with campus management for you to use the public areas of the main building at Bankstown Campus and the foyer outside lecture theatres 1 & 3 at Campbelltown for the display. You should contact campus management to obtain screens for the display should you need them. (There may not be enough screens for everybody.) Security will be sympathetic but try not to create something that will be obstructive or a hazard to the public or contains anything you would be devastated to lose. It will be assessed in the tutorial period of week 10. One member of the group should remain by the display during the tutorial period to explain it to me as I go around. The results of my assessment will be fed back to you.

Method

It is anticipated you will engage in a division of labour on this exercise and as it is a visual presentation you will credit the various contributions (photography, layout, editing, sound, camera work, artwork, interviewing) to the appropriate members of the group; naturally the research will be a delegated but common task.

Your starting point will be establishing a clear definition for yourselves of what is meant by the terms *class* and *status* from appropriate sociological sources. A one page theoretically grounded explanation of the basis for the installation, with references, must be given to the assessors at the time of display. At the outset you may refer to the course references; however, if you are dissatisfied with the applicability of the definitions that emerge here, go further afield, utilise the various dictionaries of sociology and the social sciences. The definition you come up with will define the parameters of your study and will appear on your installation as a guide to the viewers' understanding of what they are observing. As you gather your material, you may have cause to modify or critique your definition.

Sources

Material for the presentation will be gained from magazines, newspapers, photographs, television clips of the life, culture, behaviours and material attributes of the groups you are investigating. I am hesitant to guide your artistic and innovative potential too much here but some areas of investigation are suggested below.

Remember! This is supposed to strike the viewer with an understanding of the contrasts or indeed the similarities in the lives of the comparative groups so try to be innovative in getting this across. For example, do the contents of a working class woman's handbag differ from those of a middle class woman? Does the dinner table in the house at night look different? Does it mean something?

Marks and grades

Assessment is a combination of norm and criterion referencing, the essential criteria being whether students have adequately covered the requirements/guidelines given above for the execution of the project. The norm referencing will be in the comparative standard of presentation, its impact on the viewer, its concise depiction of the groups identified and the innovation of research and method in its depiction.

➤

Assessment criteria:

- visual impact,
- relation between theoretical content and coherence of presentation,
- theoretical content,
- ideas developed for presentation,
- standard of presentation/evidence of effort,
- quality of evidence for theoretical propositions,
- consistency with, deviation from guidelines, argument for deviation,
- capacity to justify choice and rationale for approach.

How these criteria are applied in practice may be clarified by the following comments on an excellent display, an acceptable one and a poor one.

Title: "Class in School" - Grade of 18

The installation was well located and organised for maximum visual impact. The viewer's attention was immediately attracted by the display of three school uniforms with prominent price tags illustrating both the distinction of the order that the pupils were drawn into but also the financial barriers to entry.

The body of the installation was divided into three parts each devoted to a different school: Bidwell High, Mt Carmel, StVincents College - in ascending order of status.

To the left of the display was a school desk upon which rested a folder entitled theory containing a series of cards which explicitly theorised and referenced the rationale for the display and expanded on the evidence available in the segments of the installation.

Each segment was composed of photos of the school environments which had been taken by the members of the group and surrounding the photos were details of staff student ratios, school fees, extracurricular activities, etc demonstrating the contrasting environments, the lifestyle and the processes of socialisation associated with the schools.

The display had coherence. The group was well informed about their objectives. It illustrated considerable organisation and effective execution and attracted a great deal of passing interest.

Title: "A Sea of Class" - Grade of 13

The display is immediately imposing with the cardboard creation of a ship emerging from its centre, illustrating the metaphor of the ship of life with the upper and lower decks demonstrating the possibilities of lifestyle and status accorded to one by wealth.

In the ship this is accentuated as the prospective passenger is seduced to aspire to the status offered by the trappings of excellence on the upper decks.

In the attached text the theme is carefully explained and the aspiration to opulence is reinforced by a quotation from Lenin on false consciousness.

Overall the display presents an imposing and coherent theme; however, it is undertheorised - a deficit the group was unable to remedy orally.

➤

Title: "Differences at Work" - Grade of 7

The installation had initially good visual impact, but did not follow up the simple message of class contrast with demonstration of the depth to which it impacts on people's lives. X's contribution of the masks has good visual impact illustrating the political nature of class conflict but failing to pursue it with a visual or theoretical explanation of what the relationships are. The collage device does not work well in this installation as it is cramped and is not explained in any way. The idea of including occupations in the central band is good but doesn't really explain anything about who takes them up. The brief explanation of class was appropriate but unreferenced. The students' explanation that observers did not want a thesis was not sufficient argument to present a piece of work demonstrating no reference to the considerable body of theory which at this point in the subject they should be familiar with.

Use of results

The assessment item is a group effort attracting 20% of marks for the course unit. It is graded on criteria and norm referencing procedure (see above).

In 1992 marks ranged from 0 to 19. The 0 was awarded to three students associated with a failing presentation who did not bother to attend the class; two others who did attend were given 5.

■

Comments

Perhaps of all the case studies in this module, this one best illustrates the marriage between content and communication style. Bounds is trying to get his students to make visual images and at the same time link them to concise statements of theory. Reading through the whole class set of comments and feedback demonstrated to us the students' quite astounding creativity; few of the projects were criticised for their presentation. On the other hand, those with middle range or lower marks did not demonstrate the ability to link and present the theory along with the images of class and status.

References

Andresen, L. (1993). "Toward a formal theory of assessment". In University of New South Wales course handout.

Angelo, T., & Cross, K. P. (1993). *Classroom Assessment Techniques: A Handbook for College Teachers*. San Franciso: Jossey-Bass.

Armstrong, & Boud, D. (1983). Assessing participation in discussion: an exploration of the issues. *Studies in Higher Education, 33*.

Bertola, P., & Murphy, E. (1994). *Tutoring in the Social Sciences and Humanities*. Perth: Curtin University.

Boud, D. (1989). The role of self-assessment in grading. *Assessment and Evaluation in Higher Education, 20*.

Boud, D., & Tyree (1980). Self and peer assessment in professional education: a preliminary study in law. *Journal of the Society of Public Teachers of Law, 65*.

Branthwaite, A., Trueman, M., & Hartley, J. (1980). Writing essays: the actions and strategies of students. In J. Hartley (Eds.), *The Psychology of Written Communication: Selected Readings*. London: Kogan Page.

Gibbs, G. & Habeshaw, T. (1992). Preparing to Teach: An introduction to effective teaching in higher education (2nd ed). Bristol: Technical and Educational Services Ltd.

Gibbs, G. (1981). *Teaching Students to Learn: A Student-Centred Approach*. Milton Keynes: The Open University Press.

Gibbs, G. (1992). *Improving the quality of student learning*. Bristol: Technical and Education Services.

Hay, I. (1994). Justifying and applying oral presentations in geographical education. *Journal of Geography in Higher Education, 18*(1), 43-55.

Hay, I. (forthcoming). Communicating geographies: development and application of a communication instruction manual in the geography discipline of an Australian university. *Journal of Geography in Higher Education*.

Hay, I., & Delaney, E. (1994). 'Who Teaches Learns': writing groups in geographical education. *Journal of Geography in Higher Education, 18*(3), 217-34.

Hounsell, D. (1984). Essay planning and essay writing. *Higher Education Research and Development, 3*(1), 13-31.

Howenstine, E., Hay, I., Delaney, E., Bell, J., Norris, F., Whelan, A., Piranti, M., Chow, T., & Ross, A. (1988). Using a poster exercise in an introductory geography course. *Journal of Geography in Higher Education, 12*(2), 139-147.

Hull, G., & Rose, M. (1990). Toward a social-cognitive understanding of problematic reading and writing. In A. A. Lunsford & e. al (Eds.), *The Right to Literacy*. New York: Modern Language Association of America.

Morgan (1989). The Socratic method: silencing co-operation. *Legal Education Review, 1*.

Nightingale, P. (1986). *Improving Student Writing*. Sydney: Higher Education Research and Development Society of Australasia.

Nightingale, P., & Sohler, C. (1994). *Considering Gender*. Sydney: Higher Education Research and Development Society of Australasia.

Norton, L. (1990). Essay-writing: what really counts? *Higher Education, 20*, 411-42.

Ramsden, P. (1992). *Learning to Teach in Higher Education*. London: Routledge.

Rowntree, D. (1987). *Assessing Students: How Shall We Know Them?* (2nd ed.). London: Kogan Page.

Shay, S., Bond, D., & Hughes, T. (1994). Mysterious demands and disappointing responses: exploring students' difficulties with academic writing tasks. In A. Angelil-Carter, D. Bond, M. Paxton, & L. Thesen (Eds.), *Language in Academic Development at UCT, 1994* (pp. 18-35). Cape Town, SA: Academic Development Programme, University of Cape Town.

Spender, D. (1982). *Invisible Women: The Schooling Scandal*. London: Writers and Readers.

Taylor, G., Ballard, B., Beasley, V., Bock, H., Clanchy, J., & Nightingale, P. (1988). *Literacy by Degrees*. Milton-Keynes (UK): SRHE and Open University Press.

Thomson, A. N. (1992). Can communication skills be assessed independently of their context? *Medical Education, 26*, 364-7.

Unwin, T. (1990). 2.i or not 2.i? The Assessment of Undergraduate Essays. *Journal of Geography in Higher Education, 14*(1), 31-38.

White, E. M. (1994). *Teaching and Assessing Writing* (Second edition, revised and expanded ed.). San Francisco: Jossey-Bass.

Wildman (1988). The question of silence: techniques to ensure full class participation. *Journal of Legal Education, 38.*

Assessment Project Glossary

A

Analytic marking/ scoring

Analytic marking attempts to judge the component parts of a task separately, assign marks to each, possibly weight them and then calculate a final grade. Analytical scoring of essays in mass testing situations has proved time-consuming and expensive, and inter-marker reliability has not been high. Holistic scoring is often preferred.

Approach to learning

Surface approach to learning

A term which has a particular meaning in educational literature, to describe a situation in which a student is motivated extrinsically to focus on selected details of content; and to study so as to reproduce these details accurately, attending to separate bits, elements or components of what they study rather than the overall picture. Learning is seen as a matter of how much is learned, and teaching is conceived as a process of transmitting knowledge. (See also "Deep approach to learning" and "Achieving approach to learning".)

Deep approach to learning

A term which has a particular meaning in educational literature, to describe a situation in which a student is motivated intrinsically to satisfy curiosity about a topic. To maximise understanding, the student reads widely, discusses issues and reflects on what has been heard and read, integrating details into broad, over-arching (or high-level) ideas which she or he is constantly trying to develop. Learning is seen as involving meaning, understanding, and a way of interpreting the world. It is the learner who constructs knowledge, not the teacher who imparts it. (See also "Surface approach to learning" and "Achieving approach to learning".)

Achieving approach to learning

A term used in educational literature, in which a student is motivated towards achievement, competing for the highest grades and optimising organisation of time and effort. This approach can incorporate either "surface" or "deep" approaches to learning. (See also "Surface approach to learning" and "Deep approach to learning".)

Assessment pattern

The collection of assessment tasks, their weightings and the timing of completion used to assess the objectives of a unit, module or subject.

Assignment

Assessment tasks that are normally submitted from work conducted during a semester or teaching session. Assignments can be formative or summative and of many forms (essays, short answer questions, computer programs, etc.)

Authentic assessment

Assessment strategies which reflect as much as possible, real world performance conditions and which assess student performance under those conditions.

C

Cognitive skills

Skills which involve significant and explicit mental activity.

Competency

Used to refer to a group of related skills, knowledge and attitudes which underlies the performance of a complex and specifiable 'real world' activity. Many professions in Australia are involved in the development of 'competency standards' which specify the competencies seen as essential for adequate performance in all the major areas of activity undertaken by professional practitioners.

Competency based assessment

Assessment designed to assess the achievement of competencies by students. Usually employed as part of a subject, unit or course designed to assist students to achieve the competencies set down for their chosen profession.

Competency standard

A statement of the competencies required for professional practice in an area. Standards are usually developed by professional bodies, and in Australia they are often approved and registered by national bodies.

Computer aided assessment

Assessments carried out with the assistance of computers. Usually used to refer to systems in which assessment questions are posed, and responses taken and analysed by computer.

Continuous assessment

An assessment pattern containing more than one assessment task with at least one, and usually more tasks due for submission during the semester or teaching session.

Contracts

Agreements between staff and students on learning activities to be undertaken, evidence of achievement to be presented and assessment criteria for a given area of work.

Criterion-referenced assessment

Assessment of students conducted with reference to specified criteria for adequate or satisfactory performance. Sometimes criteria are also articulated for performances at levels above the adequate or satisfactory level. These criteria form the standard by which student performance is judged.

Criterion referenced assessment is usually contrasted with 'norm referenced' assessment, a mode of assessment which refers to the relative performance of other students in the same assessment in order to set the standards used in the assessment.

D

Diagnostic testing

Testing designed to discover, for the benefit of teachers and/or students, gaps in learning, the nature of student mis-conceptions or other impediments to learning.

F

Feedback

Information given to students on their progress in their course/unit. The information can be in the form of marks, grades, comments, model answers, suggestions for reading, etc.

Final examination

A test, quiz, essay paper etc., whether formal or informal, set for students to complete during the official examination period at the end of a semester or teaching session.

Formal assessment

An examination or other assessment task resulting in marks/ grades which are usually submitted to the Registrar's division for entry on official transcripts of student achievement.

Formative assessment

Assessment used to give students feedback on their progress towards achieving the intended student learning outcomes in a subject or unit. Used to refer to any assessment whether graded or ungraded, which has as its primary purpose the encouragement of student learning by the provision of feedback on performance.

G

Grading

The process of ranking students' work in some order. Common grading schemes use pass/ credit/ distinction/ high distinction, or A/ B/ C/ D grades.

Group assessment

The assessment of the performance of a group of students together, rather than of individuals.

H

Higher order cognitive skills

Cognitive skills regarded as being conducted at second or higher orders, as opposed to the 'first order' cognitive skills employed in routine performances. Higher order skills usually include skills such as reflection on performance, problem solving, and critical thinking.

Holistic marking/ scoring

The assessor judges the work as a whole, considering its overall quality. There may be descriptive criteria to guide the assessor, but there is no attempt to assign marks to each criterion. Essentially the marker is judging the whole rather than the sum of the parts. A high level of inter-marker reliability can be achieved if markers discuss standards and some sample papers prior to marking.

I

Informal assessment

An assessment task conducted by the lecturer or unit coordinator which does not result in marks/ grades to be entered on official transcripts.

Integrated assessment

An assessment strategy which attempts to assess a range of the underlying aspects of a competence or ability (including knowledge, skills and attitudes), or sometimes a range of competencies or abilities, in one activity.

L

Learning outcomes

A statement, usually expressed in terms of knowledge, skills, attitudes or competencies, of what students completing a unit or course are expected to achieve. The statement of learning outcomes should form the basis of the assessment criteria used in the unit or course, especially if the assessment is criterion-referenced. Learning outcomes are sometimes written in the form of objectives.

M

Mark

A numerical value assigned to a student's response to an assessment task as an indication of its quality.

Marking schedule

A guide to markers indicating the marking scheme to be employed when assessment items are marked. Usually includes a scheme for distributing marks by reference to a number of criteria.

Mastery learning

A system of teaching which aims to ensure that all students achieve adequate performance levels (mastery) on a series of set tasks.

Multiple choice questions

Assessment questions which offer a restricted number of response options to students. Students select, from among the options offered, the choice closest to their own answer.

N

Norm referenced assessment

Assessment of students conducted with reference to the performance of the students' peers or cohort. The level of performance of peers and the cohort is used to set the standards used in the assessment.

Usually contrasted with 'criterion referenced' assessment, a mode of assessment which uses objective standards (specified criteria) in the assessment.

O

Objective tests

Tests which can be objectively marked. This is usually achieved by limiting the possible responses a student can make by using multiple choice questions, so that the student's response is clear, unambiguous and within the expected range set by the assessor.

On-the-job assessment

Assessments carried out 'on-the-job', under the normal conditions of work, including normal task, resource, time and incentive constraints. By this definition few students are assessed 'on-the-job' as part of their higher education studies.

OSCE (OSCA)

OSCE stands for 'Objective Structured Clinical Examination', also known as OSCAs - Objective Structured Clinical Assessments. Common in the Health related disciplines, it is used to refer to a range of assessment activities which attempt to provide a comprehensive and relatively objective assessment of student performance on authentic tasks. OSCEs often include less authentic assessment tasks designed to test for underlying knowledge, skills and attitudes, in addition to integrated performance assessments.

P

Peer assessment

An assessment strategy in which students assess, either alone or in groups the work of their peers. The assessment is preferably carried out with reference to criteria set by the teacher and the student group.

Performance testing or assessment

The testing or assessment of fully fledged performance usually against specified criteria, as opposed to the testing of isolated knowledge, skills or attitudes which may underlie full performance.

Problem-based learning

A method of teaching and an approach to curriculum development which employs a series of broadly authentic problems as the core organising structure for a course.

Problem based learning is a way of constructing and teaching courses using problems as the stimulus and focus for student activity. It is not simply the addition of problem solving activities to otherwise discipline-centred curricula, but a way of conceiving of the curriculum as centred around key problems in professional practice. Problem based courses start with problems rather than with exposition of disciplinary knowledge. They move students towards the acquisition of knowledge and skills through a staged sequence of problems presented in context, together with associated learning materials and support from teachers. (Boud & Feletti, 1991, p14)

R

Reliability

Used to refer to the extent to which an assessment strategy or activity yields like results in like circumstances. A reliable assessment is usually seen as one which would give the same or similar results if administered to the same students under similar circumstances.

Jim Tognolini writes for this project:

Reliability can be defined as the degree of consistency between two measures of the same thing.

A person's weight, height, etc are generally consistent irrespective of the scale or ruler used to carry out the measurement. Achievement test scores, on the other hand can vary. For example, how similar are the results of tests if students are tested at other times with the same (or a parallel) test? How similar are the results if essays are marked by a different marker? These are the types of questions with which reliability is concerned and the type of questions which permeate every form of assessment.

Unless the measurement can be shown to be reasonably consistent over different administrations of the test or over separate markings by different markers, little confidence can be placed in the results. More importantly, little faith can be placed in the grades and awards that emerge from a consideration of the scores.

We cannot expect test results to be perfectly consistent. There are numerous factors, other than the performance being measured, which may influence test scores. For example, genuine ability differences, understanding of instructions, test-taking skills, marking inconsistencies (especially in essays and checklists), guessing and item format chosen for the test can influence test scores. Similarly, temporary factors, such as health, fatigue, motivation and testing conditions will also affect the scores.

Extraneous factors like those listed above introduce error into all assessment situations. As teachers we try and control the sources of error. For example, we double mark essay tests; try and control the conditions in the examination room (we don't use lecture theatres for examinations, where students are tiered on top of each other and opportunities for collusion are enhanced); motivate our students to perform at their maximum ability; and, make instructions clear and to the point.

There is a need to estimate test score reliability so that we can judge the extent to which measurement errors might be interfering with the interpretation of the score. Because reliability can be influenced by so many factors, it is not possible to settle on a single method for estimating reliability for all testing situations. There are at least 5 methods used to obtain measures of reliability. The methods estimate coefficients of stability, equivalence and internal consistency.

It doesn't matter whether an objective test, essay, checklist, assignment, practical or problem solving exercise has been used to derive scores, regardless of the form of the assessment it is absolutely critical that the teacher has some idea of the reliability of the scores when evaluating their meaningfulness (or assigning grades).

One question which is commonly asked is 'What level of reliability should we aim for?'

There is no absolute standard for determining whether a given reliability coefficient is high enough. However, some rules of thumb have evolved over time. They are generally linked to the use of the information.

Normally reliability coefficients in excess of 0.8 (maximum possible is 1.0) are needed if the scores are to be used to make decisions about individuals and the scores are the only ones available.

Reliabilities around 0.5 can be tolerated if the scores are to be combined with other scores to obtain an overall grade. It is the reliability of the composite score that is of most concern in this instance.

S

Scaling marks

In calculating a final mark for students two sets of marks may be combined from assessment tasks which supposedly carry the same weight but where the spread of one set of marks of greater than the spread of the other set. In such a case the set of marks having the wider spread will have a greater impact on the final ranking of the students. To avoid this and give both sets of marks equal weight each set of scores should be 'scaled' or adjusted to fit within the same range of marks. See Rowntree (1987, pp220-27) for additional information on scaling.

Score distributions

The pattern of scores or marks achieved by students in an assessment activity. Distributions are usually analysed with reference to set ranges or percentile groups often derived by reference to the so-called 'normal' distribution.

Self assessment

An assessment strategy in which the student assesses his or her own work, preferably with reference to criteria set by the teacher and/or the student group, or the individual student.

Self paced learning

A method of teaching which allows students to work through the course material and other tasks and activities at their own pace. Self paced learning is often opposed to 'lock-step' learning in which all students cover the same material and attempt exercises at the same time.

Subject/unit outline

A description of the subject or unit, usually containing: the objectives or learning outcomes for the subject or unit; an outline of the content; details of assessment tasks and how they relate to the objectives or learning outcomes; set texts and other suggested readings; and other information about the subject or unit.

Summative assessment

Assessment used to gain a view (or summation) of the student learning outcomes achieved in a subject, unit or course. Used to refer to any assessment whether graded or ungraded, which contributes to the overall assessment of a student's actual learning achievements.

U

Ungraded assessment

An assessment which does not result in a graded or ranked result. Usually used to refer to 'pass/fail' or 'satisfactory/try again' assessment schemes.

V

Validity

Used to describe the extent to which an assessment strategy or activity assesses what it is intended to assess.

Jim Tognolini writes for this project:

Validity of the results of a test can be best defined as the extent to which the results measure what they purport to measure.

For a test to be valid, the scores must be reliable. Reliability is a necessary but not sufficient condition for validity.

Since a single test may have many different purposes, there is no single index of validity for the results of a test. Three main types of validity mentioned in the latest version of the Standards for Educational and Psychological Tests and Manuals lists three main kinds of validity: content, criterion and construct-related validity.

Construct validity

This refers to the degree to which the test measures the constructs on which it was based. Newble (1982) illustrates this concept by explaining that one could gauge the construct validity of a test of clinical competence by determining the extent to which scores on the test were seen to correspond to known, patently different, levels of clinical performance. For example, expert clinicians would be expected to have higher scores than recently appointed interns, who in turn should score higher than fifth year medical students.

Vu and Barrow (1994) identify this, and one other form of construct validity. The second form is usually tested by 'factor analysis'. If for example, factor analyses of clinical competence skills assessed across a range of different tasks consistently revealed two separate and independent factors (e.g. cognitive and non cognitive), then any valid test of clinical competence should incorporate separate scores for each of these distinct components of competence.

Content validity

How adequately does the content of the test cover the area about which inferences are to be made? There is no commonly used measure for by this type of validity. It is determined by a thorough and expert inspection of the assessment material. In other words it is based upon the professional judgement of the teachers.

Sometimes this type of validity is referred to as instructional validity. There should be a match between the content as specified in the objectives of the subject, the instruction and the assessment material. One way to help ensure that there is a match between the content (including the skills, abilities and processes) of the subject and the assessment material is to develop a Table of Specifications

There is an obligation on the teacher (test instructor) to be as clear as possible about what is being measured and to produce an assessment instrument that measures performance as accurately as possible.

Criterion-related validity

There are two main types of criterion related validity: predictive and concurrent validity. In **predictive validity** we are concerned with the usefulness of the test scores in predicting some future performance. For example, how useful are the scores (grades) obtained from Physics 100 for predicting success in Physics 200? How valid is the Tertiary Entrance Score (Rank) in predicting university success.

In concurrent validity we ask whether the test results can be substituted for some less efficient way of measuring performance. For example, is it valid to substitute assignments for invigilated examinations?

Typically criterion related validity is expressed in terms of a correlation coefficient. That is the correlation between the test (predictor) and criterion related score.

ANNOTATED BIBLIOGRAPHY

Alderson, C. D., & Clapham, C. (1992). Applied linguistics and language testing: A case study of the ELTS test. *Applied Linguistics, 13*(2), 149-167.

> This paper reports on the diverse views that resulted from a survey of applied linguists as to what view of language and language proficiency should be incorporated into the revised ELTS test. It also reports some of the constraints that limit the extent to which current applied linguistics theory can be implemented in language testing. It concludes with reflections on the proper relationship between applied linguistics and language testing, arguing that language testers need not feel they are on the fringe of applied linguistics, and that involving applied linguists in test development will not only help testing, but arguably may help applied linguistics even more.

Andresen, L. (1993). Toward a formal theory of assessment. In University of New South Wales course handouts.

> A handout given to an AGSM Assessment Workshop. This resource was cited as useful by Patricia Duncan whose case studies appear in Module 8.

Angelo, T., & Cross, K. P. (1993). *Classroom Assessment Techniques: A Handbook for College Teachers*. San Francisco: Jossey-Bass.

> The assessment in the title actually refers to assessing one's own teaching by collecting information on the quality of student learning at the time it is happening rather than after it is supposed to be complete. Many of the strategies could be used for grading students work as well. The manual contains many examples from practice in many disciplines.

Anthony, K. (1987). Private reactions to public criticism: students, faculty and practicing architects state their views on design juries in architectural education. *Journal of Architectural Education, 40*(3), 2-11.

> This article reports the results of research about the effectiveness of design juries in architectural education. Research consists of a case study using observation, interviews, questionnaires and diaries, plus staff surveys at a seminar attended by people from many institutions. Students report learning little from juries but find interim ones more useful than final. Students are defensive and nervous and suffer burn-out.

Armstrong, & Boud, D. (1983). Assessing participation in discussion: an exploration of the issues. *Studies in Higher Education, 33*.
> Cited by Annette Marfording (Case Study #56, Module 8).

Auckland Institute of Technology (1992). *Bachelor of Business Course Document*. Auckland: Auckland Institute of Technology.

> This document is part of the accreditation materials required for NZQA approval of the Bachelor of Business Course.

Balla, J., & Boyle, P. (1994). Assessment of student performance: a framework for improving practice. *Assessment and Evaluation in Higher Education, 19*(1).

> Assessment of student performance and the evaluation of courses and teaching are critical elements in the teaching-learning environment and are central to each higher education institution's mission of preparing students for the future. There are increased internal and external pressures for institutions to review and improve their practice in this area. While a vast knowledge-base exists to inform good practice in

assessment of student performance, change in practice seems to be slow. A framework for improving assessment practice, based in a simple quality management model, is provided as are some examples which illustrate application of the model/framework. Some suggestions are also made about support mechanisms and resources required for effecting significant improvement to practice. (Journal abstract)

Barton, J., & Collins, A. (1993). Portfolios in teacher education. *Journal of Teacher Education, 44*(3), 200-210.

This paper describes the use of teaching portfolios in the assessment of teacher education students. The authors argue for the usefulness of the portfolio on a number of grounds: it allows students and faculty to reflect on student growth throughout the course of a program; it allows an assessment of student work in the context of teaching as a complex activity; it shifts the ownership of learning onto the student; and portfolios help students become more articulate. The portfolio design used by the authors is characterised by: explicitness of purpose; integration between academic course work and field experiences; multisourced; authentic; dynamic assessment; student owned; and multi purposed. They discuss the development of purposes for the portfolio; the kinds of evidence to include; and the assessment criteria. These decisions can be made by the faculty or by the faculty with the students. They conclude by presenting two examples of the use of portfolios, one with literacy teachers, one with science teachers.

Belanoff, P., & Dickson, M. (Ed.). (1991). *Portfolios: Process and Product.* Portsmouth, NH: Boynton Cook.

Unsighted by project team - recommended in White (1994) which we have found to be an important resource

Benett, Y. (1989). The assessment of supervised work experience - a theoretical perspective. *The Vocational Aspect of Education, 109*(August), 53-64.

This article provides a theoretical perspective to the assessment of supervised work experience. It considers two key questions:
What should be assessed?
How should it be assessed?
Validity and reliability of supervised work experiences are also discussed.

Benett, Y. (1993). The validity and reliability of assessments and self-assessments of work-based learning. *Assessment and Evaluation in Higher Education, 18*(2), 83-94.

This article focuses primarily on the validity/ reliability aspects of assessment tasks in work based learning programs. It argues that given certain conditions and assessment exercises (including self assessment), it is possible to determine whether or not exercises are valid, reliable and comparable.

Bertola, P., & Murphy, E. (1994). *Tutoring in the Social Sciences and Humanities.* Perth: Curtin University.

Cited by case study contributor, John Ozolins, as useful in developing essay marking checklist.

Biggs, J. (1989). Does learning about learning help teachers with teaching? Psychology and the tertiary teacher. Inaugural lecture, 8 December 1988. *Supplement to the Gazette,* University of Hong Kong, 20 March 1989.

A very good introduction/summary of what research is telling us about teachers' conceptions of teaching and students' approaches to learning. Emphasises critical role of assessment.

Biggs, J. (1991). Student learning in the context of school. In J. Biggs (Ed.), *Teaching for Learning: the view from cognitive psychology* Hawthorn, Victoria: Australian Council for Educational Research. pp7-29.

At the core of this chapter, which focuses on learning in schools, are accessible accounts of Biggs's view of the development of competence and of the constructivist theory of learning, and the implications of these for teaching. These accounts, by helping to clarify what knowledge and understanding is, how it develops, and the implications for teaching and learning, underpin the approach to the assessment of knowledge and understanding taken in Module 6.

Biggs, J. (1994). Learning outcomes: competence or expertise? *Australian and New Zealand Journal of Vocational Education Research*, *2*(1), 1-18.

This paper discusses competency based education and training in the light of 'what we know about the nature of learning'. Biggs links CBE/T to the quantitative tradition in educational thinking, and thereby to quantitative models of assessment. These models emphasise the correct acquisition of curriculum units by students, and their arithmetic aggregation for grading. Qualitative models include developmental and ecological (function in the real world) assessments. Biggs favours the developmental framework for the definition of competence and expertise, particularly the general outline provided by the SOLO taxonomy. This taxonomy recognises three major phases of learning: pre-structural; quantitative (uni-structural and then multi-structural); and qualitative (relational and extended abstract). He offers an example of this framework applied to the development of wine tasting skills. Biggs suggests that both quantitative and qualitative aspects should be assessed in order to obtain a full picture of the development of expertise and competence. He highlights the significant influence that assessment has over the learning strategies of students, and suggests that by setting complex, qualitative goals for learning this phenomenon of test 'backwash' can 'actually be good for learning'. Biggs argues that the educational enterprise is a complex one and that the focus on outputs distorts the efforts of students and teachers, and has 'wrecked havoc on many institutions'. He points to a range of institutional trends which set up quantitative pressures which can distort the otherwise more interesting aims of CBE/T.

Biggs, J. (1982). Mathematics Profile Series, Operations Test. In J. B. Biggs (Ed.), *Evaluating the Quality of Learning: the SOLO Taxonomy (Structure of the Observed Learning Outcome)* (pp. 82-89). New York: Academic Press.

This excerpt from Biggs addresses the design and interpretation of items for multiple choice tests of mathematical ability. Biggs analyses two questions in depth, showing responses from students at different levels of the SOLO taxonomy. He shows that students operating at the most elementary and most sophisticated levels may, in some circumstances, both obtain the correct answer. The use of distractors which represent responses made from different levels of the taxonomy allows the test to be used as a diagnostic tool. Biggs argues that mathematics is included in the curriculum in order: to socialise students; to develop logical functioning; and to prepare mathematics specialists. He concludes by suggesting that, as the general population has little need of an ability to respond in mathematics beyond the relational level, the elementary and secondary curriculum should recognise this fact and target courses at this level of response.

Block, J. H., & Anderson, L. W. (1975). *Mastery Learning in Classroom Instruction.* New York: MacMillan.

Cited by contributor, Ina Te Wiata, as a useful reference on mastery learning.

Borbasi, S., Shea, A., Mulquiney, J., Wilkinson, M., & Athanasou, J. (1993). *An Investigation of the Reliability and Validity of the Objective Structured Clinical Examination (OSCE) as an Instrument for Assessing the Clinical Competence of Undergraduate Nursing Students.* University of Sydney, Faculty of Nursing.

This comprehensive report describes the development of the Objective Structured Clinical Examination (OSCE) in the Faculty of Nursing at Sydney University and documents the processes used to maximise validity, reliability, and practicality. It reports the correlations between student results on the OSCE, exam results and clinical placement assessments and the reliability levels obtained.

Boud, D. (Ed.). (1988). *Developing Student Autonomy in Learning* (2nd edition). London: Kogan Page.

Along with the revised original chapters from the 1st edition, eight new chapters have been added. The first part of the book provides a general guide to a number of issues (eg. how to introduce autonomy to students) which are illustrated in practical detail (through case studies) in Part 2. The cases are drawn from many discipline areas including, history, agriculture, engineering, and education; and from various countries including Australia. Cited by contributors of Case Studies 1 and 4 as one of the texts used to help them develop their assessment exercises.

Boud, D. (1989). The role of self-assessment in student grading. *Assessment and Evaluation in Higher Education, 14*(1), 20-30.

Discusses the question of whether student self assessments should contribute to formal assessment (student grades). The available evidence on the reliability of student generated marks suggests that most students generate marks consistent with those of staff although weaker students have a tendency to over-rate themselves and stronger students to under-rate themselves. Boud also discusses a range of strategies for increasing student marker reliability.

Boud, D. (1990). Assessment and the promotion of academic values. *Studies in Higher Education, 15*(11), 101-111.

Illustrates how many current assessment practices are incompatible with goals of developing independence, thoughtfulness and critical analysis.

Boud, D., Cohen, R., & Walker, D. (Ed.). (1993). *Using Experience for Learning.* Buckingham: Society for Research in Higher Education and Open University Press.

This book explores making sense of learning from experience. A number of questions are considered, including: how do we learn from other experience; and how can we help others to learn from their experiences? There is emphasis on the role of personal experience in learning, along with discussion as to the importance of experience in both formal and informal learning. Cited by Everingham (Case Study 1) as one of the texts used to help her develop her assessment strategy.

Boud, D., & Falchikov, N. (1989). Quantitative studies of student self-assessment in higher education: a critical analysis of findings. *Higher Education, 18,* 529-549.

> This paper focuses on one aspect of self-assessment: the comparison of student-generated marks with those generated by teachers.
>
> The authors of this meta-analysis are critical of the design of many of the studies reviewed. With this reservation, they find that there is no consistent tendency for students to under or over estimate their own performance - both tendencies may appear in particular contexts. Over or under-rating may be affected by factors such as the individual student's level of ability, the stage reached in the course and the instrument used. At the time when this study was carried out, insufficient research had been done to establish any consistent gender differences.

Boud, D., & Feletti, G. (1991). *The Challenge of Problem Based Learning.* London: Kogan Page.

> The aim of this book is to examine the current state of play on problem based learning (PBL) across a wide variety of professional areas and to identify the challenges faced when adopting a problem based approach to learning. Included are many accounts of the approaches adopted by innovators and how they met the challenges with which they were faced. The six parts of the book address the following issues: defining problem based learning; getting started; designing and implementing PBL; examples of its use in different professions; assessment and evaluation in PBL; and looking beyond PBL.

Boud, D., Keogh, R., & Walker, D. (Ed.). (1985). *Reflection: Turning Experience into Learning.* London: Kogan Page.

> Examines the nature of reflection and its role in learning and emphasises ways of assisting and deepening the reflection process. Many practical examples of implementation in educational settings are included. Fran Everingham (Case Study #18, Module 4) draws her criteria for the assessment of reflective writing from Boud, Keogh and Walker's 'cycle of reflection'.

Boud, D., & Tyree, A. (1980). Self and peer assessment in professional education: a preliminary study in law. *Journal of the Society of Public Teachers of Law, 65.*

> Cited by Annette Marfording (Case Study 56, Module 8). Peer assessment fairly consistent with teachers.

Boud, D., & Walker, D. (1992). *Reflection at Work.* Melbourne: Deakin University Press.

> Cited by Everingham (Case Study 6, Module 1), as one of the resources used to help her develop her assessment strategies.

Boysen, O. (1994). Integration of engineering and design. In P. J. Parr & S. F. Johnston (Ed.), *Proceedings 6th Annual Australasian Association for Engineering Education Conference* (pp. 247-51). Sydney: University of Technology Sydney.

> Highlights need for engineering designers to realise the importance of refinements and design modifications based on human needs and aesthetics. The major difficulty is seen to reside in the judging of the finished product or work. This arises from the inimically subjective nature of the assessor's response to creative or artistic expression- a response based in the 'emotional', 'sensual' and 'intuitive' feelings of the individuals who are called on to appraise the work.

Branthwaite, A., Trueman, M., & Hartley, J. (1980). Writing essays: the actions and strategies of students. In J. Hartley (Ed.), *The Psychology of Written Communication: Selected Readings* London: Kogan Page.

> Looking at both students' approaches to writing tasks and their tutors' approaches to marking them. There is less congruence than we would hope.

Broadfoot, P. (1987). *Introducing Profiling: A Practical Manual.* London: Macmillan Education Ltd.

> This manual like that by Law (1984) introduces the techniques of profiling and argues the case for replacing traditional reporting of student achievement by a mark or grade with a more descriptive record. There are many variations, ranging from subjective and personalised to objective comparisons of students. Some are more valid than others and some have higher reliability but all provide more information.

Brookfield, S. D. (1987). *Developing Critical Thinkers: Challenging Adults to Explore Alternative Ways of Thinking and Acting.* San Francisco: Jossey-Bass.

> Discusses the meaning of critical thinking; and how adults may learn and further develop this ability. There are a number of case studies and examples of how this ability can be applied to adult life: in personal relationships, in the workplace, in political involvements, and in responses to the media. Also included are a variety of strategies that educators and other professionals can use to help adults empower themselves.
> Cited by the contributors of Case Study 1 as a useful text for assisting with the development of assessment of critical thinking.

Brown, S., & Knight, P. (1994). *Assessing Learners in Higher Education.* London: Kogan Page.

> A very useful guide to assessment practice

Bruton, D., & Barnes, A. (1993). Design theory hypermedia studio. In *EcoDesign 2 Conference.* Powerhouse Museum, Sydney.

> Published materials that relate to Case Study 33, Module 5. The assessment task requires students to enter research data into a multimedia data base.

Buchanan, R. W., & Rogers, M. (1990). Innovative assessment in large classes. *College Teaching, 38*(2), 69-73.

> This paper addresses three problems encountered in teaching classes of 80 or more students: how to offer students an opportunity to be assessed in essay format; how to deal with students who miss an exam; and, how to generate large numbers of new, relevant examination questions on a regular basis. The authors suggest an assessment system comprising several elements. The inclusion of objective multiple choice tests, though controversial, is seen as necessary. The authors claim that research evidence shows that performance on these tests correlates well with performance on essay questions in the same area. Students are offered a choice of: four objective tests; four such tests plus an optional final examination; or three such tests plus an optional final exam. Students make their choice under the following conditions: they are told their current grade prior to the final; they are told the final can reduce as well as increase their grade; they are told the approximate percentage of students who have increased their grade in a final in the past; they may elect to take the final examination in multiple choice format, or in short answer format (a blind choice); they are told that most past students have taken the multiple choice format for the final. In the authors' experience only 10-15% of students elect to take a final under this system, and of these only 20% take the short answer option. Students miss-

ing a test are required to complete all the remaining tests or the final. Students missing two tests or the final exam fail the course, and no makeup exams are given, for any reason, to anyone.

The authors also suggest that students be encouraged to submit up to 10 questions for inclusion in the tests in a specified format. Up to two questions per student can be accepted per test, and each question accepted earns the equivalent points for the question in the test.

Budd, D. (1994). Minitests in medical science: maximum gain, minimum pain. In L. Summers (Ed.), *Quality in Teaching and Learning: 'Making It Happen'*. Perth, WA: Educational Development Unit, Edith Cowan University.

> This paper provides an assessment of the Minitest method used by Budd and included in these materials (Case Study 42, Module 5), to assess students' knowledge within a laboratory setting.

Caisley, M. (1994). Communication Skills - key capabilities. *Dialogue: the AIT Journal of Adult and Higher Education*, June, 8-11.

> Published materials that relate to Case Study 59 in Module 8.

Candy, P. C. (1991). *Self Direction for Lifelong Learning: A Comprehensive Guide to Theory and Practice.* San Francisco: Jossey-Bass.

> A comprehensive examination of the concepts underlying self-direction in learning plus practical suggestions for helping adult learners to develop skills in planning and carrying out learning projects. The development and use of learning contracts in the Health Science Education program at the University of Sydney (Case Study 18, Module 4) has been strongly influenced by Candy's work on developing student autonomy.

Cassini, C. (1994). Collaborative Testing, Grading. *The Teaching Professor*, April, 5-6.

> This piece reports Cassini's experience with collaborative testing and grading in a metaphysics class in which in-class essay tests were the norm. Cassini allowed students to consult their notes and colleagues for 20 minutes before writing their answers to the question for the remaining 110 minutes of the class. After reading and commenting on the essays Cassini invited further comments from students and a self assessed grade. Cassini considers this procedure 'student friendly' and motivating, while encouraging students to apply their knowledge to their collaborative discussions and to assess their own mastery of the material.

Chi, M. T. H., Glaser, R., & Farr, M. J. (1988). *The Nature of Expertise.* Hillsdale, New Jersey: Erlbaum.

> This volume, referred to in Module 2 (Solving Problems and Developing Plans) provides an overview of the 'state of the art' in knowledge of how expertise is developed; and in its overview section, summarises some key characteristics of experts' performances that research (particularly in cognitive psychology) has uncovered. These characteristics indicate, for example, that experts excel mainly in their own domains; perceive large meaningful patterns in their domain; are faster than novices at performing domain skills and solving problems; have superior short- and long-term memory; see and represent a domain problem at a deeper (more principled) level; and have strong self-monitoring skills. Subsequent chapters focus on a discussion of expertise in relation to certain practical skills, computer programming, working with ill-defined problems, and undertaking medical diagnosis.

Churches, A. (1989). A national design-and-build competition. In *Proc. World Conference on Engineering Education for Advancing Technology* (pp. 535-539.). Sydney: IEAust.

> Source of Case Study 45, Module 7, Section 1.

Coles, C. (1987). The actual effects of examinations on medical student learning. *Assessment and Evaluation in Higher Education, 12*(3), 209-219.

> Some research findings support the notion that student learning is largely influenced by the examinations being taken. Other work suggests the situation is more complex. This paper focuses on the kind of learning needed in medical education and the conditions necessary for its generation, arguing that once this is clarified the influence of examinations can then be explored. Cognitive psychology suggests that efficient retrieval of knowledge requires storing information about the retrieval setting along with the facts to be remembered, and that retrieval in novel settings is more likely when cognitive structures are substantially interconnected. This paper presents evidence showing that medical students can develop this kind of learning, called here elaboration, but only under particular curricular conditions, notable when they see their task as one of relating abstract information and concrete experiences. Elaborated learning occurs even when the examination arrangement is traditional. It is concluded that students fail to learn appropriately because the necessary curricular conditions are not met, not because of the examination arrangements. Educational planners need to take a whole curriculum view, and cannot expect appropriate learning to be generated merely by changing the examination arrangements. (Journal abstract)

Conway, J. K. (1989). *The Road from Coorain.* London: Heinemann/Mandarin.

> Jill Ker Conway's autobiography is cited by Case Study 23, Module 4 contributors, Robert Zehner and Michael Bounds, as a useful introductory reading for students who are preparing their own autobiographies.

Courts, P. L., & McInerney, K. H. (1993). *Assessment in Higher Education: Politics, Pedagogy, and Portfolios.* Westport, CT: Praeger Publishers.

> This book presents the authors' experience in assessing students' learning, curricula and educational programs. Its primary focus is on the use of student portfolios and the role they play in assessing students.

Cox, K. R. (1982). Measuring clinical performance. In K. R. Cox & C. E. Ewan (Ed.), *The Medical Teacher.* Edinburgh: Churchill Livingstone.

> Cox's chapter, 'Measuring clinical performance', provides a useful model for analysing which aspects of clinical performance can be assessed in the classroom, which may be assessed in simulated settings and which can only be assessed in the workplace. In general terms they propose that pre-requisite knowledge can be appropriately tested in the classroom, component skills can be tested in simulated settings, but personal attitudes and attributes can only be tested in the real-life situation. The real clinical situation is also the only place to assess the students' ability to bring together knowledge and skills in a satisfactory outcome for the patient.

Crooks, T. J. (1988). The impact of classroom evaluation practices on students. *Review of Educational Research, 58*(4), 438-481.

> In most education programs, a substantial proportion of teacher and student time is devoted to activities which involve (or lead directly to) evaluation by the teacher of student products or behaviour. This review summarises results from 14 specific fields

of research that cast light on the relationship between classroom evaluation practices and student outcomes in primary and secondary schooling. Particular attention is given to outcomes involving learning strategies, motivation, and achievement. Where possible, mechanisms are suggested that could account for the reported effects. The conclusions derived from the individual fields are then merged to produce an integrated summary with clear implications for effective educational practice. The primary conclusion is that classroom evaluation has powerful direct and indirect impacts, which may be positive or negative, and thus deserves very thoughtful planning and implementation. The author argues that deep learning should be a central goal of education and evaluation should foster its development. He also argues that more attention should be given to formative assessment and that most grading practices produce undesirable consequences for most students. Consequently he argues that most assessments should be directed at providing useful feedback, while less frequent summative assessments should be criterion referenced. Effective feedback should be: focused on student progress; relevant; specific; and related to student needs. Standards should be set and published to students; students should be given regular opportunities to practice key skills and receive feedback; evaluation tasks should be chosen to fit the goals of the course. Most importantly, the evaluation scheme should reflect the emphases of the syllabus itself.

Cross, K. P., & Angelo, T. A. (1988). *Classroom Assessment Techniques: A handbook for faculty.* Ann Arbor, Michigan: National Centre for Research to Improve Postsecondary Teaching and Learning.

> A handbook for teachers who are interested in different aspects of student assessment and educational evaluation. It includes techniques for assessment of student learning and intellectual development; for assessing students' ability to evaluate their own learning skills; and for assessing students' reactions to teachers and teaching methods.

Dahlgren, L. (1984). Outcomes of learning. In F. Marton, D. Hounsell, & N. Entwistle (Ed.), *The Experience of Learning.* Edinburgh: Scottish Academic Press.

> This chapter reviews studies into the effectiveness of teaching and assessment methods. Evidence of the failure of traditional methods to develop and assess students' understanding of fundamental principles is documented.

Davey, R., & Wheway, R. (1986). Creative design competitions as means of teaching design in first year. In *Proc. Conference on Teaching Engineering Designers for the 21st Century* (pp. 46-53). Sydney: School of Mechanical & Industrial Engineering, University of New South Wales.

> (Source of Case Study 44, Module 7, Section 1).

Ebel, R. (1972). *Essentials of Educational Measurement.* New York: Prentice Hall.

> General text in which a large variety of assessment techniques are illustrated. These cover both secondary and tertiary education. Comprehensive treatment of statistical methods for measuring psychometric properties of tests, including different aspects of validity and reliability.

Ebel, R. L., & Frisbie, D. A. (1986). *Essentials of Educational Measurement.* Englewood Cliffs, NJ: Prentice-Hall.

> Recommended for advice on issues relating to quantifying assessment of student achievement and manipulating marks statistically.

Ennis, R. (1989). Critical thinking and subject specificity: clarification and needed research. *Educational Researcher, 18*(3), 4-10.

> Addresses the problematic and controversial issue of whether or not critical thinking is subject specific, and if it should be taught separately; infused in instruction in existing subject matter; result from a student's immersion in the subject matter; or in fact be a combination of approaches.
>
> Ennis also offers a distinction among three versions of subject specificity: domain, epistemological and conceptual. He argues that the first two versions incorporate valuable insights as they share an emphasis on the importance of background knowledge. However, conceptual subject specificity is too vague to be of any use in clarifying whether or not critical thinking is in fact subject specific.
>
> This article is very worthwhile reading for anyone interested in pursuing further the vexed issue of the teaching and learning of critical thinking.

Ennis, R. (1994). Dispositions and abilities of ideal critical thinkers; and an annotated list of critical thinking tests.

> Comprises 2 handouts from the conference 'Thinking' held in Boston. One handout refers to the dispositions and abilities of ideal critical thinkers; the other is an annotated list of critical thinking tests.

Entwistle, N. (1992). *The Impact of Teaching on Learning Outcomes in Higher Education: A Literature Review*. Sheffield: Committee of Vice-Chancellors and Principals of the Universities of the United Kingdom, Universities' Staff Development Unit.

> An excellent review of the literature on student learning. Very readable and valuable introduction for university teachers.

Falchikov, N. (1995). Peer feedback marking: developing peer assessment. *Innovations in Education and Training International, 32*(2), 81-93.

> Report of implementation of peer assessment with psychology students. Few problems occurred when due care was taken to ensure process was carefully introduced and the criteria were negotiated and tested before students assessed each other's work. Useful review of the literature on peer assessment (see Module 5).

Falchikov, N., & Boud, D. (1989). Student self-assessment in higher education: a meta-analysis. *Review of Educational Research, 59*(4), 395-430.

> This paper reviews a large number of self assessment studies that compared student and teacher marks and identified factors which were significant in producing close correspondence between student and teacher marks. Significant factors included the design of the study and the preparation of students, the level of the course (advanced level students proved to be more accurate assessors) and the broad area of study (students in the sciences produced more accurate self assessments).

Feletti, G. (1980). Reliability and validity studies on modified essay questions. *Journal of Medical Education, 55*, 933-941.

> This paper outlines ways in which Modified Essay Questions (MEQs), for testing problem solving skills, can be designed, constructed and marked. Also included is an example from a students' first term MEQ paper, together with a model answer and expected minimum level of competence for the sample question.

Feletti, G., & Engel, C. (1980). The modified essay question for testing problem solving skills. *The Medical Journal of Australia* (January 26), 79-80.

> Modified Essay Questions (MEQ's) have been developed at the University of Newcastle, Australia, to assess clinical problem-solving by first-and second-year medical students. Reliability estimates (given as coefficient alpha [60] as high as 0.91 were reported for term assessment in 1979 based on MEQs. Lower estimates can be expected as statistical artifacts due to the faculty's criterion-referenced assessment of competence. More appropriate measures of reliability are currently being evaluated. The validity of assessment by MEQ was based on one model of medical problem solving and another of cognitive skill taxonomies. Internal consistency estimates (coefficient alpha) based on each model yielded some interesting anomalies on the nature of problem solving which may be re-examined in terms of cognitive preference indexes.

Feletti, G., & Ryan, G. (1994). The triple jump exercise in inquiry based Learning: A case study showing directions for further research. *Assessment and Evaluation in Higher Education, 19*(3), 225-234.

> This article describes the triple jump exercise, which according to the authors is a versatile but under-studied instrument, designed to assess students' problem identification, problem-solving and group work abilities. The article evaluates its use for assessment in a graduate course in health studies. (See Case Study #19, Module 4).

Field, L. (1990). *Skilling Australia.* Melbourne: Longman Cheshire.

> This book provides a guide to the systematic development and assessment of skills in the Australian industrial training context. The chapter on assessment discusses issues of validity and reliability in skill testing; how to select the sample of skills or competencies to be tested and the characteristics of an effective competency test.

Field, M., & Lee, R. (1992). Assessment of interdisciplinary programmes. *European Journal of Education, 27*(3), 277-283.

> This paper focuses on the assessment of the impact of interdisciplinary educational programs on students, rather than on the assessment of student learning outcomes narrowly conceived. The paper argues that the task of evaluating the impact of interdisciplinary programs is much more complex than the evaluation of disciplinary programs because the goals are not as clear-cut (the content is often idiosyncratic and not clearly specified), the conceptual framework of assessment is not as apparent (in terms of knowledge/skill acquisition), and few standardised tests are available. The paper conjectures that a 'talent development' framework may be most appropriate to these programs, but the authors have concerns that standard tests of development may be of little use in the assessment of programs with idiosyncratic content. Some programs are successfully evaluated by the use of qualitative techniques such as portfolio analysis and by essay based intellectual development instruments. One standardised test is the College Outcomes Measures Project (COMP) developed to measure student learning in general education. This instrument tests six major areas: functioning within social institutions; using science and technology; using the arts; communicating; solving problems; and clarifying values. Other standard instruments available in America include: the General Intellectual Skills test; the Academic Profile; the Test of critical thinking (which looks at: defining a problem; selecting relevant information; recognising assumptions; formulating hypotheses; and drawing conclusions); the Reflective Judgement Interview (based on Perry's developmental scheme); and the Watson-Glaser Critical Thinking Appraisal. The authors suggest that the assessment of interdisciplinary programs should: clearly tie the assessment to the curriculum and the teaching; involve academic staff in the

development of assessment strategies to build their commitment; focus on the unique goals of the program; select assessment methods to match goals; and consider using a broad array of assessment techniques.

Frederickson, M. P. (1993). Gender and racial bias in design juries. *Journal of Architectural Education, 47*(1), 38-48.

This study assesses the anticipation and interaction of various participants in the design jury process, that is, male and female jurors, male and female students, and racial minority students. Several consistently biased practices and procedures in design juries are identified and statistically examined. Among these are all-male or male-dominated juries, and differences in the communication patterns when female students are being examined.

Freeman, J., & Byrne, P. (1976). *The Assessment of Postgraduate Training in General Practice* (2nd ed.). Surrey: SRHE.

Investigates reliability and validity of different forms of assessment used in post-graduate certification of General Medical Practice in UK. The book includes detailed illustrations of assessment instruments and items.

Gardner, H. (1993). *Frames of Mind: The Theory of Multiple Intelligences.* (2nd ed.). London: Fontana.

First published in 1984, Howard Gardner's book puts forward his theory that there exist many human 'intelligences' - each with its own patterns of development and brain activity and each different in kind from the others. The intelligences identified by Gardner are linguistic, logical-mathematical, musical, spatial, bodily-kinesthetic, inter-personal and intra-personal. High levels of ability in one intelligence are not necessarily correlated with high levels of ability in all others. Gardner's work, developed as part of the Harvard Project on Human Potential has many implications for the ways in which we think about intelligence and education. His work on the inter-personal and intra-personal intelligences provides support for the idea that the development of these attributes should become a formal part of many curricula (see Module 4).

Gibbs, G. (1981). *Teaching Students to Learn: A Student-Centred Approach.* Milton Keynes: The Open University Press.

One of the basics in the literature of practical advice for teachers in higher education. Offers detailed instructions for six exercises to help students learn to learn effectively. Exercise Five (actually 4 activities are described) addresses writing and students' learning about criteria and assessing self and peers, and Exercise Six, taking examinations.

Gibbs, G. (Ed.). (1992). *Assessing More Students.* Oxford: Oxford Centre for Staff Development.

This book is one in a series which supports the UK 'teaching more students' project. Included are materials on the experience of assessment, and assessment methods and strategies.

Gibbs, G. (1992a). *Improving the quality of student learning.* Bristol: Technical and Education Services.

One of the TES manuals of good practice in teaching, including assessing and examining, in higher education. Firmly grounded in research on student learning and on pedagogy.

Gibbs, G. (1992b). Improving the quality of student learning through course design. In R. Barnett (Ed.), *Learning to Effect.* Buckingham: Society for Research into Higher Education and Open University Press.

> Reminds us of the critical role of assessment in student learning as well as covering other basics of course design.

Gibbs, G., & Habeshaw, T. (1992). *Preparing to Teach: An introduction to effective teaching in higher education* (2nd edition ed.). Bristol: Technical and Educational Services Ltd.

> Practical advice based on understanding of student learning. Aimed at novice teachers in higher education and so at the survival skills end of the literature. However, a good source of reminders about good practice and suggestions for the experienced because it can be read quickly and dipped into. Chapter 4 on assessment - especially useful pages (100-106) on setting questions

Glaser, R. (1991). Expertise and assessment. In M. Wittrock & E. Baker (Ed.), *Testing and Cognition* (pp. 17-28). Engelwood Cliffs NJ: Prentice Hall.

> This chapter examines how experts organise and utilise knowledge and understanding in different fields. Implications are drawn for developing appropriate assessment procedures.

Glaser, R., & Chi, M.T.H. (1988) Introduction. In Chi, M.T.H., Glaser, R., & Farr, M.J. *The Nature of Expertise.* Hillsdale, NJ: Erlbaum. (pp.xv-xxviii)

> This chapter provides an overview of the origins of research into expertise, in artificial intelligence and cognitive psychology. A summary follows of key characteristics of experts' performances which this research has uncovered. These characteristics indicate, for example, that experts excel mainly in their own domains; perceive large meaningful patterns in their domain; are faster than novices at performing domain skills and solving problems; have superior short- and long-term memory; see and represent a domain problem at a deeper (more principled) level; and have strong self-monitoring skills. Some implications of this for assessment are discussed in Module 2 (Solving problems and developing plans).

Gonczi, A. (1994). Competency based assessment in the professions in Australia. *Assessment in Education, 1*(1), 27-44.

> This article argues that if a holistic conception of competence underpins assessment strategies, they are likely to be more valid than current methods of assessing professionals, and equally reliable. Two case studies of specialist accreditation are presented - in law and in medicine - which demonstrate that it is possible to design strategies without much difficulty that can assess how professionals can actually perform in a variety of typical situations.

Gronlund, N. E. (1976). *Measurement and Evaluation in Teaching* (3rd ed.). New York: Macmillan.

> This general text contains numerous examples of good and poor practice in constructing question and multiple choice question items, and advice on improving traditional assessment practices.

Hager, P., Gonczi, A., & Athanasou, J. (1994). General issues about assessment of competence. *Assessment and Evaluation in Higher Education, 19*(1), 3-16.

> In simple terms, competency based assessment is the assessment of a person's competence against prescribed standards of performance. Thus, if an occupation has established a set of, say, entry-level competency standards, then these are the stan-

dards of performance required of all new entrants to that occupation. Competency-based assessment is the process determining whether a candidate meets the prescribed standards of performance, i.e. whether they demonstrate competence. Competency-based assessment has aroused numerous and varied worries and objections from many quarters, including concerns that competency-based assessment: (a) only assesses what is trivial or superficial; (b) is inherently unreliable in that it involves inference; (c) in inherently invalid; (d) represents a departure from traditional proven methods of assessment; (e) neglects the importance of knowledge; (f) focuses on outcomes to the neglect of processes; (g) relies on professional judgement, and hence is too subjective; (h) vainly tries to assess attitudes. This paper discusses each of these worries and objections and argues that none of them is decisive. While each of them points to an important issue about competency-based assessment, the discussion argues that in each case a well-designed competency-based assessment system involving integrated assessments can overcome the worry or objection. (Journal abstract, adapted.)

Hall, R. M., & Sandler, B. R. (1982). *The Classroom Climate: A Chilly One for Women?* Association of American Colleges, Project on the Status and Education of Women.

> This is one in a series of reports on gender bias in American universities. They cover many topics in addition to assessment issues, including communication patterns in classrooms, mentoring, harassment, etc.

Hamp-Lyons, L., & Condon, W. (1993). Questioning assumptions about portfolio-based assessment. *College Composition and Communication, 44*(2), 176-90.

> Unsighted by project team - recommended in White (1994) which we have found to be an important resource

Harman, R. (1992). The reasoning testlet. *Australasian Journal of Engineering Education, 3*(1), 95-100.

> This article describes the introduction of brief in-class tests, called 'testlets', within an engineering subject. These are designed to assess students' understanding of fundamental principles and their ability to reason from them. (See Case study 35, Module 6).

Hay, I. (1994). Justifying and applying oral presentations in geographical education. *Journal of Geography in Higher Education, 18* (1), 43-55.

> Argues that students need to learn oral communication skills within the context of their degree program for personal and professional development. That teachers must address fear of public speaking, help students develop skills through specific instruction, and assess those skills appropriately. Offers a checklist for assessment. (See Case study 58, Module 8).

Hay, I. (forthcoming). Communicating geographies. Development and application of a communication instruction manual in the geography discipline of an Australian university. *Journal of Geography in Higher Education.*

> Account of development, application and review of a manual intended to promote development of communication skills. Manual includes assessment schedules. Interesting discussion of the retreat from criterion-referenced assessment. (See Module 8, Section 1).

Hay, I., & Delaney, E. (1994). 'Who Teaches Learns': writing groups in geographical education. *Journal of Geography in Higher Education, 18*(3), 217-34.

> Description and evaluation of using student writing groups to give each other feedback on final draft of paper. Some problems with the process, including students coming to class unprepared (in later years participation was requirement for passing course). Students did feel process was beneficial. Teachers still thought many papers surprisingly weak. Includes a checklist and brief discussion of criterion -referenced assessment. See Module 8, Section 1.

Hay, I., & Miller, R. (1992). Application of a poster exercise in an advanced undergraduate Geography course. *Journal of Geography in Higher Education, 16*(2), 199-215.

> This paper discusses the nature and application of a research poster exercise in senior (e.g. final year undergraduate) university classes. The exercise consists of three components. First, students are involved in a piece of supervised research in which they set their own research question; design, execute and evaluate research strategies; and communicate the synthesised results of their activities to an audience. Second, the exercise is structured in such a way that it provides students with an introductory opportunity to explore the bureaucratic and competitive structure of the modern research environment. Third, student proficiency in oral, written, and graphical presentation of research results is refined. Expanding on earlier work on the use of posters in the teaching of geography at the tertiary level, the paper gives special emphasis to the rationale for conducting the research and to practical dimensions of poster production.

Hayes, J. R. (1989). *The Complete Problem Solver.* Hillsdale, N.J.: Erlbaum.

> This book has two purposes - to provide the reader with skills that will lead to better problem solving; and to provide information about the psychology of problem solving. Areas covered include problem solving theory and practice; memory and knowledge acquisition; decision making; and creativity and invention.

Heywood, J. (1989). *Assessment in Higher Education.* London: Kogan Page.

> This book focuses on descriptions of contemporary practice in assessment in higher education. Emphasis on use of objectives in determining assessment methods and marking criteria. The book is particularly useful to teachers concerned with improving marking and grading practices. Provides examples of simple statistical techniques which can be used for scaling and determining test reliability.

Higher Education Council (1992). *Higher Education: Achieving Quality.* Canberra, A.C.T.: Australian Government Publishing Service.

> Discussion papers produced by all of the key players (Higher Education Council, National Union of Students, University Staff Associations, Post-Graduate Students Associations and Australian Vice Chancellors' Committee) on the factors which contribute to quality in higher education. The paper from the HEC provides a list of the desirable attributes of graduates which might be used as a checklist in evaluating to what extent these are consciously developed and assessed in a program of study.

Holly, M. L. (1984). *Keeping a Personal-Professional Journal.* Melbourne: Deakin University.

> Readers are introduced to the potential benefits of writing about teaching and collegial interaction. This book covers: journal keeping, which includes the types of journals most commonly used and the writing process; journal keeping for professional development, which includes teacher case studies; and journal keeping - a

writer's manual, which focuses on writing for ones own benefit. This latter section covers topics such as what to write about, writing reflectively, and learning from your writing. Cited by contributors of Case Studies 1 and 6 as a useful text for educators considering assessing reflective skills, and/ or journal writing.

Hounsell, D. (1984). Essay planning and essay writing. *Higher Education Research and Development, 3*(1), 13-31.

> How students plan is less important than what planning is directed towards. Discusses challenges to the hegemony of the plan. Concludes that although students who see essay as fundamentally an interpretive task usually use some sort of planning strategy, the most important advice to students is about the nature of an essay, about expectations of academic markers.

Howenstine, E., Hay, I., Delaney, E., Bell, J., Norris, F., Whelan, A., Piranti, M., Chow, T., & Ross, A. (1988). Using a poster exercise in an introductory geography course. *Journal of Geography in Higher Education, 12*(2), 139-147.

> Published version of material used in Module 8, Section 3

Hull, G., & Rose, M. (1990). Toward a social-cognitive understanding of problematic reading and writing. In A. A. Lunsford & e. al (Ed.), *The Right to Literacy.* New York: Modern Language Association of America.

> Referred to by Shay et al as a particularly useful and sympathetic discussion of the problem of plagiarism.

Hustedt Jacobsen, R. What is good testing? Perceptions of college students. *College Teaching, 41*(4), 153-156.

> This paper reports on an investigation into students' perceptions of assessment at a private liberal arts college in Kansas. Hustedt Jacobsen reports that students valued: a methodical approach to assessment; some significant input into the content and criteria for evaluation; the freedom to fail some items; encouragement of personal involvement with the subject; and, being assessed on their own merits and not in comparison to their peers. (Paper abstracted in *The Teaching Professor*, April, 1994)

Jackling, N., Lewis, J., Brandt, D., & Sell, R. (1990). Problem solving in the professions. *Higher Education Research and Development, 9*(2), 133-149.

> The authors of this paper express the view that algorithms and heuristics may be used to help improve professional problem solving abilities provided that they are appropriately contextualised within the relevant discipline. The first part of the paper presents a basic algorithm applied to the engineering discipline. A similar algorithm applicable in the solving of legal problems is presented later in the paper. Problem complexity and related variables are discussed as are ways of teaching problem solving and integrating problem solving in the curriculum. Typical problem solving exercises are described.

Jenkins, E. K., & Holley, J. H. (1990). The interactive effect of language and question format on accounting student's performance. *Research in Higher Education, 31*(1), 61-73.

> This article reports the results of research to determine if a significant effect exists between students' linguistic background and question format on students' examination scores. Students were administered examinations made up of four subtests covering the same subject matter. The subtests were composed of four question formats: multiple choice quantitative, multiple choice theoretical, open-ended quantitative,

and open-ended essay questions. Based on analysis of variance and analysis of covariance, significant differences were observed between English as a primary language students and English as a secondary language students depending on the type of question on the examination. EPL students outperformed others on open-ended questions, both quantitative and theoretical, while ESL on multiple choice questions, both quantitative and theoretical. (Journal abstract, adapted.)

Kingsland, A. (1989). The assessment process in architecture at Newcastle. In B. Wallis (Ed.), *Problem-based Learning , The Newcastle Workshop.* Newcastle, NSW: Faculty of Medicine, University of Newcastle. pp121-30.

(Source of Case study 43, Module 7, Section 1).

Kingsland, A., & Cowdroy, R. (1991). Assessment of multiple criteria: focus on skills. In B. Ross (Ed.), *Research and Development in Higher Education* (pp. 163-167). Sydney: HERDSA (Higher Education Research and Development Society of Australasia).

Discussion of the need to expose students to the real-world practice of groups of people judging designs and of the need to make holistic and subjective evaluations taking into account many criteria simultaneously.

Kolb, D. (1984). *Experiential Learning: Experience as the Source of Learning and Development.* New Jersey: Prentice Hall.

Provides a comprehensive discussion of experiential learning. Comprises 3 sections: "Experience and Learning", historical perspective; "The Structure of Learning and Knowledge", includes a structural model of the learning process; "Learning and Development", covers theory and process of experiential learning, illustrates adaptive style inventory.
Cited by contributors of Case study 1 as a text used in the development of the program curriculum (including assessment) - part of which forms the basis of this case study.

Kurfiss, J. G. (1988). *Critical Thinking: Theory, Research, Practice, and Possibilities* (ASHE-ERIC Higher Education Reports No. 2). Washington, D.C.: Association for the Study of Higher Education.

This report examines critical thinking on the three levels by which it is most commonly taught in higher education: argument skills, cognitive processes, intellectual development. It begins with an historical background before moving onto the more recent developments in this field. It provides a good basis for consideration of the approaches taken to the teaching, learning and assessment of critical thinking. There are numerous references to other writers should readers wish to pursue particular aspects or perspectives on critical thinking.

Landa, L. N. (1974). *Algorithmization in Learning and Instruction.* Englewood Cliffs: Educational Technology Publications.

Describes how knowledge bases in disciplines can be organised and developed into sets of algorithms to promote relational learning and decision making and to develop assessment procedures.

Law (1984). *Uses and Abuses of Profiling: a Handbook on Reviewing and Recording Student Experience and Achievement.* London: Paul Chapman Publishing Ltd (1988 reprint).

Many examples of profiles and thorough discussion of why one might think of using them, under what circumstances, the ethics of profiling, reliability and validity of such reports, etc.

Marton, F., & Saljö, R. (1984). Approaches to Learning. In F. Marton, D. Hounsell, & N. Entwistle (Ed.), *The Experience of Learning*. Edinburgh: Scottish Academic Press.

> Outlines research studies into how students engage in learning tasks. The findings demonstrate that fundamental misconceptions can persist where students approach learning through memorisation. One lesson for assessors is that we may not always have demonstrated achievement of the learning outcome we think/ hope students have achieved.

McAleese, R. (1984). Video self-confrontation as microteaching in staff development and teacher training. In O. Zuber-Skerritt (Ed.), *Video in Higher Education*. London: Kogan Page.

> Cited by Fran Everingham (Case study 6 in Module 1), as a useful resource.

McGregor, D. (1960) *Human Side of Enterprise*. New York: McGraw Hill.

> This important management text of the 1960s argued that personal beliefs and values are among the most significant determinants of managers' actions in the workplace - a theme which has been taken up again in management literature of the 1990s. The theory provides a rationale for helping students in many professional areas to make their beliefs and values explicit and conscious (see Module 4).

McIntosh, H. (ed) (1974). *Techniques and Problems of Assessment*. London: Edward Arnold.

> The coverage of assessment in this volume is mostly confined to traditional methods. Two sections: first, contains detailed examples of different assessment methods, and practical advice on test construction; second, on 'problems of assessment', identifies problems teachers commonly face in assessment and outlines procedures for overcoming these.

McMasters, J., & Ford, S. (1990). An industry view of enhancing design education. *Engineering Education, 80*, 526-529.

> Students not well-prepared for careers in engineering. Identifies unrealistic notions of engineering design work and lack of teamwork skills amongst graduates entering industry. Advocates changes to engineering assessment practices towards open-ended design-related problems and projects based on collective group work.

McNally, N. (1993). Integrating two design cultures. *International Journal of Mechanical Engineering Education, 21*(3), 283-296.

> Describes assessment scheme and marking schedule for a major project in Product Design Engineering in Glasgow. Both technical and creative factors are included.

McPeck, J. (1981). *Critical Thinking and Education*. Oxford: Martin Robertson & Company Ltd.

> Discusses the meaning of critical thinking, including definitions and descriptions by writers such as Ennis, D'Angelo, Scriven and de Bono. There is also a chapter devoted to the examination of the most commonly used tests for critical thinking: the Watson-Glazer Critical Thinking Appraisal and Cornell Critical Thinking Tests.

Mezirow, J. D. (1990). *Fostering Critical Reflection in Adulthood: A Guide to Transformative and Emancipatory Learning*. San Francisco: Jossey-Bass.

> When confronting new learning situations, adults may lack the ability to see all the alternatives open to them because of inhibiting prejudices, assumptions and values. Mezirow and his co-authors offer many strategies for helping adults to recognise and re-examine deeply ingrained beliefs. See Module 4 for ways in which such self-evaluation of beliefs and values might be incorporated in programs of higher education.

Morgan (1989). The Socratic method: silencing co-operation. *Legal Education Review, 1.*

> Referred to by Annette Marfording. (Case study #56, Module 8). Female students less assertive during class discussions, potential for biased assessment of oral participation.

Murphy, B., & McPherson, J. (1988). The group assessment task: a real time test of small group, Problem Based Learning. In B. Wallis (Ed.), *Problem Based Learning - The Newcastle Workshop, held as part of the conference - Ten Years of Innovative Medical Education 1978-1988..* Newcastle (Australia): University of Newcastle. pp131-42.

> Describes the development and use of the Group Assessment Task at the University of Newcastle where it is used to assess problem based learning and group functioning in the medical degree.

Nance, D., & Fawns, R. (1993). Teachers' working knowledge and training: the Australian agenda for reform of teacher education. *Journal of Education and Training, 19*(2), 159-173.

> In Australia the policy makers are attempting to define teachers' working knowledge in terms of competencies which will form the foundation of award restructuring both for teachers' careers and for their students in industry. In the quest for increased national productivity, generic competencies may be mandated in an attempt to improve the quality of teaching. This paper discusses the possibility of rendering the working knowledge of teachers in competency terms, and the elaborated notion of competency which must be employed if this is to be successful. It argues that, since teaching is an occupation which is characteristically unpredictable and non-routine, observation of performance alone is insufficient to permit an assessment of competency. The paper proposes a codification of teacher's working knowledge, and then the use of this codification and a model of knowledge acquisition to assess "where the preservice training should be placed and to discuss the arbitrariness of qualifying competencies and advanced skills criteria".

Newble, D. (1982). The development and assessment of a new examination of the clinical competence of medical students. *Assessment and Evaluation in Higher Education, 7*(3), 216-224.

> Discusses validity and reliability of problem-based criterion-referenced examinations in clinical medicine

Nightingale, P. (1986). *Improving Student Writing.* Sydney: Higher Education Research and Development Society of Australasia.

> A practice-oriented manual for teachers in higher education to help them help their students write better in academic settings. Emphasis on writing as a tool for improving learning within all disciplines and on discipline specialists' responsibility for teaching the conventions of the discipline. Advice on alternative types of writing tasks - some not to be assessed, on establishing criteria and on giving feedback.

Nightingale, P., & O'Neil, M. (1994). *Achieving Quality Learning in Higher Education.* London: Kogan Page.

> An introduction to quality assurance for teaching and learning. Emphasises that the only good outcome measure for learning is what we discover from assessment.

Nightingale, P., & Sohler, C. (1994). *Considering Gender.* Sydney: Higher Education Research and Development Society of Australasia.

> A practice-oriented overview of the gender biases in higher education and what to do about them. Chapters on curriculum issues, classroom management issues and assessment.

Norris, S. P., & Ennis, R. H. (1990). *The Practitioner's Guide To Teaching Thinking Series: Evaluating Critical Thinking.* Victoria: Hawker Brownlow Education.

Provides a comprehensive discussion on a definition of critical thinking. Also included in this text is information on methods of assessing critical thinking including commercially available critical thinking tests, and making your own assessment instruments. The ideas of these authors formed the basis for the project team's construction of critical thinking in Module 1 'Thinking critically and making judgements'.

Norton, L. (1990). Essay-writing: what really counts? *Higher Education, 20,* 411-42.

Includes information on their strategies in essay-writing from 98 1st year psychology students in a British institute of higher education. Also interview data from 6 tutors on their marking strategies. Finally, the essays were analysed. Students were more concerned with content, but tutors claimed to be concerned with argument. Nevertheless, the essays which showed higher proportion of research based content and larger number of references got higher marks.

Nouwens, F., & Robinson, P. (1991). Evaluation and the development of quality learning Materials. *Australian Journal of Educational Technology, 7*(2), 3-18.

Learning materials development has traditionally been controlled by individual academics as distance education followed organisational models provided by traditional face to face teaching. Recent developments in both education and training have increased expectations of distance education. Increasing student participation rates, accessibility of higher education, increasing costs and exponential growth of knowledge are some factors that require development of innovative approaches to meet these expectations. Quality management literature suggests that these challenges may be met by a flexible but systematic, participative and team-based approach using quality improvement strategies. Developments in educational evaluation indicate that quality is promoted by an action-evaluation paradigm based on critical theory. Action evaluation promotes information gathering directed towards the making o specific decisions, a systems approach to evaluation, participative democracy in both decision making and evaluation and reflective practice. A marriage is proposed between action evaluation and quality management to guide the development of quality in distance education. Three strategies are suggested immediately: use of a team approach to materials development that is genuinely participative and democratic, collection of information about the quality of service, provided to students in a way that promotes systematic improvement in the quality of that service and finally examination of all relevant aspects of educational services provided. This paper discussed the initial stages of the trial of such an approach as it is being developed within the Department of Mathematics and Computing at the University College of Central Queensland. (Journal abstract)

Oldfield, K., & Macalpine, M. (1995). Peer and self-assessment at tertiary level - an experiential report. *Assessment and Evaluation in Higher Education, 20*(1), 125-32.

Authors implemented peer assessment in Hong Kong. Students' cultural origin was primarily Chinese, but results of experiment were almost exactly the same as those reported by Falchikov (1995). That is, peer assessment can work quite well if introduced carefully. (See Module 5)

Oosterhof, A. C. (1987). Obtaining intended weights when combining scores. *Educational Measurement: Issues and Practice, 6*(4), 29-37.

Explains more fully than Ebel and Frisbie (1986) the statistical manipulation of marks to avoid problems of conflation.

Paris, S. C., & Winograd, P. (1990). How metacognition can promote academic learning and instruction. In B. F. Jones & L. Idol (Ed.), *Dimensions of Thinking and Cognitive Instruction* Hillsdale, N.J.: Erlbaum.

> This chapter is about metacognition (or 'thinking about thinking') and academic learning. The central message is that students can enhance their learning by becoming aware of their own thinking as they read, write and solve problems. The twin benefits of this "consciousness-raising" are : (a) it transfers responsibility for monitoring learning from teachers to students themselves, and (b) it promotes positive self-perceptions, affect, and motivation among students. In this manner, metacognition provides personal insights into one's own thinking and fosters independent learning. Module 2 (Solving problems and developing plans) contains a note about assessing metacognitive ability.

Partington, J. (1994). Double-marking students' work. *Assessment and Evaluation in Higher Education, 19*(1), 57-60.

> This paper raises a number of problems surrounding the popular practice of double marking and argues that these problems can be eliminated, as can the need for much double marking, if marking criteria are agreed and published at the time that an examination is set. The author argues that assessment criteria and the weightings to be attached to each aspect of students' work should form part of the published syllabus which directs students' learning.

Pollard, J. (1993). Developing physics understanding through guided study. In J. Bain, E. Lietzow, & B. Ross (Ed.), *Promoting Teaching in Higher Education* (pp. 355-370). Brisbane: Griffith Institute for Higher Education.

> Outlines outcomes from a CAUT funded project in developing assessment methods for promoting understanding. Described in detail in module 6.

Ramsden, P. (1984). The context of learning. In F. Marton, D. Hounsell, & N. Entwistle (Ed.), *The Experience of Learning* Edinburgh: Scottish Academic Press.

> This chapter provides a critique of pedagogical practice in current use and argues that the major teaching task is that of producing conceptual change. Draws implications for assessment practice in terms of the need to ensure that both the assessment tasks set and students' perceptions of what is required to succeed in these tasks are consistent with promoting conceptual change.

Ramsden, P. (1992). *Learning to Teach in Higher Education*. London: Routledge.

> Already a classic text for academics who care about teaching and who want to use the results of research on student learning. Chapter 10 focuses on assessment and includes principles for improving this 'serious and often tragic enterprise' (p181).

Redmond, J. (1986). Product design and education for the art of engineering. In *Proceedings Conference on Teaching Engineering Designers for the 21st Century* (pp. 130-33). Sydney: School of Mechanical and Industrial Engineering, University of New South Wales.

> Argues for integration of the "art" and the "science" of design. Need for engineers to take account of production practicalities as well as human factors in addition to the scientific correctness of their design solutions. Develops six 'core factors' and sub-categories within each that can be applied for developing assessment criteria for product design work.

Rowntree, D. (1987). *Assessing Students: How Shall We Know Them?* (2nd ed.). London: Kogan Page.

> Thought-provoking on the issues of assessment, often challenging received wisdom and accepted practice. A "chatty" book full of stories and anecdotes but also scholarly reference to wide range of literature on assessment. This is a classic reference on assessment in higher education.

Royer, J. M., Cisero, C. A., & Carlo, M. S. (1993). Techniques and procedures for assessing cognitive skills. *Review of Educational Research, 63*(2), 201-243.

> This article surveys procedures that could be used to assess progress in instructional programs designed to enhance cognitive skills. The organisational framework is provided by J. R. Anderson's (1982) theory of cognitive skill development and by Glaser, Lesgold and Lajoie's (1985) categorisation of dimensions of cognitive skills. After describing Anderson's theory, the article discusses the following types of measures of cognitive skills: (a) measures of knowledge acquisition, organisation, and structure; (b) measures of depth of problem representation; (c) measures of mental models; (d) measures of metacognitive skills; (e) measures of the automaticity of performance; and (f) measures of efficiency of procedures. Each of the sections describing measurement procedures is followed by a discussion of the strengths and weaknesses of the procedures. The article closes with a general discussion of techniques for measuring cognitive skills. (Journal abstract, adapted.)

Samuelowicz, K. (1994). Teaching conceptions and teaching practice: a case of assessment. In *Phenomemography - Philosophy and Practice*, (pp. 343-54). Brisbane: Queensland University of Technology.

> "...academic teachers' conceptions of teaching produce influences which are felt more at the level of their practice than in the way they articulate their aims. In particular, although teachers holding different conceptions of teaching may claim to be concerned about assessing similar competencies in their students, their actual practice in assessment, and in preparing students for assessment, may demonstrate divergences derived from their contrasting underlying conceptual positions. A case study of two physiotherapy teachers is described which indicates that, although they both profess to be interested in developing higher level professional skills, one realises an assessment practice based on changing students' conceptions, while the other's practice is driven by a knowledge transmission model."

Schön, D. (1983). *The Reflective Practitioner*. USA: Basic Books Inc.

> In the words of the author this book argues for a "new epistemology of practice". The author argues that skillful practitioners demonstrate both competence and artistry, and that the "reflection in action" component of their practice is sometimes what is brought to situations of uncertainty and conflict. In his view it is this ability that needs nurturing in the professional schools, as opposed to abilities emphasised in the existing curricula. When educators better understand this ability, they are better able to design assessment strategies which require students to demonstrate it.

Schön, D. (1990). *Educating the Reflective Practitioner*. San Francisco: Jossey-Bass.

> This book addresses a question implied by the author's earlier text, *The Reflective Practitioner*. That question is: "What kind of professional education would be appropriate to an epistemology of practice base on reflection in action?"
> The author argues that professional education ought to be redesigned to include coaching in the artistry of reflection-in-action. The book is focused on reflective practice, and is intended for individuals in education or practice settings. It includes chapters

on preparing professionals for practice and teaching artistry through reflection-in-action. There are examples of reflective practicums from a number of discipline areas including architecture, music, and counselling. The book concludes with a discussion of some of the implications for improving professional education.

From the assessor's point of view, Schön's suggestions about the nature of professional expertise have implications for establishing criteria for various types of performance.

Sharp, J. J. (1990). Does higher education promote independent learning? *Higher Education*, *20*, 335-336.

> Argues that frequent continuous assessment via short tests and quizzes are likely to promote reproducing strategies. Claims that less frequent assessment based on study and investigation over extended periods is more likely to engage students in deeper approaches to study.

Shay, S., Bond, D., & Hughes, T. (1994). Mysterious demands and disappointing responses: exploring students' difficulties with academic writing tasks. In A. Angelil-Carter, D. Bond, M. Paxton, & L. Thesen (Eds.), *Language in Academic Development at UCT, 1994* (pp. 18-35). Cape Town, SA: Academic Development Programme, University of Cape Town.

> Very perceptive exploration of why students have so much trouble with what appear to be straightforward essay tasks. Three students' particular cases are discussed and placed in context of the literature on the writing process. Emphasis on interpreting the task so that it may serve as a "bridge" between students' world and the public academic one rather than as a "gate" keeping the student out.

Short, D. J. (1993). Assessing integrated language and content instruction. *TESOL Quarterly*, *27*(4), 627-656.

> Integrated language and content instruction has become a popular alternative to traditional ESL instruction. Both researchers and practitioners have recommended this approach. While considerable progress has been made in strategies and techniques that effectively integrate language and content, little attention has been paid to assessment. Neither traditional language tests nor content achievement tests are adequate to this task. This paper recommends using alternative assessment measures such as checklists, portfolios, interviews and performance based tasks for assessing integrated programs. Examples of the implementation of the framework it offers in elementary and secondary schools are also included.

Somervell, H. (1993). Issues in assessment, enterprise and higher education: the case for self, peer and collaborative assessment. *Assessment and Evaluation in Higher Education, 18*(3), 221-233.

> A summary of arguments for involving students in the assessment process and brief overview of some of the methods for doing so. Well-written and quite balanced though somewhat polemical. Believes that more emphasis on collaboration between student and teacher in setting goals for learning, criteria for assessment, and judging success will lead to better quality learning and preparation for life after education. Perspective is that too often we are "making the measurable important instead of the important measurable" (p226)

Spencer, L. M. (1984). *Soft Skill Competencies - their identification, measurement and development for professional, managerial and human service jobs.* Edinburgh: Scottish Council for Research in Education.

> Describes the 'job competence assessment' procedure - an elaborate process designed to identify the characteristics of superior performers in professional, managerial and

human service jobs. Characteristics which reliably distinguish superior performers are frequently found to be 'soft skills' such as 'accurate empathy' and 'critical thinking'.

Spender, D. (1982). *Invisible Women: The Schooling Scandal.* London: Writers and Readers.

Series of essays revealing how women's achievements have been lost from curricula in all disciplines at all levels. Raises questions about gender bias in assessing students as well.

Stape, C. J. (1995). Techniques for developing higher-level objective test questions. *Performance and Instruction, 34*(3), 31-34.

The author defines higher level knowledge as the use by the student of concepts or principles in tasks requiring illustration, prediction, evaluation or application. He then gives examples of test items that can be used to assess such knowledge. The examples provided include classification, odd one out, if-then conditionals, multiple true/false, and interpretive questions.

Stoddart, K. (1991). Lifestory: a device for dispersing authority in the introductory course. *Teaching Sociology, 19*, 70-73.

Cited by case study contributors, Robert Zehner & Michael Bounds (Case study 23, Module 4), for comments on the issue of anonymity when using autobiography as a learning/assessment tool with students.

Swanson, D. B., Norman, G. R., & Lin, R. L. (1995). Performance-based assessment: lessons from the health Professions. *Educational Researcher, 24*(5), 5-11.

Authentic or performance-based assessment has been used in the health professions for decades. This article looks at four of these methods: written clinical simulations, computer-based clinical simulations, oral examinations, and simulations using actors. It draws a number of lessons from these years of experience, including:

1) test design and domain sampling is not more straightforward just because the task imitates real-life;
2) examinees do not necessarily behave the same way in a test situation as they will/would in real-life;
3) scoring the rich and interesting behaviour of examinees can be highly problematic;
4) performance in one context does not predict performance in another very well;
5) correlational studies of the relationship between performance-based scores and other assessment methods targeting different skills typically produce variable and uninterpretable results;
6) security and equivalency of tests are extremely difficult, especially where numbers are large;
7) there are few studies of the intended and unintended impacts on teaching and learning of this type of testing;
8) selection of methods of assessment should depend on the skills to be assessed and a mixture of methods is usually to be preferred.

Tan, C. M. (1992). An evaluation of the use of continuous assessment in the teaching of physiology. *Higher Education, 23*, 255-272.

The level of understanding achieved by a class of 160 1st-year medical students was assessed from their answers to exam questions related to a series of physiology lectures in which students were taught for conceptual understanding. Questionnaire data showed that about 90% of the class perceived the subject matter to be relevant.

Information collected by interview from a sample of 30 students indicated that frequent summative assessment exerted a profound negative influence over their learning. Students adopted a surface reproductive approach aimed at passing the exams rather than at understanding the subject matter. Lectures failed to affect the way that students represented, structured and selected their knowledge, which remained encapsulated in the textbook context and was non-functional. Assessments comprised a high proportion of multiple-choice questions and emphasised low-level skills resulting in the establishment of a 'hidden curriculum'. Furthermore, the curriculum failed to provide appropriate opportunities for students to consolidate and internalise information presented in lectures. The students had inadequate abstract reasoning and integration skills and so were unable to ignore the 'hidden curriculum'. In the absence of high-level conceptual development students cannot apply theory to practice. It is argued that the early introduction of clinical experiences (in year-2) cannot promote effective integration between theory and practice and the development of an holistic attitude and heuristic thinking, when students lack prerequisite basic reasoning skills and do not know how to learn meaningfully. (Journal abstract)

Taylor, G., Ballard, B., Beasley, V., Bock, H., Clanchy, J., & Nightingale, P. (1988). *Literacy by Degrees*. Milton-Keynes (UK): SRHE and Open University Press.

> Argues that if students are to be well-prepared to write as professionals by the time they graduate, academics in all disciplines will have to accept responsibility for teaching them the conventions and styles of the disciplines. Literacy is not achieved once but by degrees. Important for assessors of student writing to understand the causes of errors.

Te Wiata, I. (1988). *Mastery Learning and Assessment.* Auckland: Auckland Technical Institute.

> Designed to help teachers plan and implement mastery learning programs. It includes a discussion of the impact on students and tutors of mastery learning programs introduced at Auckland Institute of Technology. Also includes an explanation of what mastery learning and assessment are, plus strategies for implementation, and examples of courses that incorporate mastery learning/assessment principles.

Te Wiata, I. (1993) *The Experience of Learning in Co-operative Education.* Unpublished Master of Education thesis, University of Auckland.

> The purpose of this study was to determine the effectiveness of the co-operative education system as a learning strategy, in the context of a business studies degree course. A number of themes relating to the learning experiences for students emerged from the study. The themes that were identified from interviews with the various participant groups were: thinking through confusion, providing a structure for learning, and the development of capabilities (personal and professional).
> It is argued that co-operative education is an effective learning strategy in developing certain capabilities eg. critical thinking, teamwork. This is evidenced for example, through the results of, and students' comments on the assessment tasks undertaken in the course. One of these assessment tasks is described in Case Study #1. Results from this study also indicate that students become more confident and adaptable learners through co-operative education, and are better prepared for professional practice than if they had undertaken a traditional non co-operative course.

Theobald, J. (1974). *Classroom Testing: Principles and Practice.* Hawthorn, VIC: Longman.

> Chapter 6 takes up issues of interpretation of scores and statistical procedures for combining marks.

Thomas, K. (1990). *Gender and Subject in Higher Education*. Buckingham: SRHE and Open University Press.

> Research study of male and female students' experiences in British higher education. Looks at students in subject areas thought of as male and as female preserves, finds women disadvantaged in both, including by bias in assessment.

Thomson, A. N. (1992). Can communication skills be assessed independently of their context? *Medical Education, 26*, 364-7.

> Royal New Zealand College of General Practitioners tests applicants for membership on their communication skills. Concerned that lack of knowledge about a particular case might interfere with valid assessment of communication skills, the College provided candidates with knowledge necessary to deal with the situation in the simulated patient interview. Candidates were required to conduct two interviews: they had to deal with at least one "confrontational" situation, and either a second confrontation or a situation requiring the doctor to break bad news to a patient. The correlations between results on two confrontational situations were "modest" but the correlation on two unlike situations was virtually non-existent. Communication skills are seen to be highly context dependent.

Unwin, T. (1990). 2.i or not 2.i? The Assessment of Undergraduate Essays. *Journal of Geography in Higher Education, 14*(1), 31-38.

> Argues that essay questions should be chosen to elicit a wide range of educational attainments, and should encourage the development of critical thinking skills rather than reproduction of acquired knowledge, but does not offer much practical advice about constructing such questions. Most useful section of the paper offers criteria for assessing essays. Emphasises importance of communicating these expectations to students.

Verwijnen, M., Imbos, T., Snellen, H., Stalenhoef, B., Pollemans, M., Luyk, S., Sprooten, M., Leeuwen, Y., & Vleuten, C. (1982). The evaluation system at the medical school of Maastricht. *Assessment and Evaluation in Higher Education., 7*, 225-244.

> Describes an extensive scheme for both formative and summative assessment of medical students. The wide range of testing procedures, including self assessment units, indicates the complexity of an assessment program which attempts to cover all the competency domains relevant to medicine.

Voss, J. & Post, T. (1988). On the solving of ill-structured problems. In Chi, M. T. H., Glaser, R., & Farr, M. J. *The Nature of Expertise*. Hillsdale, New Jersey: Erlbaum. Chapter 9.

> This chapter provides a discussion of seminal papers by Reitman and Simon on the solving of ill-structured problems; a presentation of the authors' own work on the solving of ill-structured problems in the social science domain; and an outline of a number of general issues that require consideration if a better understanding of the solving of such problems is to be established.

Vu, N., & Barrow, H. (1994). Use of standardized patients in clinical assessments: recent developments and measurement findings. *Educational Researcher, 23*(3), 23-30.

> Provides a comprehensive review of validity and reliability issues and outcomes in the use of standardised patients in assessing clinical competence.

Walkerdyne, V., & the Girls and Mathematics Unit (1989). *Counting Girls Out.* London: Virago Press.

> About how girls learn - or do not learn mathematics and the various interactions at home and at school that make their experiences different from those of boys. The effect of teachers' expectations and feedback on girls' learning.

West, H., Flowers, W., & Gilmore, D. (1990). Hands-on design in engineering education: learning by doing what? *Engineering Education, 80,* 560-564.

> Emphasises importance of design students having to face the practicalities of trying to build their designs as part of assessment.

Westhorp, P. (1994). The experience and outcomes of action research and reflective teaching in occupational therapy. In B. Smith (Ed.), *The experience of reflective university teachers addressing quality in teaching and learning: The CUTL action research project.* Adelaide: University of South Australia.

> This collection of reports of action research projects, undertaken at the University of South Australia, includes Penny Westhorp's account of her use of journals for the assessment of the development of empathy in student therapists.

White, E. M. (1994). *Teaching and Assessing Writing* (Second edition, revised and expanded). San Francisco: Jossey-Bass.

> Readable and extremely practical advice to teachers who wish to help their students learn to write, and who wish to assess writing fairly and constructively. Discipline specialists will need to apply the content to their own situations as the book is written primarily about teaching writing in subjects devoted to communication skills, but the message is valid for others and is very important. The new edition covers portfolio assessment as well as traditional testing and assignment writing.

Wildman (1988). The question of silence: techniques to ensure full class participation. *Journal of Legal Education, 38.*

> Cited by Annette Marfording. (Case study 56 in Module 8).

Williams, E. (1992). Student attitudes towards approaches to learning and assessment. *Assessment and Evaluation in Higher Education, 17*(1), 45-56.

> A study of 99 first year undergraduate students found that most enjoyed and found benefit in self and peer assessment provided that clear guidelines were first established. The authors also found that self assessment comments tended to be insightful and constructively critical.

Wolf, A. (1991). Assessment in European vocational education and training: current concerns and trends. *Journal of Curriculum Studies, 23*(6), 552-557.

> This paper identifies two main European concerns: to maintain and increase the validity of assessment in vocational programs (principally through forms of competency based training and the use of more practical performance based assessments); and to increase people's access to different educational tracks (through modularisation and the assessment and accreditation of prior learning).

Woods, J. D. (1994). Bridging the gap between curriculum theory and curriculum practice. In *Quality in Teaching and Learning - Making it Happen: Teaching Learning Forum 94*, pp1-12. Claremont, W.A.: Edith Cowan University.

> John Woods' account of using group work in the teaching and assessment of curriculum design. This approach is discussed in detail in Module 4, Case study 29.

Yancey, K. (1992). *Portfolios in the Writing Classroom.* Urbana, IL: National Council of Teachers of English.

> Unsighted by project team - recommended in White (1994) which we have found to be an important resource

Contributors

Lynette **Abbott**	University of Western Australia
Antoinette **Ackermann**	University of Canberra
Michael **Aldred**	University of Queensland
Arthur **Anderson**	University of New South Wales
Alan **Barnes**	University of South Australia
John **Biggs**	University of Hong Kong
Margaret **Blackburn**	Auckland Institute of Technology
David **Booth**	University of Western Australia
Sally **Borbasi**	University of Sydney
David **Boud**	University of Technology, Sydney
Michael **Bounds**	University of Western Sydney
Sharon **Bourgeois**	University of Western Sydney
Jenny **Bradley**	Murdoch University
Dean **Bruton**	University of South Australia
Dianne **Budd**	Curtin University of Technology
Mark **Burton**	Charles Sturt University
Meredith **Caisley**	Auckland Institute of Technology
Enid **Campbell**	Monash University
Mary **Chan**	University of New South Wales
Henry **Collins**	University of Sydney
Kevin **Collis**	University of Tasmania
Catherine **Dallemagne**	Queensland University of Technology
Fe **Day**	Auckland Institute of Technology
Alice **de Jonge**	Monash University
Allan **Donnelly**	University of Ballarat
John **Drinan**	University of Newcastle
Patricia **Duncan**	University of Newcastle
Ian **Dunn**	University of New South Wales
John **Eastwell**	University of Southern Queensland
Lynne **Elliot**	University of Ballarat
John **Elms**	University of Southern Queensland
Fran **Everingham**	University of Sydney
Jeffrey **Faux**	Victoria University of Technology
Grahame **Feletti**	University of Hawaii
Richard **Fuller**	Edith Cowan University
John **Goldring**	University of Wollongong
Andrew **Gonczi**	University of Technology, Sydney
Malcolm **Goodall**	Victoria University of Technology
Peter **Goodwin**	University of Queensland
Bruce **Graham**	Charles Sturt University
Ian **Griffith**	Victorian College of Pharmacy
Roger **Hadgraft**	Monash University
Anita **Hall**	University of Queensland
Jennifer **Hardy**	Australian Catholic University
Iain **Hay**	Flinders University of South Australia
Helen **Hayes**	University of Ballarat
Les **Higgins**	University of Sydney
Peter **Hobson**	University of New England
Terry **Hore**	Monash University
Lynne **Hunt**	Edith Cowan University
Michael **Jackson**	University of Sydney
Huntley **John**	University of Iowa
Barry **Kentish**	University of Ballarat
Phil **Ker**	Auckland Institute of Technology
Paul **Lennox**	University of New South Wales
Rae **Lindsay**	University of Western Australia
David **Lockett**	University of Adelaide

Godfrey **Lucas**..University of Western Sydney
Suzanne **Lyons** ....University of Newcastle
Marie **Macdonald**...Australian Catholic University
Don **Maconachie** ....University of Ballarat
Allan **Mann**..University of Ballarat
Annette **Marfording** ....University of New South Wales
Bryce **Mason**..Auckland Institute of Technology
Elizabeth **McFarland** ....University of Western Sydney
Mike **McCausland** ....University of Tasmania
Jean **McPherson**...University of Newcastle
Pauline **Meemeduma**...James Cook University
Richard **Miller**..University of Wollongong
Mick **Morgan** ....University of Southern Queensland
Monica **Nebauer**...Australian Catholic University
Joy **Nunn** ....University of Ballarat
Annalisa **Orselli-Dickson** ....Edith Cowan University
John **Ozolins**..Australian Catholic University
Barbara **Pamphilon**..University of Canberra
Graeme **Payne**...University of Queensland
Dianne **Pelletier**...University of Technology, Sydney
Jill **Perriott** ....University of Western Sydney
Barbara **Poston-Anderson**...University of Technology, Sydney
Ian **Prosser** ....University of New South Wales
Cherry **Randolph**..University of Western Australia
Melissa **Robbie** ....Monash University
Malcolm **Roberts** ....University of Newcastle
Lynne **Roberts-Goodwin** ....University of New South Wales
Peter **Robinson**...University of Central Queensland
David **Roche** ....University of Adelaide
Greg **Ryan**...University of New South Wales
Ann **Sefton** ....University of Sydney
Neal **Sellars** ....James Cook University
Susan **Shannon** ....University of Adelaide
Mark **Shying**..Victoria University of Technology
Ray **Smith** ....University of New South Wales
Anne **Stanley**...University of Sydney
Jeffrey **Stewart**...University of Ballarat
Andrew **Sturman**..University of Southern Queensland
Richard **Sutton**...University of Queensland
Roy **Tasker** ....University of Western Sydney
Jim **Taylor** ....University of Southern Queensland
Ina **Te Wiata** ....University of Canberra
Julie **Thorburn**...University of Sydney
Matthias **Tomczak** ....Flinders University of South Australia
Susan **Toohey** ....University of New South Wales
Philip **Towers** ....Charles Sturt University
Chris **Trevitt** ....Australian National University
Peter **Tutton** ....Monash University
Jim **Walker**..University of Canberra
Christine **Walton**...Northern Territory University
Jane **Watson**..University of Tasmania
John **Watts**..University of Central Queensland
Penny **Westhorp**...University of South Australia
John **Wetherell**...University of Adelaide
Jenny **Wilson**...University of Technology, Sydney
Audrey **Wilson** ....University of Wollongong
Gina **Wisker**...Anglia University
Helen **Wood** ....Charles Sturt University
John **Woods** ....Edith Cowan University
Robert **Zehner**..University of New South Wales

INDEX

T